The Woman in the Mirror

THE WOMAN IN THE MIRROR

Analytical Psychology and the Feminine

Claire Douglas

SIGO PRESS
Boston

SIGO PRESS
25 New Chardon Street #8748
Boston, Massachusetts 02114

To Mary Lee Fraser, James Yandell and Barbara Koltuv, who helped me find my own face in the mirror.

Publisher and Editor: Sisa Sternback

International Standard Book Number: 0-938434-58-6 (cloth)
0-938434-57-8 (paper)

Library of Congress-in-Publication Data

Douglas, Claire.
The woman in the mirror: analytical psychology and the feminine/ Claire Douglas
p. cm.
Includes bibliographical references.
ISBN 0-938434-58-6 : $34.95. — ISBN 0-938434-57-8 (pbk.) : $15.95
1. Femininity (Psychology) 2. Women and psychoanalysis. 3. Jung, C. G. (Carl Gustav), 1875-1961. I. Title.
BF175.5.F45D68 1990   89-21599
155.3'33 — dc20   CIP

Printed in Korea

TABLE OF CONTENTS

ACKNOWLEDGEMENTS

I would like to thank the following people who read through this manuscript in one or more of its several forms and generously gave me not only their pragmatic suggestions, comments, and criticisms, but also the priceless gift of their accumulated wisdom and support: Doris Albrecht, John Beebe, Lawrence Jaffe, Jurgen Kremer, Marcia Salner, Geraldine Spare, and James Yandell. I thank my editor, Marc Romano, for his encouragement, timely and supple editing, and his skillful midwifery. I am grateful to the Women's Group at the C. G. Institute of San Francisco and fellow candidates at the C. G. Jung Institute of New York for the discussions that have helped clarify my thinking, and for their many instances of personal support and encouragement. I am indebted to Doris Albrecht (deeply and once again), librarian of the Kristine Mann Library, NY, and Joan Alpert, librarian of the Virginia Detloff Library at the C. G. Jung Institute of San Francisco, for all the ways they facilitated my research. I would also like to thank the following instructors as well as fellow trainees at the C. G. Jung Institute of New York for several courses in which the material, its presentation, the discussions, and clinical applications, all consolidated my understanding of many valid alternate models for women and the feminine: Betsy Halpern for her course on Hindu Mythology; Sylvia Perera on Celtic Mythology; Sherry Salman on The Origin of Consciousness and on the Grail Legend; and Beverly Zabriskie on Egyptian Mythology. I alone take responsibility for my research, my point of view, and my interpretations. The backbone of this book is its earlier incarnation as a doctoral dissertation in psychology; parts of it also appeared in other forms in four articles for *The*

San Francisco C. G. Jung Institute's Library Journal. I thank the editor, John Beebe, for permission to reprint sections of these papers and for his thoughtful attention to feelings, words, ideas and text.

Grateful acknowledgement is made to the following for permission to quote from the copyrighted material:

Anchor/Doubleday for B. Ehrenreich and D. English's *For Her Own Good: 150 Years of the Experts' Advice to Women*, 1978.

Harper and Row, Inc. for V. N. Odajnyk's *Jung and Politics: The Political and Social Ideas of C. G. Jung*, 1976.

Harvard University Press for N. Auerbach's *Woman and the Demon: The Life of a Victorian Myth*, 1982.

Inner City Books for Sylvia Perera's *Descent to the Goddess*, 1981.

C. G. Jung Foundation of New York for M. E. Harding's *The Way of All Women*, 1975; *Women's Mysteries*, 1976; E. C. Whitmont's *Symbolic Quest*, 1969, 1978; "Reassessing Femininity and Masculinity," 1980.

Northwestern University Press for A. Ulanov's *The Feminine in Jungian Psychology and Christian Theology*, 1971, 1978; J. Hillman's *Myth and Analysis*, 1972.

Oxford University Press for P. Gay's *The Bourgeois Experience From Victoria to Freud*, 1984.

Paulist Press for J. Sanford's *The Invisible Partners*, 1980.

Princeton University Press for C. G. Jung's *C. G. Jung's Letters* Vol. 1 & 2, G. Adler (ed.), 1973; *The Collected Works of C. G. Jung* Vols. 2-18, Bollingen Series XX, G. Adler, M. Fordham, H. Read (eds.), trans. by R. F. C. Hull; M. E. Harding's *The 'I' and the 'Not I'*, 1965.

Psychological Perspectives for M. Nagy's "Menstruation and Shamanism," 1981; P. B. Kenevan's "Eros, Logos and Androgyny," 1981.

Psychology of Women Quarterly for M. Fine's "Reflections on a Feminist Psychology of Women; Paradoxes and Prospects," 1985.

Random House for C. G. Jung's *Memories, Dreams, Reflections*, A. Jaffé (ed.), trans. by R. Winston and C. Winston, copyright ® 1961, 1962, 1963. Reprinted by permission of Pantheon Books, a division of Random House, Inc.

Spring Publications for J. Hillman's "Anima II," 1974; "Some Early Background to Jung's Ideas," 1976; C. G. Jung's *The Visions Seminars*, 1976; A. Guggenbühl-Craig's *Marriage: Dead or Alive*, 1977; E. Jung's *Animus and Anima*, 1981; L. Fierz-David's *Women's Dionysian Initiation*, 1988.

Parts of this book have appeared in other form in articles by C. Douglas in the *San Fransisco Jung Institute Library Journal*, J. Beebe (Ed.), 1983, 1985, 1986, 1989.

INTRODUCTION

Our way of looking at things is conditioned by what we are.
C. G. Jung, *Freud and Jung — Contrasts.*

A complete and thorough examination of the literature on the feminine in analytical psychology is both necessary and long overdue. One of the main purposes of this book is to present just such an examination by means of a historical analysis of Jungian theory of the feminine from Jung to the present time. I believe this can differentiate what is of current and perhaps lasting value in the theory, what is ephemeral, what can be kept, what revised, and what discarded in light of a contemporary psychology of the feminine consonant with present needs. There are outdated aspects of the theory, contaminated by the prejudices of the time and by the writers' own biases, that are expendable, while many forgotten (often female) voices contribute a strong and enduring leitmotif that accords well with contemporary studies of gender and of the psychology of women.

Interest in Jungian psychology is growing, yet both within mainstream psychology and among many women, Carl Gustav Jung and the psychological system he founded are in some disrepute. Many of Jung's ideas on women seem old-fashioned — part of a bygone era — in spite of Jung being one of the first analysts who took women and the feminine seriously. Jung's more pragmatic father, Freud, rested his own theories on patriarchal formulations such as the primacy of the oedipal situation and the centrality of the father. Freud's genius changed the way we see and experience the world, yet his views on women remained obsessively restricted, while his psychoanalysis stringently (and pessimistically) limited itself to a man's perspective and to reductive interpretations. Jung also looked at the world from a man's point of view; however, he focuses on the primacy of the mother and explores a bountiful mother's world, polymorphously (and optimistically) open to myths, fantasies, expansive amplifications, and whatever else the psyche and the universe contain.

Jung extends Freud's work in all of these directions precisely through this attention to the feminine. Yet the potency of Jung's theory has been ignored and distorted by many contemporary, especially feminist, theoreticians who only see Jung's own distortions. Goldenberg, for instance, in her (1976) article "A Feminist Critique of Jung," writes that "Jungian psychology particularly warrants a feminist critique because it has largely become a form of patriarchal religion itself" (p. 444). She criticizes most contemporary Jungians for merely extending Jung's theories and attempting to make them more "inoffensive" and/or more mainstream (scientific), while failing to examine or question their basic assumptions. She describes these assumptions as sexist and limiting to women. She finds that the very idea of a feminine archetype, as described by Jung, favors men, limits women to a patriarchal ideal, and both reflects and justifies women's secondary status in society. "Much of Jungian thought [remains] racist, sexist, and closed to experience" (p. 448).

Such an analysis deprives contemporary thinking of those parts of Jung's theory of the feminine that are original and creative. There is a seed within his theory which contains the possibility of freeing women and the feminine from the very patriarchal formulations that surround them. Extracting this seed from all its wrappings proves arduous work, especially since much that is dated and sexist in the original theory remains unexamined within the Jungian community itself. A recent collection of excerpts from Jung's writings on the feminine (Jung, 1982), for example, makes almost a textbook illustration of Goldenberg's objections. This is partly because brief articles, though perhaps complete in themselves, cannot hope to do justice to his ideas. Jung's view of the feminine is strikingly complex and ambiguous; the enduring kernel only uncovered through a stringent rereading and reanalysis of Jung's entire body of work. Essential pieces of what he has to say about women or the feminine are scattered here and there throughout his work and one passage often contradicts another; thus one needs a sense of all the varying parts that make up the whole. Another problem is that valuable work on the feminine, building on logical ramifications of his theory, remains unknown. Reinterpretations, especially those written by women, have been forgotten. There is no consensus of what, if any, Jungian theory on feminine psychology exists and, if it does, what it contains.

Part of the reason for both the feminist blindness to the possible value of Jungian theory and the blindness (or double vision) of many Jungians themselves is that no comprehensive and thorough history of the feminine in Jungian psychology has been written. Bits and pieces of this history have been examined by such writers as Whitmont (1980), Ulanov (1971, 1981), Mattoon (1981), Samuels (1985), and Young-Eisendrath and Wiedemann (1987), but all in the service of other concerns. There has been no complete and thorough examination of the literature on this topic—neither of Jung's theory of the feminine nor of those who develop and elaborate it. Theory on the feminine in analytical psychology lacks a sense of tradition, continuity, and a common collected body of knowledge on what has already been written. Present Jungian authors are "discovering" insights already known to past researchers, and are taking credit for ideas or ascribing credit to others while ignoring prior work which examined the same issues and reached the same conclusions. Contemporary scholars and analysts sometimes adhere to and teach a one-sided and outmoded view of the feminine that is time- and culture-bound to Jung's era and the late nineteenth century, seemingly unaware of the alternatives historically available, while other analysts examine specific small areas of feminine psychology without a general overview of the entire area and without the necessary framework of historical or theoretical continuity. Our field is judged accordingly.

My second reason for uncovering the history of the feminine in psychology is frankly feminist—an effort to save and recall women's history. Because the word "feminist" reverberates in all manner of ways, and because there has been so much misunderstanding of the term, I need to spend a little time describing my sense of the word and my perspective. Feminism grants me an outlook which promotes men's and women's equal access to power, autonomy, and the manifestation of whatever mix of human qualities that were once stringently divided along gender lines. I don't mean women's wholesale adoption of traditionally masculine qualities, an endeavor which would further abjure the feminine and cause women to outman men; nor do I glorify the feminine as all good, and derogate the masculine as all bad. I don't believe that one gender is superior to another, nor even that women have distinctly separate, even superior, feeling qualities, intelligence, or moral character, nor that they should be treated and judged accordingly.

I honor some feminists' needs for separation, yet my own view of the world prefers union and reconciliation of male and female, masculine and feminine, men and women, to their division and isolation, but only when each is equally respected and equally free to do and think and be, regardless of gender. What feminism means to me is to work at understanding the underlying context that has formed and forms each one of us and our behavior; for example:

> What we now see as the "feminine ideal," defined in terms of non rational characteristics, has itself been largely determined by the exclusion of women from the ideal of reason. Thus . . . the affirmation of the value and importance of "the feminine" cannot be expected to shake underlying normative structures that support male norms and female complementarity. (Jackson, 1987, p.166)

To this end I have taken women's ideas, needs, and experience seriously, and have attempted to integrate them into a theory that has all too often been blinded to women's living reality. I see gender differences as contextual and relative, in accordance with current research and in contrast to the nineteenth century's exaggeration of differences. Its use of gender to promote control and a system of domination and subordination was bad science and psychologically damaging to both the dominant male and the subordinate female. Theories that continue this perspective need to be challenged.

In this book I endeavor to pay particular attention to women's identity and to women's writing. As Heilbrun (1988) and Miller (1988) have pointed out, the literal blindness to women's writing has profoundly troubling consequences on theory itself. Reinterpretation involves "rewriting the patriarchal text" (Heilbrun, 1988, p. 20) to include women's experience and women's reality in public as well as private arenas. Feminism for me is a point of view that tolerates ambiguity, complexity, and interactions; it notes the palimpsest of memory, language, and upbringing.

I have the feeling that if Jung and Freud were alive today, Freud would probably adhere to his original theory while Jung, responding to the material and to the changing times, would revise his. This is because there is an ambiguity in Jung's psychology: his nineteenth-century prejudices restrict women, while his underlying attitude fits many of the characteristics I define as feminist. Jung's support for individuals becoming all that it is in them to become makes him a proto-feminist whose consciousness in regard to women has yet to be raised. But Jung was also a man of his time, and his thought reflects his era. As Jung himself said "Whatever happens in a given moment has inevitably the quality peculiar to that moment" (Jung, 1950/1969, p. 592).

The purpose of the first part of this book is to attempt to both discern the quality of Jung's particular moment in time and to disentangle his ideas from past encumbrances. I first consider Jung himself and the part his character and experience play in his theory. Chapters One and Two place Jung's work on the feminine in a historical and cultural perspective through looking at his time, his culture, and his own personal life. What interests me is the ways in which Jung's life, his family, his education, and the culture around him affect and possibly bias his attitudes toward the feminine. Chapters Three and Four take up Jung's theories themselves. Here I examine the contributions and limitations of Jung's views about women and the psychology of the feminine, through an in-depth examination of his typological studies, his concepts of Eros and Logos, and the archetypes, especially the problematical anima and animus archetypes. I also reexamine Jung's theory of projection and his treatment of what he calls the dual problems of women and evil. Jung's depiction of the masculine and the feminine in his alchemical studies is especially vital to his theory. The problem of the *soror mystica* and Jung's treatment of this alchemical role is paradigmatic of Jung's attitude toward the feminine, as is his long series of seminars on a woman patient's visions. I conclude with implications from Jung's theory of the feminine that are relevant to an understanding of the psychology of women today. Original source material, primarily Jung's *Collected Works*, *Letters*, and *The Visions Seminars*, is used. Jung's work is assessed in relation to my own consciousness and experience as a woman, an analysand, and an analyst in training.

The five chapters of Part Two examine what Jung's followers have written about the feminine and the psychology of women. The chapters are organized around the following themes: definitions of the feminine and women; discussion of, attitude toward, and extension of, Jung's concept of the contrasexual anima and animus archetypes; choices and presentation of archetypes of the feminine (including key attitudes concerning women and evil, and the presence or absence of a strong, enduring, authoritative, and powerful feminine); and attempts at delineating a more or less comprehensive psychology including possible developmental theories.

The purpose of these chapters is to examine what in later writers is compatible with Jung, what incompatible, what is revised, what retained that is productive and what unproductive, and what is new. At the end of each chapter is a brief summation and conclusion in relation to the psychological needs of modern women and in light of current gender research. My aim is to present what is of use to a basic psychology of women appropriate to current socio-historical conditions. The inclusion in this book of important work by many female analysts and authors, who have often been overlooked or treated summarily, is examined for implications about theory and theory generation, including possible differences in women psychologists' theorizing, practice of therapy, and training of therapists. I believe that outdated aspects of the theory contaminated by the prejudices of the time and by the authors' own biases are expendable to the overall theory, and are detrimental both to the acceptance of analytical psychology by a sophisticated public and to the well-being of its patients. From this analysis, I have pointed out areas that require further conceptual work, promising areas of new study, and archetypes that foster a more rounded and complete view of the feminine and women.

It was a difficult question to determine which writers to include in this history and which to leave out. I finally decided to restrict my inquiry—except in the history-oriented first two chapters—to work available in English by analysts certified by the International Association of Analytical Psychology or candidates at IAAP Institutes. Maintaining clear, if stringent, boundaries avoids the danger of getting caught in an endless labyrinth of Jungian derivatives. This limitation also improves the validity of what can be said to constitute a body of Jungian theory that can be defended as rigorously within the canon. Yet defining the parameters of my subject in this manner necessarily, and perhaps arbitrarily, omits some important and revered popular Jungian writers (such as Christine Downing and Robert Johnson) who have their own place and value, but are neither trained within my discipline as it defines itself nor have an official link with a Jungian organization. I have chosen to include some unpublished material only available in Institute libraries because it is available to scholars and because it makes a significant contribution to theory. My choice of material necessarily reflects my own perception of significance. As the author of an initial history of this subject, I have to rely on my own judgment and leave it to future writers to add to and amend what I have started.

This book stems from an experiential as well as a theoretical perspective. The reader needs to be aware of the personal interests, approach, and experience that are behind this study, including my particular stance, world view, and bias. What I write is conditioned by who I am. I am, as I have said, a feminist, and I have tried to define what I mean by this. I am also part of and affected by the current flow of Jungian theory, especially as it concerns the feminine, having worked in two Institutes: as an intern at the Whitney Clinic of the C. G. Jung Institute of San Francisco and as an analytic candidate at the C. G. Jung Institute of New York. In both Institutes, I have first-hand experience of Jungians' attitudes toward the feminine and women, and have found these attitudes amazingly varied and variously informed. I have encountered traditional and revisionist theories and their merits and their shadows. Therefore, I am writing from the inside as a participant, even an initiate, who believes, questions, and doubts.

The personal question that weaves its way through this book, and that I have tried to answer for myself through writing it, is whether a theory, system, and analytic mode set up by a man in a patriarchal society—contaminated as it is by the shadows of Jung's and his follower's eras, a predominantly patriarchal viewpoint and, in fact, by our whole masculine language and symbology—is suitable either for the training of analysts or the healing of women wounded by these very things. Thus this study may be one more symbolic way of inquiring, conjecturing, and asking about myself and the appropriateness of the path I have chosen.

Behind this is a private and urgent inner search for my own feminine voice: what it means to me to be a woman living in this world today. How can I say anything about something so personal without saying too much? Part of this quest rises from the wounds all of us accumulate during our often traumatized conditioning, development, and life experience. Part comes from experiencing the healing of these wounds and the realization that, in my case and in those of many patients, I have seen that Jungian analysis works. Perhaps I was a natural Jungian from birth and this predilection needs to be brought up either as a possible source of bias or as an example of the universality of Jung's ideas. My dreams, fantasies, and fairy tales created a crucial life-line through which I discovered alternate ways of being a girl-child than I was offered by my patriarchal and warring world, and by a judgmental religion that feared and hated all sides of the feminine but one. At age twelve, during a particularly painful time, I spent hours hiding out in my convent boarding school's art room, alone with paper, a compass, and colored paints and pencils. I derived a strange comfort from creating page after page of what I called my compass worlds. I found out years afterwards that Jung had described that kind of drawing as mandala-making: depictions of what the self, often in times of stress, seeks as a centering path — both a representation of and a way to itself. So my own experience is part of this study; it joins the pain and strength of my patients, and of Jung and other writers, out of whose personal experiences, too, come the work I will be discussing, analyzing, criticizing, and forming into patterns in the following chapters.

I need to stop for a moment to include a subjective response to the task I'd set myself in planning this book. As I started writing, I was frankly overwhelmed. I had read everything that had been written on the feminine by Jung and his followers. It had taken me many years just to do this research and compile my primary data. As an introverted thinking type, all this reading, and the weaving of patterns and theory out of what I gathered, was for me much more of a joy than a burden. But I had amassed many file boxes of material, enough for books on each aspect. What should I include; what leave out; how could I organize this mass of material? For instance, even the simplest choice — organizing by chronology or topic — became complex. And what about my anger both at the external struggle women still underwent in the face of the ways they were defined and limited, and my growing realization of how much of this battle I had internalized? Part of this emerged in the aching intensity of the battle that raged within me over the writing process itself. Again and again I had to fight the odd feeling that I, who was so verbal, lacked, couldn't grasp, did not have access to words themselves: the words for what I needed to convey. I not only lacked words but found myself patriarchally questioning my right to my own voice and point of view: my right to write. Other doubts surfaced: was I a Jungian or a heretic; within the fold or without? Could I trust myself to speak out clearly without becoming, on the one side, too complexed or, on the other, playing it too safe? After all, I still was a candidate subject to evaluation by people who sometimes held very different world views than mine.

I had, it is true, formulated the general outline of my chapters but still felt at a loss. There was so much material scattered in so many different places! Little bits of new theory appeared here, more there, often

dropped unheralded into articles or books on other subjects. I was overwhelmed by Jungians' ahistoricity and disregard for temporal organization. No one had ever treated this subject comprehensively; what if I
missed something (as, in attempting a task that had never been done
before, I inevitably would)? I was feeling paralyzed, when, at the beginning of my work on these chapters, I had two dreams.

The first reflected my task quite graphically. I was at a Jungian university ("Jung U.") on a work/study program. The main gathering place
looked like a popular student hang-out from my undergraduate days.
Students crowded into the ancient wooden booths. There was laughter,
some singing and beer drinking and much animated discussion. But
the place was a mess. The kitchen itself seemed clean and the food substantial; the dishes and silverware coming out of the kitchen were stacked
and clean. However, the tables and floor were covered with dirty dishes,
crumbs and scraps of food — tomato chunks on the floor, bits of salad,
whole wheat bread, pizza crusts. As a student I needed to eat and was
very hungry; I was also a worker. I had just started my shift and had
an empathic young man with me who was eager to help. My task was
to try to bring some order to this chaos, to clean the place up a bit.

The second dream, which came a day or two later, was in several parts:
each part presented two ways of doing and being in marked contrast
to each other. In the first I again had a job to do and needed helpers.
One was a rather competitive little man with a flashlight who was busy
shining it all over the place; my task was to get him to follow my direction, not let him be the sorcerer's apprentice I felt he could turn into
if left to himself. The other man reminded me of my first analyst, a
deeply caring, introverted-feeling type. He told me or showed me how
he could help. It was through retiring to his room, playing a little sitar
music, meditating, and then sleeping on the problem. In the second
part of the dream I sailed my boat toward the shore, mooring it at a
dock right next to a boat full of music-making men. This was across
from another dock, a ghost dock — a place where ghosts could jump inside a woman, occupy her without her knowing it. My mother stood
on that other dock as a ghost and was badly ghosted herself. She and
the man with her tell me (I am now about twelve) about the culture
of the place. The practice is to saw off girls' right arms, right at the shoul-
der. This way, my mother says, makes girls easier to manage: it slows
them down and keeps them subservient. The left-handed way, they tell
me, is the right one for girls since "by nature" girls don't do things as

well as boys. Girls have inferior balance, hand-eye and spatial coordination (with the arm missing like that). This crippling, my mother insists, is especially necessary for brainy, troublesome girls like me: girls who don't know their place. Maidens aren't marriageable, they repeat, if they're too powerful. I am horrified, angry, and outraged. But then I see the San Francisco analyst, Jane Wheelwright, sitting on the other dock (where I had moored my boat). She looks at me, looks at them, then gives them a loud and disgusted hoot of derision and disbelief. I run to join her, then, adult once again, stand firmly on the dock beside her, our hands linked and both of us feeling powerful, free, and full of energy.

As I wake up, the pattern for these chapters appears. It is to show the nourishment in analytical psychology, organize and clean up a bit so that our history can be presented harmoniously, one course after the other. I also have to be alert to woman's crippling, to the ghost-filled parents and their daughters and how theory, Jungian theory, can be used to limit, restrict, and maim women as well as to heal. I need to recognize the effect of the patriarchal animus on generations of women, on my mother, and, of course, on me. I must bear witness to the effect of patriarchal mandates: how they can lead to a woman's self-hatred for her own being and how they can operate with lethal intent on a woman's and her daughters' creativity. I also need to recognize my own internal ghost-animus who disapproves, criticizes, and is never ever satisfied. The flashlight-wielding animus needs direction; he can't be left to run wild, nor to swamp himself and me with endless details. Instead, I need to look for and concentrate on whatever appears in the feminine and masculine that is nourishing and energy-releasing. I have to be alert to the tone, to recognize what maims creativity and self-esteem, what hurts a woman's soul and needs to be changed in light of present social and cultural conditions. I also need to recognize what comes from the positive feminine who is true to her own self and from the positive masculine, who, as in my dream, may appear in a man's meditative silence and openness to the unconscious, or as feeling-imbued song and music-making, or from the empathic helper in the restaurant—all these value dreams, feeling, and nurturing in their own masculine way. These will be my guides in the chapters that follow.

PART ONE
JUNG AND HIS LEGACY

CHAPTER ONE: THE VAPOR BATH AND THE SNOW

Attitudes Toward the Feminine in Jung's Time

> One still remains a child of one's own age, even with something one had thought was one's very own.
>
> Freud in a letter to William Fliess

C. G. Jung grew up in Switzerland at the end of the nineteenth century; his ideas about the feminine were conditioned by the place and period in which he lived, and by the attitudes toward women that were then current. In order to understand Jung's theories and their roots, it is necessary to examine some of these attitudes in the popular culture as well as in the more scientific thought that surrounded him as a young doctor.

Jung was one of the most remarkable, comprehensive, and creative contributors to psychology as we know it. In considering this contribution, it is valuable to learn what Jung himself required a psychologist to know. In the foreword to *The Practice of Psychotherapy,* Jung wrote:

> Psychotherapeutic practice and the historical approach . . . [are not] two incommensurable things. In psychological reality . . . we are constantly coming upon phenomena that reveal their historical character as soon as their causality is examined a little more closely. Psychic modes of behaviour are, indeed, of an eminently historical nature. The psychotherapist has to acquaint himself not only with the personal biography of his patient, but also with the mental and spiritual assumptions prevalent in his milieu, both present and past, where traditional and cultural influences play a part and often a decisive one. (Jung, 1958/1975, pp. vii-viii)

Jung's ideas and theory about the feminine need to be examined in the same inquiring spirit. Analyzing theory in this light and with caring attention to its underlying assumptions and influences helps reveal what may be of lasting value and what is unduly restrictive, perhaps part of a socio-cultural prison which acts, like a neurosis, to limit and bind Jung's view. It is possible that the theory itself, like the neurotic patient, may be extricated "from the oppressive constriction of a purely personalistic understanding . . . that cuts him off from the wide horizon of his further social, moral, and spiritual development" (ibid., p. viii).

In the first two volumes of his psychoanalytically-informed study, *The Bourgeois Experience: Victoria to Freud* (1984 and 1986), the cultural and intellectual historian Peter Gay examines the "Victorian" culture in which Jung grew up. Gay includes a vast array of primary sources: novels, journals, newspapers, diaries, letters, autobiographies, household manuals, religious tracts, medical texts, sex surveys, works of art, architecture, and even the furniture design of Jung's period. By integrating psychoanalysis with this history, Gay conveys a truer sense of the bourgeois experience of that era, including the way the social world contributes to the individual's unconscious, and the way culture permeates theory, philosophy and practice (see Henderson, 1984 and 1985, for a parallel Jungian evolvement of the same concept). A large part of the first volume of Gay's study deals with the problem of the feminine and with "the extraordinary paradox that female sexuality posed to nineteenth century middle-class society" (Gay, 1984, p. 159). Part of the problem and paradox involved woman's political, educational, and sexual place in a man's world. Another part was the astonishing ignorance about women manifested by the men who wrote about and treated women professionally. In tracing this conundrum, Gay notes that medical texts, religious advice and educational theory were all marked by unexamined preconceptions about women and by unconscious fears of the feminine.

> Men's highly charged construction of the mysterious sex in art, in literature, in society, in bed, supports my definition of experience as an encounter of mind with world, as a struggle between conscious perceptions and unconscious dilemmas. For the shifting realities of women's situation confronted most middle-class men, and for that matter most middle-class women, with a need to clarify attitudes, test prejudices, and make decisions. Men's very self-perception was at stake. The exasperated feelings all this aroused and the venomous controversies it generated should astonish only those who fail to recognize the commanding share of subterranean feelings in the making of social postures and political ideologies. (Gay, 1984, p. 171)

The split between women's authentic experience and their culture's teachings was even more wrenching than it is today. In the face of laws, rules, and social habits designed to infantilize them, women for the first time started a concerted struggle to obtain independence, self-respect, and a right to a life of their own. Knowledge about contraception began to be somewhat available, while economic conditions provided many women of the middle class with some free time and a chance for a life outside the home. There ensued a struggle for suffrage, economic parity, equal pay, some control over a woman's own money and access to higher education. A university or professional education was rare for a woman—yet this very education taught its students that the feminine was inferior. Women were depicted in the universities and in the popular press as weak, fragile, frigid, passive, docile, and morally superior, though intellectually inferior, to men—who, it was thought, had a natural right to dominion over them. At the same time women were also perceived to be enormously powerful, but their power was reduced to the negative and the erotic; consequently they were imagined to be wickedly sensual, naturally sinful, and the temptresses and seducers of men.* Women's capacities, except as mother, angel, and whore, tended to be denigrated, minimized, or denied.

Gay attributes these attitudes to men's uneasiness and fear. He describes the professionals of the late nineteenth century as mistaking for genetic and universal what was prejudiced, specific, acquired, local and questionable. Men's ignorance about women partly derived from the segregated lives each gender led. Gay describes men of the era as living a great part of their lives in a sort of exterior "clubland" world: the privileged enclaves of government, business, the professions, and the schools and universities. Gay describes professional texts about women as therefore marked by "the kind of coarseness often characteristic of man talking to man about women" (p. 149).

Fear of change in the established order accompanied the fear of women, a fear which Gay and others (e.g., Lederer, 1970; Dijkstra, 1986) assert is age-old. This fear was especially noxious during the late nineteenth century in Anglo-European societies, when—and partly because—the status of women and their psychology started to be questioned and explored. Gay seeks a psychological explanation for this problem:

The fear of women has taken many forms in history. It has been re-

---

* For an analysis of these attitudes, see Bram Dijkstra's *Idols of Perversity* (1986).

pressed, disguised, sublimated, or advertised, but in one way or another it seems to be as old as civilization itself. . . . The fear of women thus seems endemic and permanent. It is born of man's early total dependence on his mother, and his longing, frustrated love for her, his defenseless lassitude after intercourse, and the frightening aspect and portentous implications of the female genitals: for the boy who is likely to see woman as a castrated male, the absence of her penis reads like a threat to his own. The Medusa and all the dangers to man's virility she stands for are a very old story. (pp. 200-201)

The increase in woman's power and her demands for emancipation during the latter half of the nineteenth century exacerbated this anxiety and became a prominent theme in both popular novels and medical treatises. It was accompanied by a reaction formation: the anxiety-producing, powerful feminine was declared weak and inferior. Willful ignorance about her psychology was disguised behind the Romantic notion of the "mysterious" sex.

In his second volume, Gay focuses on the era's Romantic notion of love. He stresses the profound ambivalence pervading men's attitudes toward women and women's own attitudes toward themselves during this period (the time that Jung was growing up). On the one side was a Romantic ideal which newly valued women and the feminine in personal alliances. The ideal was for a companionate, witty, intelligent relationship which presupposed an equality of education and opportunity that simply wasn't there. Women themselves were trying to live up to this ideal. Many were no longer content to be just wives and mothers; they also wanted education, work, and economic opportunities. On the other side, though, came anxiety at this new valuation and its prospect of greater freedom and independence, but also greater demands. This produced a reaction which emphasized women's frailty and their supposedly innate deficiencies.

Bourgeois love "too often paraded in genteel artistic or literary disguises" (1986, p. 4), disguises which served to repress enormous energy. In Gay's view, the price of this repression was psychic strain which flowed inward into neuroticism and outward through such symptoms as prostitution and alcoholism. The repression gave rise to anxiety-provoking fears and buried wishes which found outlets in an ambivalent fascination with—as well as various serious studies of—the underside of life: of prostitutes, brothels, sexuality, and the indecorous case histories of the new psychology, as well as in the bourgeois' study of his own innermost feelings and fantasies. Gay traces the guilt felt toward women back to unresolved oedipal issues in which a man needed to both exalt and demean his first love object, his mother. Guilt about (then the attempts at reparation and rescue of) fallen, sick, or wounded women, so much a part of the conscience of the time, could psychologically be seen as an attempt to repair the denigration of the mother. Attending as an adult to fallen, sick, or wounded women redeemed, through a sort of parallel magic, the mother who could never be restored: the original wounder and wounded one. The physician, psychiatrist, reformer, or lover could escape from this original guilt through the fantasy of rescuing his mother "in whatever form he may encounter her likeness in later years" (p. 380). The male's regressive need for union with an overly powerful yet despised mother was played out in the era's flagrant ambivalence toward women and the split between the need for love and the bourgeois need for its repression. Though this oedipal situation and its many reenactments may be a heritage of all nuclear families, it was particularly prevalent during this time. The outer form this ferment took was typical of the era:

> Bourgeois in their century set certain unmistakable emotional accents . . . very much their own. I recall [here] only their rage for privacy, their impassioned rehabilitation of prostitutes, their consequential rediscovery of sexual perversions, their mobilizing imaginative disguises for sensuality, their strident slanders of women oddly combined with a new respect for her capacities. (1986, p. 389)

Gay finds the splitting and confusion in the bourgeois attitude toward women as apparent in the works of such psychologists as Freud and Jung as it was in more popular texts. J. S. Mill, writing earlier in the century about this same split, describes it in less psychological but perhaps simpler terms as a behavioral modification that was one of the consequences of the patriarchal subjugation of women by men. He concludes that the supposedly innate womanly characteristics disparaged or valued by society were not innate, but a direct consequence of distorted social conditioning.

> In the case of women, a hot-house and stove cultivation has always been carried on of some of the capabilities of their nature, for the benefit and pleasure of their masters. Then, because certain products of the general vital force sprout luxuriantly and reach a great development in this heated atmosphere and under this active nurture and watering, while other shoots from the same root, which are left outside in the wintery air, with

ice purposely heaped all round them, have a stunted growth, and some
are burnt off with fire and disappear; men, with that inability to recognize their own work which distinguishes the unanalytic mind, indolent-
ly believe that the tree grows of itself in the way they have made it grow,
and that it would die if one half of it were not kept in a vapor bath and
the other half in the snow. (J. S. Mill 1869/1979, pp. 22-23)

This distorted and ambivalent view of the feminine permeated the
sensibility of Jung's time. Two important studies of women and the literary
imagination of the nineteenth century, Gilbert and Gubar's (1980) *The
Madwoman in the Attic*, and Auerbach's (1982) *Woman and the Demon: The Life of a Victorian Myth*, look at some of the results of this
conditioning and its effect on women's psychology; they describe much
in the literature of the time which recalls what Jung found in female
patients neuroticized by their struggle with the same distortions. Gilbert and Gubar point to a distinctively female literary tradition that arose
as a result of woman's position in the culture. Some writers drew their
themes out of women's struggle to free themselves from the male-
dominated society of the time, while others derived them from their
own experience of living in such a society. Gilbert and Gubar describe
this female literary tradition as being full of "images of enclosure and
escape, fantasies in which maddened doubles functioned as asocial sur-
rogates for docile selves, metaphors of physical discomfort manifested
in frozen landscapes and fiery interiors . . . along with obsessive depictions of diseases like anorexia, agoraphobia, and claustrophobia" (1980,
p. xi).

As Jung and Freud both pointed out, myth and the lived reality often converge. Works of fiction depict the pathology of a culture often
more clearly and concisely than patients themselves, while the myth both
informs and reflects that pathology. Nineteenth century women's writing is full of descriptions of volcanic anguish and depictions of damage
done to a woman's psyche through her efforts to shape herself into, or
revolt from, the image of the feminine demanded of her by the patriarchy. They portray the same divided and conflicted view of her inner self
that brought some of her contemporaries to Jung's and Freud's consulting rooms. This view was an internalization of the ways the patriarchy
perceived the feminine: as "monstrous, deviant, excluded, powerless and
angry," (p. 387) as well as dependent, fallen, and inadequate, and of
woman as alienated from her body and her sexuality—itself seen by society as a dangerous cause of chaos and suffering.

Auerbach (1982), like Gay, examines the cultural imagination of the time and shares a psychological viewpoint with him. Like Jung, she is especially concerned with the unrecognized power implicit in the era's feminine models (what Jung would call archetypes). She focuses on the stock female characters of angel, demon, fallen woman and witch. Auerbach argues that depicting women this way showed a secret, subversive, covert acknowledgement and exaltation of women, and of their officially denied but privately feared power. Auerbach stresses the ambivalence, strength, and hidden power (rather than the "madness" of Gilbert and Gubar's formulation) latent in these nineteenth-century depictions of the feminine. Writing about England, but with a viewpoint common to the age as a whole, she emphasizes that "the Victorian culture had no firmly rooted imagination of adult womanhood and so envisioned a creature of almost infinite mobility" (pp. 138-139).

> Legally and socially women composed an oppressed class, but whether she was locked in the home, exiled to the colonies, or haunting the banks of the Thames, woman's very aura of exclusion gave her imaginative centrality in a culture increasingly alienated from itself. Powerful images of oppression became images of barely suppressed power, all the more grandly haunting because, unlike the hungry workers, woman ruled both the Palace and the home while hovering simultaneously in the darkness without. Assuming the power of the ruler as well as the menace of the oppressed, woman was at the center of her age's myth at the same time as she was excluded from its institutions. (Auerbach, 1982, pp. 188-189)

In defence of her thesis, Auerbach's study includes many of the same books Jung refers to in his study of the "infinite mobility" of the anima and in his general depiction of the feminine (e.g., Rider Haggard's *She*). Auerbach plumbs the cultural iconography of the feminine that permeated books of Jung's time. Women were supposed to be imbued with an irrational psychological energy and endowed with such an exaggerated multiplicity of seethingly conflictual attributes that it is clear they were not seen for themselves but were turned into creatures of men's imagination, both an inspiration and a focus for the creative energy of the imagination.

Ehrenreich and English (1979) and Hillman (1972) have traced the role of patriarchal imagination in the treatment of women by the medical profession. As a medical student, Jung was subject to this particular strain of patriarchal imagination; its views or prejudices about women accompanied more pragmatic studies. Hillman and Ehrenreich and English all question the belief in the "natural" inferiority of women that pervaded the medical texts of the time. Ehrenreich and English explain this belief as an effect of the market economy of the late nineteenth century, which created two separate and unequal spheres for men and women. The household was no longer self-contained with a unity of work, home, production, and family life. Instead, two separate spheres with differing and opposing values appeared. Public life became the life of the Market and of men; private life belonged to the home and to women. The Market values were rationality, self-interest, competence, competition, and impersonal business relationships, where thinking was valued over feeling. The life of the Market was considered the normal life of the world and was deemed superior to its opposite, the private sphere.

> The masculinist view of human nature almost automatically excludes woman and her nature. . . . The successful economic man, the capitalist, ceaselessly transforms life—human labor and effort—into lifeless capital, an activity which is to him eminently rational, sane and "human." Ultimately the laws of the Market come to appear as the laws of human nature. From this vantage point, woman inevitably appears alien, mysterious. She inhabits (or is supposed to inhabit) the "other" realm, the realm of private life, which looks to the Market like a pre-industrial backwater, or a looking-glass land that inverts all that is normal in the "real" world of men. The limited functions now reserved for that realm attach to woman's person and make her too appear to be an anachronism, or a curious inversion of normality. Biologically and psychologically, she seems to contradict the basic principles of the Market. (Ehrenreich and English, 1979, p. 18)

Men of Jung's era passed between these two spheres daily. In the process they tended to sentimentalize the private sphere according to the tenets of neo-Romanticism in order to compensate for the coldness and harshness of the market. They wanted the home to make up for everything that was lacking in the marketplace, while at the same time reserving priority for the external masculine realm. The place and function of woman was limited to the private realm, to her role as adjunct to the man—his wife, mistress, mother, daughter, or servant. Woman's demand for something else, and her dissatisfaction with this view of her, was turned into a problematical personal and social issue, "the woman question."

Ehrenreich and English trace the treatment accorded such women by the physicians and psychologists of this era. They conclude that the professionals by and large taught and practiced according to the prejudices of their time. They tended to handle the "woman question" by branding woman as flawed and inferior to the male norm, and by a concerted effort to limit her biologically and psychically "by nature" to her domestic and relational role. Any problems this caused tended to be privatized as the fault, disease, or neurosis of an individual woman. Much of the mismanagement of woman's medical and psychological problems by the doctors of Jung's time can be traced to this imaginary and erroneous view of her, disguised as good empirical science and objective truth.

> Claiming the objectivity of science, they had advanced the doctrines of sexual romanticism. They turned out not to be scientists—for all their talk of data, laboratory findings, clinical trials—but apologists for the status quo. (Ehrenreich and English, 1979, p. 316)

Jung found such attitudes as these in the philosophy and science he was studying, in the novels he was reading, in discourse among friends, in medical texts, and in the way he saw women patients treated. The real value of Jung's work on the feminine comes when he strives to stand a bit outside his time and can perceive a woman not as someone whose capabilities are limited by J. S. Mill's "vapor bath and the snow," but as a healthy human who can be freed from her "hot-house and stove cultivation" and assisted in finding her own individual path.

Jung's theories, though, remain tied to his history, his culture and his life; in great part his theories grew out of his education and his philosophical outlook. Unlike many psychiatrists and psychologists today, Jung had an intensive and broad classical education and was much more aware of the philosophical background of his thinking than we tend to be of ours. That education, common to his time, was one of immersion in classical Greek and Latin literature. Besides this, Jung was influenced by Romantic philosophy and psychiatry, the Protestant theological tradition and, somewhat later, by Asian philosophy (Ellenberger, 1970; Maduro and Wheelwright, 1977).

There were two major trends in intellectual and scientific thought in Europe at that time: positivism, heir to the Enlightenment, which focused on reason and society; and Romanticism, with its connection to the irrational and the individual. The influence of positivism was starting to gain ascendency in scientific education. Jung's teachers displayed the almost religious faith in science that seemed to go hand in hand with positivism and the development of the scientific method. This new science started in Germany with Wundt in the 1840s and spread outward in such divergent directions as Darwin's theory of evolution and Marx's application of it to political economics. A person of Jung's generation could trace this optimistic, linear, and ever-forwardly progressing, positivistic stance back to the classical Aristotelian idea of science (Boring, 1950).

William James describes the positivist approach which, in Jung's day, was starting to gain such a hold on science. James depicts his fellow scientists as advancing the modern scientific knowledge of the mind by attempting to stand completely outside their subject and to treat it as an object.

> This method taxes patience to the utmost, and could hardly have arisen in a country whose natives could be *bored*. Such Germans as Weber, Fechner, Vierordt, and Wundt obviously cannot; and their success has brought into the field an array of younger experimental psychologists, bent on studying the *elements* of the mental life, dissecting them out from the gross results in which they are embedded, and as far as possible reducing them to quantitative scales . . . There is little of the grand style about these new prism, pendulum, and chronograph-philosophers. They mean business, not chivalry. What generous divination, and that superiority in virtue which was thought by Cicero to give a man the best insight into nature, have failed to do, their spying and scraping, their deadly tenacity and almost diabolic cunning, will doubtless some day bring about. (James, 1890/1950, pp. 192-193)

This new method was not altogether congenial to Jung's outlook. Rather, the "generous divination," "superiority in virtue" and "insight into nature" mentioned by James form the second strong current in Jung's scientific training: Romanticism. In science this current flowed toward the study of individual cases and particular cultures and nations; it was marked by an openness to the occult, the mysterious, and the unconscious, as well as by a feeling of oneness with nature accompanied by feelings of longing, unrest, and separation (Ellenberger, 1970). This current is more circular than linear and is often pessimistic or, rather, rests upon a Platonic ideal, permanent and unyielding, beyond and behind our rational world. It can be traced from ancient Greece to the Romanticism of the early nineteenth century and its revival at the end of that century. Plato had originally hypothesized that there were certain primordial patterns of which we are more or less defective shadows; among these patterns was an original, complete, and bisexual human. In the late nineteenth century this idea of original wholeness became incorporated into a philosophy of nature where all was felt to be one. Yet all was also divided and polarized (especially the masculine and feminine), and so there was an acute sense of separation from and longing for unity and a wholeness that had somehow been lost.

This longing united with a desire to fathom the depths of the natural world on the outside and the soul within. Hillman (Roscher and Hillman, 1972) refers to this element of Romanticism as a search for the lost gods. "These depths were projected as we now say into the remote past, into mythology, into foreign dark tribes and exotic customs, into the simple folk and their lore, into the mentally alienated" (p. viii). A Romantic longing for what it conceived of as the feminine — for the unconscious and for depth, color, and feeling — was dealt with, in an age that prided itself on its rationality, by using the most advanced methods of reason, "tenacity," and "cunning" to establish the reality of the irrational. Scientists could look for all of this outside themselves while still firmly defending themselves from their own unconscious and their inner feminine; they could do this through projection and through their espousal of scientific objectivity.

A scientific interest in parapsychological phenomena and the occult, which had a resurgence in the nineties, echoed these interests and was for a time respectable. Much of the original interest in psychodynamic psychology came from people involved in parapsychological study (Roazen, 1984). Jung, through his mother's family, belonged to a group in Basel involved in spiritism, seances, table turning etc. (as was William James in the United States, and as were many other psychologists of the time). Much of Jung's outside reading during his university years concerned the occult and the paranormal. He brought this interest into his course work, lectures to his fellow students, and to his dissertation (Ellenberger, 1970; Hillman, 1976).

A Romantic outlook lay behind the rise of other sciences that attracted Jung, such as anthropology, linguistics, archaeology, and the exploration of fairy tales and myths, as well as behind the study of sexuality and of the mysterious inner worlds of the mentally ill. All became subjects of research that perhaps warmed the cold scientism of the day and attracted students like Jung, who chafed against the dryness of accepted empiricism. A Romantic outlook also led to the perception that a person could be at one and the same time "western, modern, secular, civilized and sane — but also primitive, archaic, mythical and mad" (Hillman in Roscher and Hillman, 1972, p. ix). Jung had in turn want-

ed to be an archeologist, an Egyptologist, and a zoologist, but found
medicine a more practical pursuit (Bennet, 1962). His reading of Krafft-
Ebing's study of psychology, with its bizarre and fascinating case histories, finally propelled Jung into psychiatry (Jung, 1963).

Ellenberger (1970) traces aspects of Jung's and Freud's psychology to
Romantic philosophy, such as the importance of the role of guilt (Hein-
roth), anxiety (Guislan), and sexual impulses and frustration (Ideler and
Neumann). He sees Jung and Freud's focus on the unconscious and
dreams, as well as their style of dualistic theorizing, as typically Romantic. Behind Jung's development of his theories Ellenberger finds a number
of antecedents, especially "the Romantic idea of the fundamental bisexuality of the human being" (p. 204). Ellenberger credits von Schell-
ing's philosophy of nature, his concept of the world-soul, and his idea
of the fundamental presence yet polarity of male and female, as influenc-
ing Jung's concepts of the archetypes, the collective unconscious, and
the anima and animus.

Dualistic thinking is an essential part of Jung's way of looking at the
world. "Life, being an energic process, needs the opposites, for without
opposition there is, as we know, no energy . . . The tension of the opposites that makes energy possible is a universal law . . ." (Jung,
1948/1969, p. 197). Willeford (1975) attributes the basic form of all Jung's
theories to this dualism. He examines the polaristic approach historically, concluding that though Jung was committed to the values of empirical science, his thought derived, not from mechanism or positivism,
but from the Romantics, the pre-Socratic philosopher Heraclitus, the
mystic Jacob Boehme, as well as from some deep divisions within Jung's
own nature. Willeford writes that Goethe, Kant, Schiller, and Nietzsche
were especially influential in forming Jung's ideas about the human mind.
They "illustrate a tendency, extremely pronounced in the early part of
the 19th century, to conceive difference as the result of division, which
is finally the expression of universal antagonistic principles" (Willeford,
1975, p. 223).

Jung cites these same philosophers as influences, but also adds Carus
and Schopenhauer (Jung, 1963). Goethe was a predecessor and favorite
of his (and possibly even an ancestor). Besides sharing a similar polaristic outlook, Goethe (in *Faust*, for example) was also absorbed with the
problem of evil, the possibility of metamorphosis of self, and with the
(masculine) self's relation to the feminine. Goethe was a scientist as well
as a poet, dramatist, and philosopher; he conducted a rigorous, if some-

what metaphysical, botanical search for the one basic primordial plant which he thought would prove to be the archetype and model out of which all others developed. Carus, fifty years before Jung, believed in and wrote about the creative, compensatory, autonomous, and healing functions of the unconscious; a physician and painter, Carus outlined a tripartate model of the unconscious in his book *Psyche*: the general absolute, the partial absolute, and the relative. These prefigure Jung's idea of the archetypal, the collective, and the personal unconscious.

Bachofen was known to both Jung and Nietzsche. Like Jung, he immersed himself in myths, symbols and their religious and philosophical importance (Wolff-Windegg, 1976). He wrote of an ancient matriarchal time, a world of the mothers that preceded the patriarchy. Nietzsche took this concept and his idea of a Dionysian-Apollonian duality from Bachofen. Nietzsche in turn influenced Jung through his investigations of interests and themes which were to become central to Jung's ideas: dreams, the problem of evil, sublimation and inhibition, sexual and self-destructive instincts, resentment, moral conscience, the origin of civilization, and the archetypes of the shadow, the persona, the superior person, the superman, and the wise old man. Nietzsche shared with Jung a similar sense of the tragic ambiguity of life: the potential both for good and for evil, and their presence in each human interaction (Frey-Rohn, 1974). Of the feminine he wrote, "Every person carries within a picture of woman which he acquired from his mother. From this picture, he will be determined to respect or despise women or be indifferent toward them" (quoted in Ellenberger, 1970, p. 275). Nietzsche echoes and exaggerates his era's ambivalent attitude toward women. He himself had an irrational fear of women, which manifested in a pervasive misogyny as well as in violent verbal attacks on women (Gay, 1986). Nietzsche's vituperation, however, was unexceptional, a mode of talking which accepted disparaging references to women as part of the *lingua franca* of the day. The flavor of this underlying misogyny is present in some of Jung's jokes and comments about women, especially in his lectures and more "off-the-cuff" moments (see especially the mimeographed notes of the *The Visions Seminars* [1930-1934] and *Zarathustra* [1934-1939] lectures).

Schopenhauer echoed this same misogyny in a perhaps more bitter but also more "scientific" way. His famous essay on women describes them as weak, suffering, childish, inferior to men, and incapable of rational thought. He asserts that women are governed by the irrational and by Eros; they are simply carriers of the natural (again irrational), blind force of life (Gay, 1986). Much of Schopenhauer's polarizing, alas, creeps into Jung's ideas about women, for example in Jung's concept of women's natural mind and in his dichotomies of thinking versus feeling, Logos versus Eros, the former often attributed to men and the latter to women. It also may lie behind Jung's solemnly teasing consideration about whether or not women have souls (e.g., Jung, 1925/1954, p. 198).

At the same time as he disparages women, Schopenhauer, like Jung, was strongly drawn to them, and he wrote convincingly on the idea of Eros, love, as being the heart of religious feeling. Besides writing of the power of the unconscious, Schopenhauer possessed a Romantic and pessimistic *angst*, dwelling on will, the irrational, blind force, repression, and the power of the instincts. Jarrett (1981) notes Schopenhauer's influence on the following aspects of Jung's thought: Jung's theory of archetypes; his focus on the imaginal; his belief in the reality of the unconscious, the reality of evil, and the importance of dreams; his idea of the four functions, with thinking and feeling polarized; and, finally, in his valuation of introversion. Jarrett notes both Schopenhauer's and Jung's common interest in moral issues, in Eastern philosophy, and in the possibility of individuation.

Jarrett and de Voogd (1977) differ, however, about the extent of Kant's contribution to Jung's thought. Though Jung writes that "mentally my greatest adventure had been the study of Kant and Schopenhauer" (1961/1980, p. 213) and often refers to himself as a Kantian, de Voogd argues that Kant's things-in-themselves, his innate categories, start from sensory data which are then structured by human intelligence, with Kant concluding that nothing in the mind is real; while Jung starts from archetypes and imagination and does believe in the reality of the psyche.

Boring (1950) has traced the influence of the positivistic and mechanistic psychology of this time, while Ellenberger (1970), Meier (1967/1989) and Gay (1984, 1988) stress the historical and Romantic antecedents behind Jung's and Freud's study of dreams and the unconscious. The importance of these historical antecedents to Jung's and Freud's theories cannot be stressed enough, especially when psychology itself is becoming so compartmentalized and much that rounds out theory gets erased. Jones (1955) and Fine (1979), for instance, neglect Freud's and Jung's socio-cultural milieu; instead they endeavor to build up their specific compartment of psychology ahistorically, through having their master, Freud, stand alone and out of time as the sole "discoverer of the unconscious, the Oedipus complex, the anal stage, infantile sexuality, how to interpret dreams, free association, transference and resistances" (Fine, 1979, p. 29).

Jung's Romantic fascination is apparent in the way he treated the mentally ill; this treatment was based on the close attention of the positivist but also involved concern with the individual person and the unconscious. Jung attempted to understand how a patient experienced and made sense of his or her bizarre world. Historically, Ellenberger describes Jung's approach — with its emphasis on two individuals, the doctor and the patient, and on the transference — as a culmination of a progression from priestly exorcism, to the channeling and releasing of the subtle physical fluid of Mesmer's animal magnetism, then Puysegur's and Deleuze's more scientific use of hypnosis in the early nineteenth century. From these beginnings Ellenberger traces the founding of the School of Nancy in France, the worldwide spread of hypnotism as a cure for mental illness, and the parallels between the cure and its disease, hysteria, in the work of Charcot and Janet. (Freud studied for a few weeks with the flamboyant and theatrical Charcot; Jung for a winter term with Charcot's opposite, the dedicated, modest, and intensely scrupulous Janet.) In each case, theory was constructed and generalized from patients who "were the casualties of their culture" (Gay, 1986, p. 352).

An important motif in the study of the unconscious that has received little attention (though both Ellenberger, 1970, and Hillman, 1976, note its importance) is a Romantic fascination with the depths accompanied by and expressed through the involvement of a male scientist with a female patient who became the object of his research and of his profound interest. In each instance the man explores his own depths through projection onto his subject, while the subject projects health, wholeness, and the capacity to heal onto her doctor. In this partnership the doctor takes on a strange combination of scientist, healer, explorer, and magician who seems, through evoking yet somehow controlling her secrets, to be engaging the woman's very soul in some sort of magic transformation. It was a heady combination which tended to unleash the mythopoetic functions of the unconscious, the interest of the scientist perhaps having a greater than realized influence on the flowering, as well as on the healing, of the patient's symptoms. It was also a partnership which evoked that most puzzling of things, transference-countertransference phenomena. The scientist's fascination with and longing for the repressed feminine, his projection of this aspect of himself onto the patient, the resultant transference and countertransference, all produced an unconscious collusion which allowed the feminine to break through, supposedly under safe control, in a scientific setting.

Among some of the more famous of these studies of possession, multiple personalities, mediums, seers, hysterics, trance states, and hypnosis or self-hypnosis were Pastor Blumhardt of Gottliebin Dittus (1815); Mesmer (1734-1815) of both Fraulein Oesterlin and Maria Theresa Paradis; Puysegur (1850) of Victor Race (the only male in the group—a gentle, receptive, feeling young man); Justinus Kerner (1786-1862) of the Seer of Prevorst, Friederiche Hauffe; Despine of Estelle (1836); Charcot of his *grande hystérique,* Blanche Wittman (1882); Janet of Leonie (1886, 1887, 1888); Breuer of Anna O. (1895); Flournoy's study of Helene Smith (1899); Freud of, among quite a few others, Elizabeth von R. (1895) and Dora (1900); and Morton Prince's study of Miss Beauchamp (1906). Jung was immediately drawn to this subject and avidly read the studies available to him (*The Zofingia Lectures* [1902/1983]). He wrote his own dissertation on his cousin, the medium Hélène Preiswerk. This study of her manifests many of the qualities of fascination, transference, countertransference and multiple projections that mark the other studies.

Jung's interest in this aspect of Romantic psychology is clearly visible in a course on the history of psychology that he taught in the early nineteen-thirties at the Polytechnic in Zürich—ostensibly a survey of psychology since Descartes in which Fechner, Carus, and Schopenhauer were stressed, but at root a discussion of hypnosis, the paranormal, and some of the above-mentioned case histories. Justinus Kerner and the Seer of Prevorst, along with Flournoy's study of Helene Smith, occupied much of his and his students' time and interest (Jung, 1963; Ellenberger, 1970). It was only much later that Jung observed the transference link between the doctor and his female subject and their unconscious underlying erotic relationship. What he perhaps overlooked was the link between repressed aspects of the feminine in both patient and observer and the way the cultural unconscious formed, glamorized, and empowered this deviant and wounded feminine.

What does remain of deepest interest . . . is the importance in the origin of depth psychology of these unusual women, whether those investigated by Charcot in Paris, Bernheim in Nancy, Freud in Vienna, or Jung in Basel. It was they who embodied psychic reality. And it was this fascination with the "magic" of psychic reality as embodied by these young girls, such as Hélène Preiswerk, that bespeaks the anima that was emerging via these pioneers of medical psychology into our age of psychotherapy. (Hillman, 1976, p. 135)

By the end of the nineteenth century, the powerful, creative, mythopoetic, erotic, and dramatic element of the unconscious feminine and the anima—which could be discerned behind the sober scientific studies of the researcher and his study of his feminine subject—became a theme of Romantic popular literature.

It is important to note that, beside a few good novels and plays, a multitude of popular novels and cheap literature, which are entirely forgotten today, were published in the 1880's involving the themes of somnambulism, multiple personality, and crimes under hypnosis, which certainly contributed to shaping the mentality of that period. (Ellenberger, 1970, p. 166)

More lasting works that explored the same themes were written by Balzac, Poe, Nietzsche, Wilde, Dostoevski, Hugo, George du Maurier, de Maupassant, R. L. Stevenson, Dickens, and Proust. As a Swiss student, Jung would have had access to Nietzsche and other of the earlier writers as well as to his own nation's popular literature. All of these contributed to his apperception of the feminine.

Jung's own nationality adds a particular note to this understanding. Gay describes Germany as one of the most markedly anti-feminist countries of that era (Gay, 1984, p. 195); Ellenberger finds the situation in Switzerland, especially in the German-speaking section where Jung grew up, to be even more so. He goes on to describe the important male worlds of the Swiss army, gentlemen's clubs, the business world (where even the secretaries were male), and the emphasis on the male (*sic*) virtues of ambition, aggressiveness, toughness, and self-rule. There were no female students in the Swiss universities until the 1890s, when one or two, usually foreign women, were admitted per year. A man's authority over his wife, her property and money, and over his children was unquestioned.

John McPhee (1984), writing about the Switzerland of today, describes the same atmosphere of dedication, provincialism, tradition, and male dominance. Like Ellenberger, he remarks on the social and professional importance of the Swiss army. As in Jung's time, it is exclusively male. Ten percent of the Swiss population is on regular yearly training duty at any one time, and serving as an officer is still one of the main pathways for executive advancement in the business and professional world. A citizen of Switzerland and a person who has served, or is serving, the fatherland in the army are synonymous. There is still controversy about the advisability of the recent enfranchisement of women, and women still play very little part in community or business affairs.

Being a Swiss citizen gave Jung a sense of stability; its relevance to his character has been emphasized in his autobiography and in almost all biographies of him, most notably those of van der Post (1975) and Hannah (1976). Hannah emphasizes the effect of the social and political life of Switzerland on Jung and describes the sense of responsibility and groundedness all its duties gave to him. Wolff-Windegg (1976) notes both the secure atmosphere of Switzerland and the specifically frugal and dour "sensually-averse" character of the Protestant Baseler. Jung's uniting the two strains of the Romantic and the Protestant, Wolff-Windegg concludes, helped him explore the unconscious and create an imageful psychology while remaining grounded by his nation's stability. Van der Post stresses the impact the Swiss surroundings had on Jung as a boy: the Romantic ambience of the lakes and the dark and dangerous Rhine falls and river nearby, and the high mountains distantly surrounding him. Van der Post recalls Jung telling him "that the nature of the earth itself had a profound influence on the character of the people born and raised on it" (1975, p. 65).

Jung often spoke of the beauty of Switzerland and the effect his environment and country exerted on him. He loved the water and insisted he always live near it. The other side of Jung's exaltation of the beauty and lifegiving aspects of his environment are his memories of the more ominous sides of this Romantic world. In one passage in his memoirs (1963, p. 7), Jung recalls a corpse that had been washed down from the falls upriver and temporarily stored in the family washhouse. Jung describes an almost Gothic scene of the locked washroom door, the dead man behind it, Jung as a small boy in front of it, and blood and water seeping out of the drain under the door toward him.

The influence of Switzerland's geography and government echo throughout Jung's theory. On the one hand, Switzerland is a turbulent, passionate countryside with great belts of folded rock climbing into mountains over 15,000 feet high, three wide river valleys with more than a quarter of the land covered by lakes, rivers, glaciers, and countless waterfalls; in Jung's time the land was over seventy percent productive woodland (*Encyclopedia Brittanica,* 1910-11 [Eleventh Edition]). Switzerland is a land of many climates, floods, thunderstorms, as well as an odd, neurotic wind, the foehn. There is no topographical unity, no more than

there is commonality of language. Yet on the other hand there is the
sober, pragmatic, almost constricted Swiss character, with its citizens living
peacefully in a successful confederacy throughout the most turbulent
times in European history; the towns and cities filled with frugal
bourgeois.

Like the Romantic geography of Switzerland, a side of Jung, what he
called in his autobiography his Number Two character, is immersed in
all the Romantic interest in the depths: the unconscious, the feminine,
dreams, fantasies, and the vagaries of the mind. At the same time, like
the pragmatic and sober Swiss citizen he was, Jung also had a rational
and enlightened side (what he called his Number One character) living
a respectable bourgeois life; in this role, he is the empirical scientist examining his subject. Yet Jung himself contains both with no seeming
need to integrate the two sides. Like his country, Jung has the capacity
to hold the separate, distinct parts of the psyche as a confederacy in the
inner Switzerlands of his mind and of his theory. However, both the
way the Swiss bourgeois "Number One" character sees the feminine and
the way Jung's Romantic "Number Two" character experiences the feminine become problematic for women living today and for a Jungian psychology of women, for both are suffused with the unexamined patriarchal
imagination and prejudices of the time.

A confederacy like Switzerland may be made up of separate and equal
districts, but a psychological theory built in the same way falls prey to
history and culture. What Jung read and what he experienced enters
into and affects his theory. The deconstructionist philosopher Jacques
Derrida (1976) has noted what happens to polarities in Western
philosophical systems: they become subject to a covert hierarchy that
reflects the prejudices of the time. The positivist dominates the Romantic
in the education of Jung's era; the male dominates the female in his
culture and society; the *polis* dominates nature and exploits her; and
rationality dominates feeling. In the nineteenth century and in Jung's
theories, women are equated with the Romantic, the feminine, nature,
and with feelings: each the subordinate and dominated half of the polarity. In Jung's theories of masculine and feminine, the masculine is the
norm; the supposedly equal feminine is secretly deviant. She is subject
to the same covert hierarchy, the same guilt, the same longing, the same
collective fantasy of rescue and healing that comes with this era's masculine hegemony. "From this vantage point, woman inevitably appears
alien, mysterious . . . an anachronism, or a curious inversion of normal

ity" (Ehrenreich and English, 1979, p. 18).

CHAPTER TWO: UNFINISHED BUSINESS

Jung's Personal Experience of the Feminine

Theoretical systems in psychology cannot escape the elements of a founder's own personal psychology. In this sense, every theory is a personal confession. It reflects a subjective bias, even in the very questions it selects to ask and how it sets out to answer them. If acknowledged openly and taken seriously into account, this personal bias may prove to be a scientific asset rather than a liability.

Maduro and Wheelwright, in Corsini, 1977

An examination of Jung's experience of the feminine and of women, especially his early memories and family configuration, may provide clues toward a better understanding of the psychological system he created: clues which can help separate what is transitory (and perhaps complexed) from what is more durable. History is grounded in the particular, in individual strengths and weaknesses, in wounds, their healing, their scars, and in the internal struggles and unfinished business of its participants. For Jung, his era, and analytic theory in general, the feminine is all of these, but most of all it is unfinished business.

Jung writes in his autobiography that during a time of crisis after his separation from Freud he felt impelled to open himself to his fantasies. The inner figures who emerged, Elijah, Salome, and Philemon, were to become of lifelong importance to him.

> I caught sight of two figures, an old man with a white beard and a beautiful young girl . . . The old man explained that he was Elijah, and that gave me a shock. But the girl staggered me even more, for she called herself Salome! She was blind . . . They had a black serpent living with them who displayed an unmistakable fondness for me. I stuck close to

Elijah because he seemed the more reasonable of the three, and to have
a clear intelligence. Of Salome I was distinctly suspicious . . . . Soon after this fantasy another figure rose out of the unconscious. He developed
out of the Elijah figure. I called him Philemon. (1963, pp. 181-182)

The missing human fourth in this quaternity is Baucis, Philemon's
biblical wife whom Gerhard Wehr (1987) traces, through Goethe's *Faust,*
to Philemon and Baubo (pp. 182-183). Baucis/Baubo, the crone, the
old, vulgar, sexual, and potent woman — the human form of the black
serpent — is most noticeably missing from Jung's fantasy. Jung, as a man
of his time, places his trust in the masculine and doubts or ignores his
two feminine aspects. Why was Jung suspicious of Salome, his own inner feminine, and how did that distrust of the feminine come about?
Why was the black serpent so fond of him, but her human form —
Philemon's wife Baucis — missing? How did Jung's early experiences of
the feminine, especially of his mother, affect his perception of women
and his psychological theory? These are questions that cry out for clari-
fication before a truer evaluation of analytical psychology's relevance to
women can be formulated.

Jung was born in 1875 in the little village of Kesswil, on Lake Con-
stance. The family moved to Laufen, by the Rhine falls, when he was
six months old; and, when he was four, to the village of Klein-Hunigen,
lower down on the Rhine and near Basel, a small but important cultural and business center. Water and the experience of living by a lake or
river formed such an essential component of Jung's sense of the world
that he lived almost all his life in sight of it (van der Post, 1975). After
attending the village primary school in Klein-Hunigen, he went to the
Gymnasium in Basel.

Both of Jung's parents were the youngest of large families. There were
six clergymen in his mother's immediate family; his father and two of
his uncles were also ministers. Jung's maternal grandfather, Samuel
Preiswerk (1799-1871), was a noted theologian, Hebrew scholar, and Zi-
onist. Jung (1961/1980) reports that Preiswerk and a number of other
members on both sides of Jung's family had marked parapsychological
interests and abilities. Preiswerk, in fact, seems to have mixed this interest with more personal vagaries. By keeping his dead wife's chair in
its original place solely for her weekly "spirit" visits to him (Ellenberger, 1970), he not only arrogated to himself access to both wives at once
(Jaffe, 1964) but also subtly distressed his intuitive and telepathic second wife, whose rightful place this would have normally been. He even

insisted at one period that his daughter, Emilie (Jung's mother), remain seated behind his chair as he was composing his sermons so that she could come between him and the spirits and ghosts who might otherwise interfere with his writing. Thus, even while a young girl, Jung's mother had a complicated relationship with the uncanny and its mortal permutations.

Jung's paternal grandfather, Carl Gustav Jung (1795-1864) was one of the most cultured and renowned citizens of Basel. A popular and successful physician, he also played prominent roles as rector and university professor, as Grand Master of the Swiss Freemasons, and as a scientific writer, as well as a writer of plays and Romantic poetry (Ellenberger, 1970). He was rumored to be Goethe's illegitimate son. Whatever the truth of the story, he was one of the most important figures of his day. Jung's parents, in comparison, were far less well off and had fewer advantages than their parents. Both his parents' fathers had endured severe financial setbacks by the time they, each the youngest of thirteen children, were growing up.

In contrast to Carl Gustav's worldy eminence, his son, Paul Achilles (Jung's father) became a simple country pastor who earned his living in a series of poor rural parishes. Jung's father entered the ministry neither through spiritual calling nor through scholarly interest, but, his family being newly impoverished, because the ministry provided him a way to gain an education and livelihood. This came about because a member of his extended family left some money to help a relative train for the ministry; the boy seized this chance to gain a depth of education (including a doctorate in oriental languages) that would otherwise have been beyond his reach (Hannah, 1976). Bennet (1962) recalls Jung saying that his mother must have found the life of a country parson's wife not only boring but a bit stifling, especially after her cosmopolitan and cultivated upbringing. The situation was equally unsuitable for Jung's father, who was of an introverted, scholarly, perhaps bitter nature, and from a similarly cultured background. Yet he spent his days occupied with rural, predominantly peasant, parishioners. Both Jung's parents lived far more restricted lives than their childhood circumstances predicted. Neither, it seems, fitted the environment in which they found themselves. This estrangement must have made life difficult for them, and their mutual discontent could not but have had its effect on their sensitive and intuitive son.

Jung's older brother had died when a few days old (Bennet, 1962, states, however, that Jung was the third child: *two* older boys having died in infancy; all other biographers name a single brother, Paul, named after the father). Jung's sister, Gertrud, was not born until nine years after Jung. Jung, thus, spent his youth as virtually an only child. What the effect was on both his parents and himself of his being the only surviving son, with his elder brother(s) dead in infancy, is unknown, but could have added another weight to Jung's solitary childhood. Jung describes his youth as a lonely and not particularly happy one, much affected by dreams and fantasies as well as by his environment.

Jung's companions and school fellows, until he went to high school in Basel, were mostly peasants, who, he says, were so different from him "that they alienated me from myself" (Jung, 1963, p. 19). He shared with them, however, a rural upbringing that fed his delight in the natural world. He was not only exposed to its beauty, but to its brutal side and to the natural rhythms of the seasons, the plants, and the animals. This upbringing differed from the usual sheltered one for a boy of his class and his education. It helped bring out a special earthiness and robustness in his character that provided him with invaluable practical and grounded weight and that may well have saved the lonely boy from vanishing into his fantasies and dreams. It also gave him a view about sexual matters which Jung describes as markedly different from the ignorance and naivete he found in many of his professional peers (including Freud). Jung commented that they grew up knowing nothing about nature or the facts of life. "I had grown up in the country, among peasants, and what I was unable to learn in the stables I found out from the Rabelaisian wit and the untrammeled fantasies of our peasant folklore" (p. 166).

This knowledge, as graphic and explicit as it may have been, was not altogether under Jung's conscious control, nor was he as much at ease with it as he presumes. He was much more subject to the Victorian repression that marked the upbringing of his peers than he admits. His farm experiences of animal matings and births, for example, did not prevent the nine year old boy from somehow failing to notice his own mother's pregnancy or labor (his sister was born at home), nor did it ease his discomfort at this proof of his parents' sexuality.

> I was utterly surprised, for I hadn't noticed anything. I had thought nothing of my mother's lying in bed more frequently than usual, for I considered her taking to her bed an excusable weakness in any case. . . . I was shocked and did not know what to feel. . . They mumbled some-

thing about the stork. . . This story was obviously another of those humbugs which were always being imposed on me. I felt sure that my mother had once again done something I was supposed not to know about. This sudden appearance of my sister left me with a vague sense of distrust which sharpened my curiosity and observation. Subsequent odd reactions on the part of my mother confirmed my suspicions that something regrettable was connected with this birth. (1963, p. 25)

Jung's attitude toward and experience of his mother constitute a vital element, probably the most important, of the personal background behind his general attitude toward the feminine. Themes of weakness, distrust, suspicion, and mystery (as in the above quotation), applied first to his mother and then generalized to women and sexuality, derive in part from the cultural stereotypes discussed in the last chapter. They are also deeply linked to the way Jung experienced his mother and attempted to make sense out of this experience. In this and other passages about his mother, it is unclear whether what Jung is so forthrightly struggling with is his complexed reaction or a more valid perception of his mother's psychology; it appears most often as a confusing and unintegrated mixture, with many of Jung's unprocessed fears and emotions projected onto his mother. Jung's earliest memory (age six) is of his mother as youthfully slender and wearing a black dress marked with green crescent moons. In memories of a few years later, he describes her as old and corpulent. Ellenberger suggests, rather unsympathetically (perhaps to emphasize the contrast between Jung's mother and Freud's elegant and beautiful one), that she was fat, ugly, authoritarian, haughty, difficult, and neurotic. There were at least two sides to her: at times she was sensitive and intuitive with marked parapsychological abilities, but most often she was down-to-earth and commonplace (Ellenberger, 1970, p. 662).

Jung experienced his parents' marriage as fraught with unhappiness and tension. He diagnoses his own childhood eczema as a somatic consequence of his parents' marital turmoil. When Jung was three, his father and mother temporarily separated; Jung's mother was hospitalized for several months during that time, most probably as a consequence of her marital problems. An aunt took care of the three year old boy while his mother was absent. This separation seems to have had a profound psychological effect on the boy, his mother's absence and perceived abandonment forming a basic component of Jung's underlying ambivalence about women and the feminine.

From then on, I always felt mistrustful when the word "love" was spoken.
The feeling I associated with "woman" was for a long time that of unreliability. "Father," on the other hand, meant reliability and —
powerlessness. That is the handicap I started off with. Later, these early
impressions were revised: I have trusted men friends and been disappointed by them, I have mistrusted women and was not disappointed. (Jung,
1963, p. 8)

In marked contrast to the socio-cultural mores of his time, Jung
describes his mother as the stronger of his two parents. He tended to
side with her against his father's cantankerousness. However, his mother also seems to have burdened the boy with a relationship that really
belonged to her husband. She "early made me her confidant and confided
her troubles to me. It was plain that she was telling me everything she
could not say to my father" (p. 52). Though he sympathized with her,
this made him draw further away from her. Jung states that he rejected
the role of "little husband," refusing to share her secrets. He also reacted negatively to her very style of communication, experiencing her perceptions as doubtful exaggerations of reality. This added to his initial
distrust of her, and the adolescent boy soon stopped confiding in her
entirely. He compensated for her earlier power over him with disparagement.

Jung's mother, along with most women of her day, had received little
formal education; Jung found "that in conversation she was not adequate for me" (p. 48). Through her father she had an interest in Eastern religions, which led the two of them (mother and son) to share a
very unchristian mysticism. This shared perception constituted part of
what Jung called "the 'Other' . . . my profoundest experiences: on the
one hand a bloody struggle, on the other supreme ecstasy" (p. 48). Yet,
because of Jung's mistrust of his mother, coupled with her propensity
to exaggerate (or, possibly, a propensity to give a feeling response rather
than a conceptually thought-out one), none of this was mentioned between them. They could not or did not talk together about anything
of importance that Jung was struggling with. Instead, he was left with
an even greater sense of loneliness. He found himself unable to reveal
the mystical and intuitive side of himself to her and unable to have her
accompany him in the important and strange realm that he intuited
they shared. This silence, the lack of communication between them, left
a gap and a longing in relation to his mother and the feminine which
may have been filled in his later life by his dedication to female pa-

tients who were struggling with many of the same problems.

Jung criticized his mother for praising him excessively; he found that her attitude toward her son, once he was at the Gymnasium, was extravagently adulatory and that he had to defend himself from her inflated perception of her son. Her lavish and undiscriminating approval added to his feelings of distrust and to his own lack of adequate mirroring. She failed to differentiate his true talent in the blur of her encomiums, and so made it difficult for Jung to acquire a balanced view of his own value.

In two passages from his autobiography, Jung describes her divided nature and his reaction to it. He combines appreciation for the mothering provided by her warm, animal and earthy nature with fear and awe of another, more uncanny, side. This was a side that he must have realized constituted an integral part of his own makeup.

> My mother was a very good mother to me. She had a hearty animal warmth, cooked wonderfully, and was most companionable and pleasant. She was very stout and a ready listener. She also liked to talk, and her chatter was like the gay plashing of a fountain. She had a decided literary gift, as well as taste and depth. But this quality never emerged; it remained hidden beneath the semblance of a kindly, fat old woman, extremely hospitable, and possessor of a great sense of humor. She held all the conventional opinions a person was obliged to have, but then her unconscious personality would suddenly put in an appearance. That personality was unexpectedly powerful: a somber, imposing figure possessed of unassailable authority—and no bones about it. I was sure she consisted of two personalities, one innocuous and human, the other uncanny. This other emerged only now and then, but each time it was unexpected and frightening. She would then speak as if talking to herself, but what she said was aimed at me and usually struck to the core of my being. (pp. 48-49)

> My mother . . . was somehow rooted in deep, invisible ground, though it never appeared to me as confidence in the Christian faith. For me it was somehow connected with animals, trees, mountains, meadows, and running water, all of which contrasted most strangely with her Christian surface and her conventional assertions of faith. This background corresponded so well to my own attitude that it caused me no uneasiness; on the contrary, it gave me a sense of security and the conviction that here was solid ground on which one could stand. It never occurred to me how "pagan" this foundation was. My mother's "No. 2" offered me the strongest support in the conflict then beginning between paternal tradition and the strange, compensatory products which my unconscious had been stimulated to create. (pp. 90-91)

Elsewhere, Jung describes the difference between the two sides of his mother's personality in far less sanguine and more negative terms. It seems that since his parents' marital problems and initial separation, they slept apart, with Jung sharing his father's bedroom. Jung suffered from "pseudo-croup" which, along with the eczema, he ascribes to the unbearable tension in the house. He also started having anxiety dreams about his mother and was, for a time, besieged by hallucinatory hypnogocic dreams connected to her and to his fear of her feminine power (G. Wehr, 1987). In an effort to deal with her effect on him, or to come to terms with her, Jung recalls that he split her into a sort of daytime and nighttime, good-object/bad-object duality.

> The nocturnal atmosphere had begun to thicken. All sorts of things were happening at night, things incomprehensible and alarming . . . From the door of my mother's room came frightening influences. At night Mother was strange and mysterious. (Jung, 1963, p. 18)

In contrast to an often mostly positive, though somewhat condescending attitude toward his mother's daytime character, his attitude toward her nighttime or "Number Two" character is remarkably ambivalent. She gains an archaic stature and power through these portrayals that is larger than life. She becomes like a seer, a priestess in a bear's cave, and an embodiment of the natural mind (p. 18, p. 50). His description of her "Number Two" character foreshadows Jung's experience of the black serpent in his fantasy who sought to attach herself to him, as well as his depictions of the great mother archetype in her darker aspects. It is the stuff of Romantic myth, fairytale, and nightmare. Or, possibly, since these reminiscences were written at the end of Jung's career, when he was in his eighties, they may be a projection of his theories about the dark side of the great mother archetype backwards in time onto his mother. Either way, her "Number Two" character's mythic power for good or evil over him, which Jung describes as factual, seems more like a child's response to an archetype—yet at the same time an intuitive and absorbing reaction to the force of her unlived life, her unhappiness, her neuroticism, and the stifling repressions necessitated by her milieu. Satinover (1985) has examined some of the pathology that ensued from Jung's experience of these phallic, castrating aspects of his mother and from her inability to contain his anxieties.

Jung's not altogether successful struggle to integrate these split aspects of his mother and to integrate his own mother complex in both its positive and negative aspects may be, as Maduro and Wheelwright (1977) suggest, "perhaps ultimately the source of his emphasis on a creative unconscious and man's universal need to free himself from the potentially engulfing 'World of the Mothers'" (p. 86). Negatively, however, Jung's personal reaction to his troubled mother and his unintegrated mother complex echo throughout his writings about women. For instance, a didactic passage in the *Dream Seminars* remarkably evokes the passage from Jung's memories of his mother quoted above.

> Not in vain are little children afraid of their own mothers in the night. Primitive mothers can kill their children. It is absolutely incompatible with the daytime, for then they are most devoted mothers. But in the night they take away the mask and become witches; they upset children psychically, even kill them. The more they are devoted to them in the wrong way the worse it is. (Jung, 1938/1984, pp. 144-145)

While this passage may hold psychological validity and be an antidote to the sentimentalizing of motherhood, it is a classically preoedipal view of the split good breast/bad breast. The tone seems so personally complexed and exaggerated that its general application seriously impairs Jung's empirical objectivity. It acts once again to cast the feminine in a luridly deviant light and to make women as a general class in Jungian psychology both overly powerful and overly to blame.

One side of his mother supported Jung's practical life, and the development of his own "Number One" personality; the other, his interest in psychology, mysticism, the paranormal, and the non-rational. His perception of his mother's dual character added to Jung's Swiss acceptance of his own "Number One" and "Number Two" personalities without the need to merge, blend, or integrate them. On the one hand, a scientist with a less divided and powerful mother would not have needed to struggle so to come to terms with the feminine: he or she could have just ignored it or, like Freud, relegated it to an afterthought and its secondary and inferior position. On the other hand, major elements of Jung's personal experience of his mother's psyche (especially both their denials of her bodily sexuality—her dark serpent) and of his unintegrated projections cast a shadow over Jung's future work on the feminine.

The power of this feminine was increased and Jung's struggle with it was made more difficult because of the relative powerlessness of his father. Jung writes far less warmly and directly about his father. He has

little positive to say about him, though it was his father, not his mother, whom he remembers holding and comforting him through his croup,
his other illnesses, and his nighttime terrors (Jung, 1963, pp. 42-43).
Jung manifests an unresolved father complex which leads him to be especially intolerant of his father's failures (see M. Stein, 1985 and Wilmer, 1985, for a discussion of this father complex). Jung says he felt
compassion toward his father. However, in his autobiography, he continually faults this rather ineffectual and distant though kindly man for
his immaturity, for not developing intellectually, for scattering his energy
on unimportant things and, above all, for being weak, cold, aloof, and
spiritually dishonest. Jung is convinced that his father was a hypocrite.
He thus experienced the same sense of abandonment and lack of communication with his father as he had experienced with his mother:

> There arose in me profound doubts about everything my father said
> . . . What he said sounded stale and hollow, like a tale told by someone
> who knows it only by hearsay and cannot quite believe it himself. I want-
> ed to help him but I did not know how . . . Our discussions invariably
> came to an unsatisfactory end. They irritated him, and saddened him.
> "Oh nonsense," he was in the habit of saying, "you always want to think.
> One ought not to think, but believe." I would think, "No, one must ex-
> perience and know," but I would say, "Give me this belief," whereupon
> he would shrug and turn resignedly away. (Jung, 1963, pp. 42-43)

Jung rails at his father for being intellectually and spiritually moribund, plagued by religious doubts, even, possibly, for concealing a loss
of faith. What seems to anger Jung most is that his father refused to
admit his religious doubts, instead "hypocritically" pursuing his duties
(and the family's livelihood) as pastor. Jung seems especially wounded
by his father's failure to be honest and open with him. Behind all this
may lie Jung's aggravation that his father led such a circumscribed life
and that the two could no more communicate than Jung could with
his mother. Neither parent contained him. His father lacked Jung's
robustness and intellectual vigor; he also lacked both of the Carl Gustavs'
(his own father's and his son's) creativity. He was able to be neither peer
nor guide to the lonely and imaginative boy. Stale and hollow talk seems
to have finally replaced any hope Jung had for a meeting of their minds.
(Jung describes his father as suffering from an Amfortas-like wound,
brought about by his moribund Christianity, a wound which Jung as
Parsifal could only observe, since he never found the right words to ask
about it and thus to make it heal [p. 215].)

Lacking a confidant in either his mother or father, Jung early turned to inner figures. Without a strong father figure whose intellectual realm he could inherit, Jung had to create his own theories and his own intellectual and psychological universe. Without a strong, mediating father figure, Jung's fantasies of the all-powerful and threatening feminine became psychological realities. However, again it was the very absence of the stability of a secure father's world in Jung's experience of his own father that gave him the freedom to explore elements of his own inner feminine and drew him to the feminine in others.

In contrast to the feeling of complexed irritation and depression that most often seems to lie behind Jung's writing about his father are Jung's memories of his father's many kind and supportive acts. I have already mentioned his father's care for him as a child. Later, Jung remembers that when he was fourteen and on vacation once, his father had only enough money for one ticket up the Rigi (one of the highest viewpoints in Switzerland), where they both wanted to go; his father bought that one ticket for his son, thereby letting Jung have a deeply mystical experience of his native mountains. I wonder how many other generous and enabling acts the poor father did that backed and helped his son, but which Jung has to forget because the father, though reliable and loving, is experienced as lacking sufficient masculinity, as intolerably weak, distant, and ineffectual by the virile son. His father may have ultimately failed Jung just because he failed with his wife, leaving his son with the weight of unresolved oedipal issues. Jung's defense against them then leaves the influence of Jung's uncanny mother—unmediated by relationship to the father or by a strong masculine presence—eerily strong.

Many biographers write of Jung's difficulty with his father (e.g., Ellenberger, 1970, Hannah, 1976; Maduro and Wheelwright, 1977; G. Wehr, 1987), and sometimes connect this early experience with his later problems with Freud and other men (e.g., van der Post, 1975; Lambert, 1977; Henderson, 1985; Gay, 1988). Jung was far more his mother's than his father's son. The importance of this to his "personal confession," analytical psychology, needs to be stressed, for it leaves an opening through which the power of the feminine pours through while causing, perhaps at the same time, too much of a split—overly positive and overly negative—in Jung's view of the feminine, which in turn echoes his culture's view and its too-great need for a masculine defense against the feminine. Jung's unsatisfactory relationship to his father also may lie behind Jung's need to be the hero, the son of the mother, who battles all those sons of the fathers who, perhaps, received the masculine birth-right which Jung felt he lacked. Lambert, in a memoir of Jung, writes:

> Jung told me he "had the whole problem of the father to solve," he said, "I am always unpopular—with the theologians and with the doctors. I am always *mettant mes pieds sur le plat."* (Lambert, 1977, p. 160)

Van der Post (1975) theorizes that Jung's lack of a strong father had both positive and negative effects on his life and his psychology. On one hand, he thinks it led Jung to the archetype of an internal father, the wise old man, but, on the other, left Jung without an actual example of active masculinity. This resulted in a "Number One" personality who had trouble getting on with men, who embroiled Jung in a turbulent relationship with Freud, who was the source of "a certain kind of archaic authoritarianism" (p. 79) that broke out mostly in relationship to other men; and, finally, who left Jung with an unreliable aspect of the masculine, unanalyzed, in himself. On the positive side, it pushed Jung's "Number Two" personality toward the study of and "the rediscovery of a lost feminine half" (p. 79), both for himself and for a world in desperate need of it; on the negative side, it left him as Romantically bewitched by this ambivalent feminine as he had been by his mother's "Number Two" character.

Besides Jung's experience of his mother, there is another important woman in Jung's early life who contributed to his experience of the "lost feminine half." She was the maid who took care of him and comforted him while his mother was hospitalized. Jung calls her an anima figure and writes of a powerfully sensual experience of her that became an integral part of his early experience of the feminine.

> I still remember her picking me up and laying my head against her shoulder. She had black hair and an olive complexion, and was quite different from my mother. I can see her, even now, her hairline, her throat, with its darkly pigmented skin, and her ear. All this seemed to me very strange and yet strangely familiar. It was as though she belonged not to my family but only to me, as though she were connected in some way with other mysterious things I could not understand. This type of girl later became a component of my anima. The feeling of strangeness which she conveyed, and yet of having known her always, was a characteristic of that figure which later came to symbolize for me the whole essence of womanhood. (Jung, 1963, pp. 8-9)

Jung's experience of this sensually evocative second type of woman joins with his experience of his mother's double personality to form a split perception of the feminine. Thus Jung's personal experience combines with the split socio-cultural attitudes toward the feminine to resonate throughout his theories and in his relationships with women. Before I proceed to a consideration of their effect on Jung's ideas and theories, I would like to discuss some relationships in his adult personal life that tie into and work out these early experiences, as well as contribute to his theories about women's psychology.

Jung married Emma Rauschenbach (1881-1955) on Feb. 14, 1903. From the first time he saw her as a girl, without knowing who she was or anything about her, he again had the feeling, somehow, of "having known her always," and he knew intuitively that she would be his wife. He probably could not have picked a more suitable person to complement his own character. She was intelligent, grounded, and full of common sense, yet had a sense of humor and could support and follow Jung's flights of thought. She also happened to be the daughter of a wealthy industrialist and, according to Swiss law, her money and property became Jung's. This allowed Jung to step up from his impoverished life as a young doctor with a widowed mother and sister to support, and eventually to leave his job at the mental hospital of Burghölzli. Her substantial income enabled them to build a large and comfortable house; it also gave him the financial security to embark on a novel and untried career. How much Jung's career was facilitated by this marriage is an aspect of his life that deserves attention. Jung credits her practicality, her housewifely and motherly skills for creating a comfortable setting that kept him in touch with the real world. Freud, too, has somewhat enviously referred to these skills and to the many and various supports Emma Jung provided for her husband (McGuire, [Ed.], 1974).

Emma Jung was an exceptionally capable mother and housewife, with many characteristics reminiscent of Jung's mother's "Number One," daylight character. Her practical steadiness complemented Jung's more volatile nature. Unlike his parents, she and Jung seemed to have a good relationship. Unlike his mother, Emma Jung could share his interests and understand his work. Of all the wives of the early psychoanalysts, she was the only one to become an analyst herself (Ellenberger, 1970). This was a tribute both to her interest and skills and to Jung's encouragement of women taking their place in the outside world. After her children were in school, and at Jung's urging, she started to learn mathematics, Greek, and Latin (Hannah, 1976). She also did archetypal research for Jung and some writing, especially about the Grail legend (E. Jung and von Franz, 1958/1986) and the animus and anima (E. Jung, 1957/1974). She lectured, saw patients, helped govern the new Institute, and acted as a training analyst.

Although Jung first psychoanalyzed Emma Jung, then involved her in analytic work and encouraged her to develop her own intellectual interests, he felt that she existed as his satellite. She was in his eyes first and foremost contained within their middle-class marriage as his wife and the mother of his five children. In his own personal life Jung had a nineteenth-century view of masculine prerogative. He found that his marriage did not, and did not need to, contain him (Carotenuto, 1982). In a letter to Freud written in 1910, Jung writes that for a man, "the prerequisite for a good marriage, it seems to me, is the license to be unfaithful" (McGuire, [Ed.], 1974, p. 289). In the same letter he reports that his wife is pregnant again, and that her analysis by Jung was being marred by a number of her "jealous scenes."

The justification for Jung's personal needs and character, along with the social conventions of the day, may lie behind his description of his wife, and of women in general, as the contained who live within and are satisfied by the role they find in marriage, while he states that he and most men, the containers, need outside stimulation (Jung, 1925/1954, pp. 195-196). This is one more way that the two separate and segregated nineteenth-century spheres of home and Market (Ehrenreich and English, 1979) became incorporated into psychological theory. The part of Jung's personal psychology that was affected by his experience of a split mother figure and a separate anima figure may also underlie his splitting of women into separate and exclusive archetypal modes: "One could characterize these two types of women as the 'married mothers' and the 'friends and concubines.' . . . when you are wife and mother you can hardly be the hetaira too" (Adler, [Ed.], 1973, Vol. 2, pp. 454-455). Emma Jung was required to be the "married mother," concerned with the children, her household, and Jung's domestic comfort, while a series of other women were given the mutually exclusive role of the Romantic Number Two, the anima-like Hetaira.

Of these, Toni Wolff (1888-1953) was by far the most important. Wolff, like Jung, saw each type primarily in relation to the male and worked out her psychology of feminine types accordingly. Both Emma Jung and Toni Wolff accepted, or yielded to, this division and tried to make the best of it. The two women analyzed each other's dreams (Meier, 1984);

the wife included the mistress at family dinners, and each knew of and seemed outwardly reconciled to the importance of their separate roles in Jung's life. There are intimations, however, that behind this accept-ance, both women may have been deeply wounded by the arrangement, that both suffered loneliness, and that both struggled heroically to keep themselves to the single sphere to which Jung and his culture consigned them (van der Post, 1975; Wheelwright, 1985). Both women seem to have had far larger personalities than Jung's external view of women grant-ed, yet it was his very support and encouragement that allowed this larger personality space in which to develop.

Jung's attitude toward women and their subservient status was nor-mal for the time; this role also conformed with Jung's personal needs and psychology. More original was Jung's deep (because conflicted) in-terest in the feminine and in feminine power. Jung's choice of psychol-ogy as a profession may very well have been influenced by his need to understand his mother's strange double personality, coupled with his fascination with the feminine. As I stated earlier, his university lectures in psychology also stressed this fascination as well as an equal interest in the occult. Jung's fifteen-year-old cousin Hélène Preiswerk's parapsy-chological and mediumistic abilities became the subject of his disser-tation.

Hélène Preiswerk was, in physical appearance, very like Jung's descrip-tion of the servant who held and caressed him as a child. There is a pho-tograph of her as a young girl in the end papers of a small book by her niece (Zumstein-Preiswerk, 1975) that bears an uncanny resemblance to the photograph of Toni Wolff at the 1911 Weimar Congress of the International Psychoanalytic Association, Sept. 1911 (eg., Roazen, p. 177). Both face the camera with a similar large-eyed and intense expression, both have the same olive complexion, intelligent, alert face, and huge, piercing, yet inward-looking dark eyes.

Hélène Preiswerk was Jung's mother's cousin. While at the universi-ty, Jung, accompanied by his mother and his sister, attended family se-ances where Hélène Preiswerk acted as the medium. Here he found himself again fascinated by a world which romantically mixed the femi-nine with the paranormal. During the seances, he could study another female relative with not only a normal daytime personality, but a "Num-ber Two" personality similar to his mother's, as well as a whole series of other split-off complexes manifesting as partial personalities. Van der Post writes of Preiswerk's importance to Jung's understanding of some aspects of the feminine:

> One cannot stress enough here how significant it was that in taking even this first step toward his destiny, his guide was already what one is compelled to call, for want of a better word, the abnormal and unrecognized in the feminine spirit of his day. She helped prepare him beyond all his own expectations for the dreams and fantasies of his by now well-equipped No. 1. (1976, p. 91)

The fifteen-year-old girl was clearly attracted to her cousin, and the seances soon showed the influence of this attraction. As Jung became less interested, his young cousin grew more hysterically animated, until she started faking her seances in a probable attempt to keep his attention. Goodheart (1984) has written about the transference-countertransference implications of this relationship.

Thus Jung unconsciously reproduced the situation with his mother: he discovered a woman who fascinated him, who was in touch with something uncanny and mysterious, yet whom he seems destined to find, once again, ultimately undependable and untrustworthy. Jung writes of all his subject's failings, but does not consider his part in this denouement. Nor does Jung consider what impelled him to reject Preiswerk at the end with the same force with which he was fascinated by her at the beginning (Jung, 1902/1978). This is the first example of the adult Jung's link to the feminine or to an anima figure as subject or patient which involved the two in obscure and potent transference phenomena. His anima projection onto Preiswerk was a piece of Jung's own psyche which he had not integrated; he remained, like the Salome he projected it onto, blind and unmindful, and thus similar situations tended to repeat themselves throughout his life.

The creative side of this merger and projection is evident. James Hillman (1976) writes of Jung's experience with his mediumistic cousin as seminal to Jung's development of the theory of the transference, and as an example of "the way his process of individuation consistently interiorized phenomena of his youth, transforming them into later psychological theory" (p. 133). Hillman credits Jung's study of and involvement with his cousin as central in the development of the following aspects of his work:

> The dissociability of the psyche, the projection of the repressed, the relativization of the ego, the psychology of the transference, the autonomy of the complex—more, the very reality of the psyche—first concrete-

ly evidenced themselves to Jung, neither with Bleuler at the clinic, nor with Freud, nor during his "Confrontation with the Unconscious," but through his cousin. (p. 124)

Theory, for Jung, seemed to need the alchemy provided by an ambivalent relationship to a feminine inspirer or co-worker. The alchemy was especially potent when the woman combined the body type of Jung's childhood maid-servant with aspects of the "Number Two" character of his mother: Sabina Spielrein (see McGuire, *op. cit.*, letters J. 133, 144 and 175, for Jung's confessions to Freud of his countertransference to Spielrein and of the trouble it caused him), Toni Wolff, and Christiana Morgan (the subject of *The Visions Seminars*) are three women who come immediately to mind. Henry A. Murray and later co-workers of Morgan betray a similar fascination: she is "of another order—muted, intangible, profound. . . the mere presence of her beauty. . . the natural spontaneous depth dimension that completed the whole enterprise" (Murray's postscript to Jung, *The Visions Seminars,* p. 518).

When Jung first met each of these three women, Spielrein, Wolff, and Morgan, they were deeply troubled psychologically and Jung became their doctor. Each, in marked contrast to Jung's boyhood experience of his mother, was, as a patient, in a less powerful role than he, yet also in contrast to his mother, each could explore with him her own strange "Number Two" character and talk to him about it. Jung in turn, and again in contrast to his inability to restore or redeem his mother, could help each woman heal and reintegrate her particular psychological splitness—a heady combination in which physical and spiritual attraction was acknowledged. Jung could at least partially master his childhood fear of his mother's anxiety-provoking "dark serpent" side by helping each of these women face her own inner dragons. Each woman, thanks to this reparative and transformative work and to Jung's encouragement, went on to be a sensitive and talented therapist herself.

During a particularly difficult time in his life, Jung suffered from what Ellenberger (1970) calls a creative illness and breakdown. At this time Toni Wolff did for him what his mother never could do with her own unintegrated "Number Two." Healed by Jung and brought back to the conscious world, Wolff now served as Jung's eminently trustworthy guide and lifeline for his own descent into the unconscious. Unlike his mother, Wolff was a lucid and clear companion who was able to convey her knowledge of this realm to Jung. She, again unlike his mother, could share her own knowledge and study of mysticism with him. Jung, in turn, could at last confide and reveal his innermost self, perhaps completing a return to the feminine that he had been unable to reach with his mother.

One attitude toward the feminine in these relationships derives from Jung's nineteenth-century Romanticism and its emphasis on the mysterious feminine. Jung often sounds enraptured; it breaks through in his discussions of types, cases, and in letters. An example of the consequent excess of affect both of nineteenth-century idealization of woman and of Jung's projections onto her can perhaps be seen in the following passage, written at the time when Jung was first involved romantically with Wolff. Jung describes an introverted woman who sounds very like Wolff herself. (Note that again the woman is seen primarily in the way she affects the male.)

> Why, for example, does the introverted woman read so attentively? Because above everything else she loves to grasp ideas. Why is she so restful and soothing? Because she usually keeps her feelings to herself . . . expressing them in her thoughts instead of unloading them on others. Her unconventional morality is backed by deep reflection and convincing inner feelings. The charm of her quiet and intelligent character depends not merely on a peaceful attitude, but on the fact that one can talk to her peacefully and coherently, and that she is able to appreciate the value of her partner's argument. She does not interrupt him with impulsive exclamations, but accompanies his meaning with her thoughts and feelings, which none the less remain steadfast. This compact and well-developed ordering of the conscious psychic contents is a stout defence against a chaotic and passionate emotional life. (Jung, 1921/1971, p. 154)

The extraverted feeling woman is described in equally exaggerated though negative terms (pp. 356-359). This same romantic tone is apparent in descriptions of the subject of his dissertation, Hélène Preiswerk. For example, Jung writes, "her movements were free and of a noble grace, mirroring most beautifully her changing emotions" (Jung, 1902/1978, p. 19). This tone also appears in letters he wrote to some women patients.

> Your face haunted me for a while . . . . You are always a living reality to me whereas other former patients fade away into oblivion . . . You are keeping on living. There seems to be some sort of living connection (but I should have said that long ago I suppose). You probably need a confirmation from my side of the ocean just as well.

> But my dear, dear (!!) Christiana Morgan, you are just a bit of a marvel to me. (Adler, [Ed.], 1973, Vol. 1, pp. 48-49.)

This was a letter Jung wrote to Morgan in 1927. In a letter written to Mary Mellon in September, 1941, Jung again says:

> I often think of you and I often wish I could see you again. But you are further away than the moon. . . . all your letters emanate an immediate warmth and something like a living substance which has an almost compelling effect. I get emotional about them and could do something foolish if you were not on the other side of the ocean. (Adler, [Ed.], 1973, Vol. 1, p. 304)

This tone is understandable in a man who is moved romantically by a woman to whom he wishes to give a clear and honest picture of his reactions. However, it becomes a bit more complicated when it obscures relationship and roles. In spite of Jung's genius as a psychoanalyst and his healing effect on his patients, this tone compromises Jung's position as doctor and enters into and affects his theory about women. It is also most terribly confusing to both theory and practice when Jung both seems to be eliciting a romantic transference and then rails against the "tiresome romanticism" (Jung, 1914/1970, p. 258) of his women patients and the boringness of having "to pander to this annoying romance" (p. 257). Jung's lack of his own analysis, especially of his mother complex and of its projection onto women, involves both him and his theory in an unsatisfactory and unreal relationship to women. In Jung's writing about the feminine, his time, his personal experience, patriarchal definitions of roles and role expectations, socio-culturally defined patterns of behavior and of the feminine, all impinge on both theory and process in perplexing confusion.

The women Jung treated as patients provided him with another source of information on the feminine. Soon after he finished his dissertation on his cousin, Jung started work at Burghölzli, "a world-renowned center for research into mental illness" (Gay, 1988, p. 198). What was exceptional about Jung was his interest in his predominantly female patients' inner worlds and his ability to listen and hear them out, perhaps again fulfilling a need to fathom the unknown in his mother. One of his first patients at Burghölzli was a woman, Babette, whom Freud described as "phenomenally ugly." She was a schizophrenic in whose symbolic imagery Jung, through paying close attention, found meaning and an inner coherence. She too was a guide to the world of the dissociated and the unconscious, and to a darker, more serpentine realm of Jung's and his mother's "Number Two" characters. His interest in her and other psychotics at Burghölzli belies the Romantic idea that the feminine and the beautiful are synonymous, or that Jung had to have a beautiful anima figure as a *femme inspiratrice*.

Jung acknowledges his debt to his female patients: "I have had mainly women patients, who often entered into the work with extraordinary conscientiousness, understanding and intelligence. It was essentially because of them that I was able to strike out on new paths in therapy" (Jung, 1963, p. 145). As patients, women themselves undoubtedly contributed to the evolution of this therapy and its underlying theory. The majority of the cases Jung refers to in his *Collected Works* are women. The *General Index* (1979) lists references to 103 different women patients, 77 men, and seven unspecified: however, many more of the men's cases are referred to repeatedly. *Symbols of Transformation* and *The Visions Seminars* (1933/1976) are both book-length studies of a single woman's case material (Miss Miller's fantasies and Christiana Morgan's visions). Jung himself acknowledges that women are an important source of his theories.

> Woman, with her very dissimilar psychology, is and always has been a source of information about things for which a man has no eyes. (Jung, 1928/1966, p. 188)

> What this psychology owes to the direct influence of women . . . is a theme that would fill a large volume. I am speaking here not only of analytical psychology but of the beginnings of psychopathology in general. . . . An astonishingly high percentage of this material comes from women. (Jung, 1927/1970, pp. 124-125)

He credits a woman he cured for the start of his successful private practice:

> I was a young doctor, so she took me on as a second son and said to herself: "I will perform a miracle for him." And that is what she did: she created a big bubble of reputation around me that brought me my first patients: my practice of psychotherapy was started by a mother putting me in place of her unsatisfactory son. (Jung, 193/1976, p. 309)

Women played an exceptionally large role in Jung's adult life. Besides his immediate family and his patients, the majority of his co-workers and the analysts he trained were women, as were the majority of the people in his circle in Zürich. In no little way, the actual work Jung did was inspired by women and evolved in collaboration with them. Toni

Wolff and Marie-Louise von Franz are two of his collaborators to whom he most often gives credit. Many more women devoted their lives and libidos to Jung as followers, secretaries, researchers, translators, editors, and all the other supportive roles which helped facilitate and produce his work. The man's work, in a way that is typical of the era, rises from the midst of many women's labor and support.

In a remembrance of Jung, a woman writes of this world of women from the other side:

> I didn't want to belong to the band of women disciples that surround-ed him; but the attraction of his personality would probably have been overpowering also for me. Today I think I can sense that also for him, in his great inner loneliness, the unconditional support of this band was almost a necessity. (Jutta von Graevenitz in Jensen, [Ed.], pp. 29-30)

I will bring this chapter to a close with illustrative reports of life in Zürich from three analysts: Joseph Henderson, Jane Wheelwright, and Joseph Wheelwright. I think that their experiences may not only give a good idea of the attitude toward women in the Zürich of that time, but also point to some of the results of Jung's ambivalent attitude to-ward women and the feminine.*

In two articles (Henderson, 1963 and 1985) and in an interview with me in April of 1984 and a brief conversation four years later, Henderson talked of his time in Zürich. He was there for ten years, off and on, from 1929 until World War II; it was an unstable period of history, and many people were coming to Jung in order to discover a necessary new social attitude. However, in contrast to this search, Henderson describes the Swiss as about fifty years behind the rest of the world in manners and in customs. He found Jung and his family typical Europeans, with Emma Jung appearing as a normal Swiss *hausfrau* whose life revolved around Jung. Henderson characterizes the European women of that time as much more comfortable in their traditional roles than American women. He also describes the group around Jung as, at the same time, being more outspoken and unconventional than people in the United States. He felt then that they were somehow above collective standards. In retro-spect, he thinks the women around Jung, by and large, were more open

---

* This material is taken from published interviews and other published material as well as several conversations I had with each of them in 1984 and 1988. Since this was written, I have had the opportunity of reading many more reminiscences of Jung (*The Jung Archives,* at the Countway Library, Harvard Medical School) which corroborate these interviews.

to new and controversial ideas and more conscious of the possibilities in relationship than were the men.

Henderson was very young, 26, when first in Zürich. He notes the excitement of being in on the formative stages of analytical psychology: "Some of the excitement one felt in Zürich at the time of the Dream Seminars came from knowing and not knowing what future directions the Jungian movement was going to take" (1985, p. 218). He found that the men and women in Zürich were mutually projecting their own cultural attitudes onto each other. Henderson (1984, 1985) has written of the importance of cultural layer as well as the personal and the collective layers in understanding the unconscious; in his article on cultural attitudes, he writes that "Jung has transformed his own cultural attitude into a psychological attitude which has grown out of his own life and his therapeutic experience" (1985, p. 210).

Henderson recalls that Jung honored the individual regardless of gender and was different with each individual analysand. Men and women alike, however, tended to project the stereotype of the patriarchal masculine leader onto Jung, a role Jung filled quite well. Henderson attributes this to Jung's genius; it was impossible to match him, and men seemed to get caught in a swing between inflation (when Jung was interested in them) and deflation in comparison to and possibly in competition with him. Women did not appear to have this problem. He also remarked that Jung related far better to women, possibly because of Jung's own bad relationship with his father.

Henderson concludes by pointing out the importance of Jung's work on alchemy for women because of the alchemists' inclusion of the feminine. Henderson believes there is little difference between actual people today and those around Jung in the thirties, but that there is a big change in the literature about the feminine today—perhaps because of the freedom with which women are now examining the feminine and expressing themselves, rather than as in Zürich in the first half of the century, when they were defined by men. They are now writing about the feminine from their own perspective, from the point of view of women experiencing the feminine in their own lives.

Jane Wheelwright, in memoirs (Wheelwright, 1963; Wheelwright, 1982; and Serbin, 1984) and in an interview with me in April, 1984, discussed her years in Zürich in the nineteen-thirties and her analysis with Jung. She makes a distinction between the era, the Swiss environment, and Jung's theory on the one side and the actual work he did with patients on the other. She found Zürich a place where all the conventional attitudes about women were especially pronounced; this made her feel as if she were encased in a corset whose purpose was to mold her into an unnatural and arbitrary shape that was not her own. She described Switzerland as a place where women were limited to very prescribed roles, roles that were dictated to them by men, so that women almost had to work surreptitiously in order to get what they needed. This left Wheelwright unsure of how she could fit into this environment. She also found genuine male-female relationships to be fraught with difficulty, primarily because neither men nor women understood women's psychology or knew what a woman really was.

Wheelwright describes Jung as a very powerful man with a very powerful anima. She was attracted by "his complexity, breadth and humanness" (Wheelwright, 1982, p. 98), by his sense of humor and by his earthy Swiss quality, yet she believes that Jung's relationship with the women around him was affected by the following dynamic. First, women in Switzerland at that time were taught to believe that men held all the answers. Because of this and women's awed respect for Jung, they left it up to him to define their feminine nature for them, rather than searching for it within their own psyches and enlightening Jung accordingly. Second, these women were taught and believed that women were incapable of standing alone. They seemed to expect Jung to assume the dominant role, and that they therefore could and should lean on him. In order to assure this, they projected their own power onto him. Third, and contrary to this belief, they were a group of very high-powered women with a great deal of energy, talent, potential, and ability. Many had impressive academic qualifications, did Jung's research for him, and in other ways were quite essential to him. They did much valuable work carrying out or extending various ideas or interests of Jung's—yet Wheelwright knew of no one who thought of doing something that was original and that was just for herself. In fact, Wheelwright remarked that "they tended to think his thoughts rather than their own . . . We were always told that women weren't supposed to think for themselves. They were supposed to make real and concrete men's thoughts" (Serbin, p. 157).

Wheelwright describes many of the women around Jung as powerful and sometimes even domineering. She felt isolated from these women and, in spite of envying their academic skills, nevertheless felt something was basically out of balance. The sense she made out of it, and which I find compelling, is that the women around Jung were trying to live out Jung's ideal: to put the animus to work and presumably free their female ego from animus contamination. Wheelwright adds that the animus as described by Jung was burdened with everything that Jung's era found unfeminine, which resulted in the animus being ascribed much that is now considered to be a normal part of women's conscious nature. Women could do and did do what was then thought to be men's work, but, having no feminine models, they often adopted a masculine style. As intellectuals, these women functioned with an animus sort of studiousness, drivenness, and objectivity instead of exploring what feminine intellectuality might be. Their lives were strangely neutered since they had so little contact with the feminine aspect of the self. (Wheelwright stresses the idea of the female self in which the female ego is rooted in the same way that the animus is rooted in the masculine. This is an important aspect of analytical theory to which Jung seldom alludes.)

Women's biologically potent and sexual selves were also ignored or, in the "niceness" that was so emphasized in Switzerland, this power was stereotypically conceived of as distasteful (perhaps evil) and suspect. Wheelwright also suggests that the dark and potent sides of women may well have bothered Jung, and that as a consequence analytical psychology may not have paid enough attention to the body and biological sexuality, especially female sexuality.

Wheelwright adds that Jung, following the style of the times in Switzerland, found himself obliged to tell women who they were and to analyze their dreams from a masculine perspective. Along with disciplining the animus, women's masculine side, Jung felt that women should allow their femininity to develop in relationship to men, but he didn't seem to really know how they should go about it. He left that task to Toni Wolff, whom Wheelwright considers to have been more circumscribed in her view of women than he.

Jung tried not to accept the role of the powerful god figure that these women's animi picked up and projected onto him, but Wheelwright suggests that because the figure of the goddess was as yet collectively inadequate to balance the archetype of the masculine god, Jung could not avoid such projections. In spite of himself and for the same reasons, Jung also conveyed the impression that the ideal feminine could be found, not so much in women, but through studying his own anima, his own unconscious feminine side. Wheelwright feels that it would have been better both for Jung and for an understanding of women's psychology in general if he had refused this patriarchal role; she also notes that there was no one to challenge the patriarchal bias or to question it, and that Jung's attitude was typical of his era.

She remembers recoiling at "a kind of cultism in the air" (1963, p. 226) that these projections on Jung engendered. She reacted against the "the bevy of females" (1982, p. 98), and objected to the atmosphere created around him: "women fought each other to get close to him and men railed against him because of imagined neglect . . . there was no one to contain him" (p. 98). Wheelwright considers Jung's attitude toward women and the feminine to have been both positive and negative:

> Jung was definitely the patriarch and was paternalistic . . . . But, I feel, because of his discovery of his anima and his enormous popularity with women, as well as getting support for his new radical ideas from them, especially American women, he, at least theoretically, wanted women to improve their lot and make their legitimate way into the professions. He was not, however, altogether convincing in his behavior. (p. 104)

In spite of these reservations, Wheelwright speaks and writes of the profound effect on her of her analysis with Jung. She reports feeling abysmally lost at first, for she tried to do things in Jung's way and meet his expectations. She relates that she was lucky that she couldn't. Instead, through an important dream, she found her own way. Jung had initially taken her on as a patient because he was interested in the conflict between her upbringing in a wild, natural, even primitive place (what he would have considered Romantic) and her cultured education and life. This split from, but deep alliance with, nature and the primitive echoes a split van der Post (1975) notes that Jung felt in himself; Jung was deeply drawn to the primitive, whether in Africa or in his patients' psyches (see also Osterman, 1963).

The best in Jung was brought out, however, in the analytic session, partly because Jung insisted that both analyst and analysand, whether male or female, be open to "an important rearrangement of themselves that had significance — some meaning far beyond them" (Wheelwright, 1982, p. 103). Wheelwright found that Jung had extraordinary insight into her problems; in contrast to his lectures and writing (which she found contained "a touch of authoritarianism" [1963, p. 227]), in analysis he made "what could only be described as an exceedingly warm, personal, individual contact" (p. 226). From the analysis she developed "a new attitude and new insight and sense of myself that has remained the core of my being to this day" (p. 103). It was through her analysis that she could then go on to understand his writing. She found that through the analytic work he connected her to "the stream of life... and eternal liveliness" (p. 228), and concludes that what Jung *did* in analysis was more radical in its evaluation of women than anything he ever wrote. She cites incidents which belie

> the Zürich tradition that he apparently subscribed to, namely, that women have to live through men. Times like these, and there were others, made me sense that Jung, although a product of the patriarchal society, had somewhere in him an instinctual sense that women needed to be independent of men as well as related to them. Some clever woman, had there been one in his orbit, might have brought out in him this realization. (1982, p. 100)

It was perhaps enough for his era that Jung encouraged women to release their animus energy in constructive work, and to leave the private sphere of the home for the market sphere of the professions. This in itself was of immense help to women. I concur with Wheelwright when she concludes that in spite of Jung's Swiss attitude toward the feminine, without Jung "there would be far more delay in the understanding of women" (p. 105); an understanding, partial though it was, that was Jung's specific contribution "to this next step in our social evolution" (p. 105).

I interviewed Joseph Wheelwright in May of 1984 and talked with him again four years later. He told me that Jung's work on psychological types was what initially drew him to Jung. It was the first thing that explained the differences between him and his wife, Jane Wheelwright, and confirmed them both in their "right" to be who they were: he a feeling type man and she a thinking type woman. Despite the relief the theory gave him, he found that the attitudes toward men and women in Zürich and what was expected of him were quite different. What Wheelwright calls "the odious linkage" prevailed—Eros, feeling, and women, and Logos, thinking, and men.

Because Joseph Wheelwright came from a long line of radical and emancipated women who were very active and successful both socially and politically, he had models of strong, assertive, and courageous women. This made him receptive to the same characteristics in women in general; however, this was alien to the view of women shared by the group around Jung. Because of Wheelwright's aberrant views and because he had "a trilogy of faults"—lots of anima, lots of feeling, and lots of extraversion—he describes himself as feeling rebellious, freakish, and inferior to what was expected of the masculine in Zürich. As a feeling type, he believes the Zürich group considered him effeminate. The feeling type women around Jung were at the same time being encouraged to neither express nor understand their feeling, but to become intellectuals. They were supposed to develop the animus through doing all sorts of research and other erudite "leg-work" for Jung. Wheelwright wonders if it would have been better for those women to develop an understanding of the feeling function and for all of them to have examined their own feminine centers rather than "harnessing the animus."

Wheelwright describes the atmosphere in Zürich as male-dominated, chauvinist and patriarchal, and portrays the attitude toward women there in a similar vein to Jane Wheelwright's assessment. He believes that the women around Jung were not allowed to function as full women, but were required instead to be Jung's "handmaidens," adjuncts to him and his work. Jung's anima became the only model available to them of what the feminine could be: "they were caught in a transference to him and they acted out his anima" (Serbin, p. 157). Wheelwright thinks this may be what has made the literature Jung and these women wrote about the feminine so unsatisfactory—a blurred place in Jungian thought where much work still needs to be done. He proposes that his sort of differentiated feeling may do the same intellectual work a thinking type does, but in another, no less valuable, way; he also thinks that the feeling and thinking of men of that time and now is of a different quality from women's feeling and thinking, but that, caught as everyone was in Jung's view of the psychology of women, no one had a vantage point from which to work out a clearer view.

Wheelwright feels that Toni Wolff was Jung's *femme inspiratrice;* she helped get him going and contributed much of the creative ferment in his work, especially its mystical side. He echoes Jane Wheelwright in her analysis of Wolff's typically low opinion of women, describing Wolff as a father's daughter more concerned with relationship to men than to women. "It was always implicit, both with Jung and Toni Wolff, that a woman must relate to life through a man" (Serbin, p. 157). Wheelwright remarks that Jung preferred working with women as analysands, and that he explained this preference to Wheelwright as coming from his experience that women entered analytic work for itself and were able to give themselves wholeheartedly to the work. Jung contrasted this with men's propensity to think of analysis as a vehicle toward some other goal.

In Wheelwright's own personal analysis, Jung gave him what he most valued: a full and complete authentication of himself by a member of his own sex. Jung helped him to become all that was particularly and singularly within him to become. Perhaps because Wheelwright is a feeling type, he encountered few of the problems men who were more like Jung's father ran into—though Wheelwright, on ocassion, witnessed Jung's volcanic temper.

During the last part of our first interview, Wheelwright spoke of his own discovery of the dark aspect of the feminine that, albeit unconsciously, pervaded and surrounded the Jungian matrix, and that Wheelwright believes was of central importance to Jung. This was a deep but ambivalent connection with the potent feminine. An aspect of it first appeared to Wheelwright in a dream the night after he had visited the shrine of the Black Madonna at Einsiedeln. His dream involved initiation into the religious cult of Isis, something Wheelwright consciously knew nothing about. Jung made the archetypal connections for him through amplification. After this dream, as the start of his own initiation and with both Jung's and Wolff's help and encouragement, Wheelwright made his own descent into and union with this dark form of the archetype of the feminine. Wheelwright considers Jung's openness to a connection with this level, whether in Jung's time or today, to be of immense value and to offer something to the world very different from other psychologies.

Jung's personal experience of the feminine, his wounds and their healings and scars, led to internal struggles, conflicts, and unfinished business that resonate throughout his treatment of women. His unintegrated experience of the feminine, both in relation to real women and in his own psyche, may have led to and in turn been caused by the blindness of his own anima, Salome, whom Jung abandoned as "undeveloped" (van der Post, 1975, p. 167), trusting the more developed and patriarchal archetype of Philemon, the wise old man. Yet Jung was also a Romantic; as such he longed for the feminine, and

allowed the rejected, despised, deprived and persecuted feminine in life to be his guide. It had done its work accurately . . . It is as if in that vision of Salome all that guided his yesterdays is saying to him, "Look at that girl. That is what life has done to us. It has denied us our own feminine vision and so deprived us of meaning. That is what is wrong with your so called civilization; that is the wrong so great that even you who had allowed us to guide you hither have been maimed likewise. We can do no more now. You know now what the trouble is and knowing it, you ignore it at your peril." (van der Post, 1975, p. 168)

The prejudices of the time, the lack of opportunities for women's own development, Jung's personal experiences, especially of his mother, led to the absence of the one figure who could have helped Salome and have balanced her in Jung's inner and outer psychology. This was the figure of a vigorously assertive, vital, wise, and passionate adult woman — the absent Baucis/Baubo. This potent feminine appeared archaically and monstrously in Jung's (and his era's) unconscious in the form of the black serpent; it also appeared far above the earth transmuted into the longed for, but hidden, archetype of the Black Madonna. Neither the time nor Jung were ready for her human form.

CHAPTER THREE: MAN'S OPPOSITE

C. G. Jung and his Theory of the Feminine

The end [of *Ulysses*] is a string of veritable psychological peaches. I suppose the devil's grandmother knows so much about the real psychology of woman, I didn't.

Jung in a letter to James Joyce

In terms of the magnitude of Jung's life-work, analyzing Jung's theory of the feminine is an awesome task, one to be approached with not a little humility. Part of the difficulty is that what Jung writes about the feminine is both precedent setting and, at the same time, reactionary: a cat's cradle of contradictions. Another difficulty is that his writings on the feminine are scattered throughout his work; Jung never presents a comprehensive and inclusive theory on the feminine or on the psychology of women. In fact, referring to his "theory" as I have done and will be doing may be misleading unless one also accepts Jung's view of his own accomplishment. He wrote: "I am fully aware that we are discussing pioneer work which by its very nature can only be provisional" (Jung, 1951/1968, p. 16).

Compiling or examining only a few selections of what Jung writes about the feminine omits vital parts and, through omitting complexity and contradictions, can lead to an over-simplification which stresses the time-boundedness of Jung's views on women. *Aspects of the Feminine* (Jung, 1982), for instance, which is perhaps the most comprehensive presentation of Jung's published work on the feminine and women, tends to alienate and confuse a modern reader with its initial essay—perhaps the most Romanticized of Jung's portrayals of man's inner feminine—followed by three articles full of nineteenth-century prejudices about actual women. The more practical and advice-giving the tone, and the more he considers women in the abstract and *in general* (as in these three articles), the more dated the writing appears. It is as if Jung were not talking to women but about a general class of beings whom he discusses with "the kind of coarseness often characteristic of man talking to man about woman." Jung presents a strangely distorted outside view that women did not rebut (see Jane Wheelwright, 1982, p. 100). Jung himself remarked on the general ignorance of women's psychology:

> it is a foregone conclusion among the initiated that men understand nothing of women's psychology as it actually is, but it is astonishing to find that women do not know themselves. (Jung, 1933/1980, p. 807)

In the two following chapters, I will attempt to address both the complexity and the contradictions in Jung's theory, and differentiate between what may have enduring value and what needs to be discarded as a remnant of the prejudices of his time. I have drawn from Jung's entire body of published work, plus some transcripts of seminars that were distributed privately and are now starting to become available in book form. From these sources I will look at Jung's view of the feminine as it evolved in his personality typology, his concepts of Eros and Logos, and the archetypes. Jung's theory of projection belongs in this consideration because it affects his view of women's psychology, and because projection permeates both religious and ethical views of the feminine, necessitating a revaluation of the dark side of woman. These aspects of his theory coalesce in Jung's series of seminars on a woman's visions. Jung's work on alchemy—with its reunion of opposites, especially the supposed opposites of masculine and feminine—is taken as the culmination of his exploration of the feminine. The problem of the *soror mystica* and Jung's treatment of this alchemical role brings this section to a close.

Much that Jung has written about psychology seems to me to be the most pertinent and fertile approach we have to the field. At the same time, and especially when he is writing about the feminine, in spite of the material's value, it is often marred by prejudice. Not infrequently, after passages of psychological acumen, the tone goes off the mark, holding, perhaps, an excess of affect. The result is that Jung's descriptions of the feminine and women tend to be either too personally disparaging (the positivistic, bourgeois Number One's view) or too excessively charmed (the Romantic Number Two's idealization). It is as if the nineteenth-century attitude of strong revulsion and strong fascination toward the feminine and toward women, the mysterious opposite sex, obscures and fogs Jung's sight. As Jane and Joseph Wheelwright have noted, Jung may have been introvertedly exploring the psychology of his own anima rather than the psychology of women (see also D. Wehr, 1987). In his essay, "Woman in Europe," Jung himself wrote:

> What can a man say about woman, his own opposite? I mean of course something sensible, that is outside the sexual programme, free of resentment, illusion and theory. Where is the man to be found capable of such superiority? Woman always stands just where the man's shadow falls, so that he is only too liable to confuse the two. (1927/1970b, p. 113)

> The elementary fact that a person always thinks another's psychology is identical with his own effectively prevents a correct understanding of feminine psychology. This is abetted by woman's own unconsciousness and passivity, useful though these may be from a biological point of view: she allows herself to be convinced by the man's projected feelings [and thus also accepts his definition of her]. (ibid. pp. 116-117)

Jung's tendency to organize his thinking in nineteenth-century Kantian polarizations (Willeford, 1975) is especially pronounced in his treatment of the sexes. If man be conscious, woman, his opposite, must therefore be unconscious; if man is active, woman must be passive. Psychology *per se* — man's psychology — is the psychology of the mind; woman's psychology, therefore, becomes primarily biologically determined and subject to the heart.

In this context as well as in the broader context of his era, Jung's delineation of the neglected feminine as standing for the unconscious, the receptive, the passive, and the affective feelings makes sense. These were areas which, until the advent of Freud and Jung, were seen as belonging to the private sphere and to Romantic literature rather than to the male world of the Market and its positivistic science (Ellenberger, 1970). In the early twentieth century values were starting to change. There was a certain unease with the one-sided masculine mode. Freud and Jung, on the one hand, brought up the unconscious as a counterpoint to the conscious world; on the other hand, women themselves were no longer content (if they ever were) embodying the one-sidedly "feminine" attributes required of them. Women started to be visible, active, conscious, and professional members of society who had to be taken into account. A third source of change was the increasing evidence of the pathological consequences of the era's sharp male-female split and of society's restrictions on the behavior expected of each sex. The patriarchy of Jung's time, which we inherit, projected all outward power onto men while it imposed a narrow, idealized role on women. At the same time, it looked down on woman as weak, evil, and earthy. Given this split, it was women who most often sought the psychological help of Freud and Jung, as of Charcot and Janet before them, and as women do of therapists today.

TYPOLOGY

Perhaps Jung's best known contribution to personality theory is his theory of the various psychological types, which is presented in the first book Jung wrote after his traumatic break with Freud, *Psychological Types* (Jung, 1921/1971).*

The types, as Jung formulated them, fall into two categories (which Jung called attitudes), introversion and extraversion, each having four functions: thinking, feeling, sensation, and intuition. The introvert takes objects inside, the reference point being the reality within him or her; the extravert reaches out to connect with or define reality through contact with, or direct inspiration from, exterior objects. Each of the four functions can be experienced in an extraverted or an introverted way.

> For complete orientation all four functions should contribute equally: thinking should facilitate cognition and judgment, feeling should tell us how and to what extent a thing is important or unimportant for us, sensation should convey concrete reality to us through seeing, hearing, tasting, sensing etc., and intuition should enable us to divine the hidden possibilities in the background, since these too belong to the complete picture of a given situation. (Jung 1921/1971, p. 518)

Jung's major interest, as can be seen from the book's initial subtitle, *The Psychology of Individuation,* was the process of psychological development. *Psychological Types* was and remains invaluable as a gateway toward the nonjudgmental appreciation of all the varying ways people react to, function, and develop in the world. Jung initially describes the types as gender neutral:

> As a general psychological phenomenon . . . sex makes no difference either; one finds the same contrast among women of all classes. . . .

---

* the germ for the book was already apparent in a short lecture Jung gave in 1913, where he introduced the terms extraversion and introversion and applied them to types of mental illness, to philosophy and, in the final two paragraphs, to the psychological theories of Freud and Adler. (Jung 1921/1971, appendix)

The types seem to be distributed quite at random [with respect to race, sex, class and education]. (ibid. p. 331)

In spite of this initial avowal of randomized occurrence of types, within the elaboration of the theory Jung often allocates the types along gender lines. For instance, after declaring that the types are randomly distributed, Jung narrows this view and, in the second half of the book, states that extraverted feeling occurs predominantly in women (p. 356), while extraverted thinking is predominantly male (p. 351). He defines the majority of introverted feeling types again as women (p. 388), while the majority of extraverted sensation types are men (p. 363). Extraverted intuitives, he says, are more commonly female (p. 369) while he finds introverted thinking types are more often male (p. 351). Only introverted sensation and introverted intuition are assigned no gender dominance.

What may have been true in Jung's time, no doubt influenced by socialization and custom, persists to a lesser extent today. Kiersey and Bates note that six out of ten women still show a preference for feeling as a primary function, while six out of ten men have thinking as their primary function (Kiersey and Bates, 1978, p. 200). Myers (1962) finds that only the thinking-feeling dimension tests along gender lines. Kiersey and Bates declare that any gender difference is relatively minor (*op. cit.*, p. 20). Whether this — as almost all gender differences — is a difference due to socialization and culture, or is even in part biologically determined, is open to question (Douglas, 1985), as is the effect on personality type of our extraverted thinking mode of education.

What is problematical in Jung's statements is that the more common subtly becomes the more psychologically appropriate and healthy and, finally, a universal truth. Jung tends to equate feeling with the feminine and with women and thinking with the masculine and men, no matter what an individual's particular type may be. "Feeling is a specifically feminine virtue" (Jung, 1927/1970a, p. 41). Consequently Jung gives woman the capacity, but also the restrictive burden, of functioning primarily in and through relationship and feeling. Thinking becomes reserved for men and is described as inferior and unconscious in women, deriving from their animus. Thinking gets equated with spirituality, while feeling — a question of values — is mixed up with emotionality in such a way that Jung seems to be assigning gender specificity to each. "It is an almost regular occurrence for a woman to be wholly contained, spiritually, in her husband, and for a husband to be wholly contained, emotionally, in his wife" (Jung, 1925/1954, p. 195; see also: Jung,

1935/1966, p. 188 and Jung, 1929/1967, pp. 40-41).

The fact that women of Jung's time and today tend toward being feeling types—and men, thinking types—does not require the subsequent stereotyping and limitation in Jung's development of the theme. As a thinking type myself, I have the odd and disconcerting experience, in reading Jung, of seeing my way of functioning in the world allocated to men. I am included in descriptions of a mode that seemingly belongs only to a man, while descriptions of the feminine exclude me and my feminine—albeit logical and thinking—self. Relating to the world primarily through a developed thinking function is a mode that Jung, in theory, found "open to women of all classes," but in working out his theory, he turned it into essentially forbidden territory. The thinking mode is declared inferior in women: an unhealthy and unallowed aberration. I find this both troubling and alienating. It confines men and women to a painfully restricted sense of appropriateness that echoes the prejudices of the nineteenth century rather than the reality of an individual's being and of her or his individual path. A woman who conceptualizes her own thinking as masculine (D. Wehr, 1987), or a man who evaluates his feeling as feminine, estranges and distances the function. It transfers a normal part of the self onto a taboo "other," thus adding to the pain and confusion already inflicted by conventional cultural stereotyping. Transferring it in this way also doesn't work, for the thinking and feeling of one sex don't quite fit descriptions that were tailored for the other. Nothing in Jung's initial theory demands this compartmentalization and exclusion. In fact Jung himself noted a different socio-cultural reason for the disparity, one which has nothing to do with types or gender but echoes J. S. Mill's vapor bath and snow analogy:

> When a woman is brought up to think only certain things, she cannot think at all. You cannot bring anyone up to function only in certain ways. If you hinder anyone's feeling or thinking, he will not function properly any more. (Jung, 1938/1984, p. 89)

In spite of statements such as these (and Jung's unprejudiced approach to individual patients), the working out of Jung's typological theory in practice acts, even today, to alienate those who were born with the "wrong" typology for their gender. It makes analytical psychology seem, on the surface, unsuitable to many who otherwise would be attracted to it, especially those who desire a psychology that honors and is responsive to all the complicated mixtures that constitute human individuality. Jung respects individual differences, but then seems to abdicate this respect in favor of formulations and comments which derive from the sexist prejudice of his time. This area of his theory is undergoing major revision today, though regrettably far too many Jungians pay lip service to the revisions while maintaining the more restrictive and time-bound form. This echoes something Jung noticed in his fellow psychiatrists' response to Freud's masterly reformulation of psychology:

> A few writers spoke of it appreciatively and then, on the next page, proceeded to explain their . . . cases in the same old way. They behaved very like a man who, having eulogized the idea or fact that the earth was a sphere, calmly continues to represent it as flat. (Jung, 1943/1966, p. 10).

EROS AND LOGOS

The split along gender lines which contaminates his typology extends to Jung's concept of Logos and Eros.

> It is probably Logos and Eros, impersonal and personal, which are the most fundamental differences between man and woman. (Adler, [Ed.], 1973, Vol. 1, p. 48)

> Woman's psychology is founded on the principle of Eros the great binder and loosener, whereas from ancient times the ruling principle ascribed to man is Logos. (Jung, 1927/1970b, p. 123)

> For purely psychological reasons I have . . . tried to equate the masculine consciousness with the concept of Logos and the feminine with that of Eros. By Logos I meant discrimination, judgment, insight, and by Eros I meant the capacity to relate. (Jung, 1955-1956/1970, p. 179)

Interestingly, Jung often seems to value the Romantic Eros more than the Market's Logos. He finds that Logos rests on the supremacy of the word and calls it "the congenital vice of this age" (Jung, 1957/1970, p. 286), accompanied as it is by the repression of feeling. Eros, on the other hand, is encouraged for it leads to relatedness, nourishment, and love. Jung defines Logos in terms that are similar to the Eastern concept of Yang: denoting masculinity, consciousness, spirit, thought, analysis, action, rationality, and light. Eros is given the opposite Yin attributes: femininity, unconsciousness, earthiness, relatedness, feelings, passivity, nourishment, darkness, and the material.

Jung however, along with many of his followers, confuses the concepts of Eros and Logos, and of Yin and Yang, by making the attributions exclusively along gender lines. When gender is tied to the concepts, they are impoverished (as are the function types when restricted along gender lines), leading instead to restriction, confusion, and stereotyping (Samuels, 1985). Yin, the feminine, is confused with the female gender; Yang, the masculine, with the male. In Chinese philosophy Yin and Yang are conceived of as present in everything, though one quality may vastly predominate. Jung does posit an essential and all-important contrasexuality underneath this rigorously gender-specific personality, but he also tends to parcel out Eros and Logos according to gender while linking each with the "correct" function: Eros with feeling as woman's terrain; Logos with thinking as man's domain. Yet at the same time that he limits, Jung also allows for the very opposite. He asserts the vital importance of integrating both feminine and masculine sides of the self whatever these may be. Within the psyche, Jung declares, the inner woman or man is the opposite of the other. "The supreme recognition is that a man is also a woman and a woman is also a man" (Jung, 1933/1976, p. 370).

ANIMUS AND ANIMA

Jung's concept of fundamental androgyny could potentially free analytical psychology from the stereotypical prejudices of his age. It allows individuals to experience and develop all parts of themselves, whether or not these parts are conventionally gender-specific for their time and culture. But let us return for a moment and follow the development of theory in Jung's idea of the animus and anima. Jung's formulation perceives an interior complementarity and compensation that rounds out the individual by giving him or her an inner contrasexual "other." Jung's argument for this androgyny is first of all based on the biological premise that genes in both sexes are male and female. From here he branches into the theory of archetypes, calling the contrasexual archetype in man the anima, the inner feminine, and in woman the animus, the inner masculine.

According to Jung, an archetype is a predisposition toward some image or form. It is an eternal, unchanging, primordial, and collective deposit of "certain ever recurring psychic experiences" (Jung, 1921/1971, p. 444) common throughout the history of the world. The archetype itself does not change and, because it remains in the unconscious, can never be fully expressed. However, the outward mode of presentation

and the value accorded it are subject to the vagaries of a particular time
and culture, to individual experience, and to all the varying interpretations of the conscious mind. Thus, though the archetype itself is unchanging and eternal, its manifestations can reflect the prejudices of the
time (Douglas, 1985). Archetypes are not excuses for the status quo,
though it is inevitable that people clothe the archetypes in accordance
with the fashions of their time and then tend to define them according
to the way they have made them appear.

Jung gives a definition of the archetypes of the animus and anima
in "Marriage as a Psychological Relationship" (1925/1954). I have chosen this particular passage because it contains a clear and concise definition of the construct, yet at the same time may show elements of why
this particular part of Jung's theory is perhaps the most disputed concept in analytical psychology today.

> Every man carries within him the eternal image of woman, not the im-
> age of this or that particular woman, but a definite feminine image. This
> image is fundamentally unconscious, an hereditary factor of primordial
> origin engraved in the living organic system of man, an imprint or "arche-
> type" of all the ancestral experiences of the female, a deposit, as it were,
> of all the impressions ever made by woman — in short, an inherited sys-
> tem of psychic adaptation. Even if no woman existed, it would still be
> possible, at any given time, to deduce from this unconscious image ex-
> actly how woman would have to be constituted psychically. The same is
> true of the woman: she too has her inborn image of man. Actually, we
> know from experience that it would be more accurate to describe it as
> the image of *men,* whereas in the case of the man it is rather the image
> of *woman.* Since this image is unconscious, it is always unconsciously
> projected upon the person of the beloved, and is one of the chief reasons
> for passionate attraction or aversion. I have called this image the "ani-
> ma," and I find the scholastic question *Habet mulier animam?* [does a
> woman have a soul?] especially interesting, since in my view it is an in-
> telligent one inasmuch as the doubt seems justified. Woman has no ani-
> ma, no soul, but she has an animus. The anima has an erotic, emotional
> character, the animus a rationalizing one. Hence most of what men say
> about feminine eroticism, and particularly about the emotional life of
> women, is derived from their own anima projections and distorted ac-
> cordingly. On the other hand, the astonishing assumptions and fantasies
> that women make about men come from the activity of the animus, who
> produces an inexhaustible supply of illogical arguments and false expla-
> nations. (Jung, 1925/1954, p. 198)

Jung's medieval comment about the lack of soul in woman is, alas, repeated throughout his work (see especially: Jung, 1935/1966, p. 189; 1929/1967, p. 41, and 1927-1970a, also p. 41). It is a statement, albeit perhaps a teasing one, that dates and weakens this part of his theory, one example of the type of rhetoric that alienates many who might otherwise be attracted to analytical psychology (see Goldenberg, 1976; Lauter and Rupprecht, 1985; D. Wehr, 1987).

The anima and its opposite, the animus, are another example of Jung's thinking in polarizations. Though Jung did not *in theory* see the animus and anima, no more than the sexes themselves, as inherently inferior or superior (Maduro and Wheelwright, 1977, p. 112), and though each pole is theoretically equal and no depreciation is intended, yet the comparison inevitably draws him into a socio-culturally induced hierarchy of superiority and inferiority (Derrida, 1976). Jung describes both animus and anima as extraordinarily many-sided, but the positive aspects of the anima get precedence, while the animus' negative attributes add to its inadvertent inferior status. Jung states that the paramount role of the animus and anima is as a personification of the unconscious and a bridge to it: a way toward realizing undeveloped parts of oneself. This invaluable role tends to get lost under Jung's restrictive value judgements. In his further expositions of the anima and animus, man's feminine side continues to appear in a much more favorable light than woman's masculine.

Jung discovered the anima within himself, but only later deduced the existence of the animus. He found support for this concept in the psyches of his women patients (Jung, 1963). Jung's main work on the animus and anima occurs in "The Relations Between the Ego and the Unconscious" (1928/1966), in the chapter entitled "Anima and Animus." His interest and attention, normal for a man, are devoted to the exploration of the anima (seventeen pages) while the animus receives a scant five pages at the end of the essay.

The anima sounds very like the Romantic descriptions of the feminine I outlined in the previous chapter. I will try to do justice to her (the anima) by using Jung's own words: she is "a personification of the unconscious in general, and . . . a bridge to the unconscious" (Jung, 1929/1967, p. 42). She is the soul, the *"archetype of life itself"* (Jung, 1911-1912/1967, p. 437; emphasis in the original); she contains "all those common human qualities which the conscious attitude lacks" (Jung, 1921/1971, p. 468). She is both young and old, mother and daughter, worldly, of doubtful chastity, and virginal, childlike and naive (Jung,

1925/1954, p. 199). The anima is the mother and "the glamorous, possessive, moody and sentimental seductress in a man" (Jung, 1951/1968, p. 266). She "intensifies, exaggerates, falsifies and mythologizes" (Jung, 1936/1968, p. 70). Jung adds that:

> The anima also stands for the "inferior" function and for that reason frequently has a shady character; in fact she sometimes stands for evil itself. She is as a rule the fourth person . . . She is the dark and dreaded maternal womb which is of an essentially ambivalent nature. (Jung, 1936/1968, pp. 150-151)

The anima is also the place where the symbol of wholeness and redemption appears (Jung, 1955-1956/1970, pp. 356-357) which wants to reconcile and unite (Jung, 1946/1975, p. 304).

In these and many more descriptions of the anima, the excess of affect that pervades nineteenth-century writing on the feminine is marked. "The anima is a factor of the utmost importance in the psychology of a man wherever emotions and affects are at work" (Jung, 1934/1968, p. 70). Because of this emotional weight and because Jung sought to understand woman through his own anima which, as anima, he says "intensifies, exaggerates, falsifies and mythologizes," his view of women often takes on an excessive emotional load — Jung, under the anima's influence, becomes either too personally disparaging or too excessively charmed. Instead of women and "the emotional life of women," he appears to be describing his own thinking typology's feeling type anima.

Jung's argument that the anima is single does not seem convincing. In these and other multifaceted descriptions of Jung's, the anima appears to be as multiple as the animus. However, the result of conceiving of the inner feminine as single is that it concentrates her power and makes her much more alluring than the diffused masculine of the animus. Casting the man's feminine as a single entity in his psyche gives her far more numinosity than a real woman, while the animus as depicted in his many sorry guises appears decidedly inferior to a real man. It would seem that both could manifest as either single or multiple depending on the individual. As a matter of fact, Jung, in answering a question about the possibility of a woman having a single animus figure, makes an exception:

> Many souls are young; they are promiscuous; they are prostitutes in the unconscious and sell themselves cheaply. They are like flowers that bloom and die and come again. Other souls are older, like trees or palms. They find, or must seek, one complete animus, who shall perhaps be many

in one. And when they find him it is like the closing of an electric circuit. Then they know the meaning of life. (quoted in McGuire and Hull, 1977, p. 29)

Though it solves one problem, this little-known statement of Jung's raises another. By stating that old souls have single inner figures while also teaching that the animus is plural and the anima single, Jung seems to be inferring that women, by and large, are more undeveloped, "younger souls," than men. All in all, man and his anima become the more valued half of the opposites, while woman and her animus appear decidedly inferior. Though I found many passages to choose from in describing a positive anima, in Jung's work I could find only three descriptions of a positive animus (other than the animus' invaluable role as a bridge to the unconscious):

(1) The positive animus tries to discern and discriminate. (Jung, 1946/1975, p. 304)

(2) [He] gives a woman's consciousness a capacity for reflection, deliberation and self-knowledge. (Jung, 1951/1968, p. 16)

(3) In his real form he is a hero, there is something divine about him. (Jung, 1934/1976, p. 238)

Jung often refers to the animus as the carrier of Logos for the woman and therefore to be entrusted with her thinking. Thus, again, thinking is equated with masculinity and feeling with femininity, and both are seen, *ipso facto,* as inferior when present in the "wrong" sex (e.g., Jung, 1927/1970b, p. 127). This leaves a woman of the thinking type in the odd position of already having a differentiated thinking function, yet being told to look to her animus to cultivate her most developed quality because thinking and discrimination are what she supposedly needs to cultivate most. In the same vein, a predominantly feeling type man is required to rely on his anima to further cultivate his already well-differentiated feeling. It makes more sense for there to be feeling animi and thinking animae to guide one toward the particular areas where one lacks conscious development, whatever these areas may be; both men and women who have thinking as their best-developed function can still fall into stubborn and opinionated disputatiousness, and women and men who are feeling types can also sometimes be moony and moody. The logic of the interaction between types and animus/anima is not fully worked out in Jung's pioneering work on the subject.

Given the biases of Jung's time, much of this idea (that women as feeling types would have thinking animi and that men as thinking types would have feeling animae) makes sense, but without these biases the model he presents is no longer convincing in this specific area. There is also the problem of gender stereotyping itself, and the way this infiltrates Jung's theory of animus and anima. Stereotyping is contrary to Jung's emphasis on individuality, yet it appears in his treatment of the archetypes of animus and anima and of the psychology of men and women. In his writing on this subject Jung often generalizes in the same way that positivist science generalizes. By taking the person as representative of his or her gender, Jung's theory conforms the individual to the gender-expectations of his day rather than freeing the individual to expand into all aspects of his or her personality. This contradicts the tone of his other writings and what is known of his relationship to patients.

In contrast to the anima, Jung, as I have said, most often portrays the animus in negative terms. The tone he uses is reminiscent of the judging, "spoiler," negative animus himself. Jung is at his most opinionated when he describes the animus as opinionated, unoriginal, beside the mark, argumentative, protesting, and conventional. D. Wehr (1987) has noted the anger in these and other epithets Jung hurls at the animus, as if somehow Jung were caught by the very thing he is scientifically trying to describe. He calls the animus a collective conscience, a "court of condemnatory judges," an "assembly of fathers" (Jung, 1928/1966, p. 207): critical, irrelevant, and maddening. Jung adds that: "If the woman happens to be pretty, these animus opinions have for the man something rather touching and childlike about them . . . But if the woman does not stir his sentimental side . . . then her animus opinions irritate the man to death" (p. 208). In statements such as these, Jung seems to see woman's psychology only through its effect on the male. Woman herself vanishes behind her exterior. Her ability to please or not please a man, rather than her own psychological development, suddenly becomes the central issue.

A thinking woman is described as "one of those creatures" (p. 208), an "animus hound" (p. 209) who functions in an inferior fashion through her inferior masculine, the animus. Jung finds the internal, disapproving, patriarchal voice of the animus in woman to be a natural one. It seems to me to be a prevalent voice in women even today, appearing at the beginning of therapy, for instance, and reappearing to harangue us when we are stressed, but it is not a natural one. Jung's initial description of the negative animus *names* a complex that bedevils many women. This naming is invaluable. However, Jung's negative view of the animus goes too far and implicates a woman's very sense of her own value. Rather than ascribing the negative animus to a woman's individual and inevitable failing, it seems more fruitful to understand it as the baggage we all bring with us in a patriarchy: a consequence of the status and role of women in society, and of who defines us and what voices (Jung's included) we have internalized. For instance, Horner has described this internal disapproving voice in contemporary terms as a double-bind that causes fear of success (1968). In her follow-up studies she has found the voice changing (1970); in more recent updates that examine later studies (1981 and 1989), Horner finds this voice persistent, though increasingly less powerful than in 1970. As we will see in later chapters, this same fate seems to have followed the animus over time.

One reason for the animus to be perceived and described by Jung in such a negative way may be that he is exploring his own subjective and introverted thinking masculine psychology—his discovery and analysis of his own anima's undeveloped side rather than an objective psychology of women. Jung's feeling type anima might be blind to the shadow side of his own thinking, therefore, and project the inferior part of his thinking onto women. Jung's undeveloped extraverted thinking* would carry this shadow. Another way of putting this is that the animus Jung gives to women more convincingly depicts the inferior thinking of Jung's own anima's negative animus. Jung catches a glimpse of this very problem when he writes of the individuation of a thinking type like himself:

> That last touch would be . . . realization through his inferior thinking.
> Invariably I see that the last realization, the primordial stuff from which
> the superior function is made, is the last thing to be touched by analysis.
> A thinker, for instance, has a thought morality . . . It gives one an idea
> of the enormous effort it was for man to detach himself from the inferior
> parts of his superior function in order to become human, to establish
> himself against nature . . . [Inferior thinking] is thinking, all right, but
> entirely impure; that is, thinking like nature would think, the worst kind
> of feminine thinking, like the thinking of an ignorant cook . . . the think-
> ing of a female worm. Let a man like Kant see his inferior thinking and
> he would hang himself right away. For me to admit my inferior thinking

---

* see Beebe, 1987, for further development of these typological intricacies.

is the worst thing under the sun. I would admit anything, moral insanity, incest, any vice, first. That inferior thinking is the worst. (Jung,
1938/1984, p. 273)

More often, Jung seems to project the inferior part of his superior
function onto women and accuse them of its gross and primitive defects.
However, there are also socio-cultural causes for Jung's negative and limited evaluation of the animus. One is the low esteem that men in his
era (and still too often today) held of women and women's internalization of that low opinion, contributing to the low self-esteem characteristic of many women. Another cause is women's self-consciousness
about their supposed deficits, coupled with a very real lack of educational opportunity: a place in which their thinking capacities could grow
and develop naturally. Because women were so undervalued in Jung's
time, he may have felt the psychological need to make the anima's value compensatorily high; but doing the opposite for women only ex-
acerbates their lower status and places them in double jeopardy by
undervaluing the animus to compensate for the overvaluation of masculine qualities and men in the outside world. There is also the likeli-
hood that since women of Jung's day had little chance to express their
"masculine" side, when it first appeared it may have been overdetermined and tended to manifest in a primitive and undifferentiated form
(like the new possibilities in our dreams which often turn up first in
their most negative and reprehensible shape).

Over time, as both men and women have increasingly been allowed
the expression of all sides of themselves, and as more complete humans,
both male and female, are in evidence, the animus and anima appear
as more positive and helpful. In footnotes added to later editions of
Jung's work, Jung himself began to refer to Emma Jung's (1957/1974)
writing on the animus (which presents some of the animus's more positive aspects) as more complete than his own (e.g. Jung, 1911-1912/1967,
p. 183n; 1934/1980, p. 768; 1940/1968, p. 124n.; 1940/1969, p. 30n.;
1943/1966, p. 90n; and 1948/1968, p. 247).

A final problem brings us to Jung's idea of projection. Man's propensity to project his anima onto a woman can lead to the confusion of
the anima with a woman's own psychology. D. Wehr (1987) makes a strong
argument that this confusion occurs throughout Jung's work. She says
that it causes Jung to form "a blurred agenda" where the development
of a man's contrasexual side is confused with woman's psychology *per
se*. It also can act as "subliminal advertising" so that the projection of

Jung's (or a Jungian therapist's) anima covertly informs a woman how she should really be, and so distorts her own sense of herself and impedes her discovery of her inner reality. "Since we all tend to become who we are addressed as being, men's anima projections help shape women's sense of self" (D. Wehr, 1987, p. 104).

PROJECTION

Jung noted that most people do not wish to see their own contrasexual sides. Instead they tend to project these, and both positive and negative aspects of themselves, onto someone else. In the case of what is perceived as the contrasexual, the projection is usually onto someone of the opposite sex. Projection, in Jung's theory, is the placing of one's unconscious contents onto a more or less suitable exterior object. "Projections change the world into the replica of one's own unknown face" (Jung, 1951/1968, p. 9). Jung found that men tend to place all their fear of, doubt about, and fascination with their own unacceptable feminine qualities onto women. A woman then becomes both a "soul-image" for a man and a repository of evil. Thus men can be, at one and the same time, both lovers and misogynists. Women in turn tend to give over their power, intelligence, worldly force, and assertiveness to a man, helping his success rather than developing their own capacities. There are, as Jung states, "many women who, by completely disregarding their own lives, succeed in representing their husband's soul-image for a very long time" (Jung, 1921/1971, p. 472). Thus he describes marriages and love-relationships as often taking place between people of opposite types, each of whom has developed what is yet undeveloped in the other and so carries and personifies it for the other. Jung states that an essential task in psychological development is becoming conscious of one's own anima and animus and withdrawing projections. These tasks, though, Jung comments, are very lonely ones, as projection "gives the feeling of being connected" (Jung, 1934, p. 244). It is the way most people relate to others.

Part of the harm in projection, Jung finds, is that besides leaving a person incomplete, it is also a way to escape all that one cannot accept in one's own character, including one's own complicity in the evil of the world. The core of Jung's psychology may be his wrestling with the problem of evil and his perception of the consequences of the human tendency to project internal evil out onto others. Inherent in the problem of evil are Jung's concepts of the shadow (what is unconscious, or what one cannot accept in one's self) and the archetype of evil *per se*. How these become involved in projection and scapegoating explains much that is so violently askew in our present collective attitude. Jung thinks that scapegoating and projection are inevitable consequences of the idea of human perfectibility. He traces this idea to the predominantly Judeo-Christian concept of God as an all-good being, with evil understood as a falling away from this good. Evil then has no absolute reality in and of itself, no connection to a human's imitation of Christ, and no connection to God. I will deal with Jung's concepts of evil, shadow, and projection mainly as they affect his views on the feminine, but must elaborate his ideas a bit first.

In an extemporaneous address in 1929, "Good and Evil In Analytical Psychology," Jung tried to go beyond our culture's dualism and our one-sided approach to reality. He stated:

> Good and evil are principles of our ethical judgment, but, reduced to their ontological roots, they are "beginnings," aspects of God, names for God. Whenever, therefore, in an excess of affect, in an emotionally excessive situation, I come up against a paradoxical fact or happening, I am in the last resort encountering an aspect of God, which I cannot judge logically and cannot conquer because it is stronger than me—because, in other words, it has a numinous quality and I am face to face with what Rudolph Otto calls the *tremendum* and *fascinosum*. I cannot conquer a *numinosum*, I can only open myself to it, let myself be overpowered by it, trusting in its meaning. (Jung, 1959/1970, p. 458)

What follows is a brief overview of Jung's argument, which he presents most clearly in *Answer to Job* (1952/1969). For almost two thousand years of Christianity backed by perhaps a thousand more of Judaism, Western civilization conceived of God as the *summum bonum*, only and all good, and composed primarily of masculine attributes (though Jung notes that ancient texts incorporated the feminine far more than modern history acknowledges). In these increasingly patriarchal societies, Jung writes, "the inferiority of women was a settled fact" (Jung, 1952/1969, p. 395). Evil, matter, the earth, and nature became split off from God along with the feminine. Women were omitted from the heavenly and masculine Trinity of God the Father, God the Son, and God the Holy Ghost, and were denied any part of the divine. Women were allied instead with a lower and Hell-connected Trinity: woman, earth, and devil (Jung, 1951/1968, p. 55). Women thus received the projection of all that men thought base or could not accept within themselves. The self-hatred men felt for their corporeal, ungodly, fallen selves was projected onto women, as was their "deadly fear of the instinctive, unconscious inner man" (Jung, 1911-1912/1967, p. 298). Jung sees us as inheritors of this one-sided striving for perfection and the consequent projection of all else onto the enemy, our opposite. This is accompanied by a necessary—though pathological—suppression, dishonoring, and universal denigration of women.

Jung traces this split and argues on several fronts for the reconciliation of the upper and lower trinities. To be very brief, part of his argument derives from Christian and Jewish (Kabbalistic) mysticism and part from Eastern philosophy, primarily Taoism. In Taoist philosophy all pairs of the seeming opposites are honored as made up of Yin and Yang, each of which contains the seeds of its opposite, and each of which leads into the other. In his forewords to Richard Wilhelm's books, The *Secret of the Golden Flower* (Jung, 1929/1967) and *The I-Ching* (Jung, 1950/1969), Jung elaborates on these theories and points the way to the incorporation of the feminine dimension of the divine into Western psychological theory.

Jung believes that the Roman Catholic doctrine of the Assumption of the Virgin is an early sign of the potential healing of this split. According to this doctrine, the corporeal body of the Virgin Mary ascended into heaven, which means that the feminine, through Mary, has finally taken her rightful place alongside of the masculine Trinity. In a letter to Reverend David Cox in 1957, Jung remarks: "According to what I hear from Catholic theologians, the next step would be the Coredemptrix" (Jung, 1958/1980, p. 731). This next step would add a feminine fourth to the Christian Trinity. Whatever the possibilities of this in Christianity, the longing for the feminine and Jung's vision of the feminine as an essential part of theology and psychology gives women and the feminine a weight that they did not have in former psychologies or philosophical systems. The significance of Jung's recognition of the need for a feminine that is equal to the masculine resonates throughout his work; it lies behind but is also remarkably contradictory to his positivist and bourgeois "Number One's" disparagements and insults. One has to look behind the bluster of this "Number One's" conventional sexism and Jung's own complexes, to the heart of his theory, which reveals a deep respect for all parts of the psyche and promotes individual development and completion. This is one of the main sources that make his psychology so potentially healing, especially for women, but also for all divided human beings struggling with the problem of good and evil.

A problem with this dualistic mode, though, is one common to nineteenth-century thinking and Jungian psychology: the tendency to mix up and conflate matter, the feminine, and the devil, and see all as evil. Both the feminine and the devil are equated with matter as the lower, "evil" Trinity, in what Goethe has called man's "tremendous mistrust of the titanic powers of nature" — a mistrust that has subjugated and exploited nature as well as the feminine in a disastrous way. There is a worrisome quandary in this. In all of Jung's considerations of the Trinity, he states that it is psychologically incomplete, lacking a fourth. Jung refers to this fourth sometimes as feminine and other times as evil. Logically this then equates the feminine with evil, which again leaves a woman back where she started, a scapegoat for evil in a man's world. As man's anima "she sometimes stands for evil itself. She is as a rule the *fourth* person" (Jung 1936/1968, p. 150). Although he notes these parallels, Jung starts to sound like a late nineteenth-century man filled with romantic fantasies of guilt, reparation, and rescue of that rejected, despised, sometimes deranged, fallen woman: his own anima.

I wonder if Salome, Jung's inner feminine, an aspect of his anima, is blind just because she cannot see who she really is; she cannot see her potential free of the confusion of the feminine with evil and matter, while Baucis/Baubo, her powerfully sensual old sister, a darker aspect of Jung's anima, can only exist in Jung's psyche in the form of the dark serpent. Like the temptor snake in the Bible, this feminine wants something of him. She may hold a clearer vision of women and the possibilities of the feminine outside the garden of Jung's culture and his time; "something sensible, that is outside the sexual programme, free of resentment, illusion and theory" (1927/1970b, p. 113). Jung could not taste this black snake's apple and thus make his own feminine more human and clear; his theory suffers by remaining blind to many potential aspects of the feminine that reverberate within these two unconscious figures.

When these aspects of the feminine are blinded, disowned, or banished into animal form, they become negative and as linked to evil, sorcery, black magic and snaky witches, as Jung has noted. In writing about the split between the Catholic Church's worship of Mary and society's view of woman, he wrote:

The image of woman lost a value to which human beings had a natural right . . . In the unconscious the image of woman received an energy charge that activated the archaic and infantile dominants. And since all unconscious contents, when activated by dissociated libido, are projected upon external objects, the devaluation of the real woman was compensated by daemonic traits. She no longer appeared as an object of love, but as a persecutor or witch. (Jung, 1921/1971, p. 236)

This powerful energy becomes suppressed or projected onto women and the devil by patriarchal men and by women who cannot face these strong powers inside themselves. Jung inherited this problem as the son of his age and we, as his heirs, are faced with the same deficiencies in his theory. Jung presents us with the problem of his and his era's blindness that obscures his own work on the feminine, yet, at the same time, he also gives us the key ingredients toward its healing.

Jung does see the need for a man's recognition and acceptance of his anima and for the reinstatement of the feminine to a position of respect and authority within man's psyche, but I am not clear when this applies to women and to the psychology of women. Man's anima and the psychology of real women get confused. Jung understands the necessity of both men and women reintegrating evil and returning the feminine to her rightful position of parity with the masculine. But it feels more fruitful now to bring about the redemption of the feminine through the separation and discrimination of the feminine from its emulsion with matter, with the devil, and with evil. The commixture's present indefiniteness simply adds to the power of the anima's allure and further separates both men and women from an understanding of the feminine and of themselves. Here is where Jungian psychology gets caught in nineteenth-century fantasies. Unknotting this entanglement is imperative. Clear of the confusion of the masculine and feminine, men and women can both gain better access to their earthy and spiritual parts and to their mixture of good and evil. Earth and spirit, good and evil belong neither to a specific gender nor to a specific sex.

ARCHETYPES OF THE FEMININE

In the absence of a union between the upper and lower trinities, Jung describes how the denied feminine, limited to both an unreal idealization and an equally unreal denigration, accumulates and builds up power in the unconscious. This power often turns hostile and destructive, as in the negative mother. In "Psychological Aspects of the Mother Archetype" (Jung, 1938/1969), Jung discusses the psychological effects of this archetype as it is embodied in the psychology of women of his time. He develops the multifaceted idea of the negative and positive mother archetypes, their impact on the actual mother-child relationship and their psychological effect within the child's psyche. Jung sees the archetype as manifesting itself both in the character of the mother and in what the child projects onto her. The effects of a mother complex on the daughter are thoroughly and creatively elaborated, both in their harmful and helpful aspects. Jung is uncharacteristically brief on its effects on the son: he states that possibly the positive aspects of the complex can give a woman's son access to creativity, but it can also bind him to the mother in impotence, in homosexuality, or in a Don Juan-like search for her in many women; a positive mother complex also may prevent a son from taking his place in the mundane world. The negative mother complex can lead to a hatred of women and the feminine or to an enmeshment with an equally negative or devouring woman or anima-figure. It can also lead to the development of society in general through the cultivation of the hard-working fathers' world of Logos and the Market.

The consequences for the daughter are explored more fully. Jung's delineation of them is congruent with developmental theories in the psychology of women that are still being evolved today. For instance, Jung writes about four different ways daughters can be affected by the mother-complex: becoming caught up in the mother role itself, in a sort of blind instinctual morass; reacting to it by overdeveloping an erotic attachment to the father and/or to other women's husbands; identifying to such an extent with the mother that one has no separate life; and finally, resisting the mother so that the guide for the daughter's life becomes an adamantine opposition to everything her mother is or represents. Jung does not, as do so many other theorists, place the blame for these and other negative outcomes on the personal mother. He considers the damage a consequence of the stresses on the mother and a result of making a woman carry the lopsided projections of idealization and fear that rightfully belong to the archetype. The consequent damage of a negative mother complex is well elaborated in Jung's work, as are its impersonal roots in the archetype as portrayed in history and in myth.

The positive aspects of a negative mother complex that Jung first observes and describes have been verified in modern studies of non gender-bound females (e.g., Bem, 1976). The harmful aspects that Jung cites still remain one of the problems of our age. People would be psychologically healthier, Jung avers, if the mother did not have to bear the weight of what we project onto the feminine, and if both sexes could express their cherishing and nurturing sides (this is a point thoroughly explored by Dinnerstein [1977], N. Chodorow [1978], and Rubin [1983]).

Jung sees the dark negative mother as but one aspect of the feminine archetype whose image has become exaggerated and baneful because of our socio-cultural response to her; he thus advocates the psychological necessity of incorporating all aspects of the feminine and of evil into our understanding of God (Jung, 1952/1969). Analysis provides a way to explore the dark, somewhat suspect parts of the psyche, and to absorb and redeem the negative through some accomodation to and acceptance of it. Jung explores this process from the point of view of the male (he leaves the dark masculine in woman and the dark and earthy masculine in general undealt with). Out of personal confrontation with the dark side of the feminine within woman or in the anima of a man, Jung predicts the appearance of a Sophia-like archetypal image: "Where there is a monster a beautiful maiden is not far away, for they have, as we know, a secret understanding so that the one is seldom found without the other" (Jung, 1955-1956/1970, p. 226). Evil is not relativized in the process, but is accepted as a personal and ethical problem. Along with good, with Yin and Yang, masculine and feminine, consciousness and the unconscious, evil is seen as a human quality and problem, which by virtue of its archetypal backing also transcends the spheres of opposites.

I have dealt thus far mainly with Jung's delineation of the negative mother archetype. The multitudinous forms of the mother archetype were originally described in *Symbols of Transformation* (Jung, 1911-1912/1967), Jung's first attempt to explore the archetypes as images and symbols of the collective unconscious. The archetypes of the dual mother—sometimes loving, sometimes terrible—are some of the most compelling and powerful in the book. In "Psychological Aspects of the Mother Archetype" (Jung, 1938/1969) and in "The Psychological Aspects of the Kore" (Jung, 1941/1969), Jung further portrays positive and negative archetypal images of the feminine as mother, daughter, and anima figures. He seems content just to describe these many images and hint at their power as behavioral models, leaving further elaboration of each archetype to his followers. Starting with the archetype of the Great Mother, he very briefly sketches some of her manifestations: these include the Mother of God, the Virgin Mary, Sophia, Demeter, Isis, Hecate, Kali, the Earth Mother, the Chthonic Mother, Sky-woman and Moon-lady. Archetypal images of the daughter appear as Aphrodite, Helen (Selene), Persephone and the other Kore figures. Further images of the Kore-type feminine are the unknown young girl, the dancer, and the nymph. The mother-daughter pair is also seen in animals such as the cat, bear, crocodile, dragon, salamander, and snake. Jung points to images of vessels, bowls, cities, churches, and other containers as also connected to the feminine, especially as they are portrayed in the legend of the Grail and in religious symbolism. The Demeter-Kore myth, the connection between mother and maiden, is for Jung the central myth for the feminine psyche. He describes the value of its cult of the Eleusinian mysteries as providing Graeco-Roman women with a cathartic and rejuvenating outlet, and deplores our contemporary abandonement of the myth and its associated mysteries. In that it allows a woman to live as both mother and daughter, backwards and forward in time, the Demeter-Kore myth

> extend[s] the feminine consciousness both upwards and downwards. They add an "older and younger," "stronger and weaker" dimension to it and widen out the narrowly limited conscious mind bound in space and time, giving it intimations of a greater and more comprehensive personality which has a share in the central core of things . . . We could therefore say that every mother contains her daughter in herself and every daughter her mother, and that every woman extends backward into her mother and forwards into her daughter. (Jung, 1941/1969, p. 188)

As with Jung's vision of Elijah, Salome, and the dark serpent, the third figure in the Demeter-Persephone myth (and in woman's psychology), the Crone, is largely neglected. The important Hecate/Baubo aspect of the myth frees a woman from the biological "life-stream" that Jung felt was the essential part of the myth (ibid., p. 188). This aspect forms the third stage of a woman's life and the third aspect of her psyche—the crone joins the maiden and mother; old age follows youth and maturity; while the powerful underworld queen and shaman/bawd rounds out and extends the cycle of nurtured-nurturer. The old wise woman or crone was probably too potent and loaded an image for Jung's time, though it is an archetypal image that is coming up strongly in women's psyches now; it has been left to very recent Jungian or post-Jungian work.

In his exploration of the Demeter-Kore-Hecate archetype, Jung touches on a possible difference in the individuation process for women and for men: he finds a woman much more likely to be involved in a *nekyia*, a descent to the underworld, than in a heroic fight with a dragon. A quest for treasure, or some secret, found through suffering and with the help of the instincts, is also mentioned. The connection with the earth, the underworld, the body, and even orgiastic sexuality and blood is alluded to, though again not developed (p. 184). This is one of the few places where Jung does not mix up the development of the anima with women's psychology. Here Jung's intuitive genius may have discerned a women's way of development that has no counterpart in the masculine. It is most emphatically not just something that is the opposite of the masculine. Whether or not it is some part of the feminine men can recognize in themselves is not yet clear. Men are just starting to deal with chthonic aspect of themselves that may bear some similarity, though I think Jung's statement of the archetype being singularly congruent for women remains valid. In describing this archetypal image, Jung himself seeks to differentiate it from the anima:

> But the Demeter-Kore myth is far too feminine to have been merely the result of an anima-projection. Although the anima can, as we have said, experience herself in Demeter-Kore, she is yet of a wholly different nature. She is in the highest degree *femme à homme,* whereas Demeter-Kore exists on the plane of mother-daughter experience, which is alien to man and shuts him out. In fact, the psychology of the Demeter cult bears all the features of a matriarchal order of society, where the man is an indispensable but on the whole a disturbing factor. (p. 203)

Archetypes of the feminine besides the archetypes of mother, maiden, and anima are no more than alluded to in brief passages throughout Jung's work. They extend from "the latent primordial image of the goddess—i.e., the archetypal soul-image" (Jung, 1921/1971, p. 226)—through possibilities of the feminine that are just coming into consciousness today. Many analysts who are writing about Jung's theory of the feminine seem to have forgotten them or, in developing ideas originated by Jung, forget to give him credit. However, Jung's insights remain the seeds of much of the post-Jungian and revisionary work on the feminine which I will be discussing. They also remain a strong though relatively undeveloped component of *The Visions Seminars.* These lectures delineate many aspects of Jung's view of the feminine in often creative but sometimes limiting ways.

Chapter Four: Recovery and Loss

Aspects of the Feminine in
The Visions Seminars *and in Alchemy*

There was a time when you were not a slave, remember that. You walked alone, full of laughter, you bathed bare-bellied. You say you have lost all recollection of it, remember . . . you say there are no words to describe it, you say it does not exist. But remember. Make an effort to remember. Or, failing that, invent.

Monique Wittig, Les Guerillères

THE VISIONS SEMINARS

The Visions Seminars (Jung, 1934/1976) are an edited version of lectures Jung gave to his followers over a four-year period from October 30, 1930 to March 21, 1934. The subject of the lectures are forty-four of the over one hundred visions recorded by Christiana Morgan during the end of and shortly after her analysis with Jung (Douglas, 1989). Jung uses them to teach, through specific and detailed analysis, the way the collective unconscious reveals itself in patients' material. He examines Morgan's images for their symbolic and archetypal content, and as a practical demonstration of his theories. Through Morgan's material Jung traces

> the development . . . of the transcendent function out of dreams, and the actual images which ultimately serve in the synthesis of the individual, the reconciliation of the pairs of opposites, and the whole process of symbol formation. (Jung, 1934/1976, p. 1)

The reason for dealing with these visions is that they give us a really marvelous insight into the secret workings of the unconscious. They show us how the unconscious works out certain symbols through which she [Morgan] is helped to acquire an attitude that enables her to live . . .

her own specific individual life. (p. 129)

Elizabeth Sergeant (in McGuire and Hull, 1977) gives a lively picture of the audience and the atmosphere of the seminars as she experienced them in 1931. She makes a point that needs to be kept in mind in any discussion of Jung: that what Jung said was not only an elaboration of his theories, but was geared to a specific audience at a particular time. Sergeant comments that Jung seemed to speak personally to the needs of each person in the room and directly to their complexes. She felt that he tailored the seminars to his analysands' psychology and their individual needs far more than he focused on the text (pp. 50-56).

Jung describes the process of Morgan's visions as an initiatory one, a woman's path downward and through suffering. As Morgan descends into the unconscious, the images that arise suffer and then she suffers, she swallows then is swallowed by a snake, goes through fire, bleeds, immerses herself in a river of blood, and experiences violent, sometimes orgiastic rituals of union. She encounters many fierce and transformative animals, including a ram, a black stallion, bulls, goats, and snakes. A number of psychopomps, both male and female, come to her aid, while dwarves, giants, and mechanical men impede her progress. Jung describes this path as a Yin way that involves the need "to know more about the inside of the mountain" (p. 235). He notes the connection with earth, nature, and the soil, as well as the many archetypal feminine figures encountered, one of which being the terrible mother. Jung discusses the dark, negative, and powerful aspect of the feminine but does not entirely welcome it. He does encourage the raw, erotic, and fiery parts of the fantasies in contrast to society's requirement for feminine "niceness." He thus comments that "therefore women often pick up tremendously when they are allowed to think all the disagreeable things which they denied themselves before" (p. 413).

In the visions, Morgan descends down through successive realms, assimilating their material. Jung perceives that Morgan needs to confront the unconscious in its rawest, most primitive, and painful form because she has been so cut off from her instincts. It is only in this way that she can regain unity with her body. Morgan, he feels, has to descend to these deep instinctual and vegetative levels in order to assimilate their power, their earthiness, and their unity. He contrasts these primeval levels with Morgan's background and finds them an essential compensation for her upper-class, rational, New England Protestantism.

Jung describes the visions' general pattern of descent and ascent, infla-

tion and deflation in which Morgan's animus initially leads the way; he
notes that the sacrifices required of Morgan—her passage through blood
and through fire, her enclosure in a cave, and her sacrifice of external
sight—are initiatory themes comparable to similar ones in analysis and
in alchemy. Jung focuses on Morgan's animus, her descents, the sacrifices,
the passive suffering and union. There is a vigorous and ecstatic side
to the visions which Jung notes, but then tends to ignore, in his theoretical discussions of "woman's way." The heroine of the visions engages
in assertive and aggressive activity that sometimes troubles Jung, but
which seems a necessary balance to the suffering and enduring side. The
uniting of active and passive, upper and lower in Morgan's visions is perhaps their most original, creative, and generative feature.

Jung comments on the deeply matriarchal symbolism in the visions
and their connection with women's mystery religions. The visions he
spends most time on, though, contain predominantly male images of
earthy animus guides to the matriarchy: a ram is followed by an American Indian on horseback, who is followed by a black pool, a bull, a satyr, and an animal face in which Morgan "beheld what no man is meant
to see, eyes full of beauty and woe and light" (p. 62). After further ad-
ventures, Morgan is involved in a blood ritual which leads to marriage
with a Dionysian black god and physical union "in the blood" with this
dark and passionate inner figure. This union achieved, Morgan descends
to the deepest vegetative level, where she becomes a tree with roots in
the blood and in the ground and arms reaching up into the sky. This
return to an elemental, vegetative body is paralleled by a journey down
through all the ancient matriarchal mystery religions and up again in
time to Graeco-Roman, Mithraic, and Christian mysteries. Orgiastic rituals
are alluded to "in the home of the Mothers." The outcome is that Morgan resurrects pagan and primitive mysteries and unites them with Christian ones. This union of the two, Jung asserts, brings Morgan and the
culture one step further than Christianity. He sees this as the climax
of the visions. It takes place toward the end of the first volume, after
Morgan's union with the black Messiah figure, when he, now in the form
of a snake, confronts and transforms the mystery of the Christian Mass
into a more comprehensive mystery that also includes flesh and possibly the devil: an earthly trinity (see also Sandner, 1983 and 1986).

Jung is highly creative in connecting Morgan's visions to symbols from
alchemy and from Kundalini yoga, and then connecting these to the
process of analysis. He points out that each—analysis, Kundalini yoga

and alchemy—deals with the same process of individuation, but states that Kundalini yoga is particularly suitable for women's psychological development, and for these visions, because of its linkage of earth and sky, the body and the spirit. In both the visions and this yoga, spirituality becomes chthonic as well as heavenly; Morgan's spirituality, as it develops in the visions, recovers its center within her body and uses the body and sexuality for its very expression. As Jung points out, one of the main therapeutic results of the visions is Morgan's recovery of embodiedness. The imagery of Kundalini yoga involves a body-centered ascent and descent similar to that of the visions; it is also connected with symbols of animal archetypes such as the snake, the makara, the elephant, ram, and gazelle, which are either powerfully feminine or powerfully androgynous. In Kundalini yoga, the chakras are described as energetic focal points, aligned along the spinal column in the center of the body, with the spine acting like the tree of Morgan's vision. Both are centers of vitality that actively connect and mediate between heaven and earth. The human body and the tree act as the container, the channel and the *prima materia*. Jung elucidates and amplifies many of Morgan's visions in reference to Kundalini yoga and to its particular body chakras and emphasizes their importance to the feminine.

Jung's pioneering work throughout *The Visions Seminars* concerns the value of the chthonic, the body, and the instincts in the recovery of a feminine self. Jung's work on the feminine in this area, especially as he elaborates it here, has not received enough attention. In fact *The Visions Seminars* are one of the least referred to of Jung's work (only twenty-one out of one hundred eighty-one major books and articles written by Jungian analysts since the 1976 publication of *The Visions Seminars* list them in their references or bibliography; while Sandner, 1983, 1986, is the only analyst who has discussed them at length in a form available to the public). In his analysis of the visions, Jung notes that the Judeo-Christian, and especially nineteenth-century, split—with its emphasis on the good and the heavenly—causes a particular problem for women. One aim of analytic work is to help women regain respect for and access to the earth and to instinctuality. Jung's work here holds the potential of helping several generations of deracinated women regain contact with their basic ground.

In the published visions there are twenty-one images of powerful and/or archetypally numinous feminine figures. Over the course of the visions, they slowly stand beside or replace the chthonic animus in importance.

These potent feminine figures include witches, ancient mothers, dragons, volcano goddesses, sky mothers, earth mothers, mothers who "too long have . . . fructified the earth" (p. 302), harpies, maenads, wise women, loathsome women and, above all else, women guides. Here, when Jung is talking about the appearance of the Self, an unidentified person objects that the Self image is not male. Jung notes these images' central importance by replying: "No, just not [not male], because our patient is a female. . . . the divine form in a woman is a woman, as in a man it is a man" (p. 456).

But after a descent into the unconscious and an encounter with all the figures Jung could explain, somehow Jung and his patient fall out of harmony. Things start going wrong. Jung says that "the case is getting more and more complicated" and that "things are getting reversed in a very peculiar way" (p. 438). Morgan has left analysis and Jung. He is vexed, he starts blaming the patient. He calls her too young, unsettled, finds fault with her ego-consciousness, with her return to the United States, the lack of contact between them. While at the start of the seminars he stayed close to the text and the images, now more and more of the seminar time is spent on discussions further and further away from the subject. The class grows restive. The seminars end abruptly, the excuse given that confidentiality has been breached. There is hard feeling between Morgan and Jung. Something had gone wrong in the seminars and possibly in the analysis that may be central to Jung's ideas about and treatment of the feminine, and may have led to the loss of what was being recovered.

I want to go back a bit here in order to trace some elements of the problem. A part of the visions that Jung rarely mentions is the visioner herself, Christiana Morgan. He says, "I omit personal details intentionally, because they matter so little to me. We are all spellbound by those external circumstances and they distract our mind from the real thing" (p. 2). But who Morgan was, what her struggles were, and what her associations to her material were, are all central to the understanding of her visions. Some knowledge of her is also vital in understanding the depth of Jung's problems with her, his involvement with her, and the alchemical conjunction of the two that led to the visions. The visions are an opus that needed both Jung's and Morgan's physical and psychic presence. Yet Jung's lack of involvement with Morgan as an individual person, as well as his absorbtion with her visions as universals, may account for the fact that the seminars themselves are so unsatisfactory and end so abruptly, and for the very disembodied quality that Jung faults in them. The further Jung went from his patient and her material, the more he imposed the general and abstract onto them, until, finally, the abstractions themselves and their theoretical implications replaced reality.

In the following pages I want to take a new look at Morgan and *The Visions Seminars*. Examples of Jung's blindness to Morgan's particular psychology and its implications for his own theory on the feminine can be seen in his treatment of Morgan's typology, his possible misperception of the progress of her visions and, finally, in response to Morgan's attempted recovery of her feminine self. Jung's method and theory were the cauldron in which Morgan and her visions developed, yet, as in the case of his inner figure of Salome, Jung was somehow blinded by his culture and could no more see or accept vital aspects of the feminine in Christiana Morgan's visions than he could in his missing feminine fourth — Baucis/Baubo.

The woman who created the images is described by Jung as being an American, about thirty, married and with a small child, who has recently come to him for help because of the psychic turbulence caused by some unspecified erotic problem, including a connection with a man who was not her husband (p. 2). Jung describes Morgan as being a highly intelligent thinking type, intuitive, and "exceedingly rational" (p. 1). Jung adds that:

> People with such an extraordinarily one-sided development of their thinking function have, on the other side, an inferior feeling function, because feeling is the opposite to thinking. The feeling is archaic and has all the advantages and disadvantages of an archaic function. The inferior function is generally characterized by traits of primitive psychology, above all by *participation mystique*; that is, it is peculiarly identical, or makes one identical, with other people and other situations. She [Morgan] had the feelings that circumstances gave her. She could not feel hypothetically, but she could think hypothetically. As a matter of fact, her intelligence was so highly developed that she thought the things that people in her environment did not think. (p. 1)

Since thinking is Morgan's superior function, Jung describes the way in which her inferior function, feeling, descends upon her as "a red-hot conflict" (p. 2). In a case such as this, Jung says, "people often think when I speak of inferior feeling that I mean weak in intensity. That is by no means true. It is something fearfully strong but primitive, barbarous, animal-like, and you cannot control it — it controls you" (p. 16).

Jung then goes on to explain how the inferior feeling function works: it holds the seeds of creativity and renewal on the one hand, but on the other it is undependable, ungovernable, explosive, "like a wild animal with superior strength" (p. 33); it functions best when left alone, but is so undependable that people prefer to suppress it and operate through their superior function; then, however, it often tends to break through in projection and causes no end of problems. Morgan's feeling function was insisting on its development; this happened as a consequence of her projection and "unspecified erotic problem," her subsequent analysis with Jung, and through her visioning. Yet Morgan left her analysis and returned to the United States to complete her visioning alone.

It is just where this happens, and where Jung starts blaming her in the seminars, that I think both Morgan and the visions seem to be on the right track in a search for a more comprehensive feminine, and Jung on the wrong one. Jung, having pointed the way, was stopped by his own prejudices and the blindness of his culture and his time. Part of the misinterpretation is that Jung required that, as a woman, Morgan have an animus who serves as her Logos. Again and again he describes Morgan as a thinking type with inferior feeling, yet, at the same time, includes her in the category of women, and declares that women's thinking is inferior to their feeling. In spite of the possibilities inherent in Jung's brilliant theory of psychological types, he persists in falling into the cultural stereotype: women function only through feeling and relationship. Jung makes comments such as these about this intellectual, "exceedingly rational," and unrelated woman:

> You see thinking is a Logos activity which discriminates between things, while a woman who has nothing but the Eros attitude is related to the things that sting, and is stung again and again. She [Morgan] has absolutely no weapon against it because her Eros principle always tries to establish a relationship to it. (p. 216)

> The animus statement is always peculiarly beside the mark because it is made in an absolutely unfeeling way. So this vision confirms what we have seen before, that through her contact with the animus she becomes disembodied and cold, her heart is a block of ice. (p. 217)

> But in this woman's case we usually have to deal with a very unreal form of animus, an opinionating substitute, for she was beset with animus devils. Through the process of transformation that took place in these

visions, however, her mind — what she called her mind — became impri-
soned in the earth. (p 238)

Of course, she is not really an intellectual, it is nature's wisdom speaking through her, not her own. (p. 273)

Women take a thought and force it into feeling. (p. 413)

Jung's prejudices enter his theory and become part of his construct
of reality, a construct which then blinds him to Morgan's and other wom-
en's living reality. It would have been much better for Jungian theory
on the feminine if he had stayed with his initial gender-free point of
view. But how can a man, even Jung, free himself entirely from cultural
blind spots? The stereotypes pile up as the seminars progress and flood
our vision. In the first seminar Jung declared that Morgan's animus figures
carry her feeling for her, but then Jung's time and culture and the
prejudices of his Number One and Number Two characters creep in.
Looking at the visions from a different era and with a different perspective, something new emerges. Most of the animus figures in Morgan's
visions now can be seen more clearly. They emerge full of feeling, fitting
Jung's description of feeling types. These animi value, take things to
heart, play music, dance, or express a Dionysian and chthonic sensuali-
ty. They complement Morgan's Apollonian "exceedingly rational" mind.
The animus figures Jung discusses and that aid her descent are: a Jewish musician, a Swiss boy who plays the accordion and wants to give her
music lessons, a nurturing shepherd, a Red Indian in touch "with the
womb of the earth" (p. 47), the "face" of the animal man "eyes full of
beauty and woe and light" (p. 62), a black stallion, a Chinese man, a
bull who drinks from her goblet, a green-eyed satyr playing a reed, a
beautiful dancing youth with golden cymbals, a beautiful and virile black
god lying under a tree with fruit in his hands and "singing with a full
throaty voice" (p. 136) (she follows a stream of red blood as it flows from
his heart toward her), a priest with a snake who gives her green eyes
and grape leaves for her hair, a man sitting under a tree playing a long
flute, Abraxas, an earth-sky god, Osiris and a Mexican and Indian god.
It is only the old men, the dying white giant with the rotting flesh, the
chained men, the dwarves, the soldiers in groups, and the heads without bodies (all but the giant are plural) who fit into Jung's schema as
wise old men, multiple and negative animi, or the negative and bur-
densome "voice of the world" (in the published texts there are twenty-

two figures who are probably feeling animi compared to seventeen of all the various other types combined.)

Yet Jung takes each of these figures and tries to convert him into his own idea of what an animus should be. For instance, the Jew who plays beautiful music becomes "a figure personifying the opinionating of a woman" (p. 5); the Swiss accordian player "is a sort of spirit, a sort of mental visionary, a system of views, a kind of thinking" (p. 18); the earthy, initially depressed, then ecstatic Indian "represents her unconscious opinionating . . . The representative of the unconscious mind, which means the relatively primitive mind" (p. 45). The Chinese man is called "a philosophical animus—an assumption" (p. 51); the beautiful dancing youth, "aspects of the animus representing unconscious opinions" (p. 76). The gloriously libidinous black stallion Jung constricts into another "animus opinion . . . an animus horse is libido in a certain opinionated animus form" (p. 154), and so on. This doesn't do justice to these soul-stirring figures who overflow with the primitive vigor and passion of the inferior function. In a monotonous process of reduction, Jung reduces each animus figure to one that denotes inferior and opinionated thinking. When things are going wrong, Jung describes Morgan as a "strong man" (p. 440) and says that her animus "was particularly bewildered and filled with the most extraordinary and sentimental emotions, all the emotions which she did not realize" (p. 440).

Yet supposedly it is Eros and feeling that Morgan lacks! The feeling animus as a bridge to the unconscious could and was carrying this eruptively new feeling function up to Morgan in order to enlarge her consciousness and balance her superior "strong man" thinking. Jung sees this, yet doesn't see it. He insists on interpreting the visions as if she were what he and his class defined a woman to be. He presents her animus figures, but then forces them into the role his culture requires. Jung's inability to accept her animus figures as feeling animi and as Morgan's guides to the development and reintegration of her feeling function, if this also happened within her analysis, may have been one of the forces that brought her contact with him to a stop. This lack of acceptance, combined with his requirement that she fill the Eros role and her animus the Logos role, must have appeared an impossible task. There is such weight and oppression in being expected to be something that one is not and never can be. It must have been intensely painful for Morgan to have the expert—Jung, the person who helped her so profoundly and toward whom she had such a powerfully positive and libidinal transfer-

ence, (and, who himself might have experienced an equally strong countertransference)—not be able to see her, but instead try to change her
reality to fit his expectations. Jung's ideas fitted into the expectations
of the nineteenth and early twentieth centuries, but I don't think they
fitted Christiana Morgan. In any case it was here where the mythopoetic power released from the unconscious by the relationship between Morgan and Jung had to be carried forward by Morgan alone. The final visions
in the published series are the most interesting to me, for they leave
the animus and other male figures behind and start to take Morgan down
to the realm of the mothers; the realm "that is alien to man and shuts
him out" (Jung, 1941/1969, p. 203).

Jung mapped Morgan's visions as an example of the transformation
process that can occur when the unconscious and the conscious, the analyst and the patient, work together in the mystery of analysis. Through
this work, Jung enabled Morgan to reach to the center of her own being
and her own instinctual nature. The change in Morgan as depicted in
her visions may have gone beyond what Jung understood consciously
as "woman's behavior." It is closer to something that is just starting to
enter modern sensibility; possibly a different interpretation may now
be made, one which questions Jung's standpoint. It involves a question
of mirroring. In this interpretation, Jung's concept of a woman as an
anima-type or anima-woman also comes into question. Jung states that

> There are certain types of women who seem to be made by nature to
> attract anima projections; indeed one could almost speak of a definite
> "anima type." The so-called "sphinx-like" character is an indispensable
> part of their equipment, also an equivocalness, an intriguing
> elusiveness—not an indefinite blur that offers nothing, but an indefinite-
> ness that seems full of promises, like the speaking silence of a Mona Lisa.
> A woman of this kind is both old and young, mother and daughter, of
> more than doubtful chastity, childlike, and yet endowed with a naive cun-
> ning that is extremely disarming to men. (1925/1954, pp. 198-199)

I do not think this designation accurately reflects what is really happening with Morgan or with other predominantly thinking-intuitive
women who also happen to have some physical beauty and who get labeled anima women. These women were called anima-types by Jung
because they attracted men's anima projections. Jung looked at them
from his masculine perspective and from a man's point of view. He stated that this type of woman's supposed indefiniteness could hold and
reflect a man's fantasies back and thus inspire him. Maybe the mirror

holds a different reflection entirely—one that sees these women more clearly and fairly (and is, secondarily to woman's own development, also more helpful to men). Morgan, Wolff, Andreas-Salome, Spielrein, and women of this same type today all may have seen something else in the mirror—a reflection which is just starting to emerge from the shadows. It often depends on who is doing the observing, what one's point of view happens to be, and where one stands in relation to it (it also helps to have good and unobstructed vision).

This is a major point I want to make and, in order to encompass it, need to circumambulate a bit in what may at first appear a digressive way. There is a scene, for instance, in the middle of the film *The Unbearable Lightness of Being*. In it the actual mirror that holds and frames a supposed anima-woman, Sabina, is now beneath her on the floor. She centers herself on the mirror on her hands and knees and slowly observes her own body. As Sandner said of Morgan in the visions, "she becomes her full, naked feminine self, no longer obscured by denial or repression. She is completely in her body" (Sandner, 1986, p. 11). Sabina seems to be drawing libido—her sexuality and eroticism—out of herself and up from its mirroring. Having filled herself with the body knowledge of her own passion, she desires to share this passion with the onlooker on the periphery: Tomas, who is the supposed center of the film. But he demands that he be the romantic center of her world—that she reflect him and that he dominate her. She is weighed down by his ignorance of her and by these attempts to interpret her from his perspective. She serves her own sense of being so truly that, finally, she escapes the man's patriarchal limitations of her and his denial and repression of her power. Sabina, like Morgan, leaves Switzerland for America. She ends up on some western seashore, contemplating, and then artistically reproducing the foaming waves of a vast mother ocean on another mirrored window that also reflects her own self. Both she and Morgan had to leave what had sustained them in order to try to keep hold of what they were recovering—the reality of a feminine self grounded in the womb of the dynamic feminine.

Like Tomas, Jung in the seminars generally restricts the feminine to its passive, feeling and related dimensions. In Morgan's later visions and in this film, the image of another archetype of the feminine emerges: intuitive, active, intellectually related, and passionately embodied, but serving something truer to the feminine than a man. It is an archetype I want to attempt to give words to here, because it is an element of the dark feminine and a way of feminine development that Jung saw, responded to, but finally could not accept. Many women who embody part of this archetype are unconscious of its meaning. Its power not being under their ego control, they misuse it as much as men do, unconsciously fusing and indentifying with it instead of consciously channeling it. Men can fear and belittle the power that attracts them by calling it empty or only a reflection of their own animas—an "anima-woman." Men, like Jung, can make use of the power in order to be inspired by it and then depreciate its possessor. The archetype has been abused and coopted through being misnamed, dishonored, and unmirrored.

Morgan ends the published visions with a descent to the mother. She attempts to recover something that her own mother was not able to give her: a sense of her own power along with self-esteem based on connection with a dynamic and honored, possibly maternal, feminine. If a girl child's first sensuous object other than herself is a feminine body, how deep that connection must lie in our psyches and how natural for adult men and women both to be aroused by a woman's body. For a heterosexual woman, the object doesn't just change gender, it also remains female: it is herself. When she has regained this embodied reality, she serves the erotic by being turned on by her own body and its responses. Out in the world, she serves her libido by being kindled by the spark she creates in herself, in her work, and in relationships as well as in her response to the gleam in man's eye: man's response to her. Men in their turn can be stirred and inspired, but that is not the point. The point is our understanding and honoring of this elemental power within a woman which comes to her through her own connection with the dynamic feminine. Like the Kore in the Demeter-Persephone-Hecate myth, Morgan in her visions achieved an inner union with the chthonic masculine and then was able to reunite with her inner mother and all aspects of the feminine. Fertilized, regenerated and reborn, she was full of her own divine and earthly inheritance. If this could have been held by Morgan and Jung, it would have meant a tremendous return of life, color, and energy to Morgan herself and to Jung's and his century's gray world and gray theories about their wounded, pallid, and mourning feminine.

Where Morgan and Jung and the majority of his generation, as well as many of our own, have gone astray is in not seeing this ardent libido for what it is. Instead they coopt it and demand that it be used to serve men and/or inspire them, or they give it all away, unmirrored. Where Jungians have gone astray as therapists and theoreticians may have been to diminish or obstruct this archetype's emergence by branding it on one side as infantile and narcissistic, and on the other as nothing but the charm of an anima-woman, a *femme inspiratrice*. Or, alas, not honoring its presence in ourselves, we groove on it as analysts, take energy from it in the transference, and allow these women to animate us in our work and in our writing instead of returning it back to the source from which it came, and, through mediating it and mirroring it back, help women empower themselves and regain their vital creativity.

Another aspect of the problem connected to this unrecognized archetype is the strange power and outpouring of the mythopoetic function that sometimes occur in a transference-countertransference situation in analysis, and in alchemy, between a man and a woman. Jung and Morgan are one more example of the sometimes very creative collusion between the analyst and the patient who is the object of his study, and the strange and sometimes healing worlds in which they are involved (a phenomenon I referred to in Chapter Three).

Henry A. Murray, in a biographical postscript to *The Visions Seminars,* and in an interview with me in 1987, was emphatic about the benefit to Morgan of her analysis with Jung, but also about its incompleteness. Murray wrote and spoke about his own subsequent collaboration with Morgan and her productive and creative personal and professional life. In his postscript to *The Vision Seminars,* he makes a tentative suggestion to explain the sudden flood of Morgan's archetypal and fantastic images:

> Well then, how can one explain the conduct of a woman who, contrary to her entire previous existence, suddenly manifests such a notable degree of industry and persistence, such willingness, say, to be exploited in the service of her doctor's search for truth? Wouldn't you . . . guess that love was the key to it all? (in Jung, 1933/1976, p. 517)*

Jung's and Morgan's work together was an immensely creative union of patient and therapist, in which Jung was the physician and interpreter, but both took turns inspiring and being inspired by the other. Jung encouraged the process to which Morgan put form and then was stimu-

---

* In this section of his postscript, Murray also takes note of Jung's probable countertransferential response to Morgan: "In passing, let us note (without exclamations) that measured in my scales of libidinous affection, the letter [from Jung] yields as high a rating as any letter written to any one of the more than 450 correspondents included in Jung's two-volume *Letters.*" (p. 519)

lated by her work and used it to fill out and explicate his own theories. It was a true collaboration. Jung was a highly creative healer who was both open to and interested in just the aspect of the unconscious by which Morgan was seized. Morgan, in turn, perhaps intuited the form through which her doctor could best hear what she needed to express. The visions are an alchemical opus through which elements of the feminine arose that could have instructed both the patient and her doctor. Jung was open to transference-countertransference phenomena in a way that created a container in which this valuable work could originate. He accompanied his patient as she explored the forbidden and regressed—where vital and healing energy could well up. Jung had the capacity and strength to lend himself to a patient and to enter into a process in collaboration with the patient that transformed them both. In reference to this, he wrote:

> In any thorough-going analysis the whole personality of both patient and doctor is called into play. There are many cases a doctor can't cure without committing himself. When important matters are at stake it makes all the difference whether the doctor sees himself as part of the drama, or cloaks himself in his authority . . . the doctor's whole being is challenged. (1963, pp. 132-133)

With both Christiana Morgan and Hélène Preiswerk, Jung initially involved himself fully in their dramas. He acknowledges the mythopoetic power and energy of their visions and trances and his fascination with them. He also writes of both women at the beginning in a very favorable and somewhat romantic way. As with Preiswerk, the comments Jung makes about Christiana Morgan and her visions show a different side when he grows tired of them. Jung, at the end, found that he was no longer following Morgan's visions. He then turned against them and asserted that they, not his theory, were at fault. What Jung had once praised so highly, he now finds to "flood" (p. 474), bore (pp. 263-264, 447, 471), that they are too short (p. 368), too many (p. 356), too cold (p. 217), too bloody (p. 479), bloodless (p. 365), not related enough (pp. 488-489), superficial (p. 368), not personal enough (pp. 365-366), or too personal (pp. 474-475). Finally, besides denigrating the visions and the visioner, Jung sees Morgan's visions as useful to him only when they fit his theory.

The treatment of both these women, whose dreams or trances first inspired him, marks Jung's path from initial fascination to ultimate boredom and rejection. This transit manifests traces of the secret age-old contempt men in the patriarchy have for the women who fascinate them and, perhaps, for the feminine they can't allow themselves to experience. It all sounds remarkably like that sad, worn path of a projection-full romance in which the man senses the power that the woman holds and can mirror for him. But then, possibly afraid of the power and anything to do with the primeval feminine, he seeks to diminish its holder and restrict her to his nineteenth-century definitions — definitions that in the end cannot satisfy him. She submits to this gray world, invents another, or escapes. The opus they created together inevitably loses its attraction: he cannot be satisfied with the incomplete feminine of his own invention, and his longing for a fuller, more life-filled feminine (which he can't accept) soon lights on someone else.

I wonder, in both cases, about the effect of this on the subject or the patient and her material. What happens to a woman whose analyst responds to her in the way Jung did, and then, after a time, no longer finds her or her material interesting and countertransferentially inspiring? Is it, in fact, Jung's failure of vision — his blindness to positive aspects of the dynamic feminine — that brings the process to an end? This is another way that culture and Jung's attitude (and, perhaps, character) shadow and impinge upon transference and countertransference between the sexes. I think this phenomenon has not received enough attention. An allied question arises: why do women like Morgan, who are struggling with the realization of this power within themselves, give so much and produce so much? It is as if this unmirrored feminine incessantly replicates itself in its urgency to make itself seen. Its very excess is a sign of its hunger to be known and mirrored. This is the *Arabian Nights,* shadow side of the alchemist-soror analytic model or archetype, in which the patient "tells stories designed to please and hold the analyst" (Diamond, 1988, quoting Otto Rank).

Both the flood of material and the desire to please the analyst may also be the consequence of a lack of adequate mothering, the absence of a strong mother who esteems and respects herself. Morgan's intuitive grasp of Jung's need for symbols and her brilliant production of just what might interest and help Jung may have been part of Morgan's father complex as well — an effort to gain his approval and his love. In the appendix to *The Visions Seminars* (Jung, 1933/1976, p. 517) and in his talks with me, Murray commented on the fact that Morgan's father complex was never fully analyzed or worked through with Jung, and persisted in her relationships with men throughout her life. It also showed in her lack of connection to the maternal, and her discomfort with women, as well as in her production of the visions, which not only served her own needs, but also worked as an unconscious and extremely powerful effort to keep her analyst's interest and gain a special place in his love. Instead of analyzing the complex, and how it was expressed between Morgan and Jung in the transference, Jung made use of its outward manifestation for his own benefit. I am afraid this still occurs when the alchemical collusion between analyst and analysand fulfills a need in the analyst (often in abetting *his* creative work, in inspiring him, or in healing his wounds), and so is not analyzed and separated. In a father's world, it is sometimes the price women like Morgan have to pay in order to be contained, at least until they gain the strength through the positive aspects of the analysis to go on with the process on their own.

A difficulty for women like Morgan is that women's feeling is supposed to be primary and civilized and under their control, but *isn't*. A woman's feeling function is supposedly a known quantity, civilized and smooth, and therefore neither terribly interesting nor erotic—and, besides, an analyst like Jung has, he thinks, run into it a thousand times before. So it is doubly problematic when a woman, especially a beautiful woman like Morgan, has her feelings in her unconscious. She is as unaware of them as Jung would have expected a dry old man to be (like the professor in the film *The Blue Angel*); not to speak of the impossibility of feeling being under her control. The effect was even more pronounced because of Morgan's unresolved father complex and her learning so early that she pleased men, though she wasn't quite sure why or how (Murray, personal communication; Morgan, unpublished diaries). Instead this vast, unconscious, primitive, and often barbarically erotic stuff full of bulls and snakes and black stallions and virile animi entered the consulting room with Morgan, and was soon accompanied by an even more potent feminine. This primitive feeling, just because it had not been developed nor civilized into the conventional cultural mode, still had the ability to serve as a bridge and connect Morgan back to the dynamic feminine missing for so long in her culture. It opened the way back to an aspect of the feminine that had been lost to more traditional women. It is just here that Jung must have been faced with a profound attraction and even more profound enigma. Neither Jung, the man, nor nineteenth-century theory expected this sort of power and this sort of unconsciousness in a woman. Jung (at least in the seminars) reacted by cutting himself off from Morgan; he ceased taking part in the drama, and instead "cloaked himself in his authority" on what a woman is (a feeling type) and what was going on (something "no longer law abiding," p. 438). He possibly did this to save his skin, his marriage, and his theory.

Morgan percieved what she had visioned more clearly than Jung, but she let herself be blinded by his blind Salome. The visions' promise undeciphered and Morgan unmirrored, she mirrored herself out to men. She inspired Jung and other men, but she also got caught. Morgan let them use her primitive feeling's libido and her connection to the dynamic feminine without knowing *what* they were using in her, or through her. It wasn't, as Jungian psychology would have it, that Morgan was a *femme inspiratrice;* instead, the primitive feeling archetype poured through her without grounding—without its essential connection to the dynamic feminine—and she gave it away. This is what caused havoc and what Jung couldn't help her with. I think they both may have been blinded not only because Morgan's psychology didn't fit into Jung's and his time's view of the feminine, but also, and this is a separate issue, because being a *femme inspiratrice* is what fathers expect of their daughters. The daughter's Eros in a patriarchy is expected to be in the service of the father. Morgan needed a mother who had realized this aspect of herself, a mother able to mirror and define what Morgan reencountered and help her daughter center herself in service to her own being. Without this mirroring, this type of daughter's undeveloped—though passionate—inferior feeling lies darkly in the unconscious, invisible; it then gets defined by men as an empty receptacle uncannily sucking in men's projections. It is the woman's own energy and libido that inspires, but the men take this unseen mercury as their own reflection, and reduce the container into an "anima-woman."

Jung was of immeasurable help in aiding Morgan give expression to her visions as long as he could follow them and be inspired by them. Through Jung and the visions, Morgan's feeling did get born. But Jung could not see her need for a sustained connection with a primary, strong, and powerful feminine ground. Maybe it needed a woman to value and notice this aspect and return it to its own creator. This never happened for Morgan. Jung and Morgan were also struggling with transference issues between them; Jung, not seeing his countertransference, censured and disparaged her at the end. The dynamic feminine, unmet and unmirrored, again sank out of sight, and the Kundalini energy, unchanneled, remained a dark serpent pursuing Jung.

With these aspects of analytic theory unchallenged, and with women of Morgan's type still being designated as anima-women and their feminine Self still limited to men's definitions, a model of dynamic psychotherapy based on these assumptions about the feminine may be unhelpful to women. Women need to learn to reflect themselves and to recognize and develop the hidden, inferior, and energetic parts of themselves. Jung intuited this and helped, while at the same time he was hindered by his nineteenth-century prejudices about women. Jung's Number One expected women's image and being to be at the service of the man; Jung's Number Two expected her to romantically inspire and reflect him. Women, especially women with such creative inferior functions, may need to learn that inspiring or not inspiring the people in their lives is not the point. We may need to recover and reclaim the power these women once projected onto the masculine world for ourselves so that, like alchemists, we can work equally together and discover our own reflections in the center of the alchemical retort.

ALCHEMY

In *Memories, Dreams, Reflections* (1963), Jung writes that alchemy was the precursor of his own psychology:

> I had very soon seen that analytical psychology coincided in a most curious way with alchemy. The experiences of the alchemists were, in a sense, my experiences, and their world was my world. This was, of course, a momentous discovery: I had stumbled upon the historical counterpart of my psychology of the unconscious. The possibility of a comparison with alchemy, and the uninterrupted intellectual chain back to Gnosticism, gave substance to my psychology. When I pored over those old texts everything fell into place: the fantasy-images, the empirical material I had gathered in my practice, and the conclusions I had drawn from it. I now began to understand what these psychic contents meant when seen in historical perspective. (p. 205)

In the latter part of his life, these alchemical texts and the early Gnostics gradually became the source of Jung's inspiration and superceded the dualistic eighteenth and nineteenth-century philosophers to whom he had once been so drawn. Jung started his study of alchemy in 1928 and soon amassed a library of these rare texts (Jaffe, 1971). Earlier, he had known of the psychoanalyst Herbert Silberer's 1914 book in which Silberer used Freud's theory to interpret seventeenth-century alchemy (G. Wehr, 1987). Through alchemy, Jung is able to place his own system of analytical psychology in the continuous chain of scholarly inquiry that, since antiquity, had been occupied with this "matrix of a mythopoeic imagination . . . Unpopular, ambiguous, and dangerous, it is a voyage of discovery to the other pole of the world" (Jung, 1963, pp. 188-189).

Jung uses the alchemists' symbolic formulations to elucidate his own theories about therapy and the individuation process. In the alchemical process, the alchemists, often working in solitary pairs (one male, the *artifex* or the *frater mysticum*; one female, the *artifex* or the *soror mystica*), start with a chemical substance, the *prima materia*. Through study, meditation, prayer, right living, and various chemical and symbolic processes, the alchemists work to transform themselves and their material in order to produce a "chymical marriage" of opposites within and without the retort. The goal is the union of all opposites in a hermaphroditic way, their death, decay, resurrection or rebirth, and the birth of a new and complete form which Jung calls the Self. Much of alchemy is intentionally obscure, for it deals with the incorporation of evil, the earthly, and the feminine in a way that was heretical for the time in which the alchemists lived.

Alchemy is both a mysticism of matter and of the soul. The alchemists concern themselves religiously with matter and materiality, by which, as in Kundalini yoga, the body and matter become the vehicle for incorporating the spiritual and the divine. The process is and has been open to interpretation on many levels. Jung writes in the foreword to *Mysterium Coniunctionis:*

> And just as the beginning of the work was not self-evident, so to an even greater degree was its end. There are countless speculations on the nature of the end-state, all of them reflected in its designation. The commonest are the ideas of its permanence (prolongation of life, immortality, incorruptibility), its androgyny, its spirituality and corporeality, its human qualities and resemblance to man (homunculus), and its divinity. (Jung, 1955-1956/1970, p. xiv)

In alchemy, the feminine is as important as the masculine and needs to be equally present and equally involved. Jung discusses the many representations of the masculine-feminine pairs in the alchemical opus: Sol and Luna, Rex and Regina, Mars and Venus, Adam and Eve, earth and sky, father and daughter, mother and son, brother and sister, dog and bitch, sulfur and salt, as well as the masculine and feminine alchemists themselves. Behind this mutuality and through mutual involvement and long work (and if the conditions are propitious), the Self appears, a *coincidentia oppositorum.* Jung believes that alchemists and analyst and analysand alike seek to recover the same thing—a unified or reunited Self, the archetype of wholeness that contains all the opposites. At first projected onto matter and the "other," all aspects of psyche and matter turn out to be one and, like God and/or the universe, can be found within oneself.

This enormously comprehensive point of view demands an equally inclusive view of the feminine. Jung finds the alchemists' concept of the feminine, in contrast to conventional Judeo-Christian formulations, to be extraordinarily multifaceted. For example:

> The prima materia in its feminine aspect . . . is the moon, the mother of all things, the vessel, it consists of opposites, has a thousand names, is an old woman and a whore, as Mater Alchimia it is wisdom and teaches wisdom, it contains the elixir of life in potentia and is the mother of the Saviour and of the *filius Macrocosmi,* it is the earth and the serpent hidden in the earth, the blackness and the dew and the miraculous water which brings together all that is divided. (p. 21)

Jung studied and was ambivalently drawn to all these alchemical facets of the feminine, and used them in his psychology. One of the most fertile of these symbols, for Jung, is the Luna figure. Within the retort, after the initial work of purifying, boiling, extracting, and adding had been accomplished, and if the chemistry is right, two figures appear, Sol and Luna, archetypal male and female. Luna, of course, refers to the moon and Sol to the sun. Jung uses these particular figures to explore the psychology of opposites. Luna is seen as a symbol for man's unconscious femininity as well as a symbol for woman. "The mythology of the moon is an object lesson in female psychology" (p. 175). Jung describes the cyclical quality of the moon as symbolizing the psychological aspects of a little girl, a maiden, the mother and, finally, a dark Kali-like figure. Jung tends to parcel out these various aspects of the moon symbol to separate women and type them accordingly. The texts he draws from, however, refer to their presence in the *same* person. He notes that for all women a monthly cycle occurs (though he apparently only had intimations of his own anima's mutability and her dark Baucis/serpent side). Jung comments that this cycle cannot be denied, nor can the fact that, as with women,

> things are different with Luna: every month she is darkened and extinguished; she cannot hide this from anybody, not even from herself. She

knows that this same Luna is now bright and now dark—but who has ever heard of a dark sun? We call this quality of Luna "woman's closeness to nature," and the fiery brilliance and hot air that plays round the surface of things we like to call "the masculine mind." (p. 247)

Sol and Luna and the other alchemical pairs prove useful metaphors for the masculine and feminine, but they become limited and biased when carried too far. I will not go into each aspect of the feminine that Jung brings up in his far-reaching and brilliantly evocative discussions of alchemy, but will concentrate on the ways Jung opens the alchemical world to us and recovers its vast and comprehensive view of the feminine—and then, by conforming even this feminine to his theory, once again loses much of what he had found. Jung (who is generally considered an introverted, intuitive thinking type, and true to the shortcomings of this type) pushes some very useful analogies much too far; he also attributes the wrong value judgments to them. He hooks alchemical symbology of the masculine and feminine to his *a priori* definitions—consciousness equals male; unconsciousness equals female—and to his adulation of the anima and dislike for the animus.

Jung recognizes the importance of the feminine in alchemy and is drawn to its many depictions. We are in his debt for recovering such a wealth of material on the feminine; however, he loses much of it again by denying the feminine the very equality he recovered and that his theory seems to champion. One of the ways Jung does this is by asserting that alchemy applies only to masculine psychology: "I am speaking here of masculine psychology, which alone can be compared with that of alchemists" (Jung, 1955-1956/1970, pp. 106-107). The feminine half of the alchemical work becomes, for Jung, nothing but an anima figure belonging within and reflecting a man's psyche (Jung, 1946/1975, p. 302).

Jung uses the Sol-Luna analogy in an attempt to differentiate woman's consciousness from man's consciousness. He gives consciousness a typological twist, and again an unforeseen but implicit hierarchy appears:

[A woman's] consciousness has a lunar rather than a solar character. Its light is the "mild" light of the moon, which merges things together rather than separates them. It does not show up objects in all their pitiless discreteness and separateness, like the harsh glaring light of day, but blends in a deceptive shimmer the near and the far, magically transforming little things into big things, high into low, softening all colour into a bluish haze, and blending the nocturnal aspect into an unsuspected unity. (Jung, 1955-1956/1970, p. 179)

In statements like these, Jung ascribes a romantic but nevertheless deceptive, and therefore somehow untrustworthy, consciousness to woman rather than a real one. He goes on to describe this consciousness as darker, more nocturnal, of lower luminosity than man's consciousness: one that is especially good for blurring, harmonizing, and relating (p. 180).

Apart from the value our culture puts on these two ways of seeing things, the lunar, as a mode of perception, has its own worth that is obscured by Jung's insistence that it belongs only to women. This value is also obscured by the same tone of nineteenth-century Romantic fascination, revulsion, and attraction I have pointed out before. Yet, in spite of the Romanticism and the concept's unfairness to the piercing clarity of many women's thought, Jung may be onto something. Modern studies concerning object-relations and diffusion, ego boundaries, and values point to more women maintaining what Jung would call a lunar connection with their mothers; while women generally are found to be more able to merge and combine, men tend toward a more solar type of separation and differentiation (N. Chodorow, 1978; Gilligan, 1982; Young-Eisendrath and Wiedemann, 1987). The interaction of culture, training, expectations, and typology behind these findings remains to be worked out.

The same attitude and expectations affect Jung's treatment of the *soror mystica*, but before I proceed to her, the relevance of alchemy to the therapeutic process needs to be discussed. In a letter to Olga Frobe-Kapteyn in 1945, Jung wrote:

> You yourself are a conflict that rages in itself and against itself, in order to melt its incompatible substances, the male and the female, in the fire of suffering and thus create that fixed and unalterable form which is the goal of life. (Adler, [Ed.], Vol. 1, 1973, p. 375)

Jung expands on this idea in a passage in the "Introduction to the Religious and Psychological Problems of Alchemy":

> The problem of opposites called up by the shadow plays a great—indeed, the decisive—role in alchemy, since it leads to the ultimate phase of the work to the union of opposites in the archetypal form of the hierosgamos or "chymical wedding." Here the supreme opposites, male and female (as in the Chinese *yang* and *yin*), are melted into a unity purified of all opposition and therefore incorruptible. The prerequisite for this, of course, is that the artifex should not identify himself with the figures

in the work but should leave them in their objective, impersonal state. (Jung, 1944/1968, p. 37)

In "The Psychology of the Transference" (1946/1975), Jung deals most practically yet at the same time symbolically with the problems of *arti-fex* and *soror mystica*, and of analyst and analysand. Jung sees the work as a place where two psychic systems enter into a reciprocal reaction with each other. Besides this, the pair is dealing with the unconscious, which is beyond either yet affects them both. Thus the need for the container or the alchemical retort. Within the retort, the alchemical appearance of, struggle with, and reintegration of the opposites can occur. In analysis the same process is described as happening through the transference.

In the same work, Jung chooses the sexual symbology of one ancient alchemical text, the *Rosarium Philosophorum*, to illustrate the process of psychological individuation. This is also the only place in the *Collected Works* where Jung includes a dedication on the title page: it says "TO MY WIFE" (p. 163), as if by this dedication he were at one and the same time consciously acknowledging his union, his *chymical marriage*, with his wife while trying to explain or somehow justify to her the perils in alchemy and its transference-countertransference reactions. The dedication—combined with the choice of illustrations of wooing, marriage, copulation, incestuous merging, death and rebirth—makes me hazard that the choice of these symbols may point to a quandary in Jung. They may involve his own unconscious dissatisfaction with his inadequate internal feminine and a subsequent search for union and completion. The images of masculine and feminine pairs predominate as he struggles with clinical transference-countertranference issues and seeks for his own lost feminine dimension. This reflects a general problem of his time.

The value of the *Rosarium* as an analytic text lies in the analogies Jung makes between the images and the therapeutic situation. Jung sees analyst and analysand, like the *artifex* and the *soror mystica*, working in an intense and problematic alliance toward the goal of individuation. The analysand brings the *prima materia:* wounds, depressions, neuroses, all that has been discarded and repressed. The analyst accepts these with the knowledge that they contain the gold: the possibility of healing and of the new self. Both work, often for years, at elucidating and reprocessing this *prima materia*, while bringing all the opposites up from the darkness and into the light.

Jung is not concerned with the different gender combinations possible between analyst and analysand. His description of alchemy and analysis always contains a male and female pair. I wonder, however, if the illustrations in the *Rosarium* are of more use when the analyst and analysand are of different gender. For instance, in my experience with female patients, the alchemical process seems markedly similar, but the form it takes often calls upon different archetypes from these. Images of parenting, maternal, mother/daughter, midwifing-assisting, Sophia-like wisdom-sharing, and sisterly companioning seem to be much more often constellated than the *hieros gamos* images of the *Rosarium*.

However, the *Rosarium* symbols themselves contradict Jung's idea that they pertain solely to male psychology. The images are full of domestic and relational symbols of love, marriage, union, the birth of a child, death and renewal, symbols that seem even more relevant to a woman's life cycle and development than to a man's. They represent in fact the very sphere Jung reserves for women (Jung, 1925/1954, pp. 189-201). They could just as well be feminine figures seeking individuation with the help of the animus as the other way round. Neither of these views makes as much sense as looking at them as a possible set of symbols depicting the individuation process of human beings—male or female.

As I mentioned before, two people were often involved in the alchemical work, the *artifex* and the *soror mystica*. It is of relevance to Jung's theory of the feminine that Jung largely excludes the female half of the alchemical pair, and denies the relevance of alchemy to feminine experience. Jung states that alchemists worked alone and were mostly solitary by choice (p. 372). He also remarks:

> The alchemical texts were written exclusively by men and their statements . . . are therefore the product of masculine psychology. Nevertheless women did play a role in alchemy . . . and this makes it possible that the "symbolization" will show occasional traces of their influence. (Jung, 1955-1956/1970, p. 178)

Jung declares that if alchemy were to be applied to the feminine, the symbolism would be different (Jung, 1946/1975, p. 302). In a letter to C. H. Josten in 1952, Jung writes, "His whole psychological situation then demanded the presence of the female, because usually these individuation processes are accompanied by the relationship with a *soror mystica*. That is the reason why a number of alchemists are reported to have been related to what I call an anima figure" (Adler [Ed.], 1973, Vol. 2, pp. 62-63).

Contemporary women scholars seek to regain women's history because there is cumulative evidence that this history has been suppressed in a culture that overlooks women and tends to treat their work and lives as invisible. Women's religious, artistic, literary, and scientific contributions have all too commonly been ignored or subsumed by men in ways that deny women access to power and deprive men of a perhaps unwelcome knowledge of feminine power and creativity. This seems to be the case with Jung and his treatment of the *soror mystica*.

In the eleventh edition of the *Encyclopedia Brittanica* (1910-1911), an edition of Jung's era, the source of alchemy is given as originally an area of women's knowledge, a matriarchal possession. One of the first references to alchemy, it states, was mentioned in both the Book of Enoch and by Zosimus. Both refer to remnants of the dim matriarchal past:

> Zosimus of Panopolis, an alchemistical writer said to date from the third century, asserts that the fallen angels taught the [alchemical] arts to the women they married (cf. Genesis vi. 2), their instruction being recorded in a book called *Chema*. (p. 519)

In recorded history, alchemy still kept a feminine fourth which Jung saw, acknowledged, and welcomed. The alchemists emphasized completion rather than perfection, good combined with evil, matter combined with spirit, and the feminine with the masculine. This is an emphasis that has more in common with what we know of matriarchal concepts than with patriarchal ones.

Jung recovers much of this in his studies of alchemy, but loses it again in his blindness to the presence and relevance of women in alchemy. He writes that "the alchemical texts were written exclusively by men" (Jung, 1955-1956/1970, p. 178), yet he cites the following *female* authors of alchemical texts: Maria Prophetissa (Jung, 1944/1968, p. 160, and notes 75, 76 and 77, pp. 160-161), Theosebeia, and Mrs. Atwood (Jung, 1946/1975, p. 296). Jung disproves his own statements that men alone wrote the books; his error comes from a patriarchal blindness to the role of women who are creative in their own right. Jung refers to the names of several *sororis mysticae* and their share in the work: Theosebeia, Paphnutia, Maria Prophetissa, Peronelle Flamel, Mrs. Atwood, and Jane Leade (pp. 296-297), as well as more apocryphal figures such as Simon Magus' Helen and Coumarius' Cleopatra (Jung, 1934/1968, p. 202). He also refers to a second series of pictures analagous to the *Rosarium Philosophorum* which he says represents "a certain concession to a feminine interpretation of the same process" (Jung, 1946/1975, p. 303).

Finally, and most interesting to me, is the question of what is said compared to what is seen. In an analysis of the illustrations in *Psychology and Alchemy* (Jung, 1944/1968), I find that the index lists only five illustrations of an *artifex* working with a *soror mystica*, and these are listed only under the headings *artifex* and *artifex-soror mystica* pair; *soror mystica* alone has no index listing. However there are not five illustrations of one or more *artifex-soror mystica* pairs at work but eleven: figures 2, 124, 132, 133, 140, 143, 152, 172, 215, 237 and 269. Three more illustrations possibly refer to the same pair: figures 161, 200 and 216. The *soror-artifex* pair make up by far the majority of alchemists pictured, yet more than half are omitted from mention, in a strange endemic cultural blindness — slight evidence for women's presence and the way it is overlooked by Jung and by his editors in a patriarchal culture, but evidence nonetheless.

Jung's blindness to women alchemical writers, women alchemists, and the whole feminine half of the alchemical opus — except as it pertains to men's psychological development — closes Jung from to an entire area of women's experience. It is a blind spot perhaps as much of Jung's time and culture as of Jung himself, but is detrimental to the acceptance of his psychology by women today. Salome remained blind to the presence of the feminine, and the active feminine could only appear in men's psyches in its archaic serpent form.

It is psychologically damaging to a woman to see herself and be seen as standing only in relationship to a man and only of use in *his* development. This negates woman in the same way the *soror mystica* was negated. It furthers the development of the male at the cost of the female. The *artifex* thus uses the *soror mystica*, the feminine, and requires that she mirror him. This denies women and the feminine parallel access to the work and denies them their access to their own individuation. Jung writes:

> Just as a man brings forth his work as a complete creation out of the inner feminine nature, so the inner masculine side of a woman brings forth creative seeds which have the power to fertilize the feminine side of man. (Jung, 1928/1966, p. 209)

> These hints may suffice to make clear what kind of spirit it is that the daughter needs. They are the truths which speak to the soul . . . It is the knowledge that the daughter needs, in order to pass it on to her son. (Jung, 1955-1956/1970, p. 183)

But why should such an unpalatable diet be prescribed for the queen? Obviously because the old king lacked something . . . . If contents like these are integrated in the queen, it means that her consciousness is widened in both directions. This diet will naturally benefit the regeneration of the king by supplying what was lacking before. . . . [without it] the king could then be neither renewed nor reborn. The conflict is manifested in the long sickness of the queen. (Jung, 1955-1956/1970, p. 310)

CONCLUSION

Do Jung's own blind spots and his undeveloped Baucis—his strong feminine—combine with Jung's and his era's distorted attitude toward women to make his theoretical work and the practice of analytical psychology invalid for women today? Not necessarily. I do think that the parts which were contaminated by the prejudices of Jung's age and by his own personal affects and needs must be and are being revised. Specifically, the following elements need to be revised or discarded: the impingement of the nineteenth century's culture-bound view of women into ideas about the psychology of women today; all polaristic characterizations which restrict, limit, and divide what is appropriate to men and what is appropriate to women; Jung's propensity to equate the feminine with Eros and the masculine with Logos and to limit women and men accordingly, with each kept to the separate spheres of Home and Market; Jung's idea that woman's psychology is discernible through the analysis of his own anima and can be described as opposite to and complementary to man's psychology; the linking of the feminine only to the unconscious or to diffused consciousness; the primarily negative interpretation of the animus, with the animus, and therefore the unconscious, given much that is intrinsic to woman herself—especially her more dynamic aspects; the treatment of women as if the animus were one single, inferior thinking type no matter what type the woman happens to be; Jung's relative blindness to the role of women in alchemy and the tendency of both him (in this case) and his era (in general) to treat women's work and lives as invisible or as incidental to men's; Jung's occasional tendency to take his concepts and metaphors either as absolutes or as concrete facts instead of as useful ways of organizing material—and so, as in the Morgan case, conforming the individual to the concept.

If Jung were alive today, I think he would be a Jungian in the sense that he would be one who criticizes, questions and reevaluates his own theory and thus stays closer to its own original spirit and purpose (Yandell, 1977). He might have revised his views either by listening to "some clever woman" (Jane Wheelwright, in Jensen [Ed.], 1982, p. 100), or by simply being open to the change in consciousness manifested by women in contemporary culture. Jung's theory would have informed itself as more individual women patients tapped into their own dark feminine power and as his patients and their problems changed.

There is much in Jung's theory, system, and mode of analysis that is suitable for the healing of women today, and much that can be elucidated, derived, and corrected. Jung's typology, when not gender-bound, offers women eight equally valid modes of functioning in the world. Jung's reevaluation of Eros and his presentation of Yin and Yang, Eros and Logos modes, again when not gender-bound, offer women and men valuable alternative ways of perceiving and being. The archetypes of animus and anima present the fundamental androgyny in human beings and allow for the expression of the contrasexual in each person. The withdrawal of projections gives women access to the power, intelligence, assertiveness and ability to work in the world that they so often project onto men.

Jung's intuition of the possibilities inherent in the reclamation of both the dark side of the feminine and the dark shadow side of humanity remains one of the most creative and troubling elements of his work. This recovery leads away from projections onto others and toward reincorporation of lost, powerful, and necessary aspects of the self. The reincorporation of the dark side of the feminine offers the following consequences for the psychology of women and for analytical psychology in general: it admits the value of regression and a descent into the unconscious; it makes possible the removal of the split between the "nice girl," virgin archetype that a woman was taught to be and the wicked temptress, the container of evil she was also taught to be; it reeducates men to view women and their own inner feminine in a more humane way. Women in an analytic situation, and through this reincorporation, have a chance to confront their own personal good and personal evil as well as to make friends and allies of the archetypal monsters and saints—of either sex—which appear in their psyches.

Jung was the first psychiatrist to take women's sexuality seriously and not, as Freud did, to see it as secondary to and inferior to men's. Jung, like Freud, was concerned with the damage caused by the repression of sexuality and the constant effort to be good (Jung, 1933/1976, p. 378).

His acceptance of the dark, of what we were taught in Judeo-Christianity to consider evil, especially in women, can reclaim parts of the psyche the culture has denied. The possibility of accepting these elements, along with a willingness to be open to all that is within the self and to have the therapeutic encounter be a meeting of two human beings, constitute the major sources of analytical psychology's healing power.

Jung's work on alchemy presents the individuation process in symbolic terms. It is more useful as an analogy of a therapeutic process than as an accurate portrayal of a woman's psychology. Analysis through the model of the alchemical container and journey provides a possible way through which the whole volcano of the internalization of three thousand years of repression and denigration of the feminine may erupt and be dealt with, without destroying either the analyst or the patient in the process. Alchemy also gives Jung a language through which he can convey some of the mystery of the analytic process, especially of transference-countertransference phenomena. It is also a language which, in its basic text, always seeks to include the feminine in balance with the masculine, with both perceived as equally vital in bringing the process to completion.

Much of Jung's work that I have not dealt with here rests on a deep respect for the individual and the individual's own particular path, regardless of gender. Much is also open to change. As Jung has said:

> Truth may, with more right than we realize, call itself "eternal," but its temporal garment must pay tribute to the evanescence of all earthly things and should take account of psychic changes. Eternal truth needs a human language that alters with the spirit of the times. The primordial images undergo ceaseless transformation and yet remain ever the same, but only in a new form can they be understood anew. (Jung, 1946/1975, p. 196)

> In the last analysis, the essential thing is the life of the individual. This alone makes history, here alone do the great transformations first take place, and the whole future, the whole history of the world, ultimately spring as a gigantic summation from these hidden sources in individuals. In our most private and most subjective lives we are not only the passive witnesses of our age, and its sufferers, but also its makers. We make our own epoch. (Jung, 1933/1970, p. 149)

PART TWO
POST-JUNG

Post-Jung

A systematic elaboration of my ideas which are often only sketchy is a task for all who follow me, and without this work there will be no progress in analytical psychology.

Jung, from a letter to Jolande Jacobi

The old mythologies about female psychology must be re-examined both to discard what is outdated and to save what may still be of use. The history of the feminine in psychology must be specifically re-examined with the purpose of paying attention to any writers (often women) heretofore ignored and to possible differences in women psychologists' theorizing.

Mednick, 1976.

Jungian theory on the feminine is, with few exceptions, sadly lacking in historical perspective. Many analysts writing today seem uninterested in reviewing the literature in their fields. Often writing from within his or her own introverted sense of meaning and experience, each wrestles with and creates solutions as if he or she were unaware—or it did not matter—that others may have reached similar conclusions. It is as if Jungians are, by and large, unaware of their history or their precursors apart from Jung, and consequently have little sense of the continuity and development in their field. This obliviousness to prior work leads to out-of-date theory and conclusions accepted as current, while former progress in the field is continually lost, rediscovered, and reinvented. At the same time, this leaves our discipline as a whole subject to similarly uninformed criticism from the outside (e.g., D. Wehr, 1987), and to the loss of a public repelled by some of these old formulations. This is perhaps most crucial in Jungian theory and attitudes toward the feminine.

Another troubling problem that is found not only in Jung but also in his followers is that what is written about the feminine and the psychology of women is hidden amongst other subjects. There is no solid body of critical theory; instead there are fragmented pieces of it — isolated elements strewn haphazardly over a broad field. Without a sense of history and continuity, individual writers define the feminine in idiosyncratic and incommensurable ways. An overview is lacking; without one there can be neither argument nor consensus.

In the following chapters I will attempt to gather these scattered pieces together in order to search out meaning, patterns, and form in the history of the feminine in analytical psychology since Jung. Searching for glimpses of it throughout our literature is paradigmatic of the hunt for women's history in all disciplines today: there have been few mirrors in which to find ourselves, and what mirrors we find have often been covered over, discarded, forgotten, or broken into many pieces. I will attempt to gather the fragments into a single whole, looking at each fragment in turn and then at the pattern that emerges when it is joined with other similar pieces. In this process there will inevitably be some overlap, repetition, and splicing together of incongruities which may, in this initial attempt, leave sharp or awkward edges. Since these pieces have not been assembled before, the reader can well object that there are too many individual pieces, and that other or less overwhelming shapes could be made of the same material using far fewer pieces. My introverted thinking intuitive typology *prefers* the complexity of all this material. I feel that there is much value to be gained in looking at and saving them all, and I welcome other mirrors that may yet better reflect women and our history.

The following chapters are the result of eight years of research, summary and evaluation. My goal is to present this history within an interpretative framework which stresses overall patterns, continuity and development while taking into account elaborations of theory that remain closer to Jung's own ideas. As I mentioned in the introduction, for the sake of rigor and legitimacy I have restricted the domain of this history to what has been written by certified analysts or candidates in training from IAAP Institutes.

Jung set forth a new paradigm and conducted new science insofar as his theories about the collective and personal unconscious, archetypes, complexes, typology, and the healing potential within the psyche all

combine to make assumptions that differ from those of prior psychological theorists or the competing paradigms of Freud and Adler. As
Kuhn (1970) writes,

> The proponents of competing paradigms practice their trades in differ-
> ent worlds. One contains constrained bodies that fall slowly, the other
> pendulums that repeat their motions again and again. In one, solutions
> are compounds, in the other mixtures. One is embedded in a flat, the
> other in a curved, matrix of space. Practicing in different worlds, the two
> groups of scientists see different things when they look from the same
> point in the same direction. Again, that is not to say that they can see
> anything they please. Both are looking at the world, and what they look
> at has not changed. But in some areas they see different things, and they
> see them in different relations one to the other. That is why a law that
> cannot even be demonstrated to one group of scientists may occasionally
> seem intuitively obvious to another. (p. 150)

Many Jungians elaborating Jung's paradigm today are conducting what
Kuhn calls "normal science." Contemporary Jungians most often engage
in codifying, rationalizing, clarifying, puzzle-solving, and writing in more
and more depth about smaller and smaller areas. Some of these, in their
work on the feminine, seem oblivious to social change and may even
go as far as to accept the term *Jungian* in Yandell's (1977) definition
of *Jungian-1:* "The conservative trend would be to close down the front-
iers, turn the *Collected Works* into a body of dogma, and build a fortress-
church of Jung to be defended against deviation and heresy" (p. 3).
Others, especially a number of second-generation Jungian women, may
have been constrained by social and political circumstances as fathers'
daughters in that they were "daughters of Jung": neophants in the professional and predominantly male world of work, and anxious to earn acceptance and respect. They may have been impelled to accept convention
rather than risk defining themselves in terms that could have left them
outside the pale. Whether or not the newer ideas presented by such
analysts as Hillman (1972), Hill (1978), Perera (1981), Whitmont (1982),
Wiedemann and Young-Eisendrath (1987) are indeed still within this
body of science, or are rifts which point to a new paradigm, is open
to conjecture. A reevaluation of the feminine may itself constitute a
change of the discourse, a different view and different relationship that
may lead to a new paradigm beyond the opposites.

Another complication is the personal equation. Everyone who writes
about psychology writes from within his or her own typology, experi-

ence, and psychology. As Jung himself so perceptively noted,

> it even looks to me sometimes as if psychology had not yet understood either the gigantic size of its task, or the perplexing and distressingly complicated nature of its subject-matter: the psyche itself. It seems as if we were just waking up to this fact, and that the dawn is still too dim for us to realize in full what it means that the psyche, being the *object* of scientific observation and judgment, is at the same time its *subject*, the *means* by which you make such observations. (1935/1980, p. 7)

Since Jung's time there have been an increasing number of women observing themselves and then writing about the feminine and the psychology of women; many, especially earlier writers, have tended to be largely ignored. These women do not show a particular single pattern or hold a unified outlook. They could possibly be separated into fathers' daughters who seek to mold women into what was expected, indeed required, of them and demanded of them by the patriarchy, and mothers' daughters who value women, womanliness, and the feminine in and of itself. The mothers' daughters seem to be increasing at the present time. I find that there is new warmth, passion, excitement, and personal involvement in recent women's writing. It is work that is also grounded in convincing scholarship. The combination of this type of almost lyrical intensity plus scholarliness brings something very different into Jungian theory that vivifies our field.

Women, Jungians and non-Jungians alike, are becoming individuated today through finding more comprehensive mirrors in which they can reflect themselves increasingly accurately and fully—and thereby, in turn, repair the mirror.

Chapter Five: A Transitional Space

Interpretations of the Feminine and Women

We are presently living in a transitional period—one in which it seems possible that the classic structure might be split.

It is impossible to predict what will become of sexual differences—in another time (in two or three hundred years?). But we must make no mistake: men and women are caught up in a web of age-old cultural determinations that are almost unanalyzable in their complexity. One can no more speak of "woman" than of "man" without being trapped within an ideological theater where the proliferation of representations, images, reflections, myths, identifications, transform, deform, constantly change everyone's Imaginary and invalidate in advance any conceptualization.

Hélène Cixous, *The Newly Born Woman*

Jungians' attitudes toward the feminine and their attempts at a definition of the feminine can be productively examined to see what patterns emerge out of each writer's attempt to mirror women's reality. The pattern I will be concerned with in this chapter reveals itself through Jungians' responses to a few pivotal themes: the consideration of Jung's Eros/Logos division along gender lines; woman and the feminine as debatably conscious, unconscious, or both; and the discussion, elaboration and controversies over the meaning of masculine and feminine. Included are views about typology, as well as the gender expectations of women and the sex-role attributes allocated to them—including the conflation of women and evil. These issues reflect areas of current criticism and reevaluation of Jungian theory of the feminine by contemporary writers. The plethora of this material attains coherence and form when placed in one of two main branches in Jungian thought and then, within each branch, discussed by subject and in chronological order. I have named the first branch the *conservators*; these writers essentially follow Jung, systematically elaborating, deepening, and widening Jung's original work on the feminine. The second, whom I have named the *reformulators*, reexamine, discard, reinterpret, or save in accordance with new points of view.

The Conservators

M. Esther Harding (1888-1971) was one of the earliest Jungian analysts to concentrate on feminine psychology. The aim of her first book, *The Way of All Women, A Psychological Interpretation* (1933/1975), is "to perform the entirely feminine task of showing how the knowledge of human nature made available through the study of the unconscious may be applied to everyday experience in a helpful way" (p. xi).

Harding accepts Jung's definition of normal feminine behavior in woman as the first stage in women's development: what she calls a psychologically undifferentiated anima-woman—a woman who lives a primarily unconscious life and prefers to embody a man's projections rather than discover her own reality. Harding discusses this stage and then turns to the animus (the masculine component in women); in contrast to Jung, she emphasizes positive and integrative aspects of the animus in a woman's psyche.

In the course of describing a woman's development (which I will discuss in Chapter Nine), Harding includes a surprisingly modern exposition of the many problems women face in developing consciousness. She discusses women's varied roles, tasks, and problems in work, marriage, relationship, childbearing, childrearing, and old age. She reflects on working women's need to integrate masculine qualities, and the problems and pitfalls of being a working woman in a business world set up by and for men. She also deals supportively with various issues concerning feminism, sexuality, lesbianism, abortion, and, in an invaluable and contemporary-sounding chapter, with the importance of other women's solidarity and friendship. Throughout her first book, Harding exhorts women to develop their own individual moral attitude accompanied by a sense of personal responsibility, the Jungian "law within" (p. 302). She explicitly includes women, on a par with men, in the evolutionary path toward individuation, consciousness, and the revaluation of self. Harding is concerned, in *The Way of All Women,* with women's practical problems in a changing world. She does not see women as necessarily unconscious, nor as the psychological opposite of men, nor identified with a particular role in life.

The book contains a leisurely, almost homespun psychology that is consistent with basic Jungian tenets and is full of solid, common-sense advice to women living in a man's world. In contrast to many of her contemporaries, Harding writes in a remarkably up-to-date and pro-female tone. The curious absence of such traditional scholarly apparatus as bibliography and index (added to the revised 1975 edition), plus the modest, conversational style, conceal Harding's erudition and keen psychological insight. This form may have been appropriate for the readers of her day, but leads modern scholars to take her perhaps less seriously than she merits. Her insights are remarkable for her time (for example, her appreciation of the psychological importance of other women as models, supports, and aids for a woman's personal growth), yet remain mostly unacknowledged by contemporary writers.

Harding's later book, *Woman's Mysteries Ancient and Modern, A Psychological Interpretation of the Feminine Principle as Portrayed in Myth, Story and Dreams* (1935/1976), is referred to somewhat more often as an elaboration and amplification of Jung's study of the feminine archetype of the great mother. (I will be dealing more fully with Harding's exploration of this archetype in Chapter Eight.) *Woman's Mysteries* grew out of a class project for Jung's Dream Seminars, for which Harding gave a presentation on moon symbolism that took up almost an entire lecture period (Jung, 1938/1984; Lecture VI, Nov. 13, 1929). Harding surveys stories of the various moon goddesses of antiquity for elements of "the feminine principle [which] has not been adequately recognized or valued in our culture" (Harding, 1935/1976, p. 105). For Harding, as for Jung, the moon becomes a symbol for feminine psychology. This symbol had been unavailable to modern women, Harding says, because psychology was written by men from their own masculine standpoint; a standpoint which made them blind to many aspects of the feminine.

Harding's material on the moon as a feminine symbol is useful and traditional. She continues Jung's Eros/Logos dichotomy: Eros equals feeling and is women's domain, while Logos equals spirit, thinking and rationality and belongs to men. She also follows Jung in her insistence on feminine development occurring almost entirely through subjectivity, feelings, and relatedness rather than through the "masculine" path of separation and individuation. This is in marked contrast to the more independent tone of her first book. However, *Woman's Mysteries* is original and current in exploring "the ambivalent and potent character of the feminine principle" (p. 34), and in considering the dark side of the feminine. Harding is the first of the few Jungian psychologists to consider the place of menstruation in a woman's psychology. She emphasizes the equality implicit in Jung's Yin/Yang, feminine/masculine poles, rather than her (and our) era's overvaluation of the masculine and its fear of and hostility to the feminine.

In spite of her conservatism, Harding appreciates the difficulty inherent in studying and discussing the feminine, and urges Jungians to question their assumptions about women. She writes

> In facing this subject we have to disabuse ourselves of all preconceived ideas of what woman is like or of what is "truly womanly," and approach it with an open mind. Our civilization has been patriarchal for so long, the masculine element predominating, that our conception of what feminine is, in itself, is likely to be prejudiced. (1935/1976, p. 30)

> It is a truism that we have no exact knowledge of things as they are; while we all have the prejudice that they are as we see them. Even our science, product of the masculine point of view, may well be biased and one-sided. (p. 64)

In both of her major works (1933 and 1935), Harding embeds her psychology of women within traditional Jungian concepts of the feminine, while at the same time encouraging the many positive strengths of women. In particular, she supports a woman's capacity for independence, even if it is primarily an inner one.

Later articles, speeches, and pamphlets of Harding's elaborate and amplify the major themes of her earlier books and continue her positive evaluation of feminine experience. *The Value and Meaning of Depression* (written in 1970, when she was past eighty) concerns the prevalence of depression in women. Harding makes the suggestion that this troubling phenomenon may perhaps be a woman's response to and retreat from an over-masculinized society and, as such, may be of value in the preservation and development of a feminine self.

Toni Wolff (1888-1953) joins Harding in elaborating particular aspects of Jung's theory of the feminine. For Wolff, too, the healthy woman is primarily a feeling type who embodies the Eros principle and is the holder and container for relationship. Woman's psychology is explored primarily through the ways she relates to men.

Wolff (1934/1956) delineates four personality types in women: the Mother, who nourishes and supports her husband and the family; the

Hetaira, who devotes herself, often erotically, to an individual man; the Amazon, who is independent, less related, and works alongside and as a companion of men; and the Medium, who is in touch with the unconscious and is instrumental as a vehicle through whom men can gain access to the unconscious (I will explore these types more closed in Chapter Eight). Wolff collaborated with Jung in developing the ideas behind his *Psychological Types* (Jung, 1921/1971), considering these applicable to men's psychology while her personality types are more relevant to women's psychology. She uses her own clinical experience as evidence to back up this statement and her belief in woman's relative lack of development. Along with Jung's description of the four function types, she acknowledges that her four personality types are distillations and exaggerations seldom found in pure form. Wolff notes (1941) that women of her generation usually were of a pronounced single type, while those of the following generation often combined two non-opposing types (i.e, Mother with Amazon or Medium; Amazon with Hetaira or Medium). Wolff considered the polar opposites too contradictory to be part of initial integration, adjacent types needing to be integrated first. Her theory allows for an evolving and more "complex feminine psychology" (p. 98), since it grants later generations of women the potential to incorporate more than one type. This feature of Wolff's theory has permitted its development and expansion by later writers.

Wolff's attitude toward the feminine echoes Jung's: "In a very general way feminine psychology must be understood from the point of view of relationship between man and woman" (p. 102). Yet, like Harding, her written tone is different from Jung's in that it seems more positive. This contrasts with the general view of Wolff's dislike of women which I presented in Chapter Two. The discrepancy may arise because, in her book, Wolff offers women a guide to the feminine and archetypal examples of their potential. Her personal dislike of women may have been partly due to her own personality combined with her experience in Zürich. She was introverted, shy and sensitive, and was also in the ambiguous and vulnerable social position of being Jung's publicly acknowledged mistress (C. G. Jung Institute of Los Angeles, 1982). Her relations with the women around Jung must have been far more difficult, complex, and tension-filled than her private theorizing about women and the feminine. Like Harding, Wolff serves as a model of a competent analyst who, at least in her written work, values women's and her own development, though, alas, seeing women circumscribed by and solely in relation to men.

In contrast to Harding and Wolff, Jolande Jacobi (1890-1973) reflects her era's misogyny. Publishing in the same year as the Freudian psychoanalyst Helene Deutsch (1944), Jacobi holds remarkably similar views. They both believe that the normal condition of "healthy" women is primarily passive and masochistic. Jacobi continues the traditional Jungian idea that women represent feeling and the unconscious. In *Woman and the Psyche* (1944, unpublished lectures) and *Masks of the Soul* (1967/1976, but mostly written in the war years), feminine and masculine behavior is severely compartmentalized. Women are viewed as complementary to men. Jacobi feels that women need to be subservient helpmates of men; women who pursue their own development are castigasted for attempting to start an independent "race of wonder women" (1967, p. 63). In seeking self-development, women "forget that in so doing they deprive their husband of the chance to prove himself again and again as a man by conquering and supporting her" (p. 64). A modern woman who does not follow a Deutschian model of passive and masochistic sexuality shows "psycho-sexual displacement" (p. 64) and threatens herself, her husband, and modern marriage in general.

Through showing initiative, which Jacobi also defines as masculine, a woman exerts a "deplorable effect on her sons" (p. 69). Instead, Jacobi asserts that a woman's goal should be to subordinate herself to men's needs. Jacobi advises a woman to disguise the fact that she may feel equal to, and actually be, as competent as a male, both for her own and for the man's psychological health. However, in spite of this pervasively conservative attitude toward women, Jacobi also notes the changing times and women's inner urge for individuation. She advocates, though, that women defer self-development until the second half of their lives and after family responsibilities have been met. She concludes, "of course what it really means to be a man or a woman today is a problem to which there is as yet no answer" (p. 68) and asks for an open-minded examination of the conflicts inherent in a time of change. Though Jacobi published much on women and marriage, most of these books and papers remain untranslated from German. Contemporary writers on the feminine in analytical psychology seldom cite her work in this area. What she has formulated about the feminine that has been translated (1944 and 1967/1976) seems quite dated and limiting.

Eleanor Bertine (1887-1968), in "Men and Women" (1948) and *The Conflict of Modern Woman* (1949), continues the traditional Jungian view of equating women with feeling, relationship, and the unconscious. Bertine's focus is on women's psychological problems; problems arising from the conflicts between women's "natural," traditional, feminine selves in relation to men and the family on the one hand, and women's changing status and growing consciousness on the other. Much of her work creatively extends and elaborates Jung's essay *Woman in Europe* (1927). Bertine's 1952 and 1960 articles on good and evil conceptualize evil, along with the feminine, as part of the unconscious. She advocates women's development of consciousness as well as their search for the reconciliation of opposites and a "new and conscious unity" (1952, p. 80). She believes that this reconciliation will lead to a less judgmental and patriarchal individual and society.

Erich Neumann's (1905-1960) work on feminine archetypes and feminine psychological development is far better known and far more often referred to than that of the women analysts I have mentioned. In his articles and books (1950, 1954, 1955, 1959, and 1962), Neumann uses much of the same material as Harding, treats the same themes, and employs many of the same examples. Perhaps his greater renown was partly a consequence of being a man—thus of superior status in that patriarchal era—and the greater openness to male theory and discourse. Neumann's books also seem directed more to men than to women readers. Jung's singling Neumann out from his followers may have added to his work's higher profile. In his introduction to Neumann's *The Origins and History of Consciousness* (1950/1954), for example, Jung calls him "the second generation" and declares that Neumann "starts at the very place where, had I been granted a second life, I would start myself" (p. 1). Perhaps this greater eminence was also due to Neumann's authoritative tone. There is a marked stylistic difference between the tentative, modest assertions of the women (possibly fearing an accusation of being opinionated and "animusy") and Neumann's forceful and assured stance and his splendidly grand perspective, a style and outlook unavailable to his female contemporaries.*

Neumann continues Jung's method of exploring the psyche on mythological, personal, and developmental levels simultaneously. The stages of consciousness as elaborated in *The Origins and History of Consciousness* (a book that Neumann declares is primarily concerned with mas-

---

* See Lackoff (1975), *Language and Women's Place,* or Spender (1980), *Man-Made Language,* for further considerations of the prohibitions placed on women's written or verbal expressions of power and authority.

culine consciousness) are the *uroboric* (merged and undifferentiated); the *matriarchal* (under the archetype of the great mother); and *patriarchal* (conscious, judgmental, and discriminating). The possibility that the present age could bring about a merging of both the matriarchal and the patriarchal is alluded to but not developed. Neumann, like Jung, places women and the feminine back in an ahistorical, matriarchal stage.

> One thing, paradoxical though it may seem, can be established at once as a basic law: even in woman, consciousness has a masculine character. The correlation "consciousness-light-day" and "unconsciousness-darkness-night" holds true regardless of sex, and is not altered by the fact that the spirit-instinct polarity is organized on a different basis in men and women. Consciousness, as such, is masculine even in woman, just as the unconscious is feminine in men. (1950/1954, p. 42)

In "The Moon and Matriarchal Consciousness" (1954), Neumann follows Harding's development of moon mythology as a paradigm for feminine development. His particular emphasis, however, is again on the evolution of consciousness from matriarchy to patriarchy. Neumann confuses the feminine with the matriarchal. Matriarchal consciousness, he says, is "written into a woman's body" (p. 98). He concludes from this that men are further advanced in consciousness than women, because for men the feminine is a psychological problem, while for women it remains implicitly embodied. In this book, the feminine is again described as unconscious and passive, the feminine has "no free, independent activity of its own" (p. 85), yet is necessary in combination with the masculine for wholeness of the self.

The Great Mother: An Analysis of the Archetype (1955) is, despite the title, more descriptive and historical than analytic. In it Neumann states that

> the investigation of the special character of the feminine psyche is one of the most necessary and important tasks of depth psychology in its preoccupation with the creative health and development of the individual . . . This problem of the Feminine has equal importance for the psychologist of culture, who recognizes that the peril of present-day mankind springs in large part from the one-sidedly patriarchal development of the male intellectual consciousness, which is no longer kept in balance by the matriarchal world of the psyche. (p. xlii)

In *Amor and Psyche. The Psychic Development of the Feminine: a Commentary on the Tale by Apuleius* (1962), Neumann reformulates as well as conserves. He takes up the psychology of feminine confrontation and individuation, envisioning a feminine image which transcends the patriarchy. Psyche here represents a newly active and transformative feminine, "a feminine Hercules" (p. 93). The stages in the new formulation of feminine development Neumann describes will be discussed in Chapter Nine.

Renée Brand (1900-1980) retains Jung's and Neumann's early theories on feminine psychology. She writes movingly and feelingly out of a strongly Hetaira-like stance. Speaking of Neumann's "Moon and Matriarchal Consciousness," Brand comments, "I feel that he has written a psychology from the woman's point of view" (1952, p. 1). She feels that Neumann describes woman's ego, animus, and self in new and clarifying ways. Brand refers to "the masculine function of thinking and discrimination" (p. 7), while she describes any use of the thinking function by women as a form of animus opinionating. Thinking in women, she says, "is as emotional as the inferior anima-thinking of men and as rigid as that of a man who is still father bound" (p. 10). Brand emphasizes Neumann's polarizations of the differences between men and women and in masculine and feminine consciousness and development. She also cites Neumann's gift for connecting archetypal mythology to contemporary psychology and development.

In *The Experiment* (published in 1980, but written at an earlier unspecified date), Brand reveals the intense erotic transference to her analyst through which her psyche developed. The process she describes loosely follows Neumann's stages of feminine development. Her short work is a subtle and deeply felt description of the subjective experience of analysis from the point of view of a feeling (and Hetaira) type woman. In spite of its great value as the only autobiographical Jungian work by a woman analyst on this important subject, standing as it does alone in its field, it serves to perpetuate Jung's and Neumann's depiction of a feeling and Hetaira type woman's perception and experience as the norm. This book is still referred to as the model for women's typical experience in analysis instead of as the valuable depiction it is—of one sort of experience and journey.

Barbara Hannah (1891-1986), a parson's daughter herself, found Jung's experiences as the child of a clergyman markedly similar to her own. She became one of Jung's most prescient and faithful followers, and put her own gritty and commonsensical stamp on analytical psychology. In *Feminine Psychology in Literature* (1957) and *The Problem of Contact with the Animus* (1962), Hannah continues the cultural restriction of women and feminine psychology to areas of feeling, unconsciousness, and relatedness. She includes and extends her 1957 and 1962 ideas on the feminine and on women in her more recent book *Striving Toward Wholeness* (1971/1989). In all her work, Hannah conserves Jung's original tendency to polarize what is appropriate to and characteristic of each sex. She states:

> It is true that the male-female opposites are much more basic opposites than those represented by two beings of the same sex, much more totally different and therefore in a way wider apart. Yet male presupposes female and female male, and the chances of a creative solution and union between these two opposites are therefore infinitely greater. (Hannah, 1971/1989, p. 25)

In order to be psychologically healthy, she states, women need to develop the receptive, passive and related feminine identity that Neumann and Jung described. Apropos of the Eros/Logos question, Hannah keeps the two severely divided along gender lines. Logos use by women is "under the masculine principle" (p. 29), no matter how necessary it is for women's economic and social progress. Women's life in the business world is a masculine one full of risks to a woman's feminine nature. Hannah's strongest work on the feminine is on the animus and will be discussed in Chapter Six.

Marie-Louise von Franz (1915-) is one of the last of the "second-generation" Jungians. She came to Jung in the early nineteen-thirties as a young classical scholar and paid for her analysis by translating alchemical texts for Jung. She was his closest intellectual peer and his collaborator in their alchemical studies; she filled the role of *soror mystica* perhaps more completely than any other of the women around Jung. In fact, the first German edition of *Mysterium Coniunctionis* was published as a three-volume work with von Franz as co-author ("unter Mitarbeit von Dr. phil. M.-L. von Franz"); her work on *Aurora Consurgens* made up the third volume (Jung and von Franz, 1957). Followers objected strongly, perhaps even enviously, so the Bollingen editors dropped her volume and ignored this public acknowledgement of the extent of von Franz and Jung's scholarly and alchemical collaboration. Though a helper of Jung's since the early 1930s, von Franz did not write on the psychology of the feminine until relatively late in her career, when she edited her lectures on the shadow (1957), evil (1964), and the feminine

(1958-1959) in fairy tales. Von Franz (1976, 1980a) uses fairy tales as a source of exploration of the feminine and feminine development. She is also concerned with feminine development as it manifests itself in the male anima (1970, 1971/1981, and 1980), again using myth and fairy tales as her source.

Following Jung, Harding, Wolff, and the better known of Neumann's work, von Franz views women as embodying relatedness. "The need for relatedness is of the highest value and essence of feminine nature" (1976, p. 191). The emphasis of her writing is on the *via negativa*. She tends to dwell on negative aspects of women and on the shadow side of her women patients in order to bring these difficult aspects up into consciousness. Von Franz's scholarship is brilliant; her writing has a crystalline and often devastating accuracy to it. She is such an exceptionally intelligent and conscious thinker that it is unbalancing to read her piercingly judicious descriptions of women as hazy, unconscious, ego-diffused, and denied thinking and Logos. There is a strange confusion between von Franz' clear and incisive intellectuality and what she calls women's nature. Is von Franz not, amongst other things, a woman doing her own writing and her own thinking? Under her and other of the conservators' outlooks, von Franz' strongest gift, the clarity of her writing and thinking, would be disallowed or, at most, considered a part of her unconscious animus and a way of occupying him, putting him to work. This apparent denial of a woman's right to her own good thinking is a crucial problem in the conservative reading of analytical psychology that negatively impinges on female analysands and readers, and undermines a woman's own self-esteem.

The analysts mentioned so far were Jung's "second generation" — those trained by him or under his direction and whose writing dates from the nineteen-twenties and thirties. Some, like Marie-Louise von Franz, are still writing today. Other than Neumann's final work on feminine development, their views in regard to the feminine and women seem to remain constant and conservative. These second-generation analysts adhere to Jung's original concepts and perceptions of women, in spite of recognizing the great changes in women's socio-cultural roles, women's expanded horizons, access to education and employment.

Two of the figures I will next discuss are Mario Moreno and Robert Grinnell. Though they published in the nineteen-sixties and nineteen-seventies, Moreno and Grinnell belong with the "thirties" view of the feminine, as their ideas of women are based on the cultural and social position of women in the early twentieth century.

Moreno, in "Archetypal Foundations in the Analysis of Women" (1965), attempts to integrate Wolff's four types of the feminine with Neumann's original (1959) stages of feminine development. Each stage is described primarily in reference to the male. Moreno, like Jacobi, attempts to include Deutsch's psychology within his scheme. He concurs with Deutsch that women's types are determined by "passivity (or the normal masochism implicit in feminine sexuality) and narcissism" (p. 184). He calls our present culture typical of "the masculine existential pattern" (p. 173). In line with this he speaks of women's place and the problems of women who live against their nature. He uses the phrases "woman" and "the feminine" interchangeably.

In discussing the animus, Moreno brings up the question of Logos and Eros, and the possibility of women's thinking. His conclusion is that, "in effect, the hypothesis of a feminine logos does not seem acceptable" (p. 182). Much of Moreno's article is traditional in his interpretations of the feminine, but his opinions are set forth with no substantiating evidence and little reference to clinical experience. Moreno simply states the problems caused by the patriarchal world and its rules, deriving gender-appropriate behavior from these rules. He therefore concludes, somewhat ruefully, that the way toward woman's development and

> the feminine existential pattern consists in turning oneself into object and in giving oneself to the world as mother, as daughter, as woman. . . . In the patriarchal world the woman becomes the other. Instinctiveness, emotivity, irrationality, passivity are projected on to her by the man. (p. 177)

Like Moreno, Robert Grinnell embeds his book *Alchemy in a Modern Woman* (1973) in traditional Jungian theory of the feminine. Also like Moreno and many analysts before him, Grinnell is struck by the incongruity between women's life in the contemporary world and what he was taught was women's traditional role. Grinnell finds the generic modern woman quite animus-bound and -ridden, fleeing her natural femininity, and psychologically damaging herself through her efforts to usurp a man's rightful place in the world. In regard to the particular patient who is the subject of his book, Grinnell seems to see the task of analysis as helping her regain her feminine place within the home and the world of relationship. "The problem concerns the woman who has entered as a rival into the masculine professional world and the strains and distortions to which her feminine nature is subjected" (p. 5).

According to Grinnell, a *healthy* traditional woman (in contrast to but co-temporal with the modern one) connives, belongs beside her man ("on the side where his shadow is deepest"), and realizes herself through accepting the projection of his anima (p. 5). She achieves differentiation through stereotypical feminine behavior. Grinnell contrasts her with the modern woman who has become neurotic. Rather than perceiving the neuroticism as, perhaps, a pull toward individuation, Grinnell finds that this modern woman upsets both herself and the men around her by not acting from her supposedly normal, Eros nature. She becomes easily possessed by the contrasexual, an aggressive animus, which is not only unrelated but given to "second-rate" thinking (p. 8). Grinnell states that modern woman loathes other women and herself, is subject to depression, and is also often homosexual.

The book aims to be a study of the psychology of the feminine as seen through the problems of a patient Grinnell diagnoses as a modern woman suffering from the above ailments. It is also the story of how analytic work can be used to conform a patient to an analyst's conception of gender-appropriate behavior. Perhaps this interpretation of his book is harsh. As Harding first noted, it is very difficult for women to find their own solutions to the changing world and to changing expectations of the feminine. Some women may indeed be happier and healthier in traditional roles (though current research—e.g., Bem, 1976—seems to reach opposite conclusions), and it is indeed true that women's new roles and expectations are accompanied by stress, and that the male world of the Market is a notably deficient environment. However, traditional roles no longer fit many women; the pull toward individuation involves development out of the patriarchal feminine "unconscious" and an urgent need to define ourselves more congruently and consciously. Grinnell's book is sealed off from contemporary studies of women and is fairly representative of some conservative Jungian work on the feminine. However, it troubles me when one of my patients tells me she has unearthed this book on her quest for self-discovery, and asks me if this is what I, too, believe. I wonder how other contemporary Jungian therapists react, especially if they know only the titles of the books and that they were written by fellow analysts and peers. The range of ideas and opinions about women's psychology, role, and behavior puts a burden on us to be familiar with our own literature.

The London analyst Faye Pye gave an intriguing speech before the

Fifth International Conference of Jungian Analysts; reprinted in 1974, the paper is called "Images of Success in the Analysis of Young Women Patients." Pye feels that the feminine still can be equated with Eros and the static, while the masculine represents activity, change, and Logos; in line with this thinking, she believes that women must live in submission to Eros' law. Within these concepts, Pye sensitively deals with the conflicts of her female patients, who like Grinnell's and Moreno's are caught between traditional values and their actual lives. For Pye it is a conflict women face between the pull of a Neumannesque matriarchal stasis and its feminine archetypes on one side, and the animus and ego on the other side, who push toward a more flexible, active, and changing environment. Pye notes the difference in women's lives and in values since World War Two; she gives a detailed and concrete analysis of the social problems that accompany female analysands into her consulting room, problems she attributes to the changing culture.

Pye's common-sense and willingness to consider external problems along with inner growth is refreshing and reminiscent of Harding's and Hannah's pragmatism. Pye describes a type of patient typical of this era: a father's daughter who feels empty and conflicted even in the middle of her pursuit of self-development. Emotion, marriage, motherhood, and mother are anxiously defended against because they bind and restrict. The agonizing problem of an individual and growth-enhancing solution which enables one to span both worlds remains a crucial one to women today. Pye doesn't redefine the Jungian ground in which she places these women, yet within her traditionalism she has much wisdom to offer.

June Singer's book on the psychology of Jung, *Boundaries of the Soul* (1972), contains a chapter on the masculine and feminine. Singer accepts masculine and feminine as polar opposites, and subscribes to the belief that there is a biological pattern through which female denotes *being* and masculine denotes *doing*. However, in describing traits of the masculine (active, decisive, logical, theoretical, determined) and feminine (warm, receptive, patient, and open), she puts quotation marks around the words to emphasize that she is consciously using culture-bound terms. Singer refers to the time-boundedness of Jung's work on typology, and describes his work on the feminine as "valid enough" (1972, p. 172) for Switzerland in his day. She feels that women are now breaking out of this mold and seeking new definitions of self. However, Singer, most probably a feeling type herself, still views women as primarily governed by Eros and relatedness, with consciousness dependent on these attributes. At the same time, she perceives this to be an era of "momentous change" (p. 232).

In her book *Androgyny* (1976/1989), Singer takes a historical look at this archetype and explores the possibility of the development and harmonious coexistence of the masculine and feminine within and without. She examines the sexism implicit in the old assumptions; she notes the repression of the feminine in a culture which categorized, limited, and restricted both sexes. Singer, in this one book, describes the feminine as having active and passive components. Far more important than gender, she feels, is the realization and incorporation of a person's particular individual potential.

These themes are continued in *Energies of Love* (1983). Though Singer develops her idea of the evolution of consciousness, her attitude toward the feminine seems to have returned to a more conservative stance. She increasingly stresses the importance of feeling, Eros and *being* for women, rather than androgyny. She explains her change of view by referring to (unspecified) studies by sociobiologists that influenced her and that she feels support her conviction that women "are the natural carriers of the eros principle as their leading function" (p. 120). At the same time, she, like Harding before her, notes that Jung's position on the difference in feminine and masculine consciousness, values, and attributes arose in a "man's world" (p. 280) and derived from his masculine perspective. She considers this view and its attitudes especially deep-rooted, for they constitute "the matrix from which we have entered into another level of consciousness" (p. 147). Yet Singer places a less emphatic stress on androgyny and the development of the contrasexual than in her previous book. She does discuss the importance of modern gender studies by women scholars because "they raise questions concerning the interface between innate and instinctual aspects of development, and the institutions of culture" (p. 256).

The Australian analyst Rix Weaver follows Singer in her traditional view of women and men being allied, respectively, with feeling and thinking typology. Weaver uses John Money's (1972) biological and psychological gender studies to support her 1975 paper on the feminine principle. She also notes the effect of culture which is now causing rapidly changing perceptions of the masculine and feminine. The historical devaluation of women and the feminine principle is perceived as an essential problem in both men's and women's development, as is men's fear of women. Weaver thinks the change toward more equality cannot but help psychological progress.

Writing eight years later, Anthony Stevens seems to want to actively halt this progress and restore a conservative and patriarchal status quo. His book on archetypes (1983) is a combination of popular sociobiology and analytical psychology. He holds some of the same attitudes toward the feminine as Singer seems to, but makes them more categorical. While Weaver considers gender studies to be useful in tracking sociocultural changes in behavior, Stevens finds Jung's ideas on the feminine grounded in genetic truth. He states, "indeed, both the ethological and the anthropological data tend to vindicate the Jungian position: it seems probable that significant differences between the political, social and economic roles of men and women are determined by genetics" (p. 174).

Stevens feels that gender is the most important aspect of personal identity (p. 174) and argues that "it is crucial that boys become men and girls become women and are clear about their roles and identity" (p. 201). He describes men as "naturally," and maybe even hormonally, thinking and sensation types, while women are feeling and intuitive types (pp. 194-195). He portrays men as superior physically, more adaptive, of superior intelligence, and more innovative, creative, persistent, motivated, powerful, aggressive, assertive, and more dominant than women (pp. 181-192). He quotes Goldberg's *The Inevitability of Patriarchy* (1973) to state that

> male dominance is a manifestation of the "psychophysiological reality" of our species. . . ."patriarchy is universal and that there has never been a matriarchy." Patriarchy, it seems, is the natural condition of mankind. "There is not, nor has there ever been, any society that even remotely failed to associate authority and leadership in suprafamilial areas with the male." (p. 188)

Stevens continues by asserting that women, by nature, should not try to compete with men "on masculine terms and on masculine territory" (p. 174), but instead should cultivate their genetic tendency to be contained, nurturing, affiliative, related, and altruistic (p. 190).

This attitude toward women uses faulty scholarship to confuse cultural stereotypes with "scientific" truth and to maintain and perpetuate patriarchal values. What I object to is the damage it does to women. It limits both their outer and inner worlds (maiming a woman and then seeing this as woman's normal condition). It confines women to patriarchal cultural patterns on specious grounds. It also hurts—Ulanov's "deep wound . . . the result of direct and indirect attacks on a woman's sexual identity" (Ulanov, 1981, p. 145). I worry about the effect of Steven's views on female patients, of the "atrophy of the individual person, which fails to develop beyond the limits imposed by the social role" (Odajnyk, 1976, p. 26), and on male patients when an endless emphasis on over-determined "masculine" traits such as aggressivity may also be antithetical to development.

Marriot (1983) and Mattoon (1984) in their short reviews have already criticized Stevens' scholarship and questioned his sources, as I have more extensively (Douglas, 1985), and as has Merritt (1988). Stevens' work is badly marred by using popularizations of ethological work instead of primary sources, and by using biological, behavioral, and anthropological data which have been superceded or invalidated (e.g., MacFarlane, 1977, Blum [Ed.], 1980, and Stern, 1985, present recent findings contrary to Bowlby, 1958 and 1969, on neonatology; Bem, 1976, Fausto-Sterling, 1985, and numerous other sociologists supercede Hutt, 1972, on sex differences; Arieti, 1976, is far more convincing and scientific than Hutt, 1972, on creativity; while Bleier, 1984, Lewontin, Rose and Kamin, 1984, and Epstein, 1988, marshal evidence to refute Wilson, 1975, Tiger and Fox, 1972, etc., on neurology, anthropology, ethology and sociobiology). Stevens' description of his clinical evidence and his conceptualization of male and female attributes and roles, rather than enlightening and helping individuation, seem to be an example of the "recurrent deprecations of the feminine phrased in the unimpeachable, objective language of the period" (Hillman, 1972, p. 224).

In a brief book review in *Quadrant* (1987), the New York analyst Jeffrey Satinover echoes Stevens in a passionately conservative plea for Jung's original formulations about gender and for a return to traditionalism. Having written extensively on the archetype of the puer, Satinover now takes an uncharacteristic senex view of masculine and feminine relations. He criticizes Jungians such as Samuels who, Satinover states, bend Jung's conservatism "in support of an idea to which it is frankly hostile: the identity of the sexes" (p. 81). Satinover exaggerates Samuels' stand as well as that of feminists (who are Jungians or embed their arguments in Jungian theory). He states that "the more radical femininists. . . propose a total break with a past whose myths, religions and rituals convey an unequivocal . . . discrimination between the physical, emotional, familial, social, spiritual and cosmic manifestations of the male and female principles—and this includes men and women" (p. 80). Reformulating ideas about men and women leads, Satinover fears, to modern man becoming a "wimp" who is reduced to being "nice" and "inoffensive" rather than the audaciously war-like, Nietzschean, testosterone-filled man Satinover seems to prefer—he who endures "storms" with "brute strength."

In this odd, almost lyrically evangelistic review, Satinover raises an essential quandary for Jungian theorists and analysts: how *do* men and women in modern times define their gender roles and their own masculine and feminine individuality? By opting for a Zeus-like vigor and macho attributes, Satinover resurrects essential and vital components of the masculine within men (and in women's animi), which have too often been ignored—especially, perhaps, by the many mothers' sons who are analysts or in analysis. However, it is not the only way of being masculine. Like Stevens, Satinover seems to forget Jung's emphasis on the contrasexual within each of us; he may have also overlooked the complexity and subtleness of current biological gender studies (for example, the presence and interplay of testosterone in both sexes).

What links the writers that I have mentioned so far are their traditional and conservative approach to interpreting Jung. They are further unified in seeing male and female, men and women, as polar opposites in which women and the feminine are assigned the side which encompasses Eros, relatedness, the feeling function, and the unconscious. The major value of this work is as description—often subtle, sensitive, and felicitious—of a single way of apperceiving the feminine; through this perception, writers elucidate a traditional view of the feminine and of women's psychology that remains essentially static, unchanged from their precursor Jung's own historical view.

The Reformulators

While in 1987 Satinover advocates a return to what he calls Jung's essential conservatism, one of the first Jungians, Beatrice Hinkle (1874-1953), was writing, as long ago as 1920, about the psychic costs of traditional gender roles. Clinically, she finds more differences in intra-gender behavior than in inter-gender behavior. She remarks on the harm done through "the error of confusing type distinctions with those of sex" (1920, p. 106), and through a fixity in which "all women indiscriminantly were fitted into this formula [the traditional concept of the feminine] and all men into that of the masculine concept" (p. 104).

In a chapter on masculine and feminine psychology in her 1923 book, *The Recreating of the Individual,* Hinkle reiterates her 1920 lecture; she cites anthropological and biological studies, reviews historical progress, and uses Jungian psychology in order to buttress her plea for reformulation. She criticizes Jung's reliance on putting women's animus to work as sufficient for their outer development. Hinkle argues for a broader and more individual understanding of women that remains grounded in Jungian psychology. She emphasizes the harm done to the individual when analysts identify a woman solely with the feminine principle and a man with the masculine. She finds typology far more important psychologically than gender; though she also remarks on the way gender-role modifies the expression and "alters the accent" of typology.

Hinkle celebrates women's active and passionate sexuality in passages that are vividly alive today. She was the first Jungian to note that women are neither primarily passive nor simply men's opposite. She describes the formidable difficulty inherent in a woman's breaking loose from men's definitions of her, and the intense labor involved in a woman's discovering her own individuality, self-esteem, and ego-satisfaction—all of which Hinkle sees as specifically female psychological tasks. A further major problem for women is the psychic stress caused by gender stereotyping itself and by men's ambiguous exaltation and denigration of women; she finds man's "use of women as a symbol of the inferior aspect of himself" (p. 291) especially damaging. This projection of a man's own feelings of inferiority onto a woman and his denial of a woman's individual power constitute

> a violation of her personality [that] has resulted in the greatest injury to woman; it has retarded her psychic development and fostered the infantile and instinctive reactions which are deemed her special characteristics. (p. 293)

Because Hinkle is so little remembered today, some brief remarks about her life may be appropriate. According to an article on her in *The Dictionary of American Biography* (American Council of Learned Societies, 1954), she was the first female graduate of a heretofore all-male medical school in the United States (she graduated in 1899); she was also the first female public health doctor in New York City. She studied with Jung starting in 1911. She was a small, warm, and intuitive woman whom Jung referred to in a letter to Freud as "an American charmer" (McGuire [Ed.], 1973, 269J, Aug. 29, 1911). Widowed while her two children were still young, Hinkle became their sole support. Horseback riding was a joy that she declared equalled her love of Jungian psychology.

A feminist herself, Hinkle reviewed the autobiographies of other feminists for *The Nation* (1926/1987). She comments on the creative effort that underlies women's struggle for equality, and sees feminism as a push toward individuation, which is "bringing to birth a new woman" (p. 141). Rather than the product of predetermined characteristics, personality is in her view formed through the interplay of gender, type, environment, culture, and inheritance.

Hinkle's particular approach to analytical psychology reflects her own multifaceted personality. She was a woman who was high in both traditionally masculine and traditionally feminine attributes and who encouraged these in other women as well.

Hilde Binswanger, one of the most interesting yet universally overlooked Jungian theorists on the feminine, completed her Zürich dissertation in 1955. In "Positive Aspects of the Animus" (1963), "Ego, Animus and Persona in the Feminine Psyche" (1965), and *Development in Modern Women's Self-Understanding* (1975), in contrast to most of the second generation's more conservative approach, Binswanger elaborates and reinterprets theory in a consistent but decidedly non-traditional way. For instance, like Hinkle, she notes that qualities attributed to men and women and to the masculine and feminine depend on a specific culture and era, and change as the culture changes. In contrast to other Jungians of her time, Binswanger finds women in her practice to be neither more nor less conscious than men, and equally as engaged in the same difficult journey toward individuation. She remarks, though, that the women are often more interesting and less restricted in outlook than her male patients.

Like her precursor Hinkle, Binswanger derives her theory from Jung's concept of bipolarity in both men and women; she is spirited and audacious in elaborating this theme. She decries the common Jungian error of confusing women with the feminine principle, and at the same time describes and champions a specifically feminine ego in women. Binswanger finds that women gain physical vitality and mental alertness as the culture limits them less and as they are allowed to manifest more androgynous and individual characteristics. She cites feeling type men and thinking type women as not only not aberrant, but as becoming increasingly more common as our culture develops, while the supposedly masculine qualities of strength, activity, and creativity (1965) contain both masculine and feminine aspects.

Like Neumann, Binswanger urges both men and women to become more aware of the feminine in themselves, and of men's and women's equal yet differing psychologies. Women, she says, become more relaxed and happy in analysis and progress faster when they are allowed their own dignity, value, and vitality as strong and active women. She faults the enforced passivity inculcated by a patriarchal upbringing and outlook. Binswanger notes that though educated women have been trained as men and in masculine qualities, they need to discover their own feminine qualities as well; the task is to be both feminine and intellectual, and each in an individual way. Referring to prior writers on the feminine, Binswanger attributes some of the confusion concerning feminine psychology to men's unconscious projection. Along with Harding and Singer, Binswanger finds this confusion exacerbated because most of what has been written about feminine psychology has been by men and comes from men's consciousness.

Irene de Castillejo first published a short article on the positive aspects of the animus in 1955. *Knowing Woman* (1973) updates the earlier (1955) article and includes it with a series of other unpublished lectures and articles on the feminine. This book is still recommended to women by analysts as one of the best and most complete books on Jungian feminine psychology (e.g., Mattoon, 1983; Sandner, 1983). In it de Castillejo elaborates and expands Wolff's four archetypes of the feminine in the light of traditional Jungian concepts of the feminine. However, she also advocates the development of a strong ego in women in place of Wolff's and Neumann's diffused one. Unlike Wolff, she emphasizes the importance of the various feminine personality types and psychological functions within the *same* woman. De Castillejo belongs with the reformulators in spite of joining the conservators in her allocation of feeling, Eros and relatedness as feminine and womanly, because she sees women not only not restricted to these attributes but developing out from their ground. She also makes several strong contributions to contemporary theory that had to wait until the 1980s for further development.

De Castillejo joins Hinkle and Binswanger in their understanding that woman cannot be defined as opposite to man: "woman's psyche is not just that of man the other way round" (1973, p. 165). What women's psyche actually is hasn't been sufficiently explored; she asserts that women scientists and analysts must conduct this exploration. For de Castillejo, thinking can be a woman's primary function and need not be equated with the animus. Along with Hannah and von Franz, she is concerned with women's shadow; however, she sees this shadow as a cultural problem rather than a specifically personal one. De Castillejo describes the power, depth, and rage present in a woman's shadow side. According to her, women carry three shadows: a national shadow, a personal shadow and "darkest of all" (p. 31), the shadow of being a woman. This dark shadow comes out in analysis as witch-like and full of intense rage. Through bringing this witchy shadow to consciousness, a woman regains personal authority, greater individuation, and can realign herself with the undiscovered feminine within herself. To reclaim this shadow a woman needs both an inner hero and heroine.

> I think that a woman will also turn witch today for other reasons than personal power. The deeply buried feminine in us whose concern is the unbroken connection of all growing things is in passionate revolt against the stultifying, life-destroying, anonymous machine of civilization we have built. She is consumed by an inner rage which is buried in a layer of the unconscious often too deep for us to recognize. (p. 42)

Finally, de Castillejo emphasizes that woman and the feminine do not stand solely for nature, the body, and earth, and that it is harmful to restrict and limit them to this.

> Woman is not just earth. To be told, as she often is told by psychologists, that man represents the spirit and she the earth, is one of those disconcerting things a woman tries hard to believe, knowing all the time that they are not true. (p. 77)

De Castillejo notes a strong element of spirituality in the feminine, but of a sort that has not been described nor has yet found its own voice. I will be concerned with her work on the animus and on the archetypes of the feminine in the following chapters.

V. N. Odajnyk, in *Jung and Politics: The Political and Social Ideas of C. G. Jung* (1976), applies the concept of shadow and shadow projection to the psychology of minority, colonized, and subject groups. Though his primary concern is with colonial groups, what he writes is equally applicable to women and concurs with de Castillejo's view on women's shadow. Odajnyk's theory splendidly elucidates the ways in which women have come to carry men's shadow for them and why women are so prone to scapegoating. He writes (I have changed the pronouns from masculine to feminine in order to emphasize this applicability):

> Collective shadow projections . . . activate and support various local and
> personal shadow projections, so that the recipient of the collective projec-
> tion is confronted by negative feelings whichever way [she] turns. First
> the culture as a whole defines [her] in shadow terms; then the locality
> in which [she] lives adds its own particular flavor and finally, each indi-
> vidual with whom [she] comes into contact contributes [her] own per-
> sonal shadow elements. The accumulated burden is so heavy it is not
> surprising that members of shadow bearing groups are usually demoral-
> ized and depressed. (pp. 82-83)

Odajnyk notes that people who are members of groups which are considered socially "inferior" frequently identify personally with their socially defined status and roles. He describes the pernicious results.

> The result . . . is the atrophy of the individual personality, which fails
> to develop beyond the limits imposed by the social role. And, deflation-
> ary roles also have their attractive aspects. They offer an easy compensa-
> tion or justification for personal deficiencies and a psychologically satisfying
> submergence of the individual with the collective. (p. 26)

Odajnyk thus extends the traditional Jungian idea of the shadow,
heretofore considered to be the same gender as its projector, to specific
groups, and by implication to the contrasexual. Jung wrote in *Aion*
(1951/1968) that the shadow "is always of the same sex as the subject"
(p. 10), yet at the same time, and especially when discussing projection, Jung describes the shadow as containing *everything* that a person
finds unacceptable (e.g., 1939/1969, p. 284). I see nothing in the theory either as Jung or Odajnyk develop it that necessitates limiting the
shadow to "the same sex as the subject."

A major focus of current criticism and reformulation in Jungian theory of the feminine centers around sex-roles, gender identity, the definition of masculine and feminine, the Eros/Logos dichotomy and, in
light of this, further reclamation and reinterpretation of the animus.
Jane Wheelwright, in her 1978 monograph *Women and Men*, at first
keeps to the traditional Eros/Logos dichotomy, describing Eros and relatedness as belonging more to the feminine and Logos to the masculine.
However, in her 1982 and 1984 work, Wheelwright allows for individual variances, though still stressing the differences between masculine and
feminine. She (1984) states that the original formulation goes along with
the one of the female as *being* and the male as *doing,* and explains it

as a generational one belonging to the conventions of "her day." Wheel-wright also voices openness to her daughter's (the analyst, Lynda Schmidt) different formulation, stressing the importance of individual and personal experience in creating a psychology of the feminine and a quest for women's wholeness. She differentiates between the world-view and relationship to the world of "mothers' daughters" and "fathers' daughters": those who are related primarily to their feminine and those who relate to themselves as daughters of the patriarchy.

Wheelwright's most original work is on the archetype of the maiden (1984) and the possibilities inherent in it of women having—as Harding and Wolff also concluded—more diffused egos. Wheelwright adds that women show a natural bent toward an inner committee of conscious multifaceted personalities rather than one single personality (I will discuss this in Chapter Eight). She suggests that the principle of opposites may no longer apply when defining male and female, and that there are male and female aspects of the unconscious in both sexes. She differentiates between female and male (or animus) approaches to knowledge and the spiritual, but does not develop this theme.

Ann Ulanov is a professor of psychiatry and religion as well as a Jungian analyst. Two of her two books, *The Feminine in Jungian Psychology and in Christian Theology* (1971) and *Receiving Woman, Studies in the Psychology and Theology of the Feminine* (1981), creatively integrate Jungian theory with a religious and active Christianity. Ulanov explores the equation of women with evil and the corporeal that was noted by Jung and de Castillejo. She points out that since women are thus defined psychologically, they also receive the projection of everything connected with the body and all the fears that go with sex, mortality, life, death, and bodily existence. What starts with fear of the archetypal mother (Neumann, 1955; Ulanov, 1981) continues in a double displacement from fear to hate and from the anima to the feminine in general, and then onto a particular woman.

In considering the problem of what is and is not feminine, Ulanov notes how pervasively the definitions get mixed with socio-historical bias and become obscured by men's fear and projection. Ulanov is drawn to Wolff's and de Castillejo's four feminine types; she finds each type potentially available as aspects of a single individual's personality. Ulanov extends the range of each type and adds many more feminine archetypes of both a positive and negative nature; through this multiplicity she hopes a more comprehensive understanding of the feminine can be gained.

> Our symbol systems, along with other cultural realities—what Cassirer calls the "spiritual organs" of culture, meaning, art, language, theology, science—create for us a transitional space between our private inner world and the outer world we share with others . . . . It is in the space between worlds, between inner and outer, that symbols of the feminine exist and perform a mirroring function, reflecting back to us our apprehension of a major modality of human existence. (1981, pp. 74-75)

Ulanov stresses our culture's, especially Christianity's, fear and hatred of the feminine and its compulsion to subjugate women and keep the feminine unconscious. "A deep wound [to the woman's ego] is the result of direct and indirect attacks on a woman's sexual identity" (p. 145) brought about by this attitude. "A woman who elects consciousness must fight almost indomitable sexual projections, her own and others" (p. 154). Ulanov champions the recovery of the feminine, the exploration of its meaning, and its incorporation into full humanness as essential for our culture, for Christian theology, and for the healing of our own psyches. "The change in our consciousness of the feminine and our relation to it is so radical because it changes our consciousness of what it means to be human" (p. 139). Ulanov's later work on the feminine is on archetypes which stand behind and elucidate complexes involving feminine potency, rage, envy, and jealousy; these will be discussed in Chapter Eight.

James Hillman's major work on the feminine appears in *The Myth of Analysis: Three Essays in Archetypal Psychology* (1972). The purpose of the book and of his archetypal psychology is "freeing the psyche from the curse of the analytic mind" (p. 3). Hillman approaches the feminine through a discussion of the history of misogyny, its accompanying myth of female inferiority, and both of their permutations in analysis. Writing of this "mytheme of female inferiority," Hillman, using the plural voice, says:

> We discover that this idea is basic to the structure of the analytical mind, basic to the kind of consciousness which we find in both neurosis and its treatment. Misogyny would seem inseparable from analysis, which in turn is but a late manifestation of the Western, Protestant, scientific, Apollonic ego. This structure of consciousness has never known what to do with the dark, material, and passionate part of itself, except to cast it off and call it Eve. What we have come to mean by the word "conscious" is "light"; this light is inconceivable for this consciousness without a distaff side of something else opposed to it that is inferior and which has

been called—in Greek, Jewish, and Christian contexts—female. (p. 8)

Neurosis becomes compensatory to the one-sidedly masculine, scientific, and technological world of the patriarchy. Hillman calls for a new consciousness based on a different archetypal structure, one in which the Dionysian is as inherent as the Apollonic, and the feminine equal to the masculine. In a search for this new structure, Hillman decries the lack of Eros in the present world and the lack of the erotic in men and their erroneous projection of Eros onto women. He reviews Neumann's (1962) study of Amor and Psyche and emphasizes Neumann's distinction between matriarchal (Aphrodite) and individuated feminine (Psyche). For the feminine to be individuated, a new view is required:

> The transformation of our world-view necessitates the transformation of the view of the feminine. Man's view of matter moves when his view of the feminine moves. . . . The idea of feminine inferiority is therefore paradigmatic for a group of problems that become manifest at the same time in psychological, social, scientific and metaphysical areas. (p. 217)

Hillman calls much of psychology a fantasy:

> Perhaps still more fundamental are the fantasies which afflict the male in regard to the female when male is observer and female is datum. . . . they are recurrent deprecations of the feminine phrased in the unimpeachable, objective language of the science of the period. (p. 224)

Hillman traces these fantasies and myths historically, starting with the Biblical Adam and Eve through Apollonic Greece, the eras of witchhunting, the rise of nineteenth-century psychology, and the study of hysteria, ending with psychoanalysis. His conclusion is that all contain and exemplify the same myth of feminine inferiority, and that science, psychology and our culture still "know next to nothing about how feminine consciousness or a consciousness which has an integrated feminine regards the same data" (p. 249).

In opposition to the prevailing masculine definition of consciousness, Hillman proposes Dionysian and bisexual, androgynous consciousness, a synthesis rather than division, and an equal respect for the unconscious and the conscious. In a book that could well have been revolutionary in its reformulation of the feminine and that echoes some of the same historical analysis that Ehrenreich and English (1972, 1973) use in a feminist way, Hillman, even here and even at this time and contrary to the findings of his own research, still describes the feminine as representing only the inferior, incomplete, imperfect, passive, empty, introverted, slower, sadder, cooler, the inert, depressive, and noncreative "durable weakness and unheroic strength" (p. 293). He omits the feminine as positive, creative, powerful, initiating, gestating, birthing, and mothering. He equates the feminine and bisexual consciousness with body-consciousness and an experiential somatic awareness of self. He notes, along with Whitmont, that the inclusion of the feminine in analysis would involve more body-oriented and group involvement than is generally practiced (p. 294).

Depth psychology is criticized as having an Apollonian method but a Dionysian substance. "If our aim is 'more light' [more consciousness] can we ever reach . . . the union with dark materiality and the abyss?" (p. 293). Hillman asks for the abandonment of both terms, "conscious" and "unconscious," especially when, as he describes occurring in depth psychology, the use of such terms results in an emphasis on a masculine, Apollonian consciousness to whose supposedly higher level the feminine unconscious must be transmuted. "It seems unjustifiable to give the name 'consciousness' to that dried and sunlit condition of the psyche" (p. 289).

In conclusion, Hillman proclaims that

> The end of analysis coincides with the acceptance of femininity. . . . The termination of analysis . . . coincides with the termination of misogyny, when we take Eve back into Adam's body, when we are no longer decided about what is masculine and what feminine; what inferior, what superior, what exterior, what interior. (pp. 292-293)

In a lecture, Gareth Hill (in Dieckmann, Bradway, and Hill, 1974) remarks on the problems created by Jungian jargon and the unconsidered assumptions in the Jungian community about thinking/feeling, animus/anima, and Yin/Yang, and the deplorable penchant for linking them to gender. He considers them "largely culture-bound images" (p. 16) that are mostly free of sex-linkage, though affected by norms, statistical probabilities, and stereotyping. He cites the confusion in Jungian circles between archetype and cultural stereotype. Another aspect of the problem, Hill suggests, is that it was thinking men who did most of the original writing on the feminine. What they were drawn to and portrayed was their opposite—the classical model of the feeling type woman. In his 1978 dissertation, Hill describes and elaborates on the concept of dynamic and static feminine and dynamic and static masculine qualities. Again he deplores modern analysts' ignorance about the feminine and their acceptance and endless emphasis of Jung's original time-bound formulations.

> In the traditional, patriarchal culture pattern, then, the classical developmental formulation of analytical psychology is not apt for women, and this has led to a tendency toward confusion among analytical psychologists when modern women's development is described. (p. 18)

Hill's original and creative reformulations of Jungian theory are as yet unavailable in published form, which has kept his valuable and exciting contribution out of mainstream awareness. This points up a critical problem in the development of Jungian theory: much that creatively reformulates our discipline remains unavailable to all but the most assiduous researchers. In any publication of Jungian ideas on the feminine, Hill's work would constitute one of its most important chapters.

In his 1975, 1976 and 1977 work, Willeford points out that Jung's tendency to think in a dualistic and polarized way is especially pronounced in his treatment of the masculine and feminine. Willeford traces the historical roots of this polarization (1975) and argues for a reevaluation and reinterpretation of the feeling function (1976, 1977). He criticizes Jung for an absolutism that derives from the emphasis on opposites. In place of this, Willeford stresses the *relative* differences between the masculine and the feminine, their continuity, complementarity, and complexity. He points to the compatibility of these supposed opposites and the more salient "gradations, transitions and coherences" (1976, p. 45) which become evident through differentiated feeling. Willeford alludes to the differences brought about by time and culture, and criticizes those writers and analysts who take Jung's intuitive formulations for law.

Guggenbuhl-Craig also considers the Eros/Logos bipolarity problem and decries the limited archetypes used to define masculine and feminine attributes. In contrast to Stevens and Satinover, he calls this type of conservatism naive and misinformed:

> This misunderstanding has led, for example, to the assumption in Jungian psychology that masculine is identical with Logos, and femininity with Eros. It is assumed that the essence of femininity is personal, related to one's fellow man, passive, masochistic, and that the essence of masculinity is abstract, intellectual, aggressive, sadistic, active, etc. This naive assertion could have been made only because the masculine and femi-

nine archetypes that were dominant at that time and in that culture were understood to be the only valid ones. (Guggenbuhl-Craig, 1977, p. 48)

Should the whole range of the new archetypal spectrum actually break through, however, the relationship between men and women will be reformed in many new ways. (p. 57)

In a concise and cogent presentation, the London analyst Judith Hubback, in her important article on the psychology of women (1978/1988), brings Jungian ideas on women into the mainstream. She finds that the core intrapsychic problems that form gender identity and sexuality—the basic early mother-infant, oedipal, and sibling conflicts—happen to both male and female infants equally. Both are equally subject to the forces of human creativity and destructiveness. The difference lies in the manner in which men and women express these conflicts and the solutions they find. Hubback considers three major themes in women's psychology: the question of whether or not anatomy is destiny; the effect of social and cultural factors on women's potential; and the need for research on the true nature of women and on the psychological similarities and differences between the sexes. The sex of the person doing the research, writing about, and interpreting women's psychology, is for Hubback a crucial variable that needs consideration. She also stresses the obligation analysts have to educate themselves about current studies in women's psychology and to know something about pragmatic reality—the world which contemporary women inhabit.

It is most valuable, in my opinion, for the analyst to know the facts about the [twentieth-century] women's movements in various countries and to appreciate the general climate of opinion here, as being the world where people are living. (p. 177)

E. C. Whitmont presents the most comprehensive, exhaustive, and caring consideration of the feminine in analytical psychology to date (especially 1979, 1980, 1982a and 1982b). Following Neumann, he sees consciousness progressing through uroboric, matriarchal, and patriarchal states. Whitmont posits the end of patriarchy and the emergence of a new integrative era which evolves beyond, though includes and synthesizes, the matriarchy and patriarchy. He insists on the necessity of both males and females going through each stage, and concurs with Ulanov on the socio-historical causes for the changes in our view of the feminine, presenting an even wider array of archetypal examples of the feminine — types which had been overlooked, suppressed, or rejected during the period of the patriarchy.

Like Hillman, Whitmont traces the myth of the inferiority of women and of the feminine from antiquity to the present. He integrates this myth with three other patriarchal myths which "unbeknownst to us, . . . still underlie to a large extent our modern world view" (1982a, p. 78). These are the myth of divine kingship which underlies the Christian religion and its lack of a feminine principle; the myth of the loss of paradise (loss of the feminine as represented by the natural world and the body), and the myth of the scapegoat (in which the feminine receives the projection of everything which the masculine perceives as negative). The Grail myth is seen as an antidote to these harmful myths and as a way of honoring, serving, and reincorporating the feminine.

Whitmont (1979, 1980, 1982a) presents an extensive list of what he considers feminine and masculine attributes. He prefers the terms Yang and Yin to masculine and feminine, but redefines them to include "the idea of exteriorization, diversification, penetration, and external action for Yang and inherence, unification, incorporation, activity and existence for Yin" (1980, p. 112). He proposes the eradication of the Eros/Logos division for feminine and masculine, calling this division "terminologically and psychologically inappropriate" (1980, p. 109). Thus both masculine and feminine are allowed their related and unrelated, active and passive aspects. He notes the social conditioning which encourages women to be passive and related, saying "this is but a persona gesture" (p. 111). However, he keeps Logos as masculine, replacing Eros with the term "Medusa" to designate Logos' powerful, seemingly chaotic opposite. Whitmont equates the Medusa with Neumann's (1962) transformative aspect of the feminine.

P. B. Kenevan, in her article "Eros, Logos and Androgyny" (1981), continues Neumann's and de Castillejo's differentiation of focused and diffused consciousness. She seeks to update and reformulate it, though, in what she terms a pro-feminist way. She finds both Eros and Logos androgynous; while disconnecting them from gender, she does give them specific attributes and ways of manifesting along gender lines. She criticizes the confusion many Jungians make between "sexual differentiation and the differentiation of psychological types" (p. 9), but calls the confusion unavoidable given the traditional equation of Eros/Logos with feeling and thinking and women and men. She describes feminine consciousness as having a diffused, holistic, related, and circular Logos and a focused, personal, concrete, subjective Eros. She gives masculine consciousness a focused, analytic, atomistic, linear and logical Logos and the feminine a diffuse, impersonal, abstract, objective Eros. She argues cogently for the reevaluation of diffused consciousness as a necessary and complementary addition to focused consciousness. She deplores the devaluation of what she calls the feminine and of women's way of thinking, and wants women to assert the value of their own mode of thinking:

> It seems that people with strongly developed masculine logos misinterpret completely the thinking of feminine logos and call such thinking *feeling*. I believe they do so through a projective mechanism. Since their own *feeling is diffuse* and holistic, they confuse the categories of eros and logos and assume that, as their *feeling is diffuse,* the diffuse thinking of feminine logos is similarly *diffuse feeling* instead of *thinking*. This is reinforced by their assimilation of thinking to the focusing capacity. (p. 17)

The value of this lies in restoring respect for a feeling type person's thinking and clarifying its processes. The problem of Kenevan's reformulation, however, is that women and the feminine are conformed to this feeling type, which is then defined as feminine consciousness. The focused thinking of a thinking type woman is not allowed except as a manifestation of masculinity. Separated from her own categorical confusion, Kenevan's theory elucidates a feeling type person's thinking. Kenevan also clarifies the supposed lack of feeling in men. She notes that what she calls feminine consciousness, and what I would call a feeling type woman, considers the diffused Eros of masculine consciousness as a deficit, a manifestation of an inability to relate and as a sign of absence of feeling. Kenevan points out that this is not so, but instead is a different and more diffuse way of expressing feeling.

Mattoon, in her powerful book *Jungian Psychology in Perspective* (1981), reviews prior work on the feminine in less than ten invaluable pages of rare historical analysis. She notes the prevalence in Jungian psychology of what Joseph Wheelwright has called that "odious linkage" of feminine/Eros/feeling/related/unconscious (or diffused consciousness) /woman. She describes Eros "as synonymous with the female principle" (p. 94) in most Jungian work. In this chapter she mentions the work of Jung, Harding, E. Jung, Wolff, Neumann, Ulanov and Guggenbuhl-Craig, omitting most of the writers who have taken a different stand, perhaps because consideration of them would unnecessarily muddy the impressive clarity of her text, making her explication of Jungian psychology less available to her reader. The result, though, reinforces a conservative and static Jungian view of the feminine. Mattoon does point to the confusion of cultural stereotypes with innate qualities. She also reviews type-test results that place women as generally but not preponderantly more in the feeling than the thinking spectrum.

In her two lectures in San Francisco (1983a and b) and in her 1987 article, Mattoon cites feminist criticism of this static and conventional view of the feminine and talks of her own personal and intellectual difficulty with it. In her second (1983b) lecture, Mattoon presents traditional Jungian views of the feminine; while finding them unsatisfactory, she limits new alternatives to those which derive from a positivist and empirical reworking of the concepts. In her first (1983a) lecture, however, Mattoon presents an exciting reinterpretation of the animus in response to her own and others' deep dissatisfaction with the original Jungian interpretation; her 1987 article dynamically elaborates her reworking of the concept and grounds it with references to some other past and contemporary reevaluations of the concept.

Bradway reviews research on typology as well as some of the same research on gender differences that Anthony Stevens used, but reaches markedly different conclusions. She remarks that "linking traits to gender can perpetuate the stereotyping that women initially recognized, and that men have increasingly seen, as potentially limiting to the development of both sexes" (1982a, p. 279). Bradway concludes that though there *is* an important difference between men and women, the difference is affected by changes in cultural standards, and thus the polarity current in Jung's era has become increasingly less prevalent. She notes both the positive and negative aspects of the varied masculine and feminine elements present in all women. In a very brief reference to prior work, she cites Neumann, Whitmont, and Hill on the elaboration of the dynamic and static poles that occur in both the masculine and the feminine, as well as Bolen, Guggenbuhl-Craig, Hillman, Schmidt, Whitmont, and Philip Zabriskie on the variety of feminine archetypes. She reviews the arguments against the Eros/feeling/Yin/feminine/woman and Logos/thinking/Yang/masculine/man equations. Yin and Yang, she finds, are terms that are especially misused by Jungians: intrinsically Chinese concepts, embedded in Chinese culture and philosophy, Yin and Yang encompass far more than simple masculine and feminine qualities, so that taking them merely as such falsifies and obscures. In Bradway's research on women who work and those who stay at home, she finds that each need at some point to develop what had been left undeveloped by their lifestyles: thinking and possibly outside work for the home group, feeling and perhaps a sense of the home for the professional group. This is explored in Bradway's 1978 study of the Hestia and Athena archetypes and will be included in Chapter Eight.

In an earlier monograph (in Dieckmann, Bradway and Hill, 1974), Bradway focuses on the primary importance of a woman gaining identity as an individual person rather than as a member of a particular gender. She writes:

> I am particularly interested in how women experience themselves. I believe that the psychology of women is still evolving, and that it is not just a neat counterpart of male psychology. I wholeheartedly agree . . . [that] males and females are not opposite from each other, but different from each other. (pp. 9-10)

Bradway is one of the few Jungians to note the patriarchal bias in our language and to emphasize how language affects the way women are perceived and see themselves. She deplores the use of so-called feminine traits as an excuse to exclude women "from certain educational, occupational and social opportunities" (p. 8). In her later work Bradway advocates a clear separation of terminology between masculine/feminine on the one hand and men and women on the other. For both analyst and analysand, appreciation of the functioning of the masculine and feminine in both is "essential for Jungian work" (p. 279). In a deeply moving 1984 talk, she stresses the new approach in therapy demanded by the increasing number of women who are in touch with, but confused by, a new dynamic and powerful feminine spirit rising within them.

A number of valuable contributions on the feminine get lost because their titles do not reflect what is contained within them, or because (as in Bradway's 1984 lecture) they have not been published, or because the work is contained in a review on a similar subject, but the reviewer inserts her own experience or theorizing. In a 1983 article, "The Archetypal Masculine," Barbara Greenfield subtitles her work: "Its Manifestations in Myth and its Significance to Women" (1983). The subtitle tends to be left out of indexes and bibliographies, so her valuable contribution on the feminine escapes notice. In this article, Greenfield considers the long history of gender stereotyping and the historical permutations in what is allocated to men's or women's psychology. Socialization, biology, and the differing cultural positions of men and women all have an impact on individual psychology. Though she is primarily concerned with elaborating varieties of archetypal roles available to men and the animus, Greenfield also focuses on the consequences of stereotyping. She feels that, as categories, the terms masculine and feminine "take on a life of their own" (p. 33) until a whole new mythos comes about through the vast cultural elaboration of a very few differences. Greenfield concludes that

> if we are to be concerned with modifying these stereotypes, then we must begin by attempting to understand as deeply as possible not only the nature of our cultural myths and categories, but also their significance for the psychological development of the individual. (p. 33)

Both Naomi Lowinsky and Suzanne Banford have written long reviews for the *San Francisco Jung Institute Library Journal*, in which they consider the feminine and the psychology of women with a felicitous mix of personal and clinical experience combined with deep knowledge of their field. This mixture adds invaluable depth to a reformulation of Jungian theory, yet their creative and original work remains buried in reviews of other people's writing. Lowinsky, in "Why Can't a Man be More Like a Woman?" (1984), a review of a Jungian-inspired popular psychology book, goes deeper than the book she is reviewing toward making a significant contribution to Jungian theory on the feminine. She does this through "telling it like it is": she focuses on her own experience and on the psychology of her female patients. She is intensely aware of the psychological consequences of patriarchal tradition and stereotyping and their cost to women. The lack of adequate female models of maturity adds to the problem. "The painful themes that run through my clinical work have to do with women's negative self image and enormous self-doubt" (p. 23). Women's therapy has to acknowledge and support women in their struggles with these issues. Lowinsky finds that the problems inherent in patriarchal culture and its traditional gender roles and choices resonate within her own experience and that of the patients she and all of us see daily in analysis. She concludes that women's current needs demand a restudy and reformulation of Jungian ideas on the feminine.

Suzanne Banford continues this reworking of Jungian attitudes toward the feminine in her 1982 review. She focuses primarily on the problems of modern women (including herself) when they break away from being the fathers' daughters that families, society, and Jungian hierarchies often seem to expect. Banford speaks with urgency and a depth of perception based on strong grounding in her field, clinical sensitivity, and personal experience. Her conclusion is that the circular path toward wholeness leads away from old formulations. Echoing Neumann's *Psyche*, Banford finds that women who progress beyond the patriarchy and seek to embody their own authority and sense of themselves follow a profoundly solitary and problematic path, on which they are often unsupported; their rejection by the collective and its traditional views and expectations of women may cause them great anguish. She urges a reformulation of Jungian thought which includes an understanding of the deep injuries patriarchates — whether personal or institutional — inflict on their daughters.

Andrew Samuels tends to be more theoretical and less personal than Banford and Lowinsky. I would imagine him to be most at home gathering all sorts of disparate material together out of which he formulates patterns and spins theory, thus making a strong contribution to Jungian literature. His writing draws upon many other people's work, which Samuels consolidates somewhat in the spirit of a Jungian Boswell. In spite of Satinover's review to the contrary, Samuels lucidly defines and clarifies current trends and representative ideas in Jungian psychology. In his book on the developments in Jungian psychology since Jung (1985), Samuels has a chapter on gender, sex, and marriage, in which he surveys some of the same areas as I am doing here (his chapter also appeared in *Anima* 11, *2*, 1984, under the title "Gender and Psyche").

Samuels has a finely tuned historical sensibility, though the breadth of his book limits his consideration of the feminine to one chapter. He briefly credits the prior work on the feminine of Binswanger, Wolff, de Castillejo, Emma Jung, Harding, Whitmont, Hillman, Perera, Ulanov, Woodman, Singer, Mattoon and Moore. Jung's cultural bias has to be taken into account, especially on gender issues; Samuels believes that Jung's theory, as well as that of the analysts who followed him, reflect "a particular personal and historical context" (p. 216) which must be acknowledged. He also finds this bias the cause of much of contemporary Jungians' dissatisfaction with Jung's work on the feminine.

Samuels comments on the marked conservatism he finds in many women analysts (especially Harding and Emma Jung) when they write about women. He proposes three essential themes in rethinking analytical psychology's approach to gender (these reflect Hubback's earlier but unacknowledged 1978 article): definitions of masculine and feminine and whether they are absolute; the range and degree to which individual men and women are masculine and feminine, neither sex necessarily limited to one rather than the other; the way in which stereotyping limits and congeals, while freeing from stereotypes promotes psychological growth and healing through allowing humans all their potential. Besides these themes, Samuels questions the innateness of heterosexuality itself, arguing that polymorphous perversity is perhaps more intrinsic to human behavior. Samuels buttresses his argument with some review of biological work on gender, plus a dash of Lacanian Freudianism and social learning theorists (i.e., Chodorow on the effect of gender on same or different sex mothering). In this chapter and in the introduction to his (1985) book, Samuels argues for the necessity of a refinement in Jungian theory in which gender and sex are no longer synonymous (this is evocative of the cogently argued differentiation that Hinkle, Binswanger, and de Castillejo make between separation of the feminine principle from actual women). He goes so far as to disengage Jung's concepts of Eros and Logos, animus and anima, and masculine and feminine archetypes from any sex or gender connection (echoing but also extending Willeford's 1975 plea for an end to polarized thinking in opposites and for differentiated, subtle, and more sophisticated theory).

Polly Young-Eisendrath's 1984 book on couples therapy and her *Female Authority* (1987), written in collaboration with Florence Wiedemann, reformulate Jungian ideas on feminine psychology in a vigorous, active and feminist way. After critiquing psychodynamic theory in general and Jungian theory in particular for their androcentrism, these analysts validate external criticisms of Jung (such as those of Goldenberg, D. Wehr, and Rupprecht and Lauter). At the same time, they offer a new theory embedded within Jung's general principles but freed from patriarchal attitudes. Chapter two of *Hags and Heroes* (1984) is called "Feminism and the Psychology of C. G. Jung"; it is the theoretical basis for much of their 1987 book.

Young-Eisendrath and Wiedemann present the first really comprehensive Jungian review of other disciplines' theorists and scientific research in the field of gender studies. They use these findings to critique earlier Jungian theory, to propose their own alternative, and to integrate Jungian and feminist psychology. However, prior work on the feminine in analytical psychology is markedly absent. In the 1984 book, Young-Eisendrath only refers to Harding's book *The 'I' and the 'Not I'* (1965), and to C. G. Jung, Perera, Stevens, Wolff, and Woodman (the San Francisco analysts William Goodheart and Arthur Coleman are also mentioned, but in relation to general analytic technique or to couples therapy). In the 1987 book, de Castillejo, C. G. Jung, Neumann and Stevens are the only analysts referred to. This leaves the Jungian ancestry of the authors' ideas sadly invisible. Thus their books lack a ground within their own discipline in which to embed their detailed, valuable, and creative reformulations.

In spite of this, their plea for the urgency of freeing analytical psychology from its negative and limiting views of women is strong, timely, and cogent. In particular, they decry the Jungian emphasis on female passivity, masochism, and the inferiority implicit in Jungians' sex-role stereotyping and sexual bias. Labeling, as in the term "animus-ridden," also opposes women's access to their own competence. Young-Eisendrath notes that "women consistently face a double bind when they speak with authority or insistence" (1984, p. 25). Both of these books fit in with mainstream psychology of women in advocating therapy and theory based on individuation through working toward autonomy, self-esteem, authority, competence, and independence. The authors masterfully delineate the ways this can be accomplished within an analytic framework. I will return to their elaborations of the animus/anima theory in the following chapters.

The formulations I have attempted here reflect my own introverted thinking intuitive typology. The confusion of a writer's typology with what she is describing is an ever-present hazard which has not received enough attention. Thus Emma Jung and Binswanger describe their own sensation type thinking—objective and concrete—and then apply this to women's thinking in general, while feeling type writers like Singer and Kenevan explain women as reflections of the writers' own feeling function. The reformulators' point of view is closer to my own and therefore I see more value in it, especially for its emphasis on the fluid and changing possibilities inherent in humans, though I also believe there is a difference between the ways men and women live in, perceive, and respond to the world. I also think that gender and typology affect each other. Specific types (as I discussed in Chapter Three) tend to be generally more common and more encouraged in specific genders according to socio-cultural conditions. More important, the ways these types are influenced by gender produces a different quality to their expression whatever their theoretical stance—whether conservator or reformulator.

Among both the reformulators and the conservators discussed in this chapter there has been growth in theory since Jung, which involves some shift away from viewing women only as adjuncts of men and toward seeing them as independent. This started with Harding's and Hinkle's working woman and Neumann's transformative one, was developed by Binswanger, and reached full acceptance in Hill, Hillman, Whitmont, Wheelwright, Bradway, Young-Eisendrath and Wiedemann today. Among the reformulators, there has been a shift away from pigeon-holing women along stereotypical "gender-linked" lines and from defining women as the opposite of whatever is male. This shift has been accompanied by increasingly convincing arguments against Eros/Logos and type linkages with gender.

Both groups continue to expand Jung's understanding of the presence of the contrasexual within each person, and to extend his exploration of the possibilities open to the feminine. There is a growing interest in the study of women themselves, and an emphasis on personal experience as a basis for theory. Within both groups there is also a new exploration and valuation of what may be essentially feminine: a feminine voice which has been suppressed and is just now surfacing; while others are specifically interested in and encourage power and strength in women. The reformulators, especially, criticize prior work on the feminine that omits attention to culture, circumstance and time. Yet Jungian theory on the feminine continues to be, with few exceptions such as Mattoon, Hillman, Willeford, Samuels, and Whitmont, sadly lacking a historical outlook. Many of the writers remain oblivious to prior work and seem to be writing from within their own introverted world.

Few women writing today hold to the conservator stance. I feel that the conservators' evaluations, useful as they might have been in Jung's time, need to be revised in order to be of use to contemporary women: they are representative of a historical view belonging to a specific and past era, there is no convincing evidence to support them, they seem not to make use of the increased knowledge available about the psychology of women, and they are restrictive and potentially harmful to the full development of personality. The following ideas are especially in need of revision: that the feminine and women's psychology can be reduced to only one correct way of being—connected with Eros, feeling, the contained, diffused conscious or unconscious, related and passive Yin mode; that the feminine and women's psychology is opposite to and complementary with the masculine and men's psychology, and can be described solely in these terms; that there are separate (though possibly equal) spheres for men and women; the limiting (in spite of theoretical contrasexuality) of women to the feminine and men to the masculine; the limiting of woman and the feminine to socio-cultural stereotypes, the description of these stereotypes as normal and necessary for woman's psychological health and as accurate depictions of her reality; all the varied terminological confusions between typology, gender, and the feminine and the masculine principles.

What needs to be kept is the assumption that there *is* a difference between the masculine and the feminine and between men's and women's psychology. These are, again, differences of kind and perhaps of quantity, not of value. However, what these differences are and how they arise remains unclear and needs further investigation. Probable differences in biology and in the experience of same and different sex mothering may prove crucial. Many other differences, accepted as innate, are transitory, dependent on the time, culture, and social conditioning. Jungian concepts of the contrasexual in each gender, of typology (when not gender-bound), of honoring both Eros and Logos ways of perceiving and being, of exploring the masculine and feminine through symbol and myth, remain forceful and generative elements which can lead towards a modern interpretation.

Women are becoming individuated through mirroring themselves increasingly accurately and fully, and through finding more comprehensive mirrors. As the critic Harold Bloom has said in another context, perhaps the most important aspect of being fully human is a person's ability to contemplate himself or herself objectively. By looking clearly at themselves, humans can change and so "beget what they yet will be" (1989, p. 54).

Chapter Six: The Passion of Unlived Life

The Animus and Anima — Part One

> In considering the anima and animus, we must always keep in mind that these figures stem from a very deep source in the unconscious and are only partly available to consciousness. In addition to being parts of the personality, they partake of the nature of the archetypes. Jung has called them border phenomena, standing at the junction of the personal and collective unconscious. We can describe them only to the extent that they are manifested in consciousness; we cannot delimit them completely; and so we are dependent, as we really are in all psychological investigation, on empirical data.
>
> M. Esther Harding, *The 'I' and the 'Not I'*

An archetype, as Jung has characterized it, is not representable but is a primordial, unchanging pattern, "instinct" or motif that rests in the collective unconscious. It is a predisposition, propensity, and readiness toward a certain expression in image, affect, and action rather than the concrete form itself. Images of the archetypes have appeared in differing socio-cultural forms throughout history in myths, religions, dreams, art, visions, legends, fairy tales, and certain basic behavioral patterns.

The outward form of the anima and animus archetypes, attitudes toward them, and descriptions of them have probably generated more response and more controversy than any other of Jung's formulations. It is important to note that though the archetype itself does not change, its manifestations conform to custom, attitude, and circumstance and are modified accordingly. This makes them both very much alive and subject to various interpretations. Those who adhere strictly to Jung's definitions of the animus and anima archetypes may be falling into a concretistic mistake that departs from the spirit of his work, while those who seek to dismiss the whole subject miss out on a potentially accessible and fertile way for Jungians to contribute to the turbulent realm of sex-role and gender studies, and the relationship between men and women. Jung's subtle, ambivalent, and exciting paradigm is endlessly evocative, providing mirrors within mirrors to reflect our own sense of our masculine and feminine selves, yet what he has written about the animus, especially, alienates many readers. It is as if his general idea strikes one with its intrinsic rightness, but the details mislead and repel.

Since there has been so much written about the anima and animus, these chapters will concentrate only on those analysts who have significantly added to, elaborated on, or modified Jung's initial observations. The writers I will be discussing portray the animus and anima as archetypes, as structures of the psyche, as dynamic processes, and as crucial factors in individuation and in treatment. Analysts sometimes fail to distinguish which aspect they are delineating. This results in some confusion and makes a clear, chronological picture of the development of these concepts particularly difficult. I will attempt to point to the differences between content and process issues as they occur.

Emma Jung was the first to strongly rework, elaborate, and expand on C. G. Jung's descriptions of the animus; her work appears in a paper, "On the Nature of the Animus" read before the Psychological Club of Zürich in November of 1931. In both that paper and "The Anima as an Elemental Being" (1955/1981), she portrays the development of positive and negative animus and anima figures. In contrast to C. G. Jung, who seemed to consider the animus with no little aversion, Emma Jung's more balanced perspective serves as counterpoint and corrective. As I mentioned in Chapter Three, in later editions of his work Jung refers to and recommends her work for its valuable amplification and addition to the original concept.

Emma Jung emphasizes the way the three factors behind the manifestation of the animus and anima — latent contrasexual characteristics, the individual's experience of representatives of the opposite sex, and the socio-cultural image of man or woman — all coalesce into a psychic entity which affects process. The anima or animus

> behaves as if it were a law unto itself, interfering with the life of the individual as if it were an alien element; sometimes the interference is helpful, sometimes disturbing, if not actually destructive. (1981, p. 2)

Her purpose, she says, is to understand and demonstrate the ways in which the archetype "appears in relation to the individual and to consciousness" (p. 2). She, like Jung, defines the animus as representing Logos, "the quintessence of the masculine principle" (p. 3). She graphically portrays this Logos as it progresses dynamically through stages dependent on a woman's psychological developmental level and natural talents. The animus first appears in forms representing primitive physical power; these evolve into an animus of deeds. Words and ideas become the central motif and attraction in the third stage; in its most developed state, the animus personifies and incorporates a woman's search for spiritual meaning. Emma Jung draws attention to the helpfulness and potency in the figures of each stage, without neglecting the negative sides so emphasized by her husband. She concludes that the earlier two phases of animus development (power and deed) were integrated by most women in the culture of her day; the stages of word and spirit, however, still prove troublesome because of women's relatively new extension of consciousness. This new consciousness in women derives, she feels, from energy released spiritually by the loss of the patriarchal church's power, and biologically by women's release from constant childbearing and manual labor. Women's rise in consciousness joins with the general widening of consciousness to suit what Emma Jung describes as *kairos,* the right moment for it. The animus and this greater energy and awareness interact so that

> if woman does not meet adequately the demand for consciousness or intellectual activity, the animus becomes autonomous and negative, and works destructively on the individual herself and in her relation to other people. This fact can be explained as follows: if the possibility of spiritual functioning is not taken up by the conscious mind, the psychic energy intended for it falls into the unconscious and there activates the archetype of the animus. Possessed of the energy that has flowed back into the unconscious, the animus figure becomes autonomous, so powerful, indeed, that it can overwhelm the conscious ego, and thus finally dominate the whole personality. (p. 6)

Emma Jung finds that development necessitates understanding and integrating the animus. Integration demands the withdrawal of a woman's projection of her own potential onto men, her involvement in useful and creative work, and, finally, the recovery and development of her own strong sense of the inner feminine. Two intertwined problems make all of this very difficult. The first problem is still a compelling one: "this now superannuated veneration of men, this overvaluation of the masculine" (p. 24). This induces a woman to relinquish her own power as well as other vital aspects of herself. Instead of a woman claiming this power as her own, she surrenders to an idealized masculine or to her animus. The second problem, more prevalent in Emma Jung's generation, was a woman's relatively constricted or sheltered life and generally limited education and opportunities—all of which resulted in lack of experience, whether in thinking for herself or acting in the world at large (see Virginia Woolf's *A Room of One's Own* [1929/1957] for a crucial and darker view of the consequences of these same constrictions). The search for and reclamation of the feminine, Emma Jung believes, will also liberate the masculine so that both can become conscious parts of a woman's personality.

> What is really necessary is that feminine intellectuality, logos in woman, should be so fitted into the nature and life of woman that a harmonious cooperation between the feminine and masculine factors ensues and no part is condemned to a shadowy existence. (p. 13)

Emma Jung makes further important contributions to the theory and understanding of the animus. She finds the animus's propensity to overwhelm the feminine a cause of the prevalence of depression in women, while it also excells in separating woman from relationship. In Emma Jung's view, the animus is more prone to wishful or magical thinking than to realistic thinking. She seems to describe from the inside, the way the negative animus can involve a woman in recurrent compulsive brooding that can become a form of self-torture. However, when differentiated, discriminated and given a subordinate role, the animus can turn into a familiar, a servant, a teacher, and a guide who "initiates and guides the soul's transformation" (p. 33). She states that integrating the animus within the psyche has an unexpected positive effect opening a woman to relationship with the feminine and with other women.

> I have had occasion to observe that as the animus problem became acute, many women began to show an increased interest in other women, the relationship to women being felt as an ever-growing need, even a necessity. Perhaps this may be the beginning of a feminine solidarity, heretofore wanting, which becomes possible now only through our growing awareness of a danger threatening us all. Learning to cherish and emphasize feminine values is the primary condition of our holding our own against the masculine principle which is mighty in a double sense—both within the psyche and without. (pp. 41-42)

Emma Jung's theory of the animus includes a conception of animus development through power, deed, word, and spirit stages; seeing the animus as mediator to women's access to energy and opportunity; and an emphasis on culture as well as on a woman's particular psychology.

Emma Jung's work on the anima, though felicitous, lacks the passion and urgency that underlies her writing on the animus; she is clearly less personally involved. She elaborates on a particular manifestation of the anima: the nature spirits of nixies, fairies, swan maidens, mermaids, and nymphs of legends, myths, and fairy tales. In the process she finds these to be *multiple* figures, disagreeing with Jung's idea of the anima as a specifically single figure. She describes the anima as erotic, irrational, receptive yet elusive; the anima has a gift for magic, prophecy and second sight, and is both close to the unconscious and close to nature. These anima qualities manifest themselves in a man in a positive or negative way depending on his attitude and actions. The anima often requires capture, rescue, or redemption by him. Emma Jung finds that the task of integrating the anima is quite different from integrating the animus. Integrating the anima requires an abasement toward the demeaned feminine, which most men perhaps consider an inferior part of themselves. The integration of the anima therefore requires man's humility, service, and possibly even a voluntary lowering of his consciousness. Emma Jung ends her book with a startlingly contemporary statement:

> When the anima is recognized and integrated a change of attitude occurs toward the feminine generally. This new evaluation of the feminine principle brings with it a due reverence for nature, too; whereas the intellectual viewpoint dominant in an era of science and technology leads to utilizing and even exploiting nature, rather than honoring her. . . . In our time, when such threatening forces of cleavage are at work, splitting peoples, individuals and atoms, it is doubly necessary that those which unite and hold together should become effective; for life is founded upon the harmonious interplay of masculine and feminine forces, within the individual human being as well as without. Bringing these opposites into union is one of the most important tasks of present-day psychotherapy. (p. 87)

Esther Harding, in two articles in *Spring,* "She: A Portrait of the Anima" (1946) and "Anima and Animus" (1952), further develops these concepts, both in their manifestations and in their process. The first article is an example of what was to become a common form in Jungian studies: the retelling and amplification of a single story or dream for its analogies and relevance to one or more aspects of analytical psychology. It may have derived from Jung's Zürich seminars, which tended to follow this form. Harding interprets the novel *She* by Rider Haggard as a case of a man possessed by his anima and as an example of the failure of anima differentiation by a man with a markedly undeveloped feeling side. The novel depicts a negative, powerful, alluring, and despotic anima figure who is ultimately destructive and is herself destroyed. Harding scans the story for examples of the characters' attempts at differentiation from and union with the anima—and for all the ways this process goes astray. "The ever-recurrent problem," Harding concludes, "is, how can man so relate himself to life that this energy shall be reviving and reinvigorating, instead of destroying?" (1946, p. 73).

Harding focuses on a typical failing of men in her time. She states that the men in the book have lost all contact with the Eros principle, which therefore remains unconscious: the bitter result is an unbalanced relationship between the sexes. In an incisive statement, Harding sums up the consequences; her tone seems redolent of years spent (whether in the consulting room or out) dealing with the misery caused by this unbalance and man's lack of Eros, where:

> no commitment is made, no interchange on a human level or in the realm of ideas is possible, and no sharing of life is expected of the man; the woman does all the adapting; she gives up her former way of life without expecting or receiving any guarantee of his faithfulness or of receiving a place in his future plans. This represents the Victorian man's idea of love! (p. 78)

Harding (1952) incorporates anima and animus stages in a developmental theory which will be discussed more fully in Chapter Nine. A woman, she states, starts as a psychologically undifferentiated anima-woman living a primarily unconscious life. In this stage she holds and embodies a man's projections rather than living her own life. The animus only starts to develop in the second stage. Like Emma Jung and in contrast to Jung, Harding emphasizes the animus' positive and integrative aspects.

Harding's contribution to theory, besides her further elaboration of positive animus figures, is the division of animus and anima identification into two types: active and passive. She states that the passive type is common in people who have developed neither a satisfactory ego nor a persona. She calls the passive type an animus-man or anima-woman;

both exist, however unconsciously, in reference to another: the animus-man through relating to women's projections or to the feminine side of men, and the anima-woman acting primarily in response to men or in order to attract them. Active identification with the animus, by contrast, produces in women "mannish" activity, opinions, and mannerisms, but also can result in hard and creative work in the business and professional world. A man's active identification with the anima in turn produces "effeminacy," moods, and a type of sensitivity and artistic creativity which rests on aesthetic and emotional value judgments. Harding notes that people progressing from the passive to the active stage do not necessarily show much growth of personality; in both stages, however, the anima/animus are contaminated in different ways with shadow qualities. Harding finds that differentiation of the animus/anima from this shadow contamination and integration of the shadow aspect of the unconscious itself are profound moral as well as psychological problems. With better integration and the proper relation to the animus/anima archetypes, she sees a change in the forms of their manifestations; images that depict increasingly wiser and more helpful figures make their appearance and actively assist the individual. Harding concludes that a developed anima or animus mediates, interprets, and differentiates experience dynamically within the psyche.

In a 1965 book for a popular audience, *The 'I' and the 'Not I',* Harding adds a great deal to the practical and theoretical understanding of the animus and anima. She describes both as soul-figures and, in an important statement that solves a logical inconsistency in Jung's original formulation, states that both anima and animus appear as multiple figures in people who are immature, but become more unitary, even single, as people develop. Thus she finds the animus can exist within the psyche as a single figure as well as the multiple figures Jung most often envisioned.

Harding emphasizes the practical effects the animus and anima exert within a relationship. The positive aspects of projection of the animus or anima help in transforming, developing, and maturing the psyche, because "in actual life, the anima and animus start to 'live into' the conscious situation instead of remaining merely possibilities in the unconscious" (1965, p. 117). She states that the animus and anima are attracted by the combustible, energy-filled, or troublesome spots within a relationship; even though painful, this can be beneficial to the relationship when it is consciously mediated. In contrast, the negative aspects of projection cause tyrannical demands on the other, irritation, reproaches, and quarrels which can drive a couple apart.

Harding perceptively delineates the negative effects the anima can have on relationship (perhaps compensating for Jung's emphasis on the negative animus). What she described in 1965 is current and pertinent today, and is for a woman perhaps the negative anima's most menacing and troublesome aspect: the capacity the negative anima has for separating a man from the woman to whom he is attracted. Harding demonstrates the way this negative anima demands that a man only accept part of a woman — that part which reflects his own anima; whatever else belongs to the woman, but deviates from the anima, is ignored, despised, or hated, the woman herself becoming a threat. The negative anima also causes moods, "subtle dishonesty, unreliability, and autoeroticism" (p. 111). This is especially so when a man has not developed a sufficiently masculine stance; then the anima suffuses him with resentment and rage accompanied by feelings of helplessness, yet fantastically effortless entitlement. The woman, in this case, is caught in the middle and has hell to pay; she often defends herself from what feels like a killing attack by letting her negative animus unsheathe its sword and take over the fight. More positively, and when both people in the relationship have become more psychologically developed, Harding also describes the animus' and anima's contribution to the alchemical *coniunctio:* here the two outer "I's" and inner "not-I's" reach a corresponding and constructive union.

Harding gives animus and anima qualities a dramatic and convincing depiction. Her original contribution to theory lies in her delineation of active and passive stages in animus/anima development, in relating the multiplicity or singleness of the figure to the level of an individual's integration, and, finally, in her graphic analysis of the animus/anima's — especially the negative anima's — effect on relationship.

Elizabeth Howes, in an unpublished series of lectures on the animus given in San Francisco in the nineteen-forties, presents a synopsis of Emma Jung's Zürich seminars and then adds her own ideas. She stresses the extent to which individual experience modifies the various manifestations of the archetype, as well as the importance of biological contrasexuality. She notes that women need the animus not only to become conscious of their own Logos qualities, but to contact Eros qualities as well. Howes is the first analyst to make the important link between function type and the form the animus takes. She concludes that women in the nineteen-forties were moving away from the animus-dominated stage described by Jung, in which the negative animus acted predominantly in a critical, undermining way or as a repressive censor, and toward a more positive, creative, and innovative stage in which the animus actively assists the ego as inner analyst, guide, shepherd, messenger, king, and hero. It is a loss that this innovative and perceptive work remains unpublished.

Linda Fierz-David follows Harding's pattern of exploring masculine anima development through the amplification of an ancient story. Her *Dream of Poliphilo* (1950/1987) is a carefully worked out description in mythological terms of the process of individuation and of the development of the anima. This uniting of modern analytical developmental psychology with ancient myth has played an ever-increasing role in the Jungian elaboration of psychological motifs from Jung's time to the present. Fierz-David makes use of it here to focus on the psychological importance of a man's proper and balanced attitude toward the feminine within himself. Such an attitude allows the anima to develop in a positive and helpful way. Like Emma Jung, she traces this development through stages of increasing sophistication.

Barbara Hannah's (1948, 1951/1962, 1957, and 1971/1989) views of the animus remain constant and close to Jung's original formulation. A lecture, "The Problem of Women's Plots" (1948), contains Hannah's best and almost forgotten work on the animus (I thank Barbara Koltuv for drawing my attention to this paper). It is one of the strongest and most useful depictions of the ways in which laziness, unconsciousness, and the negative animus conspire to undermine a woman. In a brilliant analysis of a contemporary book, Hannah explicates a profoundly troubling element in a woman's psyche—the way in which a woman can compartmentalize so that she allows the negative animus to plot against her, letting herself fall victim to the devastation schemed by him. This comes about, Hannah says, when a woman who lacks self-esteem and grounding in a conscious sense of the feminine self allows the negative animus to become encapsulated within one compartment of her consciousness, almost, but not quite, sealed off from consciousness. Hannah emphasizes that the woman knows, in one compartment of her psyche, exactly what is going on, yet overtly and at the same time shuts this knowledge off so that she acts as if the rest of her doesn't know; part of her thus colludes with the negative animus in plotting her own destruction. The film *Looking For Mr. Goodbar* could be analyzed for the same menacing process today; it is a flagrant example of the negative animus festering and plotting in its own split-off place, but always aided by the woman's anger and her low opinion of her own worth. This is a destructive process that reveals itself again and again to a therapist alerted to it by Hannah's crucial, valuable, and mostly forgotten paper.

In *The Problem of Contact with the Animus* (1951/1962), Hannah describes the animus as neither good nor bad but potentially double — capable of both. She states that the positive and negative attributes of the animus derive mainly from shadow contamination and that the general negativity of the animus is a cultural problem rather than a specifically personal one. With this link to culture, Hannah frees women from the onerous sense of personal guilt and responsibility that accompanied Jung's formulations. Hannah describes "having it out with the animus" (1971/1989, pp. 24-25) as a necessity, the first step in this fight being the differentiation of the animus from the shadow. She stresses the manifestations of the negative animus and calls it "the blamer."

> Although there are exceptions, most women — when they have experienced the reality of the animus beyond all doubt — feel exceedingly negatively towards him. He is apparently forever thwarting our intentions, spoiling our relationships, replacing our sound instincts and feelings by a mere collection of opinions and altogether preventing us from living our lives naturally as women. (1951/1962, p. 21)

Hannah makes several suggestions to help women develop a more positive animus. She promotes active imagination as the best method to differentiate the animus from shadow, to come to terms with the animus, and to both listen to the animus and to inform it; she also advocates using feeling and love (and tears) in this dialogue. Without this work, she feels that the animus takes over and fills any vacuum left by the woman's own lack of consciousness.

In Hannah's 1957 article and 1971/1989 book, she explores positive and negative animus figures in fiction. She uses the work of R. L. Stevenson, Mary Webb, and the Brontë sisters to give examples of a great number of positive and negative animus figures. (Her analysis of Heathcliff as an animus figure is perhaps the most formed. Like her 1948 paper, it is another valuable elucidation of the psychological complexity of one type of animus figure and of women's attraction to it.) The Brontës' lives and work are also examined in terms of anima/animus conflicts, with Hannah considering what can be learned through them about various problems of feminine identity and of women's rapprochement with the animus.

Renée Brand (1952), in an article on Neumann's "The Moon and Matriarchal Consciousness," suggests that all of a woman's thinking is done by her animus. She follows Jung's interpretation of the animus, except that she sees some developmental process behind negative animus manifestations. She finds the negative animus to be "not a natural feminine function, but a misdirected . . . attempt at survival, a cultural achievement" (p. 42).

Irene de Castillejo first published a short article on positive aspects of the animus in 1955 entitled "The Animus: Friend or Foe?" She credits Hannah's 1951 article as helping to turn the tide toward a better understanding of the negative animus through stressing the animus's collective and impersonal nature. In this way, the undifferentiated negative animus stops being looked upon as a woman's personal disgrace. It became, in de Castillejo's words, "not your devil, not my devil, but *the* Devil" (p. 1).

De Castillejo argues that the animus is far more complex than Jung described. She separates the animus into three essentially different manifestations: the aggressive animus; the belittling imp animus; and the helpful animus. The characteristics of the animus "can and should be changed" (p. 16) and enlightened actively by a woman through honest and sincere dialogue (a process Barbara Hannah also stressed). This dialogue serves to inform the animus about a woman's feminine perception and individual stance; it also assists a woman in seeing that she does not have to be subject to its tyranny. Given an appropriately subordinate position and the data it needs in order to be helpful, the animus can become a positive inner force which helps a woman clarify and stand up for her own values and feelings. De Castillejo calls the helpful animus "a torchbearer" who is able to focus, analyze, and discriminate, providing the focused consciousness to balance what de Castillejo, following Jung, describes as women's diffuse consciousness. As I mentioned in the last chapter, de Castillejo is one of the few Jungians to believe that thinking can be a normal, healthy woman's primary function and need not be equated with the animus nor with what she terms masculine focused consciousness.

De Castillejo follows Harding and Hannah in emphasizing the sociocultural determinants behind the negative animus. In *Knowing Woman* (1973), she points out that men's fear of women and men's hatred

of the feminine within themselves have become internalized by women
and are the source of the negative animus's most pernicious and subtle
voice—a voice which constantly attacks any feeling of self-worth.

> In the unconscious of men, the appearance of the amazon is still both
> feared and hated. I can find no other explanation for the persistence of
> the inner voice in every woman I have ever met which dins into her ears
> the words, "You are no good!" I believe this is her negative animus pick-
> ing up man's collective unconscious fear of woman's rivalry, and his pas-
> sionate desire to keep her in her place. If men could become more
> conscious of their inner disdain, women might become less aggressive
> in self-defence against this insidious unconscious erosion. (p. 66)

De Castillejo states that through integration the animus helps a woman
live more independently and become more conscious. This poses a difficult and perhaps insurmountable paradox in de Castillejo's work, since
she defines woman as needing an essential contact with the unconscious
not only for herself but for the benefit of men. She believes that a woman
needs to take on a role which seems to me more appropriate to man's
anima; she states that "woman. . . . knows her role to be, as it always
has been, mediator of the unconscious to man. Through her he finds
his soul" (1955, p. 11). It is this sort of statement of de Castillejo's which
makes her such a transitional figure. She goes far in her understanding
of women, argues decisively to free women from some of the more limited
aspects of Jungian tradition, yet restricts them to others, such as being
the embodiment of relatedness and the mediator through whom a man
can advance his own individuation. De Castillejo does state that the soul-
image for a woman is a woman, not her animus, and argues for the withdrawal of a woman's projections of the animus onto men. Yet she doesn't
take the next step: that a woman's priority is to herself, not to her mediating role for men, and that men too must withdraw their projections
from women and search within themselves for their souls.

In *The Father Archetype in Feminine Psychology* (1955/1985), Amy
Allenby continues the emphasis on those positive aspects of the animus
that she has observed clinically in patients' dreams. She finds that the
animus, in its most developed form, presides over and unifies the opposites. She makes an urgent plea for the need to study women's psychology for its own sake and in order to better understand the animus.
Historically, she says, it "is a comparatively recent development of analytical psychology to study the feminine psyche as such rather than treat
it as a variation of the human average which is typical of both sexes"

(p. 135). Allenby mentions the contributions of Harding, Wolff, and Neumann in this respect. She is the first woman to examine in depth the role of individual negative father-daughter relationships in producing the traditional negative stereotype of the animus. Allenby concludes that "in my opinion an excessive attachment to the father commits a woman, perhaps for life, to the impersonal—though the specific nature of this committment depends on her personal psychology" (p. 151).

Florida Scott-Maxwell (1957) portrays the animus and anima as reflections of the cultural moment Emma Jung found so significant. Scott-Maxwell sees the present time as reflecting an especially painful quandary for women, in which the animus mirrors a woman's own confusion over whether or not she has the right to exist in and of herself. She finds modern women split by their new roles and new demands. "The less a woman recognizes and honors her masculine side the more primitive it is" (p. 38); however, when the masculine is more developed, then the animus tends to take over and women copy masculine nature, losing contact with their own. Scott-Maxwell considers women in general to be more differentiated than men because they no longer want "men to live their masculinity for them" (p. 33), while men still expect women to live men's femininity. This causes the average man's anima to be far less developed than the woman's animus, and often to appear infantile and mother-bound. Scott-Maxwell acutely observes that men's continued anima projection exerts a regressive and limiting effect both on themselves and on the women on whom they project, while women's integration of the animus causes a positive and unsettling advance.

> [Women's] craving for differentiation is both creative and destructive, and will take a long time to satisfy, for the masculine side of women has the passion of unlived life, and it has the numinous quality of the unknown. It fascinates. . . . The change that is taking place in women naturally disturbs everyone. At present men are almost as much at sea about it as women are. Men can feel they have a natural right to something that is being taken from them. (p. 73)

Marie-Louise von Franz investigates aspects of the animus and anima as part of her 1958-1959 series of lectures on the feminine in fairy tales. Her work (1958-1959/1976, 1958-1959/1980a) uses fairy tales as a source of exploration of the feminine and feminine development in the psychology of women. In these books and in *Puer Aeternus* (1971/1981), von Franz is also concerned with feminine development as it manifests itself in male anima development. According to her, "feminine figures in fairy tales are neither the pattern of the anima nor of the real woman, but of both, because sometimes it is one, and sometimes another" (1976, p. 3). Von Franz (1976) uses eight of Grimm's stories, some as familiar as Snow White and Cinderella, others as little known as the Beautiful Wassilessa, to outline the process of feminine psychological development. In all her books von Franz stresses the negative; she explains that this is an area which demands psychological work, in particular the confrontation with what she calls "the nastiness" of animus/anima manifestations. Von Franz also points to the role hurt feelings may play as the predecessors of "animus attacks" (where the woman is taken over by the animus and it speaks through her in an unintegrated and unmediated way), as well as "animus attacks" as disguised and conflicted appeals for love. Von Franz examines the process through which a father passes his anima problem onto his daughter, who then has to deal with the consequences of her father's anima projection as well as her own animus problems.

In her chapter in *Man and his Symbols* (Jung, 1964), von Franz reviews Jung's ideas about the animus and anima. Her own contribution is her emphasis on the power complex as especially potent within the negative animus; she describes how this animus acts upon the ego to produce "brutality, recklessness, empty talk, [and] silent, obstinate, evil ideas" (p. 203), endless ruminations, "a web of calculating thoughts, filled with malice and intrigue" (p. 202), as well as its serving as a cocoon for the desires and judgments with which it fills the ego. Von Franz adopts Emma Jung's four process-stages of animus development (physical power, initiative, word, and spirit/meaning). For von Franz, the positive animus provides "the masculine qualities of initiative, courage, objectivity, and spiritual wisdom" (p. 206). It serves as a bridge to the unconscious, helps creative activity, and is redeemable through love and attention. However, like Jung, she focuses on the benefit of this to men because "the creative boldness of the positive animus at times expresses thoughts and ideas that stimulate men to new experience" (p. 207). She equates the animus with women's thinking and the anima with most of what goes into men's feeling:

> The anima is the personification of all feminine psychological tendencies in a man's psyche, such as vague feelings and moods, prophetic hunches, receptiveness to the irrational, capacity for personal love, feeling for nature, and—last but not least—his relation to the unconscious. (p. 186)

Von Franz emphasizes the decisive effect of the mother on the anima; she finds that the form in which the anima manifests itself is largely dependent on the character of the man's mother. If she is a highly negative figure for instance, the anima may produce an equally negative voice which demoralizes him (in what seems to me a strikingly similar but moodier way than a woman's negative animus) through reiterating, "I am nothing. Nothing makes any sense. With others it's different, but for me . . . I enjoy nothing" (p. 187). Von Franz points out that negative experiences of the mother can cause a man's anima moods, dullness, fear of disease, impotence, accidents, sense of oppression, or can make him bitchy, waspish, venomous, and devaluing. If the man has a positive experience of his mother the anima isn't much improved. According to von Franz, the anima then will be "effeminate," touchy, sentimental, over-sensitive, and/or may trick the man into arid intellectualism. The anima is most often discernible in man's erotic fantasies and through his experience of love, both of which von Franz ascribes to the man's anima (and thus to his unconscious) rather than allowing them to belong to the man himself. This idea about the anima leads to no little confusion. For instance, it is the anima through which a man experiences love, yet it is also the anima who jealously guards him from that very experience and makes him unconscious of love.

Von Franz follows Emma Jung in describing the positive anima as it progresses through four stages, ultimately developing into a mediator and guide. The best way to achieve this development, von Franz concurs with Hannah and de Castillejo, is through therapy, the use of active imagination, and through a man taking his feelings and fantasies seriously. In a 1974 lecture, "Jung and Society" (published in 1986), von Franz includes a further listing of the negative behavioral manifestations of unconscious anima and animus possession. She concludes that after the anima and animus are more integrated into consciousness, people get on much better with the opposite sex.

Though her work on negative aspects of the animus and anima adds much to the literature on the subject and though she has written extensively and cogently on anima development, von Franz seems closest to Jung in her generally negative tone — it is almost as if she has inherited her spiritual father, Jung's, anima problems with the feminine and with women, and uses an even more brutally judgmental negativity than his when dealing with the negative animus. Reading her work may be salubrious in drying out the too moist anima and searing an intransigent and brutal animus, but one longs for the empathic affection for women and a quality of mercy for and optimism about the belabored animus that marks the work of Emma Jung, Harding, and de Castillejo.

Cornelia Bruner wrote a classic study of the development of the anima in the dreams of one patient, *The Anima as Fate* (1963/1986). She compares the course of development of the anima in the work and life of Rider Haggard with that seen in the dreams of a middle-aged physician. Besides providing a sensitive dream analysis, the author clarifies the connection between the gradual development of her patient's inner anima figure and his outer signs of growth. Bruner's attitude toward the anima is open and not pinned on prior descriptions or to conventional function type. For instance, she portrays her male patient as an extraverted intuitive feeling type and traces his reunion, through the development of his anima, with both his animal instinct and toward a more consciously spiritual (and logos-enhancing) attitude. The initial (undeveloped) anima images are plural; they are of multiple goddesses and nixies, who are slowly transformed into a single companioning and mothering figure as the patient himself matures and becomes able to show "a capacity for human relatedness within the concrete world" (p. 262). Bruner's clinical example helps validate Harding's paradigm.

Hilde Binswanger (1963, 1965 and 1975) elaborates traditional Jungian theory more optimistically and positively than Hannah and von Franz. Her 1963 article, "Positive Aspects of the Animus," contains important new thinking both about women and the animus. Binswanger is most interested in what the animus means "subjectively, in the inner experience of a woman" (1963, p. 83), and what the animus might have been like before its cultural transformation into its generally negative form. She is concerned with the reasons why the animus became a negative manifestation in the first place. She remarks on the preponderance of negative animus figures that appear in dreams in the initial stages of a woman's analysis, and cheers the gradual change that ensues as analysis progresses, the destructive figures transforming into positive and helpful ones.

Binswanger makes a significant differentiation between two components of the masculine she finds within a woman: one is the animus who is a manifestation of the woman's inner images of men; the other is a woman's own naturally masculine side, which Binswanger takes to be not only biological but also to include a woman's understanding and her consciousness. She links this understanding and consciousness to

Eros rather than Logos. She proposes that these two, the animus and woman's masculine side, may follow a process of opposition and counteract each other. A woman at first struggles to resolve the contradiction of the two aspects by projecting both her inner images of men and her masculine side onto someone in the outside world, or else either the animus or her masculine side tends to turn negative and oppressive within the woman's own psyche. The goal of therapy involves integration of both these aspects together. In a strong reworking of Jungian theory, Binswanger questions its basic limitations of the feminine and of women; this comes after she reviews Emma Jung's process-stages of animus vigor, action, word, and meaning as adequate representations of masculinity, but then asks:

> Are they exclusively and fundamentally linked to it? Are these not really common or central human qualities which have been attributed (or projected) to the masculine because men were the first to differentiate them in their own minds and so give them a typical masculine slant? Could it not be that . . . as women also develop their minds and become conscious of their own special qualities, there might develop a specifically masculine and specifically feminine vigor, a masculine and feminine word, masculine and feminine action and masculine and feminine meaning? (1963, p. 87)

Binswanger, the precursor of later Jungian feminists, answers her questions with a strong affirmative which had to wait over twenty years to be reenunciated, and then as if for the first time. Her feminist tone can be seen in her plea for a reevaluation of the animus based on a better understanding of the masculine and feminine, and her view of negative animus manifestations as being a consequence of the devaluation of self, and the feminine, and the over-valuation of the masculine by individual women and the culture at large. She describes the way the animus within individual women echoes and apes male values; it devalues the feminine in the same way men and society devalue it. This animus echoing and devaluation, becoming tyrannical and annoyingly superior, overwhelms the ego and consistently denigrates women. In contrast, Binswanger requires women to integrate so-called masculine values within their own psyches while maintaining and cherishing their own feminine qualities. In order to be able to do this, women need to develop a strong, friendly animus who can help uphold and assist women's own creativity, activity, strength, and vigor as well as give them a more disinterested perspective. With this accomplished, she believes women will be more integrated and human, both more feminine and more masculine; the animus providing moral as well as spiritual support.

Along with Emma Jung and de Castillejo, Binswanger perceives the culture-boundedness and mutability of the many qualities attributed to men and women and to the masculine and feminine. Other qualities, though, she finds more constant. These she examines at length for their biological antecedents, primarily in analogy to the different characteristics of sperm and ovum. In her 1965 article, "Ego, Animus and Persona," Binswanger continues her positive evaluation of the animus, but here is specifically concerned with the animus's contamination with shadow and with persona, "the animus climbing the steps of the persona" (1965, p. 5) to take over the personality and block growth. To counteract this contamination and separate the animus from both shadow and persona, Binswanger points to the value and assistance offered through a developed and friendly animus and through a woman realizing her own value as a woman.

The development of the feminine with the aid of an integrated animus is the subject of her 1975 address, which recapitulates her earlier work; she concludes (as Howes did before her in the nineteen-forties and Hinkle in the twenties) that the era of over-valuation of the masculine is past, the feminine once again coming into its own. With this new valuation of the feminine, she finds that the animus loses much of the negativity it manifested in Jung's time and takes on increasingly positive forms.

Binswanger's work on the animus is comprehensive and dynamic, yet seems to be all but forgotten. Her major contribution to theory, besides her actively supportive, therapeutic, and feminist stance, is her separation of the animus from a woman's own masculine nature, and her linkage between persona and animus. Her idea of specifically masculine and specifically feminine forms of vigor, action, word, and meaning is both bold and persuasive. Jungians in general lag far behind her and are only now catching up; no one has yet provided the fleshing out and practical interpretation of what this precursor envisioned.

Vera von der Heydt's (1964) pamphlet *On the Animus*, although it follows Binswanger's initial work on the subject by two years, could have been written at the time of Jung's initial development of the theory. It reiterates Jung's statements, but includes Emma Jung's emphasis on animus as spirit. Von der Heydt recapitulates Binswanger's biological analogies (without giving her credit), but makes these absolute. Without mentioning Binswanger, the pamphlet seems to be a systematic refutation of her ideas. In direct contrast to Binswanger, von der Heydt remains convinced that outer and inner masculine and feminine exist as fixed, complementary or warring opposites, always in tension with each other. She reverts to Jung's opinion that the anima is single while the animus has plural manifestations; she finds this especially true in dreams. Von der Heydt does note some changes in the status and condition of women in the outside world since Jung's day, but she says that these changes have not and will not reach the more conservative psyche. She concludes that culture may affect style, but that "essentially the animus problem is bound to remain the same at all times though it may appear in different forms" (p. 17). She seems unaware that growth, development, or change in sex-roles or gender relations might increase harmony between the sexes, or that animus problems might be mirrors to and reflections of changing attitudes toward the feminine and women.

In an unpublished paper, "Depression in Women" (1968), William Alex considers the animus' role in depression. He does not mention Emma Jung's prior work on the connection between depression and the negative animus, but reaches the same conclusion. He also connects depression with an essential stage in Neumann's theory of feminine development, finding it a developmental consequence of a woman's patriarchally impaired or traumatized childhood, during which the archetypal image of the parent has itself been injured. The result is a malfunctioning animus image which gains power over a deprived, weakened, or structurally deficient ego; its tyranny grinds the individual down both with its power drive and its criticisms—depression ensues.

This formulation is remarkably consistent with Seligman's (1975) theory of learned helplessness, in which successive injuries, especially to self-esteem and self-efficacy, create vulnerability to new forms of victimization and to depression. In Alex's Jungian terms, the negative animus is the tyrant who victimizes the patriarchally weakened feminine ego, with depression as the result. This is another place where Jungian theory is in step with and can significantly add to current theorizing about the psychology of women.

E. C. Whitmont (1969/1978) describes his book *The Symbolic Quest* as an "attempt to present a systematic survey of the theory and practice of analytical psychology" (p. ix). He devotes about forty-five pages, roughly fifteen percent of his book, to the subject of the psychological differences between the masculine and the feminine. He has three chapters

on this: one on the male and female, one on the animus, and the third
on the anima. His chapters on the animus and anima are based on the
definitions of masculinity and femininity explored in my previous chapter.
He radically reevaluates these in his more current thinking (1980 and
1982a), which I will discuss with other work of the nineteen-eighties.
Whitmont's initial definition is that

> anima and animus are the archetypes of what for either sex is the *totally
> other.* Each represents a world that is at first quite incomprehensible to
> its opposite, a world which never can be directly known. Even though
> we carry within us elements of the opposite sex, their field of expression
> is precisely that area which is most obscure, strange, irrational and fear-
> inspiring to us; it can best be intuited and "felt-out" but never completely
> understood. (1969/1978, p. 185)

Whitmont equates the animus with Yang qualities and the anima
with Yin. He differentiates both from the shadow, the shadow typifying repressed personal characteristics, while the animus and anima "personify the *general* human *a priori* unconscious instinct patterns upon
which many of these personal characteristics are based" (p. 185). Each
individual manifests a different form of the animus and anima which
acts like a different, individual sub-personality.

In discussing the two archetypes of animus and anima, Whitmont
makes useful distinctions between the world of each, its numinous image, its behavioral pattern or manifestation, and its pattern of emotion.
He explores many varying archetypes of the masculine and feminine as
essential for the understanding of the animus and anima. Identity with,
inflation from, and projection of the animus and anima are all discussed
as problems in the process of their assimilation. Relationship to the opposite sex is seen almost invariably, at least initially, as a case of animus
or anima projection.

The animus at first tends to appear negatively, as rigid and dogmatic. Whitmont describes its statements and actions as based upon an error in the judging process itself. He quotes Jung regarding the animus'
negative manifestations, then traces the animus' dependence on influential men in a woman's life. Whitmont considers the integration of the
animus the major task in woman's individuation process. This integration requires "consciously active initiative" (p. 213), and the development of discrimination, clarity, independence, responsibility, rationality,
and the capacity to endure tension. As with Jung, Hannah, von Franz,
and de Castillejo, the objectification of the animus through active im-

agination is stressed as a way of solidifying animus images into actual figures within the psyche with whom a woman can converse. Whitmont considers the ability to actively question the animus as if it were a real person, and the ability to ask it the right questions, as key elements in its integration.

Whitmont observes that the anima, as well as the animus, occurs in multiple forms. The anima is most often split between a dual virgin and whore archetype, though she also appears in combinations he names after Wolff's feminine types. By including so many aspects of feminine archetypes and the varying behavior produced, Whitmont brings out the differing possibilities inherent in each. He emphasizes men's inevitable need to project their anima qualities. Perhaps because he is a man looking at this from a masculine perspective, he tends to be harder on the "anima-woman" who receives these projections than on the projector; he describes her as acting through a drive for power and a need for security and persona identification. A man's need to withdraw these projections, confront the anima, and establish a relationship with it, are all essential to his development. A man's acceptance of his anima's autonomy within himself and his service to her changes her from an enemy into an ally. Active dialogue with the personified anima within the psyche is again stressed.

> By paying attention to her unpredictable reactions one can discover what one's real emotions happen to be, regardless of will and intent. Such awareness transforms blind emotions into genuine feelings, opens the doors to the soul, to the integration of spontaneity, sensitivity, receptivity, adaptability and warmth, but also to the assimilation of aggressiveness and the inferior functions, hence of the ability to direct one's temper constructively. (p. 199)

Whitmont looks at aspects of the anima in the outside world. Like Emma Jung, he is concerned with the socio-cultural and political ramifications of psychology.

> The anima constitutes a problem for the world at large no less than for the individual. Fear of the anima historically and collectively led to the degradation of women. Today this fear expresses itself in the masculinization of the world and the attending disparagement of femininity which is defined exclusively in terms of mothering and homemaking, hence the low ebb of woman's true self-regard as a woman, rather than as an imitator of male functioning. Failure to integrate the Yin world culturally has led to the widespread rigidity of abstract mental attitudes, resulting in

the sterile, instinct and feeling-dissociated, overrationalistic society of our day. Compulsive anima invasions occur collectively in all expressions of mob psychology, mass psychoses and hate psychoses, which inexplicably erupt ever and again in our "enlightened" and "sensible" modern world. (pp. 199-200)

In "The Animus and Impersonal Sexuality" (1970, later expanded as a chapter of his 1973 book *Incest and Human Love*), Robert Stein concurs with Whitmont that the animus and anima are both split in the modern psyche. Stein distinguishes a sensual and a spiritual component of each, explaining the basic split through analogy to their Apollonian and Dionysian aspects. Apropos of the negative animus, Stein believes that the animus will remain negative and will cut a woman off from her feminine side until and unless this split is healed.

Stein portrays the spiritual sides of the animus as aspects of the Father, the Brother, and Son archetypes, and describes the Father archetype as conservative and contemplative, providing the urge to understand and formulate meaning, to create order and form, and to be concerned with love — both in order to humanize culture and further spiritual development — and, finally, as underlying the urge to care for the dignity and freedom of the individual soul. The Son archetype is spontaneous, curious, imaginative, playful, daring, and explosive; it represents the principle of renewal for the Father. Stein describes the Brother archetype as carrying the Eros principle and as inseparable from the Sister archetype. Together, Stein says, they form the Brother-Sister archetype, the Incest archetype, which he describes as governing soul-connection with another, romantic love, and marriage. "A woman's connection to this aspect of her animus is therefore central; it makes it possible for her to experience her totality in a loving soul-to-soul meeting with a man" (1973, p. 100).

Stein terms the psychic effects of this archetype the "incest-wound," which he says is caused symbolically by the lost connection with the Brother archetype, and also by the lack of a woman's incestuous inner connection with her spiritual animus. This is a very problematic statement, pointing to an area in which a type of Jungian theorizing repels the modern (especially female) reader. The use of the term and concept *incest* seems unreflective of women's experience of the archetype; it fails to communicate what really goes on within a woman in reference to her perception either of integration or of incest. Woman's inner experience of herself as revealed in therapy and in woman's writing and theorizing has a far different relationship to incest. Stein's conventionally Jungian usage also seems a potentially damaging conflation of the animus with an ill-defined idea of incest. This points to the general problem of Jungians' sometimes unexamined and unfeeling use of loaded terms, which in this case is especially off-putting and potentially damaging to the many patients who have experienced the trauma of actual physical or psychological incest.

The concepts of the animus and the problem of incest are vital subjects in the psychology of women. Stein, along with many (often male) Jungian analysts, confounds an abstract and theoretical construction concerning self-connection through the animus with the *fact* of incest and all its concrete horrors and traumatic psychic sequelae. This mixing of categories blurs both reality and theory. It alienates a victim of real incest from her own reality—her ability to face and deal with her own often denied, rejected, and repressed sense of what happened to her in actuality. It serves to shield her from herself and her reality by covering them over, as her own experience was covered over, with some fuzzy intellectualized concept and with an unthought-out saccharine approval of incest disguised as archetype, and by the designation of a necessary developmental process as "required incest" with the animus. It also may lead to a therapist's failure to take the fact of actual incest and its psychic wounds seriously. The flight into abstract and intellectual categories that accompanies this unfeeling and ungrounded usage of such a loaded term may also mask repressed and unprocessed incestuous impulses toward the patient within the therapist himself, disguised as the therapist's conscious effort to promote connection with the animus. The indiscriminate confusion of the symbolical and concrete ways in which the word incest is used by Jungians and this usage's discordancy with the profound wound that comes from actual incest deserves serious reevaluation.

Victims of incest, whether in childhood or repeated in therapy, often learn secrecy and subterfuge in order to conceal the extent of their pain even from themselves. They are often not in a position to defend themselves nor to evaluate the impact of being told, following Jung's formulations in *Psychology of the Transference*, that incest is really a union with one's own self and is the main content of the transference. Victims of incest need help in calling things by their real names. They require a trusting relationship in which they can work through actual incestuous experience; women need to learn feminine self-esteem and self-efficacy rather than "required incest" with the animus. They also need help in recognizing, and allowing themselves to recognize and cope with, potential abuse either from their analyst or from their negative animus. Clinicians owe it to their patients to learn about current findings and theory about the psychological impact of early sexual and psychological abuse and change their language and theorizing accordingly.

Stein notes the sensual aspect of the animus: its phallic, priapic, and aggressive side. To Stein, this side appears impersonal, inhuman, ruthless, and vital. Both the spiritual and the sensual aspects of the animus require connection, "obeisance" and service from a woman (1973, p. 101). Neither, he says, can be realized without the other, while both help connect the one with the other. Stein believes that creative imagination in a woman is masculine and derives from this sensual animus. Without union of the two, the sensual animus and the spiritual animus both can make a woman feel guilty and cheap about her own sexuality. The sensual animus alone, Stein says, appears as an impersonal and unconnected raw drive; the spiritual animus alone makes prudish or puritanical comments about a woman's sexuality. Stein advocates personification of these animus figures and urges inner discourse with the images. He proposes that women stand up to the sensual animus through "being on the same familiar terms with her phallic sexuality as he is" (1970, p. 132). Once a woman frees herself of guilt and allows active imagination and sexual imagery as part of her own psyche, she can

> accept this type of mental sexuality as belonging to her nature, the attitude of the animus will also change: he will no longer demand that she always be open, related and loving; he will begin to accept the fact that she can be imaginatively creative in areas other than human relationship and still be womanly. (1970, p. 132)

> A woman can never realize her creative potential and her individuality if she allows only related sexuality to enter her consciousness. (1973, p. 105)

Why this vital, unrelated, and active sexuality comes from the sensual-phallic animus and not from the dark, sensual, unrelated parts of the dynamic feminine is not explained. The archetype or model of a vigorously erotic embodied female, whose eroticism rises within the mirror of her own bodily self, is missing. I would guess that, besides men's general fear of the powerful feminine and her powerful sexuality (a woman's biological birthright), these aspects are missing because, even when arguing for a woman's unrelatedness, Stein still sees women ambivalently and from a masculine perspective; he expects the feminine to be what the fathers taught: related, feeling and serving men's needs.

Ann Ulanov (1971/1978, 1981) also explores the animus for its role in balancing the relatedness and feeling of the feminine psyche. She emphasizes the helpful and positive aspects of the animus. Ulanov writes that these positive aspects are encouraged by the development of a personalized and conscious relation to the animus through active personification and inner dialogue with animus images. Most of her work on the animus updates that of Emma Jung, Harding, and de Castillejo, in that she sees animus development as occurring in and through the same stages as they do (though Ulanov credits these stages not to them but to Neumann). Ulanov adapts Neumann's idea of the feminine as potentially developing past the patriarchal stage; in her fourth and final stage of development, she envisions women emerging from the patriarchy and developing a new consciousness. This is marked by integration of the animus at the highest level, and also propels Ulanov's theory into the post-modern world.

Ulanov extends the work of Emma Jung, Fierz-David, Brand, and von Franz in her interpretation of the anima. Like them she stresses the importance of a man's proper and balanced attitude to the feminine within him, which then allows the anima to develop in a positive and helpful way. She makes a strong and valuable differentiation between the anima and actual women, and describes anima manifestations as being more passive, sentimental, vain, soft-headed, and less tough than real women; the anima also appears as more exaggeratedly good or evil than actual women. Ulanov stresses Jung's remarks about the effects on the anima and on women of the Judeo-Christian equation of the feminine with evil and the corporeal. She makes the important observation that since women are thus defined, they consequently receive as men's anima projections everything connected with the body and all the fears that go with sex, morality, life, death, and bodily existence; what starts with fear of the archetypal mother continues in a double displacement from fear to hate and from the anima to the feminine in general to a particular woman. In the same work Ulanov echoes her precursor, Harding, in her description of the damage done to both men and women by men's fear and hatred of their own repressed anima. Ulanov traces the sequellae in a way that makes a significant contribution to current psychological theory about violence toward women:

From the dread may come a need to see the feminine as entirely second-ary, inferior, less stable than the masculine. If a man remains unconscious of his fear of the feminine element in his own being he may compulsive-ly act it out by projecting its threat onto actual females. From such project-ed fears spring some of the most hostile attitudes and prejudicial acts against women. (1981, p. 81)

Problems arise when men think women duplicate and therefore de-serve the same mistreatment given to their anima. (p. 126)

Ulanov's clear and thoughtful delineation of animus and anima de-velopment as part of the development of the psyche in general empha-sizes their dynamic, progressive, and process aspects. Her recapitulation of earlier work sets her own contribution firmly in context and updates Jungian theory with examples from her own practice and from a con-temporary perspective. Ulanov's emphasis on socio-cultural determinants, especially Christianity's, on animus and anima projections is especially valuable, as is her important linkage of anima theory to violence against women. She makes a strong contribution to theory through combining Neumann' final feminine stage of development with animus/anima in-tegration and the acceptance of a possible new, and post-patriarchal, stage of consciousness.

June Singer's (1972) book *Boundaries of the Soul* is an attempt to show "the Jungian analytic process and how it works" (p. xiii). In her chapter on the animus and anima, she presents the archetypal, biologi-cal, and sociological components of these two archetypes. Along with Binswanger (though not citing her), Singer stresses biological differences as an important source of animus and anima variances. She uses the same biological metaphors of sperm and ovum that Binswanger and von der Heydt used to elucidate masculine and feminine behavioral differ-ences (like them, she ignores the ambiguous biological reality that both sperm and ova have significant active and passive patterns).

Perhaps more than other writers, Singer stresses the conjunction of opposites, the inner marriage—a term far more congruent and less ex-plosive than Stein's *incest*. She emphasizes the compensatory function of the animus and anima for the way each balances conscious masculine or feminine attitudes. Like Ulanov, but to an even greater degree, Sing-er provides many examples, dreams, anecdotes, and personal experiences which are used to embody and ground Jung's theory and give it con-temporary relevance. The theory incorporated in the chapter derives from Jung's and shows little influence of others who have written on the animus and anima since his time. However, Singer does note that, "what Jung stated in this connection nearly half a century ago is still basically true, although I believe that we are now standing on the brink of momentous change" (p. 232).

In *Androgyny* (1976/1989), Singer focuses on part of that great change. In her preface she states that the book rose out of the unfinished business of her (1972) chapter on the animus and anima. Singer develops a theory of human sexuality based on androgyny, which continues her interest in the inner marriage, "the harmonious coexistence of masculinity and femininity within a single individual" (1976/1989, p. x), but which, unlike Harding's work on the *coniunctio,* has little to do with animus/anima concepts as such — in fact there are only fifteen references to the animus or anima in the index. Singer includes a brief feminist critique of the original animus/anima theory. She acknowledges that this formulation of Jung's is "where Jung has received so much criticism from those who have been striving for an equalization of opportunity and status " (p. 258). She then attempts to explain the deficits in the theory through reference to Jung's description of his "Number One" and "Number Two" characters: the "Number One" competent, practical and worldly; the "Number Two" interested in the mystical and unearthly. Singer ascribes Jung's tradition- and time-bound statements to what he wrote out of his "Number One" character. She thinks Jung's alchemical and transpersonal work derived from his "Number Two" character, as does the concept of the contrasexual animus and anima — but that the concrete working out of the theory and the examples given are a result of his "Number One" reflecting the conditions and prejudices of his era.

> Jung's descriptions of the annoying and irritating qualities of the *anima* and *animus,* which evoke so much resistance from those who read them today, are those very personal qualities that are bound to emerge in a raw and unrefined state in an individual because they have been so long repressed and denied their natural development. (p. 257)

Singer concludes that Jung's exploration of alchemical symbolism as an example of the differentiation and then integration of the masculine and feminine remains the most important part of his work. In it, she states, he laid the spiritual foundations for androgyny. "If the problem of the opposites is solved within the individual, a step will be made toward the better understanding of all warring opposites — between individuals, and between the wider systems to which they belong" (p. 262).

In her 1983 book *Energies of Love,* the references to anima and animus decline to three. They do show a further development, though, in the direction Singer suggested in 1972. One of the few Jungians who ever incorporates a historical outlook, Singer gives an invaluable but brief personal overview of the ways the animus developed over time within herself and in her peers in Zürich, and then in the United States (Singer's animus development helps validate Scott-Maxwell's theoretical formulation). Though Harding is not cited, Singer uses her stages of animus development as a model. She traces her own and her contemporaries' growth from expressing a negative internal animus and projection of its positive qualities, through a struggle with the animus, to living and expressing the animus and masculinity, to a search for both the feminine and the spiritual, culminating with an inner unity of both the masculine and feminine. In the world at large, Singer finds a change in consciousness:

> What has been happening, it seems to me, is that the archetype of the contrasexual that Jung saw as a deeply unconscious psychic factor is no longer as unconscious as it once was. The shift began with the emergence of a more dynamic consciousness in women, but it has been swiftly followed by reciprocal changes in the consciousness of men. (p. 236)

So far I have traced the development of the animus and anima concepts from Jung's initial formulations to more comprehensive ones. Before I go on to examine current work that may show some change in consciousness, I want to sum up the extensions of Jung's ideas.

First and perhaps most important is a new evaluation of the feminine principle and a feeling that women's development is perhaps generally ahead of men's. Major corrections of inadequacies in Jung's working out of the original theory include a more balanced representation of the animus and anima with both their positive and negative attributes elaborated equally; this has necessitated more positive evaluations of the animus and more negative evaluations of the anima. Developmental stages in the integration of the animus and anima have been formulated, with the realization that this development includes the figures becoming less multiple and more unitary as they become more integrated.

Perhaps because more women are drawn to the subject than men, perhaps because their animi are a more active challenge, or perhaps Jung's outline of the animus was particularly deficient, more constructive and creative work has been done on the animus than on the anima. Important extensions of theory include giving the animus both active and passive components, separating it according to stage and type, as well as separating it from a woman's own biologically masculine side. When looked at developmentally, a clear progression has been seen and clinically verified, with the animus starting as plural and negative and ending more unitary and positive. Some work on the anima duplicates these findings, with the anima also linked to developmetal stages. The relation between social and cultural conditions and the form of animus and anima manifestations is significant and convincing.

In working on this chapter, I have been surprised at the capacity these women, especially the early writers—Emma Jung, Harding, Hannah, Howes, de Castillejo, and Binswanger (though Ulanov, too, somehow joins their rank)—have to move me, and how deeply moved I have been. I think what most impresses me is their astonishing courage. Writing from deep within a patriarchal system and an androcentric time, their work resonates with a personal struggle to free women and themselves. It is in their descriptions of the animus, that inner patriarchy, and through their gentle though emphatic insistence on their *own* sense of the animus, that both the struggle and the victory are achingly apparent. Reading behind the texts is often necessary, phrased as they are in the cadences required of these women who labor to express their own truth within a discipline and structure that, no matter how much it honors the feminine, remains patriarchal.

Reading in this way, I want to restate some of these women's findings. The psychological impact of women's unequal treatment as a class speaks through the negative animus. Both the negative animus and man's anima projections onto woman are linked to men's unconscious fear and disdain of women. Violence against women is connected to men's mistreatment and mistrust of the anima and to androcentric hate of the feminine. The misuse of power by men in the patriarchy and by the negative animus is implicated in the right both think they have to control the feminine or use women for their own needs. The negative animus recapitulates the androcentric idea that the masculine is free to dominate an "inferior" feminine and disregard women's own rights. This echoes in both men's and women's devaluation of women and the feminine, and in violence toward women, nature, and humankind. Much in animus/anima theory clarifies and explains some of the unbearable skewedness of life and gives at least an outline of a way to regain our balance. Animus/anima theory also augments other theories concerning learned helplessness, the origins of depression, and issues of man's destructiveness. There is a reciprocal need to integrate theory about the psychology of women into our field and our conceptualizing of animus and anima as well.

Above all, there is the need not to forget the valuable work these fore-mothers have already done. There is little continuity in animus/anima theory and much repetition, confusion, and neglect of prior work. This derives in large part from Jungians' lamentable ahistoricity. Finally, as is true of what does come down to us as history, much valuable work by women is forgotten or abandoned. This is a serious loss for Jungian theory as a whole, for ourselves, and for our critics. Much that would make Jungian theory—especially on the animus and anima—understandable, current, and serviceable, especially to women, lies neglected in forgotten files and old journals, the passion of its unlived life, its potential to be of use to us today, ignored.

CHAPTER SEVEN:
ON THE BRINK OF MOMENTOUS CHANGE

The Animus and Anima — Part Two

> A delight in difference, in multiplicity, in continuous awareness of 'the other' within the self.
>
> Sandra Gilbert, *The Newly Born Woman*

With changes in the culture and with men's and women's increasing knowledge about each other — possibly even with some growth of consciousness — the forms the animus and anima archetype take push and rub against narrow definitions. The concepts seem to have expanded and no longer fit into former molds. Something new and far more ample, larger-hearted, strives to make itself known.

James Hillman, true to his usual style, gives the concepts of animus and anima a good jostling. This is particularly true of his two part-essay "Anima" in *Spring* 1973 and 1974 (later published as his part of an alternately-paged duet with Jung in Hillman's *The Anima*, 1985). In his earlier (1971) work on the feeling function, Hillman starts to separate the anima from feeling and the animus from thinking. He states that the anima's only special relationship to feeling is that it is often responsible for feeling disorders. Kinder to the anima than Harding, von Franz, and Ulanov, but not yet its champion, Hillman here describes anima-feeling as being too sensitive, sincere, polite, light, charming, vacillating, autoerotic, aesthetic, materialistic, personal, undirected, and irrelevant. It distorts sexuality by suppressing negative feelings. Animus-feeling shares this capacity to be off-the-mark in many of the same ways.

Where the anima-feeling does help the feeling function, however, is precisely through these difficulties, for the anima brings conflict, disorder and falsification, providing the feeling function a place to exercise its main activity: the discrimination of values and the elaboration of relationship. (1971, p. 129)

The purpose of Hillman's essay on the anima in *Spring* is to look at the "phenomenology of the *notion* of anima" (1973, p. 97) or "an anatomy of a personified notion," as he subtitles the 1985 book. He finds (overlooking the occasionally strongly feminist subtext emphasized in the last chapter) that previous work on the anima only reiterates and elaborates Jung's work. In exploring this "notion," Hillman makes ten major points which radically expand and transform the initial concept.

(1) The anima is not the contrasexual side of man, nor is it present only within the psyche of men. This idea came from Jung's "fantasy of opposites" (1973, p. 99), which was relative to his time and culture and can now be discarded as obsolete.

(2) The anima is an archetypal structure of consciousness that reflects the soul, not Eros. Much confusion has resulted in putting Eros in place of the soul and in placing "anima events upon the altar of Aphrodite" (p. 108). This has resulted in the sexualization of the anima concept, the error of mistaking Aphrodite-images for anima-images, the erotic conceptualization of transference phenomena, and further confusions of thinking polluted by the anima's affect.

(3) The anima is not the archetype of the feeling function and should not be equated with feeling. In fact, the anima tends to lead away from human feeling, not towards it.

(4) The animus and anima are archetypes in the psyche of both men and women alike, and may be neither singly masculine nor feminine. Woman's psychological development takes place through the cultivation of the feminine and her neglected anima, not through animus development, nor is anima a shadow manifestation in a woman. "The *per definitionem* absence of anima in women is a deprivation of a cosmic principle with no less consequence in the practice of analytical psychology than has been the theory of penis deprivation in the practice of psychoanalysis" (p. 117).

(5) The concept of anima leads toward psyche and away from the personal. It, the anima, is the true base of consciousness, not the ego. The ego's (and analytical efforts) to integrate the anima to an ego's idea of consciousness are misguided.

Instead of regarding anima from the viewpoint of ego where she becomes a poisonous mood, an inspiring weakness, or a contrasexual compensation, we might regard ego from soul where ego becomes the instrument for day-to-day coping, nothing more grandiose than a trusty janitor of the planetary houses, a servant of soul-making. (pp. 127-128)

(6) A helpful depersonalization of the anima comes about through a voluntary return to the archetype behind the image, through relinquishing personal identification with both outer and inner events and abandoning the belief that the ego is paramount. Negative depersonalization, both internal and external, is caused by loss of soul, loss of contact with the anima. The anima acts through images, gives a sense of personal reality, and can be called upon therapeutically.

(7) The integration of the anima is neither a hero's task nor an ego one. The anima's own individualization is the centrally important concept. "The recognition of the anima as a personified numen" (1974, p. 121) leads not, as Jung and prior Jungians theorize, to integrating her into consciousness, but, instead, to joining her on her own terms — integration *with* her. This occurs through internalization and sacrifice, not through suppression nor through drawing the anima up into greater ego-consciousness.

Integrating the anima, which means becoming an integer or one with her, could only take place by our remembrance that we are already in her. Human being is being-in-soul (*esse in anima*) from the beginning. Integration is thus a shift of viewpoint from her in me to me in her. (1974, p. 124)

(8) The anima is mediatrix to the unknown, the unconscious. She mediates through images, not words or dialogue. As such she is the archetype of psychology and soul-making.

The deeper we follow her, the more fantastic consciousness becomes. Then in dreams she reveals herself as psychotic, a wraith with queer eyes, an "inmate" of my nightly asylum. Union with anima also means union with my psychosis, my fear of madness, my suicide. This conjunction is purged by her salt and her sweet sentimentalities, for it is a conjunction with the craziness of life that is at the same time my own craziness, mediated and personalized through her, bringing home a "me" that is an oddity, peculiar and mine, or what Jung calls self. (1974, p. 126)

(9) Neither the anima nor animus is specifically single or plural; both

can occur as either. However the notion of anima unity is a helpful one to Hillman because it keeps to one numinous soul-image and prevents sloppy usage which calls anything feminine an anima-figure. "We may call 'anima' only that particular gestalt which precisely, continually, and specifically signifies the core quality of my soul" (p. 134).

(10) The anima is always paired with the animus. This pair is called the divine pair, the *syzygy*. "To be engaged with the anima is to be engaged simultaneously with animus in some way or another" (p. 139). Each is the vantage point for the other, and thus it is through the animus that the anima has been investigated. Within this internal syzygy projections can also occur, so that each anima figure constellates a particular animus figure and vice versa. The incursion of soul into spirit and spirit into soul in the interior and exterior worlds through the animus and anima is what Hillman calls the syzygy in action — the *coniunctio*.

I find this close examination and reevaluation of Jung's work on the anima and animus brilliant. Besides, or maybe because of, turning various formulations inside out and questioning what others have accepted at face value, Hillman provides an invaluable critique of the animus and anima concepts. It would take several chapters to wrestle with each point Hillman raises. He is the first person to bring the delineation of the anima archetype, for better or worse, firmly into the post-modern age. It has been over fifteen years since these essays were written and yet no one has sufficiently addressed the problems they raise, nor have Jungians integrated the perhaps revolutionary revitalization of the term. No one has built much upon his work, though a few writers on the same subject are starting to refer to it, often simply mentioning his alternative view of the animus and anima, then reverting to prior usage, as if both Hillman and his notion of the anima have dropped into the unconscious. Points six, seven, and eight are not worked out with enough clarity; acceptance of their premises would, I believe, require a radical shift in both the practice and form of analytical psychology (a possibility that Hillman seems aware of in his development of an "archetypal" rather than "analytical" psychology).

Point seven is especially moving and compelling and is what, perhaps, most deserves the term "post-modern." This is because Hillman argues here for the acceptance of "the craziness of life," not its therapeutic (and arrogant) eradication. Hillman laughs at modern psychology's urge to empty out, clean up, and rationalize; instead, he champions the relinquishment of some ego-consciousness for the sake of integration with the anima on her ground and on her terms. This stance of Hillman's balances the common and weighty patriarchal devaluation of at least one aspect of the feminine, and rights the injury done her by the original theory's implicit androcentric bias. As such it offers an invaluable adjustment to modern Jungian theory. However, the very excess of Hillman's sublimely lyrical approach to the anima adds a wildly Romantic exhalation of its own that also needs its counterpoise (as well as, as Hillman perhaps knows too well, its conjurer).

Point ten, the syzygy of animus and anima, is manifestly plausible, but its formulation needs grounding and some attention to detail. For instance, just stating that the anima can only be seen through the animus and vice versa is not convincing—nor is his statement that the two are true opposites, yet also beyond what he calls Jung's "fantasy of opposites." Hillman's belief that by discussing the anima exhaustively one also has included the animus could be considered remarkably similar to Jung's dealing with the animus as an "inverted" anima. As the feminine cannot be included as a simple reverse of the masculine, neither can the animus be described only in reference to, and accompanied by, the anima. The concept of the animus merits its own reappraisal. Yet at the same time, the idea that the animus/anima may be one single archetype kindles excitement and generates further inquiry.

Gareth Hill builds on Hillman's work in his lecture "Men, Anima and Feminine" (1975), which he further develops in his 1978 doctoral dissertation on archetypal patterns in development. Like Hillman, he reviews Jung's work on the anima; Hill finds Jung's description to be that of the particular anima of a particular thinking-type man, Jung, himself, and reflective of his specific socio-cultural era. In contrast to Hillman, who finds the best picture of the anima in the archetype of psyche, Hill, like Whitmont, finds it in the archetypal predisposition toward the experience of otherness. In setting out this argument, Hill starts with what he calls the archetypal patterns of masculine and feminine, the Yang and Yin, and gives a long list of attributes for each. He then attempts to make a clear distinction between the anima and the feminine. In this he explores the anima in reference to Jung's basic work, to its behavioral manifestations, and to its psychological development.

Hill deplores the confusion of anima with feeling, Eros, and relatedness, and refers to Hillman's (1974) distinctions between each of them. He describes the interaction between anima and different typologies, using the negative anima manifestations of each type as examples. He criticizes Jung's categorical error of confusing the socio-cultural with the archetypal. In contrast, he suggests that personal, historical, cultural, and biological aspects of the anima and animus—the other—all need to be considered separately.

Hill concludes with a plea that the feminine and masculine both need redefinition today in light of changing times, though he does not consider the possibility of animus and anima both being present within a single gender. He subscribes to Jung's ideas about the contrasexual as the basic polarity from which all else can be deduced, yet, like Singer, also advocates androgyny as a term or concept which allows men and women to explore their own feminine and masculine in keeping with the evolving culture. He does not address the logical error of androgyny within polarity—how a monistic idea can exist within an essential dualism—a philosophical ambiguity in Jung's theorizing as well. Because of Hill's adherence to the polarity of animus and anima, he also applies his theory of the anima to the animus in reverse. In spite of these incongruities, Hill's work is a crucial and strong step toward freeing men and women from many of the restrictions imposed by the original construct.

Whitmont is another analyst who has recently rethought the anima and animus concepts. In *The Symbolic Quest* (1969/1978), Whitmont portrays the anima as generally equatable with Eros, feeling, and emotion, and the animus with Logos, thinking, and judgment. In "Reassessing Femininity and Masculinity: A Critique of Some Traditional Assumptions" (1980) and *The Return of the Goddess* (1982a), Whitmont refutes this equation. Instead he stresses the cultural relativity of these concepts and argues for their change. Like Hillman, he finds relatedness and unrelatedness common to both men and women. He differentiates archetypes of the masculine present in men and in the animus into types he names after Eros, Ares, Mars, and Hephaistos, all with differing Logos qualities. He differentiates archetypes of the feminine present in women and the anima into Lila, Pallas Athena, Luna, and Medusa types (see the next chapter for a further discussion of these archetypes). Moreover, he states that all of these archetypes can appear in varying constellations in both men and women.

Whitmont reexamines the basic idea of the animus and anima in relation to consciousness and gender, joining Hillman in making the following comprehensive and important reassessments of the Jungian theory of the animus and anima (reassessments that are in remarkable congruence with the theorizing of the women in the forgotten works I mentioned in the last chapter):

> On the strength of clinical experience accumulated since the time of their early formulation by Jung, their limitation to the unconscious dynamics of one sex or the other no longer appears quite practical. . . . It was during the dominance of the patriarchal, androlatric culture and only in terms of the patriarchy that masculine values, patterns of perception, feeling and behaviour shaped the structure of consciousness because they were given supreme value. In the patriarchy feminine standards were devalued and rejected hence repressed and reduced to unconscious determinants. Masculinity then represented consciousness.
>
> In our time we witness a re-emergence of feminine Yin and anima qualities in the collective value system. They are becoming cultural determinants again and co-shapers of a new consciousness for both sexes. Psychopompic figures appear in unconscious productions as frequently if not more so in feminine shapes as in masculine ones. (1980, p. 119)

> Masculine traits can also be part of the nonpersonal unconscious potential in men and be obsessive, animus fashion; so can feminine traits in women. Instinct, soul and spirit, anima and animus are archetypal principles that pertain to both sexes equally. Men are not necessarily more spirit oriented than women. Neither do women have a monopoly on soul and instinct. Spirituality as a predominant male characteristic and woman as the embodiment of soul are heirlooms of 19th century romanticism, still dominant in Jung's day but no longer valid in our generation. Women can be and always could be deeply involved with and psychologically determined in their conscious outlook by Logos and out of touch with their affects; men can be immensely sensitive to instinct, feeling, and affect and quite at loss in respect to Logos or for that matter to any other of the masculine archetypes.
>
> Either sex may partake in any of the masculine or feminine determinants in various constellations or degrees, comparable to a zodiacal wheel in which any of its sections can be accentuated to different degrees in different people. (pp. 120-121)

Whitmont, together with Binswanger, Hillman, and Hill, provides a modern reworking of Jung's thought on the anima and animus that holds promise of future development. Other analysts who have been writing on this subject since then have elaborated some parts of the idea, but by and large write as if these analysts' vital and important work had not appeared.

Ujhely (1973), Kluger (1974), and Hubback (1978) continue the work of Emma Jung, Binswanger, and de Castellejo in exploring characteristics of the positive animus.

Gertrud Ujhely, in an unpublished paper, notes that the positive evaluation of the animus is a cultural phenomenon concomitant with increasing acceptance of the feminine and of women. She adds further examples of the negative animus voice which reiterates such undermining comments as: "You can do better," "You should have done it differently in the first place," and "What's the use, you'll never succeed." Ujhely notes the detrimental effects of this animus, externally when it is projected and internally when it abets the tendency to give up before one starts, promoting futility, hopelessness, and depression. She also gives valuable clues as to how to change and develop the animus. She pays significant attention to the problem of the mother's animus on her daughter, and notes women's need for stillness and periodicy as opposed to the negative animus' clockwork linearity.

Philip Zabriskie (1974) accepts the multiplicity of anima figures. Andrea Dykes (1976) points to the witch archetype as a manifestation within the child's psyche of the mother's negative animus. She objects to the all too common analytic practice of blaming the patient for her animus rather than working *with* the patient toward animus development. Hubback, in a long and valuable article on the psychology of women, finds that in spite of socio-cultural change, what C. G. and Emma Jung wrote about the animus remains valid "even if the sociological aspect and coloration now seem dated" (1978, p. 183).

Wesley (1977) and Alex (1977), writing in their encyclopedia articles on animus and anima, also keep to the old interpretations, though Alex does mention Hillman's questioning of them. Sanford's *The Invisible Partners* (1980) also mentions Hillman's work and accepts the possibility that the psychological makeup of both men and women contains manifestations of animus and anima. He refers to Hillman's distinction between Eros, feeling, and anima, and Logos, thinking, and animus. However, when not concerned with Hillman, he reverts to the general idea that the anima and feelings and relatedness go together. He also falls into what Hillman calls an Aphroditic error by including as anima-figures many confusing images which Hillman would designate as belonging to Eros or Aphrodite rather than to the anima as soul. Sanford's book follows in the line of Harding's *The Way of All Women* as well as *The 'I' and the 'Not-I'* and Scott-Maxwell's *Women — and Sometimes Men,* in that it is a book more for the lay reader than for experts. It is also blessed with the same type of humor, down-to-earthness, deep feelings, and common sense of the earlier writers. On the new ideas about the animus and anima, Sanford concludes:

> These issues cannot be decided here and now, and that is as it should be, for anima and animus remain somewhat borderline concepts, verifiable in experience, useful in therapy, practical when we apply them to ourselves, but at the same time not capable of being precisely defined . . . For practical purposes, it is perhaps better to stick with Jung's original definition and reserve the anima as a term for masculine psychology, but it would be a mistake to cast this into the form of a dogma and *insist* that this be so. For in dealing with the anima and the animus we are dealing with figures that are largely unconscious to us. (1980, p. 111)

The tide has recently turned toward more radical reevaluations of the animus concept. Linda Schmidt (1980) hides a remarkable review and reworking of the animus concept within an article on marriage and the brother-sister relationship. In a discussion of the literature on the animus since Jung, she mentions Emma Jung, Wolff, Kluger, Binswanger, and Harding as well as her own adoption of their contributions to the theory. She agrees with Harding that the development of ego and of animus consciousness go hand in hand. Schmidt disagrees with Wolff, citing Wolff's feminine typology as more reflective of men's anima than of actual women. She points to the harm done to women when they are led to model themselves on anima figures such as these, rather than on real women. Schmidt sees this type of anima women encouraged by, and the consequence of, being a father's daughter. In development, a father's daughter progresses from being a naive carrier of projection to a sophisticated, increasingly aware one; she then liberates herself, becoming more conscious and independent. The difference for her and for women today, Schmidt thinks, is that instead of being shielded from the masculine world—and thus, instead of the shelteredness Emma Jung noted behind women's lack of animus development, women are now "immersed in conscious animus experience from childhood" (p. 22). She concludes that the theory must change in order to take modern reality into consideration.

Mary Ann Mattoon (1981) briefly restates Jung's ideas about the animus and anima. She finds his work typical of his time, but criticizes it as too negative in its delineation of the animus and not sufficiently appreciative of women's capabilities. She suggests that opinionatedness is found in both sexes and more likely results from undifferentiated thinking than from animus thinking. Mattoon very briefly reviews Harding, Emma Jung and Wolff on their extensions of Jung's ideas. She may have misapprehended Bradway's (1978) study comparing women patients who worked with those who stayed at home, calling it a study of animus-women and anima-women. Mattoon cites the confusion prevalent in Jungian circles where, all too often, cultural stereotypes are mistaken for innate qualities. She notes the Eros-feeling-anima-woman linkage and its opposite, but adds that the animus/anima concept is being challenged in this respect, and for its link to contrasexuality.

In her lecture, "Is the Animus Obsolete?" (1983a), Mattoon reviews Jung's work on the animus, calling it a marked advance over other contemporary theorizing on the feminine, but regrets Jung's negativity toward the animus. Mattoon finds that most writing since his time and most usage of the term in practice remain pejorative. This negative evaluation is a socio-cultural limitation of Jung's era that is obsolete. She cites feminist objections to the term and deplores the detrimental effect of the animus concept when it is used to limit women to socio-cultural gender-specific "feminine" behavior.

Mattoon draws her evidence for the presence of the animus from anecdotal, clinical, subjective, anthropological, and biological examples. However, as a model and a concept she criticizes its usage. She cites some former work on the reevaluation of the animus, notably Emma Jung's work, and notes most Jungians' neglect of this reappraisal. Mattoon herself neglects contemporary work on this reappraisal; she mentions only Sanford and Ulanov and their more traditional approaches.

In contrast to her 1981 book, in the 1983 lecture Mattoon makes a strong plea for modification of the concept and for its separation from thinking. She elaborates her 1981 idea concerning the confusion of so-called animus thinking with its reality, inferior thinking, which both men and women may employ. She also briefly explores the confusion of masculine and feminine with thinking and feeling. This differs from her textbook on Jungian psychology (1981), where her purpose is to record the more traditional views. Mattoon updates her historical and theoretical overview of the animus in a definitive 1987 article (Mattoon and Jones, 1987) which I will discuss with work done in the late eighties.

Genevieve Geer chooses a quality of animus manifestation, humility, as the subject for her dissertation in analytical psychology *The Humble Animus* (1981), for the C. G. Jung Institute of New York. The aspect she concentrates upon is based on E. Jung's and de Castillejo's description of the helpful worker and servant animus. Geer traces this form of the positive animus in her own psyche and in dreams as well as in fairy tales, myths, and fiction, finding it to be an aspect of the animus that has been overlooked by men because of the Western dislike for un-heroic masculinity. Women also tend to overlook it, undervalue it, or take it for granted, paying more attention to heroes and villains. Geer believes that the integration of this aspect reconnects women to lost feel-ings and to concrete everyday life, helping relationships through guarding against projection and unrealistic expectations. It also leads to the ac-ceptance of new non-patriarchal values of both masculine and feminine roles and behavior.

Geer briefly refers to the major points in Whitmont's (1980) article but neither criticizes nor evaluates them other than to state that she finds them radically divergent from Jung's formulations and thus dif-ficult to incorporate. She accepts the idea that thinking and feeling be-long to both sexes, but prefers the animus in its simpler and more traditional form. She gently criticizes Whitmont for not paying enough attention to the personal animus.

Katherine Bradway, in her valuable and insightful article "Gender Identity and Gender Roles" (1982a), briefly reviews some prior work on the animus. She notes Jung's initial negative description of the animus, but also emphasizes the revolutionary quality of his ideas about the con-trasexual animus and anima in an era of rigid gender roles. She stresses the continuity in the view of the positive animus, from Jung's idea that the animus could be a creative power and a bridge, to Harding's idea of the animus as focuser, and de Castillejo's as torch-bearer and enlight-ener. She finds Hillman and Whitmont responsive to changes in cul-tural conditions in their conception that each gender contains both an anima and an animus in the unconscious. In reviewing the work of Jung, Neumann, Hillman, and Whitmont on the contrasexual—the animus and anima—Bradway focuses on some gender-studies which echo these findings. She criticizes work that limits men and women to a definition of behavior appropriate to Jung's socio-cultural era, and advocates more awareness of the difference between the socio-cultural and the innate. In the process she supports a clear separation in analytical terminology between the words masculine/feminine and animus/anima and men and women. For both analyst and analysand, appreciation of the function-ing of the masculine and feminine in each of them is "essential for Jun-gian work" (p. 279).

Joseph Wheelwright has a chapter on the animus and anima in his *Saint George and the Dandelion* (1982), which is based on a series of training seminars on analytical psychology. It is a discursive, personal, and immensely appealing book, reminiscent of the popular work by Harding, Scott-Maxwell, and Sanford mentioned above. Elsewhere (Schmidt, 1984), Wheelwright interjects a comment about "that odious linkage" of Eros/feeling/feminine/anima/woman and its opposite. Here he neatly dispatches the linkage, I hope, once and for all. He cites Hillman's efforts in the same direction and calls for further work on the differentiation of anima and the feeling function. As a feeling type himself, Wheelwright points to but does not elaborate the difference between his feeling, which relates and evaluates, and his anima, which does not (p. 75).

Wheelwright calls the animus/anima phenomenon "one of the gravest American problems" (p. 42). He focuses on the patriarchal legacy of valuing the masculine over the feminine and the contribution of this imbalance to the pathological development of anima and animus. He finds the lack of a strong, clear, or valued feminine principle to be the main cause of much abnormal animus development. Wheelwright indicates the way in which typology, undeveloped functions and the shadow all impinge upon and affect the way the animus and anima function in the individual.

The value of the anima/animus chapter in *Saint George and the Dandelion* lies mainly in its personal tone. Wheelwright *cares* about actual problems between the sexes and delineates the ways in which the unintegrated animus/anima affect relationships, especially familial and love relationships. Much personal material is used as the source of what Bateson has called, in his foreword to the book, "Jungian theory at work . . . a solvent for all the nonsense of daily life that inhibits the communication of love" (p. xii).

Three analysts, Te Paske, Beebe, and Woodman, have focused on particular aspects of either anima or animus problems. In his *Rape and Ritual: A Psychological Study,* (1982) Te Paske, echoing Ulanov, describes the anima as

the first crucial factor in rape. Without a fundamental recognition of this archetype, rape as a problem *within* men will never be grasped. As has already become quite clear, the male *fantasy* of woman is the primary factor. As the bearer of the anima in projection, woman appears as the highest and lowest which man stands existentially over against. (p. 79)

Te Paske thus finds that a man's attitude toward the feminine is dependent upon the degree to which his ego has emerged from matriarchal consciousness and advanced through patriarchal developmental stages. The former consciousness results in unconsciousness and mammoth fear projections, while the latter can lead to loss of soul. Anima identification with shadow phenomena is traced to both of these consciousnesses, as is "the fierce ambivalence toward women" (p. 118) prevalent in contemporary culture. Equality and union of the inner and outer masculine and feminine, withdrawal of projections, development of the ego and the soul, and socio-cultural change toward a more integral era are his solutions to the problem, which he does not think will be easily resolved.

John Beebe's strikingly original paper, "The Father's Anima as a Clinical and Symbolic Problem" (1984), focuses on the archetypal aspects of the various difficulties produced by one particular type of anima—the patriarchal anima and personality. Beebe is specifically concerned with the clinical and personal effects a father's anima has on his son. He gives four examples of the problem of "anima-fathering" in the patriarchy. In different ways, each impedes the son's Eros or Logos growth. Beebe describes the dilemmas that ensue as problems caused as much by the father's anima as by the son. These are successfully solved only through the son's struggle to develop a more differentiated external or internal anima. The task in each of the four examples is for the son to relate to the problem in such a way that he can reclaim the energy ensnared within the father's anima. Beebe's view of the patriarchal anima is that it is similar to what Hillman has called the Aphrodite type, personifying Eros qualities. For Beebe, this anima best fits with classical Jungian terminology. He writes, "I find it helpful to think of the anima as the emotional attitude a man takes toward any thing he reflects upon" (p. 10). Beebe, however, also stresses a heretofore neglected side of the anima: its mercurial, trickster form, which he describes with insight and humor. This aspect of the anima has seldom been mentioned in the literature on the anima (Jung, Hillman, Hill, and Beebe are exceptions), but may be the essential component that frees the anima from its restriction to contrasexual manifestations.

Nora Moore, in an important paper, "The Anima-Animus in a Changing World" (1983), reflects on the changes in the concept. She reexamines both the archetype and its images in light of culture and time; current anthropological, sociological, and gender studies buttress her work. She concludes that these studies show men and women to be more similar than different, though she also acknowledges that "gender differentiation is global, but follows no universal rule" (p. 202). Moore, following Hillman, reflects on the archetype as a single one (animus-anima) free of traditional gender attributes and as free of the thinking/feeling dichotomy as men and women are in the culture today. Along with Whitmont and Hillman, Moore sees anima and animus in both sexes, the form the archetype takes being opposite to the individual's persona. Each sex, however, tends to project its opposite, finding members of the other sex to be more unconscious and unaware (more animus or anima-like) than individuals of that gender really are. Moore considers the traditional differentiation of anima and animus too polarized for modern reality; instead, she sees animus-anima as counterparts and conjunctions of opposites that may need to be split apart in order to develop. Along with Hillman, Hill, and Beebe, she views the trickster as a vital component of the archetype. Moore concludes:

> Images of the anima and animus are dependent on culture, and are becoming less polarized, more fluid, and partly overlapping, so that, as the roles of men and women approach each other, so images of anima and animus appear not as opposites, but as different aspects of one archetype: anima-animus. (p. 194)

Barbara Greenfield (1983) also considers the impact of gender stereotyping, socialization, biological differences, and the different positions of men and women in society as psychologically significant. All impinge on the forms the archetype takes, while minor differences are elaborated into what she calls a whole "mythos" of opposites. If the stereotypes are to be modified, the "nature of our cultural myths and categories" (p. 33), their importance in psychological development, and their impact on us must first be understood. To this end, she is concerned with the animus, but is more traditional in her basic view of the archetype than Moore. She retains Jung's and Neumann's categories for the masculine and feminine, but within these she makes a valuable contribution to the types and meanings of many varieties of animus in women. Personifying the archetypal image, Greenfield depicts the archetypes of the trickster and of the father as the most developed form of the animus of modern women, especially when they exist together. Initial stages of the trickster are the boy and Don Juan; the trickster in turn can develop into the hero and then into the father. The wise old man is the ultimate manifestation of the archetype.

Greenfield finds this last manifestation of the archetype to be beyond the experience of most adults, but also and most importantly beyond questions of gender, so that she too ends up with an androgynous figure as the final form of the archetype. She not only explores each figure in depth, bringing out its positive and negative sides, but she also looks at woman's psychological relationship to these figures and the way they are projected and internalized. Her article has the brief title of "The Archetypal Masculine" and is subtitled "Its Manifestation in Myth, and its Significance to Women," yet the subject of the work is really the animus. This is one more example of how Jungians make it difficult to do research on the psychology of women, and how easy it is to miss papers relevant to one's specific subject.

Marion Woodman (1980, 1983) returns to a more traditional interpretation of animus and anima. She discusses these concepts ahistorically and only insofar as they affect her central focus: the relationship of eating problems to the repressed and devalued feminine. As Beebe wrote of the importance of the father's anima in the son's development, so Woodman writes of the negative effects of the mother's animus on her daughter. Women with eating problems, Woodman writes, often have animus-possessed mothers—witch mothers—who inculcate predominantly male values in their daughters and disparage or neglect the feminine. Their fathers tend to follow patriarchal values, denigrating older women in favor of younger women or their own daughters. A father tends to project his anima upon the daughter, and consequently sees and values her not for herself but as a representative or image of his own anima. Woodman describes eating disorders as a variety of animus possession through which the woman is driven and hounded by perfectionism, and during which the power-witch-animus rapes the creative spiritual one. "The image of perfection in the culture and the internalized idealization of masculine principles in a woman create a desperate split in her nature and her perceptions of the feminine principle itself" (1983, cassette recording).

Jane Hollister Wheelwright (1984) eloquently describes the straitjacket that stereotyped and limited women's behavior in Jung's era: "Freedom for me to be myself was absolutely forbidden" (p. 3). She points out that many attributes natural to women but not fitting the stereotype were ascribed to the masculine and to the animus. Wheelwright believes that some animus identification is inevitable on the way toward its integration; she alludes not only to an integrated creative, light animus, but also to a positive, dark, and earthy one. "The primary business of the animus is to be a creative tool. Its secondary role is to give the necessary stamina to all endeavor" (p. 53).

Wheelwright, like such analysts as Harding, Binswanger, and Ujhely before her, traces the development of the animus in dreams; she describes how male figures in womens' dreams tend to change over the course of analysis, from violent oppressors and cruel judges to friendlier, more helpful figures, then to equal or supporting figures that stand beside the dreamer or even behind her, and finally become integrated so that feminine figures display positive characteristics that once belonged to the animus. Old age, Wheelwright adds, is a great time for integration.

Polly Young-Eisendrath and Florence Wiedemann (1987) present stages of animus development that are different from Greenfield's, though they use a number of the same figures (some of their work is based on Young-Eisendrath's 1984 book). The animus is an alien "other" in the first stage of development, the father, god or patriarch in the second, the youth, hero or lover in the third, the "partner within" in the fourth, and finally the androgyne in the fifth stage. These stages, the authors insist, need to occur in sequence; no stage can be missed. The authors loosely follow Emma Jung's, Harding's, and Neumann's developmental schemes, though without referring to them; instead they ground their theory on Loevenger's important work on ego development.

Young-Eisendrath and Wiedemann criticize Jung's original work on the animus and develop their theories in reference to it. They object to Jung's androlatic bias, his negative view of the animus, his confusion between the anima and real women, and his lack of attention to social context. They find that Jung and many of his followers share a tendency to use animus theory to belabor women, which hurts women's self-esteem and thus hinders, rather than promotes, psychological growth: "Jung contributed to much popular thinking about the inferiority of women's moral and intellectual capacities" (1984, p. 33). Young-Eisendrath and Wiedemann have little use for the constructive reworkings of the animus that have been made since Jung, and seldom refer to the work of other Jungians. Neither Young-Eisendrath's 1984 work nor Young-Eisendrath and Wiedemann's 1987 work is meant to be historical; the authors are concerned instead with immediate clinical problems, with promoting attitudes toward women which emphasize, empower and promote female authority. Most significantly, these two books present the first strongly feminist reworking of Jungian theory since Binswanger.

In 1984, 1985, and 1986, brief insights into the animus appeared in books and articles on other subjects. Jean Bolen (1984) criticizes the entire concept; she finds the animus not essential to women's psychology, and advocates doing away with the term, replacing it with feminine archetypes such as Athena and other dynamic goddesses. By using feminine figures to personify active, insightful, generative, and spiritual qualities, Bolen believes women can better regain their own strengths and powers; handing these over to the masculine, even to an inner masculine, further vitiates women's belief in themselves. In her discussion of Lilith, Vogelsang (1985) notes the way culture has for centuries opposed animus activity, labeling it as evil and systematically trying to eradicate it. According to her, bringing the creative animus back to life will help restore women's energy and creativity.

Andrew Samuels (1985) emphasizes the fluidity, permeability, and flexibility of the anima-animus concepts, finding them still useful, not as opposites, but as expressions of otherness and difference. He sees their greatest value as indications of the unconscious bases of the individual's particular form of positive or negative projection. Linda Leonard (1986), like Harding, Scott-Maxwell, and Singer, reflects on anima and animus problems as they come into play within relationships; she finds that working on anima-animus projections in a love relationship can involve the individual in a developmental process through which the two archetypes meet, unite, and lose their polarity. The inner and outer *coniunctio* of man and woman, anima and animus, holds the potential for a new existence in which men and women can be independent equals.

Verena Kast's (1986) view of the animus and anima in relationship is less optimistic than Leonard's, but more theoretically grounded. Her book, *The Nature of Loving,* is concerned with many of the same issues Leonard deals with. Kast belongs with the post-modern Jungians— Hillman, Hill, Whitmont, Beebe, and Moore—in that she considers animus and anima archetypes available to both men and women equally. Like Moore, she sees the archetype as a single one involving both the anima and the animus in a "couple constellation." The interplay between the two archetypes is primary. Kast strongly opposes gender stereotyping and stereotypical roles; instead she advocates questioning concepts in light of their psychological relevance and value. Her greatest criticism, which echoes Mattoon's and Bolen's, is the use to which animus theory is put by fellow analysts.

In the use therapists make of the Jungian anima-animus theory, the theory is sometimes simplified — often falsified — and in this simplification a fundamental assumption is more frequently expressed than in the more differentiated formulation of the theory. (p. 89)

Kast also criticizes the use of the concept to disqualify women's accomplishments, giving them over to the animus (a point Bolen, too, might have been contending with in her advocacy of feminine archetypes in place of the animus). Like Mattoon and Young-Eisendrath, Kast finds the term still too often used to disparage instead of to encourage conscious human potentiality. Hers is a strong and cogent addition to modern theory.

I am one of the Jungians who is guilty of burying theory within articles on other subjects. In my review of three books on the feminine (Douglas, 1986), I included an eight-page synopsis of the history and theory of the animus. It was the most comprehensive to date, but it was hidden in a form that made it inaccessible to scholars researching Jungian theory (it now forms the backbone of the present chapters).

In "Is the Animus Obsolete?" (1987), Mattoon and Jones present an insightful and up-to-date critical review of Jung's work on the animus, and then briefly refer to Emma Jung, de Castillejo, Neumann, Hillman, Whitmont, Woodman, Bolen, Leonard, Young-Eisendrath, and Douglas as part of a new wave of interest in and reevaluation of the concept. Mattoon and Jones point out the opposition of some feminists and critics to the dogmatic and traditionalist use of the term. They fault the traditional view as being bound by time and culture, not empirically established, inferred second-hand from the anima, leaving little room for individual differences, and being unbalancedly negative. After reviewing the reworking and updating of the concept, the authors determine that the animus is *not* obsolete, but has evolved in a useful way, as can be verified by psychological studies, anthropological data, and through subjective experience. They conclude, with the other post-modernists, that the animus is what is repressed and "other"— that it can lead toward androgyny, and reflects individual rather than primarily gender differences. Depotentiation of its negative aspects and integration of its positive ones helps women reclaim their full potentiality.

Much elaboration of the initial concept of anima and animus has occurred since Jung's time, while significant reinterpretation has taken place. Most of the reconceptualization of Jung's ideas has been aimed at making the archetypes' form and process more fitting to our culture and time, and less specific to that of Jung. Positive aspects of the animus have been increasingly emphasized. The role the culture and the patriarchy play in the rise of negative aspects of the two archetypes has been clearly delineated. An attempt has been made to free the archetypes from their link to one specific gender and exclusion from the other; efforts to rid the animus and anima of their linkage to certain types and to Eros and Logos accumulate. Though Hillman stands pretty much alone in his radical reassessment of the anima, Moore, Mattoon and Jones, Young-Eisendrath, and Kast have begun to do the same thing for the animus. Work on the animus follows a more consistent path and may therefore be more stable. However, even this work would benefit if the writers were more aware of (and cited) theory that underlies their own. It would make for better science if this became more common Jungian practice — because, as Mattoon has put it,

> the development of theory is enhanced, and perhaps is only possible, when theorists build on each other's work, either confirming or modifying, and each providing empirical support for the chosen position. (Mattoon, 1986, p. 24)

Further work in terms of this reassessment will undoubtedly consider the animus as separate from thinking and Logos, and define the difference. The anima/woman/feeling/Eros/Yin/relating/feminine linkage is no longer applicable, if it ever were. These concepts must be separated from each other, as must the animus/man/thinking/Logos/Yang/creating/masculine linkage. Different manifestations of the animus in relation to typology need to be explored. An area of great interest to me is the role of the animus as a mediator to the feeling function (Douglas, 1989). Aspects of the animus that would be consistent with this but remain unexplored would be the animus as earth father, nature spirit, peace bringer, gardener, nurturer, poet, storyteller, music maker, dancer, and playful, committed lover. As the masculine changes in its outward manifestations in our culture, its inward ones also change. Through cultivation of these new images of the inner masculine, their appearance in the outer world may possibly increase.

The archetype of Mercurius, the trickster, is suggested by Hillman, Hill, and Beebe as an element of the anima. Moore and Greenfield have shown its applicability to the animus. I believe, with Moore, that the trickster is an archetype that enlivens both animus and anima. Its application to the animus needs further non-traditional exploration; its consideration in terms of the anima remains rudimentary. I would suggest that the trickster archetype contains much that adds to and clarifies both concepts and their interrelationship without bringing in the confusion of gender-specific attributes. The trickster offers an archetypal approach to a contemporary treatment of animus and anima that holds the potential for including all the elaborations listed above. The trickster may also be the archetype that can unite a strange and divided age. It is an ambivalent, enigmatic, and subtle force that has the capacity for uniting opposites; at one and the same time, the trickster calls us back to a wild and magical level while leaping forward to embrace the new. The trickster and the shaman both transcend what we have been taught about our own psychology; the inclusion of the trickster also adds a note of antic humor to leaven and enlighten our reflections about ourselves.

The use of the terms animus and anima as pejoratives and as limitations on the range of individual behaviors must stop, as must any consideration of the feminine as inferior to the masculine, or vice-versa. Jung's descriptions of the animus and anima need to be seen as specific to his personality, to his era and its attitudes about the sexes. Wholesale adoption of his ideas as theory serves to ignore socio-cultural relativity, to maintain and perpetuate early twentieth-century gender roles, to limit the psychological development of patients, and to make Jungian theory retrogressive and unacceptable to feminists of either sex. The classical usage of writers limiting themselves to what Jung wrote is too strict, too tidy, and too simple; it is not appropriate for real people leading complex lives.

In spite of this criticism, I agree with Mattoon and Jones that the use of the concepts of animus and anima as a model remains of value, particularly in the exploration and expression of the "other" (one manifestation of which is the contrasexual), and the hold this "other" may have on us all through its varieties of projection and possession. It remains useful as a way of talking about the contrasexual and as a way of exploring the impingement of culture on self-development. For example, through exploration of the animus I can, as a woman of this culture, regain access to some of what I have repressed. This must be defined individually. Each manifestation of animus and anima—its strengths and weaknesses—are as idiosyncratic as each individual personality. The archetypes of animus and anima remain unconscious and incapable of full delineation. Examination of their images—which change with culture, with the growth and development of consciousness, and with individual needs—enriches and deepens our understanding of ourselves.

CHAPTER EIGHT: A FEELING OF POWER

Archetypes of the Feminine in Analytical Psychology

Like all life, tradition is a vast passing away and renewal.
  Robert Curtius, *European Literature and the Latin Middle Ages*

The situation of women today is especially hazardous because they are detaching themselves from a small group of archetypes and approaching a large group of them, but the new group is not yet clearly visible. Should the whole range of the new archetypal spectrum actually break through, however, the relationship between men and women will be re-formed in many new ways.
  Adolf Guggenbuhl-Craig, *Marriage: Dead or Alive*

The use of archetypal material continues to be one of the most fertile and accessible areas of Jungian psychology. Through it, abstract thought arrays itself in stories and images; archetypal forms add physical detail, they give a feeling of relationship and immediacy, and evoke direct response in the same way that pictures and stories have wakened the senses and the imagination since the beginning of human time. Recently there has been a burgeoning amount of books and articles on feminine archetypes, the feminine itself being a problematically insistent concern in analytical psychology. Guggenbuhl-Craig (1977) posits that, "there are dozens, if not hundreds, of feminine and masculine archetypes" (p. 48). He adds that there are many more than can be imagined, many also which only emerge in and are appropriate to particular socio-historical periods.

Since Jung's time, material from cultures antedating the Graeco-Roman era has become increasingly available and increasingly mined; these sources expand our awareness of the variety of feminine archetypes and give a wider mirror in which the feminine can reflect itself. They are often more useful than patriarchal myths because their ideas of the feminine tend to be less limited by androcentrism and are thus better suited to a freer, more comprehensive view. Some images are chosen by a culture, others remain hidden or latent and have to wait until the culture can receive them. Even though the time span I am covering is only about sixty years, a relatively short time historically, there has been both change and a pattern to that change which reflects and possibly abets a marked growth in the appreciation of the feminine.

Initial work by Jung and his early followers explored the idea of "archetype" itself and proposed examples. Jung, for example, wrote of the Great Mother, the maiden, the anima, the wise woman, and of the alchemical symbols of the feminine, especially its lunar motif. His material is based largely on Graeco-Roman myths, or, in the case of alchemy, on medieval texts. His immediate followers—Toni Wolff, Esther Harding, and Erich Neumann—each looked at feminine archetypes under differing organizational principles: feminine personality types, the feminine as a unity containing multiple cyclical characteristics, and the feminine within the mother-daughter continuum.

These three approaches represent three branches into which most subsequent investigations of feminine archetypes seem to flow. The first originated in the work of Toni Wolff, who proposes a theory of feminine psychology based on four different archetypal forms of the feminine. The second received impetus from M. Esther Harding's contemplation of the moon and moon goddesses as representative of the archetypal feminine and its cyclical structure. She sees the moon as a single entity containing separate phases. Her attention to and reevaluation of the dark side of the moon has been particulary generative for women writing and thinking on the feminine today. The third main branch derives from Erich Neumann's elaboration of Jung's initial work on the mother archetype and the mother-daughter archetype; Neumann adds an enormous amount of historical and mythological amplification, yet enfolds the feminine in a circular mother-daughter continuum within a linear theory of development of consciousness.

This chapter is organized around these three themes, with writers placed in one of the three categories according to the overriding archetype that seems to inform their work. Later writers struggle with, amend, expand, and elaborate particular areas of Wolff's, Harding's, and Neumann's basic forms. There is some inevitable ambiguity and overlap in this pattern, but it contains enough verisimilitude so that a seemingly fragmented plethora of images forms itself into these three comprehensive channels.

Personality types

Toni Wolff (1934/1956, 1941) organized woman and the anima according to four archetypal personality types she believes are representative of all feminine psychology. She prefers these personifications to Jung's psychological types (thinking, feeling, intuition, and sensation) as basic "structural forms of the psyche" more relevant to women than the function types. Her reason is that she finds women of her time less differentiated than men, governed by soul rather than spirit, and in need of an accessibly comprehensive and tangible form in place of Jung's more consciously articulated yet abstract formulations. In Wolff's model, woman's psychology is explored primarily in reference to the ways in which she relates to men. The four archetypes are the Mother, who nurtures men; the Hetaira, who relates to them as lover or mistress; the Amazon, who works alongside them and is a companion and a sister; and the Medium, who serves as a pathway to the unconscious for men. These four types also represent a man's anima, one type predominating and the others more or less developed.

Wolff presciently underscores one source of psychological problem by noting that though each of these archetypes is crucial, a woman's particular type may not suit her situation or the culture in which she lives; the type may even be one the culture disdains or fears. If the fit is wrong, psychological problems are apt to ensue, as they are if the feminine becomes divorced from the sacred. Before Wolff proceeds to explicate her structural forms, she writes of the sacred and deplores the loss of this aspect of the feminine in Christian and Judaic cultures and the imbalance this causes in many women's psyches.

In her exposition of types, Wolff portrays both the positive and negative aspects of each archetype. Her first type is the Mother, who primarily nourishes, guides, and protects, helping growth in her positive aspect. In her negative one she can overprotect, restrict differentiation and separation, and infect those in her care with unaccepted parts of her own personality. The Mother relates to the institution of marriage and family rather than to a particular man or child. Her opposite type is the Hetaira, who, in marked contrast to the Mother, relates to an individual man and the individuality of her children. "The function of the Hetaira is to awaken the individual psychic life in the male and to lead him through and beyond his male responsibilities toward the formation of a total personality" (1941, p. 6).

The Hetaira does this positively through her intensely individual focus, negatively by overemphasizing individuality and uniqueness and thus causing a man to lose his persona and his contact with outer life. Another negative possibility Wolff reflects on is that a woman may be unaware of her Hetaira nature and its effect on her children, so that she unconsciously treats her children as lovers. Wolff states that in marriage the Mother type acts as the "contained," the Hetaira as the "container." Both embody the relationship side of the union for the male.

The third type, the Amazon, is independent, holds many of the same values as men and works in relationship to culture rather than to a specific individual. Wolff depicts the Amazon-identified woman as having a strong ego and best realizing herself in work in the world and as a comrade to men. She incites men to action and inspires them. Negatively, Wolff describes this type as manifesting many of the same characteristics Jung gave to an animus-possessed woman: she can be driven, opinionated, over-masculinized and male-identified.

The fourth type is the Medium, whom Wolff places opposite the Amazon. The Medium "is immersed in the psychic atmosphere of her environment and the spirit of her period, but above all in the collective (impersonal) unconscious" (p. 9). On the positive side she helps put a man in touch with these aspects; on the negative she can embody the collective unconscious' shadier and more evil characteristics, and can be overwhelmed and possessed by them even to the point of insanity. Wolff states that a major danger for the medial woman is her very openness to the forces of the unconscious; they may weaken her ego and draw her into losing herself in her role as a conduit for others.

Wolff believes that all aspects of these four archetypes are potentially available to women, but that, as in function types, women tend to be a single type outwardly while having a secondary one as an inner possibility. The developed form and the less developed are companions, not opposites; for instance, the Hetaira is never paired with Mother, the Medium never paired with the Amazon. If completely one-sided, the form tends to manifest in an especially negative way. Wolff concedes that women may now be starting to integrate more aspects of these psychic forms and may be less one-sided than women of her generation; she applauds this development, but focuses on describing her observations of her peers.

The outer Hetaira, inner Medium combination is the most clearly and convincingly portrayed of all of Wolff's types. This may be because this combination was closer to Wolff's own psyche; perhaps the intensity of the descriptions arose because they meant so much to Wolff personally. One reading of her article is that Wolff created her typology out of her own battle to make sense of her relationship with Jung. Wolff's insistence that a woman could not be both Hetaira and Mother, but that each type played an essential yet different role in a man's life, legitimizes her own painfully equivocal role as Jung's mistress. Through her theory, Wolff could view herself as the Hetaira, whose task it was to awaken, inspire, and promote Jung's individual psychic life, while Emma Jung enriched his collective role in the community and family. Emma Jung fitted Wolff's description of the opposite and antithetical type, the outer-Mother inner-Amazon, almost as if it were based on her.

The flaw in Wolff's concepts is their restrictiveness; they leave out a woman's existence as an independent entity. Wolff portrays woman living only in a dependent relationship to something outside herself. Her structural forms constitute a model analogous to Jung's typology, but are more limited. The Mother is similar to the extraverted feeling type (with sensation secondary), the Hetaira to introverted feeling; the Medium is an example of extraverted or introverted intuition, the Amazon of sensation; a woman's thinking function is largely ignored. Each form reflects the socio-cultural limitations of the position of women of Wolff's time; they legitimize women's imprisonment in relationship and subservience to men's needs and interests. However, as Wolff's personal confession and as her effort to make sense out of the actual socio-cultural world in which women were confined, I find this work extremely moving. This is how Wolff and women of her generation must have had to live if they wanted to relate to men or have a place in the world at all. As concrete examples and personalized embodiments of some of the functional types, the Mother, Hetaira, Amazon, and Medium archetypes would probably be more appealing and understandable to predominantly feeling types. As a thinking-intuitive type, I prefer the freedom, logic, and expansiveness of Jung's typology.

Since Wolff's time, many analysts writing about the feminine have been drawn to her formulations, and their investigations of feminine types continue today. In *Knowing Woman* (1973), de Castillejo elaborates on Wolff's four types of the feminine in the light of traditional Jungian concepts of the feminine. She portrays the types as archetypal roles possible to women, and amplifies their positive and negative manifestations in the contemporary world. Like Wolff, she focuses on women and the feminine primarily in relation to men (though in a note to the 1973 edition, the editor adds that de Castillejo was planning to include a section on relationships between women, but died before she could). In contrast to Wolff, who focuses more on the Hetaira, de Castillejo writes most penetratingly about the Medium—a type with which de Castillejo can be identified. She builds on Wolff's idea of the gradual growth of consciousness in women as the century progressed, to both criticize and expand her typology:

> It is not enough today for any woman to be limited to one personality type any more than it is enough for a man to have only one psychological function at his disposal. The inner process which demands wholeness is as vividly at work in women as in men. When stuck in one personality type something forces a woman to develop a second, then a third and finally a fourth. (1973, p. 70)

De Castillejo explores the witch archetype as the negative of the Medium and as a product of our culture. She is one of the first Jungians to acknowledge and try to make sense of the anger she finds in her women patients. In a remarkable passage, de Castillejo gives a strong interpretation of this phenomenon.

> I think that a woman will also turn witch today for other reasons than personal power. The deeply buried feminine in us whose concern is the unbroken connection of all growing things is in passionate revolt against the stultifying, life-destroying, anonymous machine of civilization we have built. She is consumed by an inner rage which is buried in a layer of the unconscious often too deep for us to recognize. (p. 42)

Ann Ulanov, in *The Feminine in Jungian Psychology and in Christian Theology* (1971/1978), recreates Wolff's four feminine types in her own exploration of women's psychology. Ulanov does not refer to de Castillejo's work on the same subject, but does make extensive use of Moreno's (1965) theory of feminine development which combines Wolff's types (unaltered) with Neumann's developmental theory, Jungian animus/anima development, and a Deutschian perspective on feminine narcissistic-masochistic "adult" sexuality (see Chapter Nine for further discussion of Moreno's work).

Ulanov is specifically concerned with Wolff's types in women rather than in the anima. She expands on Wolff's original idea by dividing the types into active and static poles and into their positive and negative manifestations. She explores these psychologically in relation to a woman's attitude toward men and toward her animus. Ulanov, following Moreno, lists the dominant archetype behind each type. The Great Mother is the dominant archetype for the Mother type, The Great Father for the Hetaira, The Virgin for the Amazon, and the Wise Woman for the Medial Woman. Like de Castillejo, Ulanov sensitivly elaborates the positive and negative aspects in each type and emphasizes the potential presence of each type in every woman, noting, in an important extension of theory, that woman's "wholeness requires the fullest integration and exercise of all four modalities" (1971/1978, p. 195). Referring to Deutschian theory, she remarks on the masochistic, highly feminine female of the Mother type. By including Deutschian theory but restricting it to one type, Ulanov makes a subtle and innovative distinction that Freudians who adhere to Deutsch and feminists who despise her both overlook—the reality of one cultural form that has molded the feminine. Ulanov ascribes a passive, reactive role to the maternal that often extends into the unconscious, while, in this early book, she generally ignores the dynamic, active, initiating, heroic aspect of the mother.

Ulanov's description of the Hetaira follows Wolff's, but Ulanov expands it through equating her with the *puella aeterna*, the father's daughter, and then convincingly linking the Hetaira to masculine rather than feminine archetypes. She adds to the extensive work done by Wolff and de Castillejo on the positive aspects of the Amazon and the Medium, and expands on their negative possibilities. She writes perhaps most movingly of the Medium and the serious problems the Medium can cause through her very gifts—her natural intuitiveness sometimes stifling the potentialities of those around her.

Ulanov is drawn to Wolff's archetypal types rather than to Jung's function types, like Wolff finding them more characteristic of women's psychology. She adds another reason for her preference: the types are more descriptive as images of the particular manifestation the archetype takes, and these same images can shift outward form to suit varying cultural contexts. The cultural context Ulanov is concerned with in this book is the feminine in the United States of the nineteen-fifties and early nineteen-sixties. However, at the same time she sees beyond this to offer women a vision of a more comprehensive model of feminine individuality.

If a woman is aware of the archetypal dynamism underlying her own femininity, she knows more of herself. If she knows herself, she can avoid developing her own stereotypes of women and avoid having those of others foisted upon her. She falls neither into the trap of thinking and acting as "just a housewife," or "only a career woman," etc., nor into the opposite horror of being unable to accept the pluralism of the contending forces within her that might lead her to be more than one kind of woman. If she responds to the archetypes underlying her nature, then she can respond to the deep motivations that the archetypes provide, which can only enrich her life, her relation to others, and her contributions to her society. (1971/1978, pp. 210-211)

In "The Witch Archetype" (1977), Ulanov amends and extends her (1971/1978) examination of the Medium by looking at (as de Castillejo did so briefly before her) one aspect of its manifestation—the much-maligned witch. Ulanov finds positive elements in the witch archetype as well as the more conventionally negative ones. She brings the archetype dynamically alive through her study of the witch's voracious appetite, her unconventionality (marked by a distancing from the human community), aggression, sexuality, and her interest in power. Ulanov makes an invaluable psychological interpretation of the reasons behind the witch's presence in modern women. In contrast to her 1971 work, Ulanov emphasizes the constructive and compensating function of the witch archetype in a woman's psychology, finding that the witch typifies the "negative" and rejected aspects of the feminine which currently cry out for redemption. She demonstrates that the witch has a great deal to teach a woman, including the witch's capacity to nourish herself rather than others, her ability to say *no* to outer demands, her isolation from the crowd and its varied holds on her and her retreat into a dark, introspective, solitary place of renewal, which results in the recovery of her own power, sexuality, and her full self. Ulanov speaks out passionately for the redemption of these witch-like characteristics which Judeo-Christian culture has heretofore denied women. She affirms that the restoration of these elements recovers woman's efficacy and power while also helping to constellate and affirm feminine intellectuality and assertiveness.

Ulanov does not ignore the negative manifestations of the witch, a negative that becomes all the more potent as the archetype is culturally and personally rejected and split off. For instance, Ulanov finds that eating disorders can accompany the witch's voraciousness. (She also writes of this in a 1979 article "Fatness and the Female".) Coldness and rejection are the negative sides of distancing, while a power complex and animus possession are the negative aspects of the witch's assertion and her sexuality. Irritability, fretfulness, bad temper, and malevolence also signify the witch's presence; however, if the witch's power is openly acknowledged and confronted, then she becomes transformed into a helper. The witch abjures the "feminine" requirement to be relentlessly receptive and giving and thus teaches a woman how to nurture, feed, and give to herself. Ulanov makes a strong argument for the incorporation of the witch, along with the other attributes of the feminine, as key to psychological growth. She finds that if the witch is not integrated, the feminine risks possession by this remote, archaic, and primitive archetype.

Ulanov's sensitive and courageous exploration of the witch archetype is an important addition to Wolff's description of the Medium and adds a dynamically potent aspect to woman's psychology. In *The Witch and the Clown* (1987), she and her husband, Barry Ulanov, expand on her earlier work on the positive and negative aspects of this archetype, dealing now with the anima as much as with women. They examine the two archetypes in relationship with each other and focus especially on issues of sexuality. The influence of the witch archetype in masculine psychology is especially well developed.

In *The Wisdom of the Psyche* (1988), Ulanov is concerned with a feminine approach to religious discovery; here she stresses the "fierce force of the feminine" (p. 75). Her chapter on women's wiles extends her work on the witch, especially on the aftermath of incorporating this aspect: "the calm wise authority [that] springs from facing the witch" (p. 77). Moving away from Wolff's types, she concentrates on the archetypal images of Eve and of Mary to portray another form of the developmental path that incorporates the negative and moves from wiliness to a vigorous, daring, and aggressive femininity. In this book Ulanov extends Wolff's and her own understanding of the relationship between the feminine and the divine; she sees the spiritual and potent feminine as well able to contain the energy inherent in the redeemed or undistorted witch archetype she has helped us to appreciate and revalue.

Instead of Wolff's more general types, Philip Zabriskie (1974) chooses five particular Olympian Goddesses—Aphrodite, Hera-Demeter, Artemis, and Athena—as archetypes that constitute a typology of the feminine and also represent a totality of what the feminine can be. Though he states that his work is applicable to both women and the anima, Zabriskie's choices of type and descriptions are particularly helpful in gaining a better understanding of the anima. Like Wolff, he also considers varying combinations of his types. Zabriskie emphasizes what lies behind the choice of archetypal image: "We look for images with power, images which evoke or connect with powerful feeling, for such images move the psyche" (p. 34). He cites the five archetypes he has chosen as each containing different possibilities "of a genuine, anciently valid mode of the feminine" (p. 36) which can guide contemporary women's varying paths of development. Zabriskie finds that women or men's animae, through studying and meditating on these goddesses' variety, can find what mirrors them best, and then use this to model themselves on a compatible type; they can thus also better accept their own individual ways of being and expressing the feminine.

Guggenbuhl-Craig (1977) reviews earlier work; he concludes that current attitudes toward the archetypes are marred by "too limited a vision" both of the archetype and of its possibilities. He regrets that Wolff's types were portrayed simply through their relationship to men. He extends and adds to Wolff's and de Castillejo's interpretations, partially freeing them from their relational dependence. He divides Wolff's maternal archetype into its chthonic and spiritual aspects, each of which he sees as bipolar — the chthonic mother nourishes and devours; the spiritual inspires or maddens. He adds a Hera type and a Mater-Dolorosa type to Wolff's concept of the mother. Guggenbuhl-Craig views the Hetaira archetype as a companion and equal, intellectually independent yet not hostile to men. To these two Wolffian types, he also adds Aphrodite, the archetype of the desirable beloved, and Athene, the archetypal image who is wise, energetic, self-sufficient, not especially sexual, "a most interesting" archetype he finds pertinent to many happily widowed and divorced women. The Amazon whom Wolff limited to comrade and inspirer of men, Guggenbuhl-Craig finds far more independent. He combines this archetype with Artemis and the Vestal Virgin as types that have been neither sufficiently valued for their independence nor sufficiently permitted in our culture. Negatively, this archetype manifests itself as the femme fatale and Belle Dame Sans Merci. Instead of blaming the woman who lives out these images in a negative way, Guggenbuhl-Craig echoes Ulanov in restoring an important historical perspective to archetypal images and to their "pathology." In doing so he relieves some of the burden women bear for being out of step with their world.

Many of the so-called neurotically false attitudes are not the result of an unfavorable psychological development, as we usually understand them, but the image of a particular archetype which cannot be lived with a good conscience because it is rejected by the collective. Practically whole archetypal patterns of feminine behavior which do not relate to men are relegated to "should not be," and are seen as neurotic and sick. . . . Archetypes need certain circumstances and spiritual movements in a particular historical period in order to be activated and lived. (1977, p. 51)

Guggenbuhl-Craig finds the dominance of the maternal archetype to be declining, as is the fund of energy women have for its various manifestations. This decline has been accompanied by a rise in once rejected archetypes. For men, however, he finds not much has changed—the same archetypal patterns dominating men's roles in 1977 as in Jung's day. These patterns once offered men many more choices than were available to women; once they liberated but now they bind men, whereas women are freeing themselves through embracing many archetypal images and roles. The possibilities open to women today mark a major transition. Guggenbuhl-Craig views this transition as a time of crucial and stressful life-passage in which the power released by these new archetypal images needs to be humanized and domesticated.

In "The Amazon Problem" (1971), René Malamud updates one of Wolff's types, the Amazon, as an example of self-sufficiency and independence. He finds this archetype particularly suitable for both men and women today, and amplifies the archetypal images connected with the Amazon, especially as depicted by the goddess Artemis. The major problem connected with her integration is misconstruing the archetype as one of enmity toward men rather than of a way toward necessary detachment from them. Malamud feels that the conflict between the archetypes of Aphrodite and Artemis, the mother and daughter, is especially marked today by misunderstanding, hatred, and a refusal of each to examine the other—her own shadow side.

Linda Leonard (1973, 1978, 1982), echoing Ulanov, includes the Wolffian Amazon type with the *puella* under the archetype of the daughter. Her work on the father/daughter relationship culminates in her 1982 book, *The Wounded Woman: Healing the Father-Daughter Relationship*. Leonard is concerned with the need for a deeper appreciation of the feminine. She finds that valuing the feminine heals the wound inflicted by the father and by "the patriarchal society which itself functions like a poor father, culturally devaluing the worth of women" (1982, p. 3). Leonard examines the Iphigenia legend as an archetypal symbol for the culturally-extolled sacrifice of the daughter. She writes of the *puella* (the eternal girl) and the Amazon as two archetypal poles present in women in a patriarchy. Clinically, she describes the *puella* and Amazon as suffering from low self-image and faulty development that derive from a damaged relation with the personal father or the patriarchy, or both. Leonard thinks that the *puella* archetype is one consequence of a positive father complex, since the *puella* gains acceptance through adopting her father's and the culture's idea of women. She accepts and lives out masculine projections rather than developing her own individuality or strength. Leonard divides the *puella* archetype into four patterns: the darling doll, the fragile girl of glass, the Donna Juana and the misfit. Each of these is dependent; each lacks a balanced relationship to limits and boundaries; each avoids commitment. Leonard perceptively outlines ways of transforming the archetypal image into something more positive; she finds that it requires women to become conscious of specific negative patterns, examine them, overcome the underlying despair and self-loathing present in each pattern, gain strength, and ultimately value their own selves rather than the projections.

The other side of the *puella* in a father-daughter complex is the Amazon. In her splendidly elucidated differention of Wolff's original description, Leonard explores three types of the Amazon which result from a negative father complex. The Armored Amazon unconsciously lives the masculine — she dons it as a dynamic or driven persona in order to compensate for a passive, ineffective father, and to offset the horror of his inability to protect her. The Dutiful Daughter expunges feeling and passion and replaces them with a rigid sense of duty imposed by someone else, often the father. The Martyr "petrifies" in an armor of long-suffering, limitation, and resentment — she is often the daughter of a fascistic, authoritarian father. A fourth type, the Warrior Queen, a potential Psyche figure, is more positive and evolved than the others; she is a strong and determined fighter, yet is often trapped in the fighting, raging aspect of the archetype, misdirecting her energy in fury at her weak and irresponsible father. Leonard portrays all these Amazon types as rejecting and devaluing the feminine side of themselves through their imitation of what they deem the superior masculine.

Leonard describes the healing that can occur for both the Amazon and *puella* through a woman's full experience and expression of her rage and grief at her own and the general feminine condition today, and then through a search to discover her inner and outer feminine. Leonard concludes with the image of Psyche searching for the feminine spirit. Her work is an invaluable contemporary study of the wounded feminine in archetypal and clinical form. It is stronger, often searingly strong, in its delineation of the problem rather than in its resolution (which Leonard attempts in her 1986 book *On the Way to the Wedding*). Her work proposes some first necessary steps toward reclaiming the feminine. What the feminine spirit is, though, is not articulated, though its many archetypal forms are extensively explored.

In her article about the psychological problems of tomgirls in our society B. K. Fowles (1978) rejects the word "tomboy" as sexist, limiting, and inaccurate. Like Malamud and Leonard, she focuses on the Amazon, explicating this single Wolffian type; while at the same time criticizing and reinterpreting Neumann. Fowles regards the Amazon archetype as a potentially healing symbol which provides active, vigorous, and adventurous girls with an active feminine model for these qualities. In unpublished dissertations, Martha Harrell (1983) and Susan Schwartz (1985) also focus on aspects of the *puella* archetype. Harrell sees the archetype as an image emblematic of the psychic split in women; this is especially exemplified in a type of double *puella:* a father's-daughter handed over to the patriarchy by a patriarchally-identified mother. Harrell sensitively examines the syndrome through its archetypal imagery and in clinical material; she give a vivid description of an outwardly conscientious and efficient type whose feminine self remains hidden, even frozen, behind her spurious identity as a good girl—cut off from her own power and sexuality, and preternaturally subservient to men. Healing comes about when the feminine self is paid attention, honored, encouraged, and related to in a feeling way.

Jean Bolen (1982 and 1984) chooses seven Greek goddesses as images of archetypes active in women today, and describes each with great thoroughness. She employs a format similar to Zabriskie's original one (1974), portraying each goddess as a model suitable to a particular type of woman and her individual development. Like Zabriskie, Bolen explores the archetype's relevance to contemporary women's lives and to their psychological problems. In *Goddesses in Everywoman* (1984), she briefly examines the underlying archetype of the goddess, often stressing its pre-Greek origin. She speaks of the difficulty inherent in differentiating between the ways the feminine manifests itself in a patriarchy and what the feminine is in itself. Bolen divides the seven goddesses into three major categories that diverge from Wolff's quaternity: the virgin goddesses, Artemis, Athena and Hestia, who are independent and active; the more traditional and related vulnerable goddesses, Persephone, Demeter, and Hera; and the one alchemical and transformative goddess, Aphrodite (Bolen's other precursor, Guggenbuhl-Craig, 1977, also introduced Aphrodite as a necessary addition to Wolff's types). Bolen takes Aphrodite as a model for a more complete and independent feminine than offered by the other archetypes. Like her contemporaries, Ulanov and Zabriskie, and in contrast to Wolff, she considers it normal for a woman to have access to each archetypal image, drawing on its values and variety as she needs them. Bolen concentrates on the more positive aspects of each archetype rather than on the negative—a side which is not denied, though it and its reclamation don't receive the same passionate intensity that Ulanov bestowed upon it. Bolen seems more intent on increasing women's acceptance of themselves; she buttresses a sense of self-worth and esteem through women's alliance with congruent archetypal images. She is writing for a general audience, and her book serves as a popularization of the Jungian idea of feminine archetypes. Her work is well researched, containing salient examples of the applicability of her concepts to her clinical practice; it is a valuable expansion of Wolff's typology and an important popular Jungian contribution to feminist literature in general.

Following Wolff, de Castillejo, and Ulanov, E. C. Whitmont (1979, 1980, 1982a) divides the feminine according to type; he portrays the four types in a broader context than did the earlier authors. Rather than limiting women to one or two types, he finds his types manifest in and available to all women, and to men's anima-natures. Whitmont describes the types as autonomous in the individual (rather than defining them in relation to the masculine); consequently he renames and reevaluates them. His first type is Luna, whom he depicts as the empathic supporter of concrete life and feeling, of measure, rhythm, and the claims and needs of the body. He describes Lila as the "dance of the senses"; she dances and plays with the world of opposites and is full of lightness, charm, and poetry; she is also as changeable as Maya. Pallas Athena works, creates, and strives in the world; she holds well-considered convictions and concerns herself with new patterns of being and relationship.

Whitmont credits Perera for the first comprehensive exposition of his final type, Medusa, who on one side represents the healer and medium, while on the other is the abyss of transformation, annihilation, emptiness, and depression; unconnected and unrelated, she typifies the descent into the underworld. She also symbolizes a capacity for letting go and surrender which, he says, women recognize though they may repress, but which for men represents "a death-like threat. . . a temporary loss of soul" (1982a, p. 141). As in most recent delineations of Wolffian types, Whitmont considers their active and passive sides as well as their positive and negative aspects. He makes the strong suggestion that the integration of the feminine, especially the dark Medusa side and the ecstatic Dionysian side, is perhaps the essential individual psychotherapeutic and cultural task of our time.

Whitmont's typology resembles Wolff's in that Luna's characteristics are similar to Wolff's Mother type, his Lila similar to the Hetaira, Pallas Athena to the Amazon and his Medusa to the Medium, but its effect is immediately and strikingly different. Autonomous and free of societal restrictions, these feminine types are far more exciting, intense, and immediate than their Victorian foremothers. The heightened intensity of their affect, or else the poetic sensibility underlying Whitmont's descriptions, seems more evocative of the anima in both men and women than denoting a woman's typical mode of being. These may in fact be the best depiction to date of the structural forms of the anima.

Katherine Bradway, Betty Meador, and Jane Wheelwright, in lectures or workshops given in 1984, remark on the new sense of power in the archetypes of the feminine emerging in studies and in women's dreams, as well as the increasing awareness of that sense of power by many women whom they see as patients. Bradway (1984) puts this succinctly:

> In the past year there has been a new phenomenon in my analytic work: one woman after another has come to my office with the statement that she is aware of a feeling of power. It seemed to just suddenly start happening. They say, "I feel a kind of power I never felt before." They are both excited by and afraid of this power. What may happen? They have trouble identifying what kind of power this is. It feels like something personal. Perhaps it is sexual, but it doesn't feel like that. It feels like something more extensive. It has energy. These women don't want to get rid of the feeling, but they want to become more conscious of what it is. They want to use the energy and passion that comes with it without being afraid that it is dangerous. It doesn't sound as if there is a desire to wrest power from another person, or that it is connected more with destroying than with creating. It seems like a special type of woman power that has been waiting in the wings and is now being cued in by our evolving culture. I think it is connected with a freeing from inhibitions—a kind of freedom to be themselves—to feel anger and hate as well as caring and love. Women are finally feeling permitted to experience and claim

the full range of their affects, even the demonic affects of the dark feminine as described in *Descent to the Goddess* by Sylvia Perera. Such experiencing brings with it a feeling of strength — a feeling of power — a
feeling of effectiveness. (pp. 3-4)

Wolff's typology continues to attract attention and amplification. Two
recent articles or books have been studies of single extensions of her types.
Woolger and Woolger (1987) further explore the Amazon-Athena archetype for its active vigor, but now link the Amazon with its Medusa side
to produce "a fully developed adult woman — able to fight and create"
(p. 27). They make the significant point that this archetype, thus rein-
terpreted, challenges prior assumptions and efforts to keep women limited
to traditional Jungian definitions of femininity. The archetype presents
a strong model of an extraverted, companionable, modern working woman. They conclude, however, that "a whole new psychology of the intelligent, creative woman in the world needs to be written" (p. 28).

Laurie Shapira (1988) explores Wolff's Medium type in relation to a
specific hysterical pattern. She finds that this pattern deprives the medial
woman of her power by splitting it off; hysteria catches a woman between a patriarchal animus-identified ego on the one side and a powerful negative mother complex on the other, with both acting in place
of a feminine ego. Shapira equates mediality with a function type that
is predominantly feeling, though informed by intuition and sensation.
Without references to other work, Shapira declares that feeling is wom-
en's primary function. She uses Cassandra as an example of the archetypal
image of the Medium in its undeveloped form and as a personification
of a complex that can arise when a medial woman gets caught in the
conflict between matriarchal and patriarchal values. Shapira notes a
progression in the development of feminine ego and feminine self, to
describe which she uses the archetypes of Athena, Demeter, Persephone,
Hecate, Artemis and, finally, Themis as the most developed.

Toni Wolff's idea was to translate Jung's typology into archetypal images of four personality types for women and the anima. There has been
much updating and reworking of her feminine types. These include
elaborating, modifying, or reevaluating the four types; adding additional
or new possibilities; focusing on one particular type; redeeming the negative side of one or more types; applying a particular archetype to a particular psychological problem; and the growing use of pre-patriarchal
mythology. The general evolution of Wolff's typological ideas is toward
making the types more autonomous and freeing them from cultural

stereotypes. Negative elements, especially, have been reclaimed to add needed power and complexity. Their strongest use encourages women's own individuality, way of being, and self-efficacy. Some of these same processes recur in the development of Harding's and Neumann's initial work.

The Moon and Its Phases

Another way of looking at the feminine is to see it as representative, not of a composite of one or more differing personality types, but as a central and specific unity which now reveals one aspect, now another. This unity manifests different views and sides of a single concrete entity, in the same way that the moon remains constant, though its appearance changes. Harding was the first Jungian to explore the moon goddess in all of her varying phases; her purpose is to present the many sides of the feminine within this context, especially sides which her culture ignored or devalued. Harding's emphasis on these devalued aspects contributes an important balance to the one-sided view of the feminine of her era. Harding endeavors "to reinstate the goddess in the individual life, through psychological experience" (1935/1976, p. xv). In his introduction to Harding's *Woman's Mysteries: Ancient and Modern* (1935), Jung describes her purpose as "an attempt to present certain archetypal foundations of feminine psychology" (Harding, 1935/1976, p. x). In fact she goes further. Through presenting the lunar goddess in all her cyclical multiplicity, Harding has created a lasting and comprehensive model from which to understand feminine psychology and development. In her first articulation of this model, Harding includes the idea that the initiatory element in women's lunar mysteries is similar to women's experience of analysis. She makes the analogy between ancient times and ours and notes that both require an initiation into the feminine mysteries. Harding stresses the need for initiation as a way to redeem our external or internal wastelands through the restoration of a fertilizing spirit. She believes that the symbol of the moon provides a unifying link that has validity for the present time as well as for the past.

> The ancient religions of the moon goddess represent the education of the emotional life as taking place, not through a course of study, not even as the result of a system of discipline, but through an initiation. The interpretation of the moon mysteries . . . links our modern life problems to those of the ancient people. (p. xiv)

Harding examines archetypes of the feminine in the early lunar religions, ranging from Graeco-Roman examples to the far earlier ones of Babylon, Assyria, and Phoenicia. Her chapters on Ishtar and Isis contain important depictions of the active feminine generally unrecognized in Harding's day. Aspects that Harding stresses are the active feminine's cyclical nature, its mutability, its multiple nature, and its power as an independent symbol. The virgin archetype present in these lunar goddesses, in the feminine and in an individual woman, is like the moon one-in-herself; she is also sexual, procreative, and creative. Harding's emphasis on the power of the archetype and her depiction of it as a strong and important symbol of the feminine stand in implicit contradiction to Jung's and Wolff's view of a related and subservient feminine. Her words cry out a very different reality to theirs.

> The Moon Goddess belongs to a matriarchal, not a patriarchal, system. She is not related to any god as wife or "counterpart." She is her own mistress, virgin, one-in-herself. The characteristics of these great and powerful goddesses do not mirror those of any of the male gods, nor do they represent the feminine counterpart of characteristics originally male. (p. 105)

Harding examines the relevance of the lunar archetype to the psychology of women and the anima. She finds it an apt symbol of inner psychological change. The dark sides of the goddess and her capacity for what our culture excludes or terms "evil" — the unrelated, magical, underworld qualities — are included and honored. Harding emphasizes that these are necessary aspects in both men and women, but may be harder for men to assimilate. She explains women's greater knowledge of their darker side and their relative willingness to accept it, through what Harding calls woman's easier access to the unconscious and through a woman's biological knowledge of her own moon-like cycles and all the changes that occur in menstruation, pregnancy, and birth.

> The contradictory character of the Moon Goddess is thus resolved. For her good and evil aspects are seen to be not absolute but relative. Her power works evil under certain circumstances but good under others. To men whose nature is in opposition to her cyclic character she is apt to be particularly dangerous. To women who have within them this same peculiar quality which the Moon Goddess epitomizes, the power she wields is far less likely to be destructive and indeed if the woman is in right relation to this principle of her own nature, the goddess blesses her with fertility and with magic power. (p. 116)

Harding makes the perceptive observation that the cultural and psychological loss of rejected aspects of the feminine results in a loss of contact with the deeper levels of humaness. The regaining of what was once excluded, she concludes, produces a revolutionary and revitalizing inner change. Harding finds that the reclamation of what had been banished constitutes both a major individual and a major collective problem. A woman's access to what was excluded provides an inner source for her own feminine strength; a man needs the same access in order to have a proper relation to his anima and to regain what Harding calls his lost Eros. The son, she says, needs to have a mother who knows both her negative side as well as her positive side so that she can say "no" to him as well as "yes," and give him a push toward independence as well as nurturance. This seems to me to be crucial for daughters as well as sons.

"Eros" appears to be a rather limited term to cover the huge realm of the feminine Harding explores. Eros is considered the archetype of love and often of relatedness; the lunar archetypes Harding describes embody a far wider range than this single archetype. This usage, however, seems to be the unexamined convention of Jungians of Harding's day, and her adoption of it may have made her much more comprehensive view of the feminine more acceptable — because on the surface she speaks the same language, honoring feminine Eros and relatedness, and thus apparently accords herself with her contemporaries' theorizing. Hardings's depiction of the psychological and collective problems rising from the loss of contact with the feminine remains valid and applicable today. If one replaces the term "Eros" with "feminine," Harding's conclusion, her hope, and her grief appear achingly modern:

> Today the goddess is no longer worshipped. Her shrines are lost in the dust of ages while her statues line the walls of museums. But the law or power of which she was but the personification is unabated in its strength and lifegiving potency. It is we who have changed. We have given our allegiance too exclusively to masculine forces. Today, however, the ancient feminine principle is reasserting its power. Forced on by suffering and unhappiness incurred through disregard of the Eros values, men and women are turning again towards the Moon Mother, not, however, through a religious cult, not even with a conscious knowledge of what they are doing, but through a change in psychological attitude. For that principle, which in ancient and more naive days was projected into the form of a goddess, is no longer seen in the guise of a religious tenet but is now sensed as a psychological force arising from the unconscious, hav-

ing, as had the Magna Dea of old, power to mold the destinies of mankind. (p. 241)

The inclusion and reevaluation of the dark and "negative" lunar side of the feminine that Harding emphasizes continues to be one of the most fertile developments in analytical psychology. There is much contemporary interest in the dark side of the feminine and of archetypes that represent the often unrelated, inward and downward-turning, dark moon side of feminine nature. This is often depicted as a black side, and has tended to be considered negative and evil, sometimes even split off from Harding's respect for it as but one of the moon's necessary phases.

In the discussion that follows, the writers' emphasis is on the blackness or darkness of the image and on an implicit or explicit acknowledgement that it is but one phase of the feminine; these archetypes thus fall more naturally in with the moon archetype — here in its dark phase — than with Wolffian typology and its separate emphasis on witchiness *per se* or as part of the Medium type.

Leopold Stein continues the reevaluation first started by Harding in his 1955 article on the loathsome woman archetype; this is the basis for his less clinical book *Loathsome Women* (1959), a study of four patients whom he diagnoses as possible witches because of a certain uncanniness he felt in their presence and because of their weird capacity to fascinate and repel him. He felt they were living out something dark and obscure within them. His fascination with these women led to his study of witches in general. It is unclear, even after a rather close re-reading of his book, whether what Stein relates may not also involve transference and countertransference phenomena and projections similar to those constellated by those women in medieval times who were also labeled witches because of their oddity and deviance.

Hosmer (1968) follows this reevaluation with a long descriptive study of the Kali archetype. Andrea Dykes, in a 1976 lecture that was later printed in Tuby (1983), elaborates on the Medusa archetype today. She notes that Medusa was originally one of three connected sisters; originally beautiful, she was turned loathsome as a result of Athena's anger. Dykes informs the reader that the name Medusa not only denotes a witch but also means queen, ruler, and mistress. She writes of both the negative and positive aspects of a woman's psychological encounter with Medusa and this strange archetype's ability to possess or to transform, to be witch or queen, depending on her phase, attitude, and stage of development.

Guggenbuhl-Craig (1977) writes of other "archetypal images of man-killing aggressivity" which he considers to be unrecognized or patholo-gized parts of women's nature. He mentions Penthesilea, Clorinda, Britomart, Juturna, Marfisa, Bradamanta, Camilla, Belphoebe, and Radigund as archetypal images of a side of the feminine that has been misinterpreted and therefore designated incorrectly as unfeminine, mas-culine, or androgynous. His point is that they represent *feminine* charac-teristics. They are aspects of a vigorously aggressive dark feminine side that is culturally prohibited and out of fashion. It is an archetypal pow-er of the dark feminine which seems very hard to metabolize and calls up images of fierce destruction. Guggenbuhl-Craig concludes that "the recognition of primary murderous aggressivity will bring a colossal en-richment of conscious experiential possibilities to mankind on one hand, but countless complications on the other" (p. 60).

The blood imagery in this archetype, brought out in Hosmer's study of Kali, Dykes' exploration of the Medusa, and Guggenbuhl-Craig's gory viragos, goes back to the moon, its phases, and its connection to wom-an's monthly menstrual cycle. Though Murray Stein (1977), in perhaps his most feminist and significant contribution to feminine psychology, expressly states that Hera is far more than a lunar goddess, he links her four aspects to the four phases of the moon and grounds the archetypal image in instincts and in woman's bodily reality. He champions Hera as fourfold and complete, in turn virgin, perfect or fulfilled, widow and, finally, "the secret one" during her menstruation. Stein emphasizes that Hera's value as an archetypal image lies in her (and woman's) cyclical access to all four of these characteristics throughout her life. It is the bloody, fiery, and infernal side of the archetype that occupies most of Stein's attention, and that he elucidates so splendidly. He deplores the patriarchy's attitude to the widow and menstruating sides of Hera and of the feminine, and blames patriarchal times and attitudes as the cause of the very negativity they revile. Stein gives a strong reinterpretation of Hera's "down side"—her being unclaimed, he states, means that no androcentric man is up to her demands for equality, while her secret, menstruating state affords access to the underworld where she reigns as queen.

Penelope Shuttle's and Peter Redgrove's (1978) study of menstruation is another original and far-reaching reevaluation of the dark side of the feminine. These writers connect Harding's dark lunar archetype with the premenstrual and menstrual phases of a woman's hormonal cycle, including the varying aspects of the feminine (which type theorists such as Wolff parcelled out to different women or different times of the life-cycle) as representative of normal cyclical hormonal patterns present, to a greater or lesser degree, in all women. Shuttle and Redgrove look at all phases of the moon in relation to women's cyclic behavioral and hormonal patterns. They find the dark lunar, premenstrual and menstrual stage has particular psychological value; it contains an inward-turning, unconnected, and often depressive aspect which can provide a woman (or demand from her) a time for contemplation and retreat. Shuttle and Redgrove and Stein are among the very few writers who give enough emphasis to the importance and value of menstruation in the psychology of women. They cite such Jungians as Emma Jung (1981), Harding (1935/1976), Hannah (1951/1962), von Franz (1958-1959/1976), and Ulanov (1971/1978) as their predecessors.

Marilyn Nagy (1981) connects menstruation with shamanism, citing the archetype of initiation in a woman's menstrual cycle. Along with Shuttle and Redgrove, she finds that menstruation allows time for retreat and interiority in which what she calls "feminine Eros" can develop. She describes the psychology of women as reflective of their biological rhythms.

Betty Meador (1986) writes of the Thesmophoria as a woman's ritual "centered around the mystery of blood" (p. 36). She relates the ritual to the round of life, connecting women with sacredness, their bodies, menstruation, and menopause. Along with Harding, Stein, Nagy, and Perera, she emphasizes the importance of the downgoing from which women's creativity can rise. Through returning to the depths in a psychological ritual similar to the Thesmophoria, Meador finds that a woman can regain contact with a form of spirituality deeply connected with primal life. Meador makes an important link between a woman's sense of inner strength and her connection with her lunar cycles—the daily, or lunar, round of existence.

Perhaps synchronistically, Jutta Voss' unpublished Zürich Institute thesis, "The Wild Pig Goddess and Her Blood of Life" (1986), deals with the same themes as Meador. Voss also writes of the Thesmophoria and includes a historical treatment of attitudes toward menstruation. Voss connects the loss of contact with feminine power with the cultural change in attitude toward female blood. Once honored as a healing power, women's menses became cursed in the patriarchy at the same time as men's blood became honored. Rituals of the Thesmophoria and of the wild swine goddess recall that honor and lost power. Voss focuses on the cosmic uterus of the wild swine goddess as a uterus of regeneration and rebirth; she traces this goddesses' blood rituals in many cross-cultural parallels, and for their vital and empowering effect on women.

Philip Zabriskie (1979) extends Leopold Stein's consideration of the loathly woman archetype in a neglected but important study of Cundrie, Baubo, and other supposedly negative aspects of the Great Mother, such as the Medusa and Baba Yaga, modern examples of the dark archetype in literature, dreams, and in clinical case material. He reclaims the value of the loathly woman, finding that her "horribleness is partly the fury of the oppressed and repressed matriarchal era or feminine principle" (p. 52). Perhaps less under the spell of this archetype than L. Stein, Zabriskie (like Murray Stein) examines it more comprehensively as being far from stereotypically wicked or evil but, rather, typifying a certain fullness, authority, and helpfulness that potentially holds great promise toward rounding out a more complete sense of the self. Zabriskie stresses the importance of the struggle with, and acceptance of, the dark and the ugly, and of this archetype's usefulness as a guide and a source of wisdom.

In a collection of articles in Stroud and Thomas' *Images of the Untouched* (1982), the virgin archetype is revalued both for its quality of being vital, holy, and alive yet untouched (Harding's "ever-renewing moon" and the woman who is "one-in-herself"), and for the virgin's darker, more chthonic aspects. The virgin archetype is revealed as a variable, complex, and multi-dimensional image that is neither unknowing nor unphysical. In this collection, Patricia Berry-Hillman writes of some negative consequences of the virgin archetype in her aspect as the untouched one. She explores this negativity in the stories of Hippolytus, Narcissus, and Cassandra, all of whom come to disaster through cleaving solely to the bright side of things, and who all lack darkly lunar ambivalences and an embodied relationship with the archetype.

Gustafson (1979) focuses on the uncannily powerful dark-moon side of the archetype in its most positive form. He traces this in the Christian worship of its Black Madonnas, especially the statue at Einsiedeln in Switzerland. He makes the important point that there is a worldwide equation, among black people as well as white and in all cultures and at all levels of sophistication, of the color black and of the dark with night, the earth, the underworld, the uncanny, and with power and magic. Through these black and powerful virgins, who often display magical healing, protective, and spiritually constellating forces, he connects Christianity to ancient forms of goddess worship.

Ean Begg (1986) is concerned with the same Black Virgin archetype. He traces the archetype geographically and culturally, finding it a survival of the ancient lunar goddess in a form full of great mystery and power — especially sexual and healing power.

> The return of the Black Virgin to the forefront of collective consciousness has coincided with the profound psychological need to reconcile sexuality and religion. She has always helped her supplicants to circumvent the rigidities of patriarchal legislation and is traditionally on the side of physical processes — healing the sick, easing the pangs of childbirth, making the milk flow. She knows how to break rigid masculine rules. (p. 28)

Begg connects the Black Virgin to Lilith, the Queen of Sheba, and Hagar of the Old Testament, as well as to the Celtic Cerridwen, Moriggan, and Loathly Damsel. In other cultures he finds aspects of the Black Virgin in Innanna, Kali, the Black Isis, Neith, Anath, Hathor, Sekmet, in Artemis of Ephesus and in the triple goddess, Hecate. His book is lyrical — while Zabriskie and Murray Stein honor their dark-moon figures through examination and explication, Begg's book reads like a song of love to the Black Virgin and to independent feminine strength. Begg himself writes how the repressed parts of the archetype in history and in individuals tend to "take their captors captive" (p. 37). He finds Lilith emblematic of the rebellion against the patriarchy's treatment of women and its denial of women's equality and freedom. Writing of the combined pairs of opposites, Begg considers one side of the pair orthodox as the Matronit, Mary, and the White Virgin, while the contrasting side are the heretical Lilith, Mary Magdalene, and Black Virgin. He considers the latter to be of great psychological use today, as the patriarchal system dies and signs of a new system start to emerge.

The archetype of Lilith continues to be one of the most darkly enigmatic and intriguing forms of the lunar archetype. She is the unseen one — the moon with its face turned away in rage at earth's usurpation of her light. She is also the rejected Moon Mother, fantastically and menacingly obscured by our own dark fears of her. Barbara Koltuv (1980, 1983, 1986) has done most to recall Lilith to our memories and to our psyches as a crucial though profoundly ambiguous feminine power. Koltuv analyzes the rejected yet potent dark-moon side of the feminine represented by Lilith and traces this archetype historically. She describes

Lilith as opposite but equal to and counterposing the Judeo-Christian, masculine, all-good God, calling her "the feminine transpersonal shadow" (1980, p. xi). In an important analysis of the archetype, Koltuv depicts Lilith as an archetypal phase of the feminine that is dark, wounded, bitter, fiery, hostile, and raging because it has been neglected and rejected for so long in the patriarchy. Koltuv links Lilith with Hecate as a crossroads goddess and strongly reclaims the power of both in women's lives. As goddess of the crossroads, Lilith (Hecate) is a passionate and intense presence indispensible at the instinctual crossroads of women's puberty, menstruation, orgasms, conceiving, birthing, motherhood, and menopause. Yet Koltuv is also concerned that this archetype is one that has been especially suppressed and unintegrated; as such it embodies "the sense of irredeemable loss and betrayal in the deepest places of feminine psyche" (1980, p. 13). This is an observation that amplifies and makes more conscious de Castillejo's image of "the deeply buried feminine . . . consumed by an inner rage which is buried in a layer of the unconscious too deep for us to recognize." As a representative of the feminine's loss, betrayal, and rage, it is clear that Lilith holds much that reflects women's deepest feelings, try as we might to obscure her light with our own shadow projections.

Colonna (1980) also connects Lilith with images of the darkened moon. For her, Lilith represents the deviant, the witch, and the outlaw; she is transformative as well as demonic. Like Koltuv, Colonna notes that honoring and reintegrating Lilith results in the restoration of energy and vitality—a gift of this archetype to a woman's body. It also provides access to an instinctive and passionately creative side of the psyche that goes far beyond Eros. However, Colonna realizes that it is just this released feminine energy which the patriarchy finds so threatening and intolerable. Colonna does not refer to Koltuv's more comprehensive work on the same subject (perhaps developing the same theme independently, as happens when an archetype emerges into collective consciousness).

E. W. Vogelsang (1985) cites both Koltuv and Colonna in her study of the conflict between Adam and Lilith. She, too, regards Lilith as an important archetype newly emerging into consciousness. For her this reemergence is a sign that women have grown beyond Eve and the more traditional biblical roles for women. Vogelsang considers Adam and Lilith to hold the potential for a true partnership of the masculine and feminine. She describes Lilith as strong, angry, and aggressive. Though men may still reject Lilith the way Adam did, Vogelsang feels that women are now being impelled to develop their Lilith side. She feels this development to be an individuation process like Lilith's own, where nothing happens linearly or in order; in fact the process has its own idiosyncratic order, much more lunar than patriarchal.

The cross-cultural scope of the dark side of the moon archetype is shown in Ruth Knipe's (1982) article on Pele, the Hawaiian goddess of volcanoes, and in Vera Bürhmann's (1987) studies of the feminine in witchcraft in Africa. In a fascinating study, Bürhmann portrays this dark feminine archetype as the force behind psychological healing in African witch religions, menstrual cults, and in their New World Voodoo counterparts. She finds part of this archetype a good image for a specific shadowy side of many women. She describes the same uncanny feeling of "an evil presence" as L. Stein (1959) did in his study of modern witch-like women. She adds that the witch can also be a type of trickster feminine, and refers to Neumann's ideas about the terrible mother aspect of the great mother archetype.

Marion Woodman (1980, 1982, 1983) describes many of these same lunar aspects of the feminine. Like Koltuv and Colonna, she portrays them as manifestations of an archetype of devalued feminine energy which is constellated when the power of the feminine is repressed and suppressed. Woodman has a horrific insight into this aspect of the feminine, depicting it as having been subjected to generations of rape by the external patriarchal culture and by the internal negative demon-lover animus. Like Ulanov, she calls the feminine aspect that results from this the "witch" archetype. Woodman, in contrast to Ulanov sees the witch as negative, an inner enemy, and relates its deleterious effects to the clinical problems of anorexia and bulimia. She presents much clinical evidence as well as moving case histories to back her conclusions.

In *The Owl Was a Baker's Daughter* (1980), Woodman focuses on the negative mother complex that she believes underlies many eating disorders. Woodman describes the daughter's self-blame rising from a disturbed primal relationship with her mother, or when she has been rejected by her mother in the outside world. Woodman pictures the daughter responding by developing a voracious inner Terrible Mother; living this out, she also rejects her own inner child. The father complex adds to this problem, as does the rejection of the feminine by society as a whole. In order for women to regain access to the feminine, Woodman finds the archetypal images of Dionysus, the Eleusinian mysteries, and the Mysteries at Pompeii of great psychological use. She cites Fierz-

David's prior work on Pompeii, but is apparently unaware of the English translation of her lectures that were, until recently, only available in Jungian libraries.

In *Addiction to Perfection* (1982) and in her 1983 workshop on the same subject, Woodman concentrates more on the father complex. She again sees the witch archetype as the typical manifestation of the rejected feminine in our culture today. She describes this manifestation as Medusa-like, driving and possessing women in many different and compulsive ways of which eating disorders are the most obvious. The archetypes of Sophia and the Black Madonna are proposed as counterforces emerging in contemporary consciousness. Sophia is representative of the full-moon feminine of wisdom and balance, the Black Madonna of the synthesis of the "dark" carnal, the earthly and the spiritual. The round of the Great Mother, mothering and being mothered (as in da Vinci's portrait of Saint Anne), has been especially important in Woodman's own therapeutic work, which she describes as a vigorous combination of analysis with dance, massage, and body-work. "Extraordinary changes take place once the Goddess is accepted. Whereas the body was a bulwark against the feminine, it now becomes the instrument through which the feminine plays" (1983, p. 168).

In *The Pregnant Virgin* (1985), Woodman reemphasizes the importance of ritual, body work, and feminine grounding combined with more traditional analysis. The pregnant virgin harks back to Harding's moon goddess who is one-in-herself. Here, Woodman focuses on the split between the masculine and the feminine; she finds that women are often cut off from their bodies while men are cut off from women and the feminine. Woodman includes her own personal journey and healing; she uses the archetype of the chrysalis as a healing symbol whose pattern she and many of her patients follow.

In "Emergence of the Feminine" (1987), Woodman returns to the problems of the devouring mother and its connection with women's starving and bingeing. She also makes use of the Demeter-Persephone myth and cites Perera's (1981) work on the Sumerian myth that antedated it. She differentiates her analytic work from Perera's:

My work with obese and anorexic women, especially if they are fathers' daughters, has made me very aware that women contending with an inner Medusa/demon lover have a different psychology from those contending with an Ereshkigal, the dark side of the Sumerian Goddess, whom Sylvia Perera so clearly describes in *Descent to the Goddess*. Their paths of healing are quite different. It becomes increasingly important to recognize which archetypal pattern is at the center of the neurosis, because if a woman is trying to contact her instincts through Ereshkigal, when in fact she should be trying to take the head off Medusa, she can find herself in paralyzing despair. (1982, p. 174)

I find these different paths possibly indicative of Woodman's and Perera's differing personal psychologies, function types, personal experiences, and analytic approaches. Certainly Woodman focuses more on one aspect—the concrete fight with the witch, the pathology, and the bodily battle—in a way which somewhat distances her, perhaps, from Harding's lunar continuity. Sylvia Perera, like Harding, Nagy, and Meador, is concerned with a slower, darker, more intuitive and introverted subterranean journey. Perhaps because of a type similarity with Perera, I find her *Descent to the Goddess* (1981) more useful than Woodman's book in my own therapeutic work, even with women with eating disorders. Perera's book is a comprehensive and deeply moving study of the psychological value in, and the healing quality of, the dark, depressive archetype. Perera uses the Sumerian myth of Inanna and her descent to an underworld belonging to her shadow and sister, Ereshkigal, in order to elucidate the need, both in therapy and in our culture, for recognizing and regaining the potency of all the dark, repressed sides of the feminine.

Ereshkigal represents an archetypal feminine potency which Perera describes as timeless, abysmal, messy, full of affect, ugly, and impersonal; she uses terms similar to Shuttle and Redgrove's description of the menstrual archetype. It is only in the patriarchy, Perera concludes, that this aspect has been split off from the upper feminine and thus manifests itself as terrible mother, dragon, and witch. Perera's important reevaluation emphasizes the psychological necessity of withdrawal, descent into the unconscious, and even a possibly severe depression in a woman's individuation process. She notes the crucial need for this realm of the disdained and repressed, for it is in this blackness that psychological healing, empowerment, and creativity may lie. She equates our suppression of woman's dark side with contemporary shadow projection onto anything feminine that reminds us of it, and with our society's fear of death, birth, and the body. Perera joins Woodman in emphasizing that in her analytic practice the recognition of this archetype seems to demand more body-oriented or body-involving modes of therapy, in addition to traditional verbal analysis.

Perera's strong and valuable work recalls an essential link between the reclamation of this dark lunar archetype and analysis. She delineates the initiatory process of analysis in terms of Inanna's descent, her ritual revival and rebirth, with its sprinkling of food and water as libation.

> In analysis we see this feeding in the necessity to offer validation over and over to the untrusting analysand in small, immunizing doses, until she or he can bear the experience of acceptance. It means guarding against haste, staying with the endless affects and events of daily life in all their detail until the flow of life energies returns to the stricken soul.
>
> Inanna is restored to active life and rises from the underworld reborn. But she returns demonic . . . She has met Ereshkigal and knows the abysmal reality: that all changes and life demand sacrifice. That is exactly the knowledge that patriarchal morality and the fathers' eternally maiden daughters have fled from, wanting to do things right in order to avoid the pain of their own renewal, their own separate being and uniqueness. Inanna comes up loathesome and claiming her right to survive. She is not a beautiful maid, daughter of the fathers, but ugly, selfish, ruthless, willing to be very negative, willing not to care. (p. 78)

Perera uses a more patriarchal archetype in *The Scapegoat Complex* (1986) perceiving the Hebrew scapegoat ritual as the archetype behind victimization and projection. "The scapegoat phenomenon is a particular expression, along with Cain, Ishmael, Satan, witch-hunting, minority persecution and war, of the general problem of shadow projection" (p. 98). Perera notes that women, as the devalued sex, almost always have to struggle with identification with the scapegoat projections they receive. Healing of the complex involves a woman in a long journey of inner growth and authentication, accompanied by the development or discovery of the feminine ego and feminine self Perera writes of so movingly in *Descent to The Goddess.* Her work is significant and profound because of the way she grounds the archetypal image clinically in psychological theory and case material, and the way each illumine and kindle the other.

Betty Meador (1984) presented a weekend workshop for the San Francisco Jung Institute on her work on the same Sumerian archetype that Perera used in *Descent to The Goddess.* Meador describes the conflict between the Inanna and Ereshkigal in each woman; she sees these two as shadow and sister archetypes. Meador interprets their reuniting as an inner search for the neglected, suppressed, wounded little girl and this child's growing up and union with the more accepted feminine. Meador views this reunion and reevaluation of the dark side of the feminine (which our culture has erroneously called "negative") with the light (which our culture has, again erroneously, depicted as "positive") as the great task in consciousness today. She warns that it is a hazardous task now carried out by women, and one denoting a huge movement of the psyche out of and away from the patriarchy. In her delineation of the archetype, Meador draws on the Demeter-Persephone myth, women's mysteries of initiation, and the black goddess. To these she adds the red (and menstruating) goddess, the Tantric Dakini of sexuality.

Meador describes a three-fold archetype of the feminine, all aspects of which can be found in and through a woman's own body consciousness and her "passionate bodily connection to the divine female ground." The white goddess, whose animals are the white sow and the white mare, is the goddess of birth and growth. Christianity and the patriarchy have accepted part of her in the image of Mary. The black goddess is the underworld goddess of prophecy, divining, and fate which the patriarchy banished as a witch. The red goddess is the potent Yin aspect of the erotic and of women's sexual power. Meador describes this aspect as being suppressed and denigrated by our culture more than any of the others; it is an essential archetype which combines the erotic, the sexual, and the spiritual in a significant and feminine way. Making a free translation of the Sumerian myth, Meador has enacted the poems with a group of women in a modern form of the mystery religions. The most powerful of these poems are in praise of female genitals, of earthy, feminine sexuality, and of woman's desire for and sexual meeting with the masculine on equal terms.

The linkage of the body, especially the female body, with the moon is self-evident. Harding first wrote of this in the nineteen-thirties, and it has continued to be a strong part of the lunar-feminine connection ever since. A less obvious link with the moon as archetypal image is that the body too goes through cycles and yet, like the moon, is also a symbol of wholeness, the unity that holds and grounds us in all our phases. Body work, embodiedness, bodily disturbances, and body therapy all recall us to our earthly selves and to the pull the moon exerts on our corporeal existence. Recollecting the moon in turn restores the crucial importance of our bodies to our own sense of who we are. Both give a woman back her body—a crucial return to wholeness—which had been subsumed by the patriarchy. A discussion of archetypes that have to do with body therapy, the body, or body as archetype, thus belongs with the archetype of the moon and its phases.

In the nineteen-eighties more and more attention was paid to the neglected corporeal body in analytical psychology. One focus of this attention on weight and eating disorders started with Ulanov's (1979) "Fatness and the Female" and received a great impetus through Woodman's work. Eating disorders are interpreted as an expression of feminine hunger for real nourishment in a society that often fails to provide it. Many Jungians now perceive these disorders as a feminine issue exaggerated by the demands of the patriarchy for anima-like youthfulness (the maiden) and indicative of a "disordered relation to the archetypal feminine of our world and our attempts to re-order it in new ways" (Ulanov, 1979, p. 19). Berry (1982) notes the connection of anorexia and compulsive eating with archetypal and chthonic rites, ritual, and taboos. She thinks these diseases represent both bodily enactments of a symbolic and psychological problem and a search for its cure.

In "The Concealed Body Language of Anorexia Nervosa" (1983), Bani Shorter gives a sensitive portrayal of the anorexic as under the spell of an unintegrated Medusa/Athena archetype, at once too dark and too bright. She equates the anorexic with a father-identified, Athena-like maiden. Living the Athena side, this type of woman always guards against her dark Medusa phase; as she heroically attacks and strives, she is also ever alert to avoid facing herself as the biological (Medusa) woman she also happens to be. As Athena, she identifies with the aggressor and with the patriarchy, and resists being a woman, especially a mother.

Polly Young-Eisendrath (1984) returns to the concept of the loathly woman addressed by Stein and Zabriskie. She concentrates on one particular loathly women archetype: Lady Ragnell. Her book, *Hags and Heroes,* is about the reclamation of the hag; this reclamation results in a woman's greater sense of power and efficacy and a more equal relationship between the sexes. Young-Eisendrath portrays the unredeemed hag as typical of the undervalued feminine principle behind the negative mother complex. She writes of the problem of women's self-hatred of their own culturally reviled hag qualities. The recognition and acceptance of the loathly woman leads both men and women toward autonomy, independence, and toward embracing all aspects of the repressed feminine.

The growing use of body therapy has been written about and practiced by Anita Greene (1984) and Joan Chodorow (1984). Penny Bernstein (1980a, 1980b, 1981) studies the archetype of the moon goddess, medium, and earth mother for its special relevance to the healing poten-

tial inherent in dance and body therapy. She describes the lunar archetype's value for dance and movement therapy; she also finds the archetype behind the union of gestalt technique and active imagination in
Jungian movement and body therapy of analysts such as Woodman,
Greene, and Chodorow, each of whose work rests on an embodied view
of the feminine.

Single archetypal myths stand behind other recent work on specific
psychological problems that arise from non-acceptance of the full round
of feminine experience. Jan Bauer (1982) writes of alcoholism and women,
using the archetypal conflict of Apollo and Dionysus in myth and in
a woman's psyche. She sees Aesklepios, the wounded hero, as a recon-
ciling and healing symbol for women who are dealing with the problems of alcoholism. Lynn Cowan (1982) considers the religious and
archetypal components of masochism; she (like Bauer) uses primarily
masculine figures, such as the medieval Flagellants and the mythological Prometheus and Dionysus, to exemplify various aspects of the problem (which also contain its healing). Her conclusion, through a study
of Dionysus, is that sadomasochism is masochistic at its center, deriving
from desolation, over-dependence, and hatred of dependency. The sa-
dist or masochist is psychically split and involved in shame-filled and
forbidden excesses of duality, rather than in a more moderate phase-
like linkage (like the dark and light sides of the moon). "A shift in perspective, from either/or to both/and would help us move out of the vicious cycle" (p. 23) and toward allowing rapture and ecstasy.

Nancy Qualls-Corbett (1988) returns to the archetypes of Mary, Mary
Magdelene, and the Black Virgin, as well as to the more ancient lunar
Great Goddesses. She finds aspects of these goddesses and their female
followers in the archetype of the sacred prostitute, whom she depicts
as a previously forbidden "moving, changing, transformative aspect of
the feminine that is associated with the goddess of love" (p. 57). Qualls-
Corbett connects this aspect of the dynamic feminine with Harding's
moon goddess and sees it as contributing to a woman's knowledge of
both her light and her dark sides and to the expansion of the perception of the feminine.

Core work on the feminine derives from, or is enlightened by, the
archetype of the moon. From Harding through to the present, this archetype offers an image of wholeness made up of parts which are also wholes;
it allows for an image of a feminine containing multiplicity, cycles, and
change within one self—one moon. The archetype has abundant room

for all that a woman can be and all that the feminine can represent. Through work suffused by prior endeavors, analysts using elements of this archetype have built up an impressive reevaluation of the feminine, work which involves reclaiming feminine power, anger, vitality, the rejected, dark, bloody, and corporeal as well as strength and sovereignty. It also reconnects us to our own home planet and its nearest companion in an image of sublime beauty. This is in marked contrast to the impoverished glimpses of a constrained and truncated feminine too often presented in traditional Jungian theory (and traditional culture).

The Mother and the Mother-Daughter Pair

A third unifying theme in Jungian treatment of archetypal imagery of the feminine is more relational and personal than the other two. In it, writers portray the feminine in terms of a Mother-Child continuum or in images of the Mother archetype alone. Though the archetypal image itself is circular like the moon, it is unlike the moon and its phases because the cycle is depicted humanly and in time. Perhaps because Neumann was the first to explore this image in depth, a parallel idea of stages of consciousness and linear development often accompanies it.

Erich Neumann (1950/1954, 1954, 1955) contributed much valuable material to the elaboration of more traditional aspects of the feminine — especially on the archetype of the Great Mother. His work on feminine archetypes is, perhaps, better known than Harding's, though his ideas initially take a dimmer view of the feminine as carrier of psychological progress. In *The Origins and History of Consciousness* (1950/1954), he posits three archetypal stages of consciousness. The first stage is the *uroboric* — primordial, unconscious, thoughtless, and wordless. In it everything is merged and undifferentiated. The second stage, the *matriarchal*, values the feminine over the masculine, and is again mostly unconscious. It expresses itself in a timeless round of experience and falls under the archetype of the Great Mother. The *patriarchal* is the third stage. In it a person or a society splits off and differentiates from the mother toward increasingly individual, personal, rational, and linear experience; in the process, the matriarchal stage and the feminine are devalued. In his article "The Moon and Matriarchal Consciousness" (1954), Neumann builds on Jung's idea of lunar consciousness as diffused, unfocused consciousness, and applies this to women. He also examines the moon archetype as symbolic of the matriarchal stage of consciousness, and describes it as quintessentially feminine and useful

for understanding women's psychology. Yet Neumann's idea of the moon
lacks immediacy. It also lacks Harding's and her followers' vital grasp
of its (and women's) completeness; instead, he limits the moon to a shim-
mery, indefinite quasi-poetic image. Perhaps Neumann's idea of the lunar archetype is more fitting to the feminine in men of his era than
to most women. In one review, Marilyn Nagy may have found the apt
words for the unease Neumann's article engenders.

> When *The Moon and Matriarchal Consciousness* was published in Zurich
> in 1953 it caused a discontented stir among the women analysts of the
> Jungian community, who thought that it was a study not so much of femi-
> nine psychology as of a projective state of consciousness in a man when
> the anima is constellated. I've thought about the women I know. Do they
> behave like the images of the attractive, mysterious, self contained god-
> desses in Neumann's . . . books, with their deep, inner sense of timeless
> rhythms, and a knowledge of life which is instinctively felt rather than
> verbally formulated? . . . we don't feel very magical or very powerful.
> (Nagy, 1981b, p. 109)

In his next work on the feminine, *The Great Mother: An Analysis
of the Archetype* (1955), Neumann continues his exploration of feminine archetypes. His purpose is to make a structural analysis of the Great
Mother as an example of what analytical psychology means by archetype. It is also an investigation of the feminine and the female psyche
as a "contribution to a future therapy of culture" (1955, p. xlii).

Neumann thinks the inclusion of the feminine is crucial in order to
balance "the one-sidedly patriarchal development of the male intellectual consciousness" (p. xlii). This book is far longer than Harding's; its
examples derive from the Primordial Goddess primarily in her role as
mother or—as in the archetype of Demeter and Persephone—in the
mother-daughter pair. He splits the Great Mother and feminine psychology into two characters, the elementary and the transformative. The
elementary has two sides, a positive and a negative, each of which can
manifest itself within a woman's psychology in a sort of unconscious *par-
ticipation mystique.* The transformative element also has its positive and
negative sides. Positively, it aids growth and renewal and leads away from
the elementary. Negatively, it can be hostile and provocative, yet even
so, cause tension and change. Other than this concept of tension and
change, Neumann, unlike Harding, does not reevaluate the dark side
of the feminine archetype.

Neumann comments that men's and women's experience of the feminine within them and in projection are different. For the woman, he describes the expression as external and in relationship; he says, "the transformative character—even her own transformation—is from the beginning connected with the problem of the *thou* relationship," but occurs naturally and unreflectingly (p. 31). For a man, though, it is internal: "the anima is the vehicle par excellence of the transformative character" (p. 33). Like Harding, Neumann focuses on woman's mystery religions and their connection with biological experience.

> The instinctual mysteries revolve around the central elements in the life of a woman—birth, menstruation, conception, pregnancy, sexuality, climacteric, and death—the primordial mysteries project a psychic symbolism upon the real world and so transform it. The mysteries of the Feminine may be divided into mysteries of preservation, formation, nourishment, and transformation. (p. 282)

In this work, Neumann seems to conclude that women are both less evolved and less conscious than men. He also sees "feminine" closeness to nature and bodily experience dualistically, as the opposite of, and below, the "masculine" spiritual, with the result that women appear inferior and more primitive than men in their psychic evolution. However, Neumann asserts that this very instinctuality holds power, magic and "mana" that men need and can use for their own evolution. Neumann's idea of the mother-daughter archetype limits the feminine to a matriarchal cycle where the mother births the daughter, who then becomes a mother herself in an endless and repetitive matriarchal round that requires neither wholeness nor the push toward individuation implicit in the moon symbolism.

Neumann describes the Eleusinian mysteries (which recall perhaps the greatest mother-daughter myth—that of Demeter and Persephone) as women's mysteries that are midway between the matriarchal and the patriarchal; they are still "predominantly emotional and unconscious" (p. 323). Neumann offers them as a model of a way for woman to reach an understanding of herself, and describes them as a mystery during which the daughter separates from and then is reconnected to the mother, having only a brief and aberrant contact with the masculine world, resulting in the birth of a son. To be fair to Neumann, he does say in a note that he is describing archetypes; their relevance to women would "require a 'psychology of the Feminine' to consider in full" (p. 305n).

The value of the book lies in its wealth of detail and its many exam-

ples of the archetype of the Great Mother from prehistory and across
many divergent cultures. There are 185 pages of illustrations of the archetype. As proof of the prevalence and power of a single archetype in the
human world, it is a conclusive work. Aside from its tendency to mix
an exploration of an archetype with a theory of consciousness which confuses an actual conscious woman with matriarchal consciousness, the book
remains an excellent depiction of the archetype of the Great Mother.

> The Archetypal Feminine in man unfolds like mankind itself. At the be-
> ginning stands the primeval goddess, resting in the materiality of her
> elementary character, knowing nothing but the secret of her womb; at
> the end is Tara, in her left hand the opening lotus blossom of psychic
> flowering, her right hand held out toward the world in a gesture of giv-
> ing. Her eyes are half closed and in her meditation she turns toward the
> outward as well as the inner world: an eternal image of the redeeming
> female spirit. Both together form the unity of the Great Goddess who,
> in the totality of her unfolding, fills the world from its lowest elementary
> phase to its supreme spiritual transformation. (pp. 334-335)

Neumann's dualistic and evolutionary mode of seeing a linear growth
of consciousness from the primitive, earthy, and predominantly womanly to the spiritual, heavenly, and predominantly manly seems very
typical of his time. In *Amor and Psyche* (1962), however, Neumann took
a great leap forward from this early twentieth-century outlook. In this
remarkable book he portrays a far more active developmental psychology of women that is marked by confrontation and a quest for individuation. In striking contrast to his earlier work on the feminine, he presents
Psyche as an archetype of an active, transformative feminine who creates her own redemption rather than passively waiting for it. Psyche
separates from the Great Mother, engages in tasks of individuation, and
evolves along conventionally masculine lines toward greater consciousness; but, unlike masculine individuation, she manages to accomplish
this and still reunite with the Great Mother. This book mainly involves
a developmental theory which I will discuss in Chapter Nine, as I will
the work of Fierz-David (1988).

Linda Fierz-David is perhaps the most consistently overlooked writer
on the psychology of the feminine. It is only thanks to her sons that
her lectures on the frescoes at Pompeii were saved and privately published in their original typewritten form. She uses the frescoes of the
Villa of Mysteries at Pompeii as the basis of an archetypal analysis of
woman's psychological development, positing the images of Dionysus,

Ariadne, Pasiphae, Phaedra, Medea, the Kore, Sophia, and the Roman
matron Livia as different archetypal aspects of feminine stages of consciousness that are relevant to both the anima and the psychology of
women. A strong mother figure guides the initiation and comforts, but
does not protect, the daughter initiate in her ordeal and development.

In this development of consciousness, Fierz-David sticks very close to
Jung's ideas about the feminine, relatedness, and the need for spirit.
However, her choice of a women's mystery that was solely for and by wom-
en uses a very different set of archetypes and a different form from the
alchemical marriage symbols Jung used for the same purpose in "The
Psychology of the Transference" (1946). In contrast, the fresco symbols
emphasize the uniting of the earthly with the spiritual, the higher with
the lower, the sexual with the divine, in a way peculiarly suited to wom-
en's psychology. It is also a set of symbols mediated by the feminine,
and seems more appropriate than Jung's images when applied to an analytical relationship where both analysand and analyst are female. The
Mysteries involve an initiatory process that Harding, too, equates with
analysis. Fierz-David contrasts the archetypes of the feminine she is
discussing—which, like mother and daughter—emerge from and gain
their strength from relationship to each other, with Toni Wolff's personality types, which she criticizes for being one-sided in that they are
related only to men and to society. Fierz-David suggests that because
of this one-sidedness they carry an unrecognized and powerful shadow
in which the unrelated feminine becomes solely negative: Freud's *terrible mother* is the shadow of the Mother; the prostitute, the shadow of
the Hetaira; the destructive witch is the shadow of the Medium; the
power-driven matriarchal despot is the shadow of the Amazon.

> None of these types can give us an impression of how it looks when the
> woman rests purely and solidly upon her femininity; none can give us
> an indication of what this can mean. In our Pompeiian mystery cult, how-
> ever, we have an archetypal image of the deepest significance for just this
> femininity resting entirely upon itself . . . the *forsaken Ariadne-
> Persephone on Naxos.* (1988, p. 157)

From Neumann's work on feminine archetypes descend a quantity
of work on the mother and mother-daughter archetype and their many
permutations. The androgyne archetype belongs with and is allowed by
the Mother-Child archetype in that the mother includes, combines and
unites; she also permits a polymorphous complexity that the more du-

alistic, hierarchical, and gender-conscious father archetype abhors. Androgynous archetypes are heralded by Carol Rupprecht (1974) and June Singer (1975, 1976) as an antidote to the limitations imposed by gender expectations. Singer focuses on the healing potential of the androgyne archetype. Ulanov (1971), Hillman (1974), Black (1978), Bradway (1982a), and Whitmont (1982a) briefly consider the androgyne archetype as a counter to the psychological damage caused by the split and repression resulting from our stereotypical gender-linked patterns of behavior. Berry (1982) believes gender to be archetypal, but also that Jungians often err in making gender distinctions dogmatic and oppositional (while some feminists use them defensively). When the archetype of gender is used to justify personality, then it is restrictive and hinders development. Instead, Berry argues for the archetype's manifestation in its androgynous polymorphous perverse form—a form which predates gender consciousness and can teach how to play with gender roles and how to combine pleasure, sexuality, and play. She feels that this archetype of infancy can be returned to and reintegrated at a more developed level, while freeing it from infantile feelings of inferiority. Hillman discusses the alchemical and material archetype of salt as an androgynous image for feeling, Eros, and soul available to men and women alike. Its positive side is solidly felt experience; its negative, the danger of fixation. For the *puer* or *puella* "the puer comes not only on wings of flight and in games of love; he comes, too, smarting with a memory of beauty and what one is on earth for" (Hillman, 1982, p. 122).

Hillman's major work on the feminine is contained in *The Myth of Analysis: Three Essays in Archetypal Psychology* (1972). He builds on Neumann but prefers the archetype of bisexuality—the androgyne as emblematic of a further development of consciousness. He approaches the feminine through a discussion of the history of misogyny and its accompanying myth of female inferiority. He reviews Neumann's (1962) study, *Amor and Psyche,* and emphasizes Neumann's distinction between the matriarchal archetype (Aphrodite) and an individuated feminine archetype (Psyche). For the feminine to be individuated, Hillman thinks that new archetypal consciousness is required. In opposition to the prevailing masculine definition of consciousness, he proposes two archetypal symbols: Dionysus and the bisexual androgyne. These promote synthesis rather than division, and carry an equal respect for the unconscious and the conscious, the masculine and the feminine.

Rivkah Kluger (1974, 1978) extends Neumann's work by examining female characters in the Old Testament for the presence and absence of feminine archetypes. She finds that the neglect of these feminine figures is closely related to contemporary women's spiritual problems. She notes that strong mother-daughter figures do exist in the Bible, and depicts Sarah, Leah, Rachel, and Rebekah as models or archetypal images that are still potent.

Black (1978) analyzes Jung's comments on the priestess archetype, whom she sees as a symbol for a spiritual mother — a figure more useful to women in their search for spirituality than the father, or priestly, archetype. Writing at the same time as Kluger, she does not mention her, but instead finds Judeo-Christianity lacking in appropriate female archetypes. Lynda Schmidt (1980) notes Kluger's work and builds on it, identifying a progression from Sarah to Leah and Rachel, then to the prophet Miriam, all as forerunners of modern women in a mothers' lineage. She separates the mother-daughter pair by contrasting the images that are positively connected to the mother (mother's daughters) with archetypes of father's daughters, such as the Virgin archetypes of Artemis, Athena, the angry Amazon, and the seductive Aphrodite, all of whom have a negative relationship to the mother. She proposes Artemis/Apollo and the alchemical soror/adept as paired brother-sister archetypes who can be models for less stereotypical relationships and who may hold, perhaps, more developmental possibilities. Kotschnig (1968-1969) extends this examination of spiritual problems to myths. Rachel Hillel (1987) retells the story of Ruth and of other neglected mother-daughter or feminine-identified figures in the Bible, and applies them to contemporary women.

Berry (1975) reanalyzes the Demeter/Persephone myth for its relevance to modern mothers and daughters as well as for its connection to neurosis and to rape. In *Echo's Subtle Body* (1982), she extends this work. She uses the archetype of Gaia, the Great Mother, as an image for honoring the formlessness, chaos, materiality, and darkness within therapy (rather than their too quick abreaction or interpretation). She notes that Gaia represents both mother and matter through an archetypal image whose form is often ignored or only shamefully acknowledged; this results in women's loss of energy and the loss of the psyche's assistance. The wordly mother, as represented by Demeter, is, for Berry, a less realized and far more human figure than Gaia. Berry studies Demeter's immersion in daily experience and her depressive and neurotic ties to her daughter, and notes that archetypal images such as Gaia and Demeter can

"appear just as easily pathologically (abnormally) as they do normally
. . . in the same archetypal pattern lie both the pathology and the therapy" (p. 20). Demeter's mourning becomes sterile, and is in danger of
becoming suffering for suffering's sake, losing its connection to the divine. Berry notes that Hecate and Persephone were once linked; she argues for the reclamation of Hecate's dark and outlawed former power
into the myth and into our psyches. Luminescence, fertility, nursing,
nourishing, bawdiness, and bitchy energy are found in and through the
Hecate archetype. Each of the archetypes in the Demeter-Persephone
myth can be seen as a part of, and the other side of, the other. In this
book, Berry also writes of Echo as an archetype of longing for introspection, self-reflection and nuance, the meaning behind, and in contrast
to, the worldly Hera archetype.

Koltuv (1975) further and more positively examines the mothering
and housewifely archetype of the Hestia/Vestia aspect of the Great Mother
as a counter to the trivialization of this role. She stresses the dignity
and worth inherent in a much maligned, often invisible role. Bradway
(1978) extends this portrayal of the archetype in her study of Hestia and
Athena modes. She compares two groups of women, housewives and
career women, using these archetypes for their positive implications, concluding that each develops a need to integrate the qualities implicit in
the other archetype; she sees one of her analytic roles as being an aid
to integration. Her (1982b) work elaborates on Fierz-David's monograph
on the Mysteries at Pompeii as a feminine-grounded and aided archetypal
pattern for women's individuation in analysis. Bradway thinks these mysteries manifest an archetype for woman's psychological development
(which I will discuss in Chapter Nine).

Pauline Napier's unpublished Zürich Institute thesis, *Demeter of Villarosa, Sicilia* (1985), is also concerned with the initiatory mysteries that
Fierz-David and Bradway examine. Napier studies Demeter as what she
calls a mother-woman and a soul-shadow, then focuses on the Black
Madonna as this archetype's redemptive form. She extends this study
to mother-daughter mysteries in general and to the women in her own
Sicilian family, ending with a moving examination of a single patient.
In each, she describes a progression through initiation, suffering, and
relationship.

Besides the positive mother in the mother-daughter archetype, some
analysts have looked at complexes that can arise when either the archetypal
image has lost value or the archetype of the bad mother is constellated.

Young-Eisendrath and Eisendrath (1980) follow Berry's (1976) article "What's the Matter with Mother?" with the aptly-titled "Where is Mother Now?" In it they also deal with and cite Neumann's themes of the Great Mother and the archetypal relationship of the actual mother to matter, *Mater*. They survey the nineteen-fifties to seventies and find the role of mother and the actual mother demeaned, scapegoated, and stereotyped to the point that the archetypal image seems to have lost soul. Yet, at the same time, they describe the role as often a loaded and exaggeratedly important one. This is abetted by fathers who abdicate their own role, leaving the household surreptitiously or overtly matriarchal. Young-Eisendrath and Eisendrath write incisively of the subsequent love-hate relationship with the mother, the huge responsibility of the role, and its lack of cultural rewards. They conclude that the whole undervaluing of the archetypal feminine, and especially the archetype of the mother, leads to destructive materialism (Berry's negative Demeter) and to hostile yet infantile dependency on the human mother. All the guilt this devaluation and demand incur is then projected onto the individual mother, who is blamed for everyone's psychological deficits.

Hillman continues this dialogue in his 1983 article on "The Bad Mother" (the three articles—Berry's, Young-Eisendrath and Eisendrath's, and Hillman's—enlighten each other and belong together). He states that "the altar at which much of psychology worships is the shrine of the Negative Mother" (p. 168). Hillman differentiates the *experience* of bad mothering from the archetype of the bad mother and connects the experience to the archetype of the child-imago who reacts to the mother. It is these latter two (the bad mother and the child imago archetypes) who act in tandem. This results in the idea that all good belongs to the child (as Divine Child) and leaves the bad to the individual mother, who then takes on the negativity of the Negative Mother archetype. Hillman traces this one-sided treatment of the archetypal bad mother divorced from the child-imago in the work of Jung, Harding (rather than Neumann, who writes more about the Terrible Mother), Baynes, and Layard, and to the psychological theories of Freud, Klein, and the London School's Jung-Klein hybrid. He makes the important conclusion that the bad mother, having suffered from very bad press, is, in reality, perhaps less damaging than an idealized image of the good mother. In this statement Hillman reclaims wholeness and balance both for the archetypal image of the mother and for those who use the Mother archetype, consciously or unconsciously, as a model.

As a human event, bad-mothering belongs to any mother and to the Great
Mother. This archetypal perspective leaves a mother less alone with her
badness and, so, less driven to repress it and then be forced to act it out.
(p. 170)

Fairy tales have been an important source for archetypal stories about
the feminine and its many mother and daughter figures. In *The Mother: Archetypal Image in Fairy Tales* (1988), Sibylle Birkhauser-Oeri looks
at images of the great mother in fairy tales and examines their psychological meaning. She follows Neumann's definitions of the feminine,
contrasting feeling, Eros, feminine nature, and nature with the spirit
of the father. She is concerned with the mother and her problems in
the actual world, and argues for a recognition of the light and dark sides
of the archetype. She does not limit the archetype to a human carrier,
but also takes an object—a stove—as an aspect of the fiery, aggressive
side of the archetypal mother. By including this aspect, Oeri leaves room
for a more active feminine than tradition espoused. She also writes of
the need for the mother (or mother-representative) to believe in the child,
not cut him or her down, and to allow and encourage the child's fantasy.

Hart (1978) extends von Franz's studies of the feminine in fairy tales
from an evolutionary and developmental perspective. Von Franz, Ulanov,
and Dieckmann are perhaps the analysts who have used fairy tales most
tellingly as a source from which to study various archetypal manifestations of the feminine (since von Franz wrote mainly about them as anima and animus representations, I have included her work in Chapter
Seven). In *Cinderella and her Sisters* (1983), Ulanov uses the fairy tale
as a way to explore envy. In this important work, she demonstrates that
envying and being envied are part of the same complex; she examines
the story from each of the two vantage points, while also seeing the story as a deeper conflict between the ego and shadow in an individual
woman. Ulanov describes Cinderella as lacking an earthly mother-
daughter relationship and the protection afforded by this feminine-
identified ground—Cinderella's own mother is dead and a fairy-
godmother fills this role for her. Ulanov's Jungian treatment of this un-
mothered state and the heroine's search for a strong feminine ground
reminds me of Heilbrun's (1988) feminist analysis of the effects of a
mother's absence on a woman's need for self-realization and achievement. Dieckmann (1986) writes of the fairy tale itself as archetype, citing its many figures of feminine submissiveness, but also its search for
feminine independence and development. For him, the memory of an

early favorite fairy tale may be recapitulated (and/or distorted) in a person's life and in neurosis.

Schmidt (1983) and Wheelwright (1985, 1988) write of the mother archetype in animals and nature. Schmidt finds her own reconciliation with her mother and the mother's world indicative of a general cultural shift away from the masculine principle toward reclaiming a feminine heritage. Wheelwright and Schmidt each write of the archetype of the Great Mother in the ranch on which they were raised; both mother and daughter found that the ranch itself acted as mother and as model of the female world. Wheelwright concludes that "we were touched more deeply than we ever suspected by a land that was not always a loving, embracing earth-mother kind of place" (1985, p. 94).

R. D. Newman (1986) extends this archetype of the Great Mother as natural world to its exemplification in James Joyce's *Ulysses*. He finds Molly Bloom naturally fertile, generative, protean, and elemental, like an earth mother and earth goddess, and compares the way she glories in her body and her sexuality with the way the Great Mother goddesses did before her. He notes that Molly Bloom is perhaps more an anima figure than a depiction of a woman. Wheelwright and Schmidt choose a mother-identified geographical place to explore a facet of woman's psychology, while Newman chooses a literary figure created by a man through which to examine the same facet in the anima. For all three, however, it is the natural, generative biological energy that is the transformative center of their work.

In *The Nature of Loving* (1986), Verena Kast emphasizes the importance and value of mother goddesses as models for women's development and strength, and applauds women's renewed interest in these archetypal images. She looks at some myths as archetypal models of relationship and at the possibilities and problems in each pairing of characters. She tells the myth, relates it to clinical material, and then discusses the myth in reference to relationship. She organizes her inquiry through looking at the following archetypal pairs: Shiva and Shakti, the ideal of union of creator and the energy of creation; Pygmalion and his statue, the creator and created; Ishtar and Tammuz, the goddess and her youthful lover; Merlin and Vivian, the wise old man and young girl; Zeus and Hera, a couple in conflict; and, finally, the more modern and egalitarian brother-sister pair typified by Solomon and the Shulamite. Referring (like Ulanov and Perera) to the problems caused by women's passivity and tendency to live a scapegoated or victim role, Kast sees

the need for women, whether in or out of relationship, to develop their
strength, vitality, and awareness through identification with a strong and
maternal feminine model. She concludes that the woman then

> becomes very conscious of her womanhood and her worth. It is not by
> chance that women today are rediscovering the ancient mother goddess-
> es in their splendor and magnificence. If a woman can identify herself
> with these mother goddesses, who are, after all, also creators of culture,
> they then lose their Cinderella complex. (p. 37)

Recently the three basic archetypal images of the feminine that have
attracted Jungian interest—Wolff's personality types, Harding's moon
and its phases, Neumann's mother-daughter pair—all seem to be con-
verging very generatively. Jane Wheelwright (1984) combines Neumann's
work on the Great Mother with Harding's idea of the moon, in that
she sees the archetype of the Kore essentially a representation of the
mother-daughter pair while also being representative of a whole com-
prised of many parts. She examines the archetype of the Maiden, the
Kore, for elements of its power, believing the archetype to be an image
capable of returning complexity and wholeness to women. She finds the
Kore to be essentially a mother-daughter archetype rather than just an
image of the daughter. Wheelwright traces the archetype back to its image
in Paleolithic times before it was split into two; she describes it as a pre-
patriarchal symbol of the Self for both men and women. The pairs
Demeter-Persephone, Ariadne-Dionysus, Inanna-Ereshkigal, Psyche-
Amor, and Adam-Eve (plus the positive serpent), along with the Orphic Mysteries, the Eleusinian Mysteries, and Wheelwright's personal experience as a daughter and with her daughter, contribute to her exciting
amplification of this archetype.

The key importance of the Kore archetype, Wheelwright proposes,
is that it is a totality, inclusive of all feminine deities. Facets of it were
split off by the patriarchy into all sorts of fragments and types. The Maid-
en archetype can appear as daughter, sister, young mother, virgin, goddess, prostitute, psychopomp, priestess and much more. She adds
timelessness, continuity, growth, achievement, progress, and evolution
to the mother archetype, and thus completes her. Wheelwright believes
that it is the realization of this archetype which leads to woman's understanding of her real nature and to a stage beyond patriarchy—the
"missing ingredient needed to balance a lopsided world."

Wheelwright synthesizes her precursors' work on the archetype into

a new and significant model. She describes the
merging in its complete form. Psychologically, it
hind what Wheelwright calls "the multiple whole
women. She credits Wolff's four structural types w
and restrictive, were a first attempt to explain the
woman's personality. She also credits Harding for her depiction, through
moon imagery, of the normality inherent in the mutability of the feminine. Wheelwright briefly suggests the Navajo goddess Changing Woman
as an unexplored example of this archetype. Changing Woman, a lunar
goddess, is complete in herself though also periodically intensely related. She is maiden, mother, middle-aged, and old, over and over again
in a way that is not merged nor unconscious but, instead, is highly
differentiated.

Wheelwright considers the idea of change, incubation, descent to the
underworld, the reuniting of upper and lower, younger and older, mother
and daughter, to be the path to women's wholeness. She makes a strong
case for a therapy and analysis which reflects this wholeness and argues
for it necessitating a new holistic feminine analytic approach to replace
the splintering and often destructive aspects of the androcentric analytical attitude. In Wheelwright's vision of this therapy, the complicated,
more democratic nature of women's psyches is validated and receives more
accurate mirroring; she feels that women are better treated as heroines
in a full-length novel than as "cases" to be analyzed.

A final element in Wheelwright's presentation of this archetype is
the inclusion of personal experience. She and her daughter, Lynda
Schmidt, together presented a workshop on the mother-daughter in
which they explored their relationship and the working out of their particular mother-daughter reunion (Schmidt's contribution is personal rather than archetypal; her mother's is theoretical as well). The theory and
its personal elements and the way these affect practice were thus united
in an example of feminist methodology in action. When this important contribution to theory is published, I believe it will help bring about
a much needed reevaluation of the feminine and of therapeutic treatment of women in analytical psychology.

The most recent work on the Demeter and Persephone myth underlies Young-Eisendrath and Wiedemann's developmental scheme (1987)
and will be discussed further in the next chapter. These two analysts
also see the archetypes in terms of pairs: Demeter and Persephone, Pandora and Zeus, Amor and Psyche, Ariadne and Theseus/Dionysus. They

...te of women's need to integrate both the masculine and feminine parts of each archetype.

The historical pattern of Jungian work on archetypes of the feminine marks a progression that first examined a single archetype (Harding's work on the moon and Neumann's on the Great Mother), then explored all the many split aspects of the feminine that were fragmented and polarized by the patriarchy, and then applied these to particular women and particular problems. The aim now is, as in Kast's and Wheelwright's work, to unite the single and the complex at a higher level of integration. The tendency at first was restrictive. With exceptions such as Harding, it designated only one particular aspect or pattern of the feminine as the prevailing one in a particular woman's psyche, and limited a woman to a particular form of consciousness and a particular mode of functioning. Since Jung's time, writers have portrayed increasingly diverse possibilities for the feminine and for women, culminating in Wheelwright's theory of multiple personalities under a single, complex archetype.

As with Whitmont's theory of consciousness (matriarchy followed by patriarchy followed by an integral era), the pattern of archetypes presented during the past sixty years starts with a depiction of the unconscious, primodial unity of the matriarchal feminine. It then reflects differentiated facets of the patriarchal feminine. Current theorists are now attempting to reintegrate both matriarchal and patriarchal images at a higher level of consciousness in order to regain a feminine whole that includes the individuated feminine. Under this overt pattern is a strong and dissenting subcurrent that was always present and is most apparent in those analysts, like Harding, who have chosen the moon and its phases as subjects of their discourse. They conceive of the feminine already including its own feminine-centered and feminine-grounded completeness; its adequate uncovering and mirroring is seen as the essential task in women's individuation.

A significant pattern in Jungian work on the feminine archetypes can be discerned by sorting it into one of three areas: personality types, the use of the archetype of the moon and its phases, and the use of the mother-daughter archetype. The use of archetypal forms themselves gives an image, a picture, a sensuous and embodied reality that grips the imagination. The feminine archetypes demonstrate a multitude of diverse expressions of the feminine in contrast to the earlier limited patriarchal delineation; they offer models of a profusion of types and patterns that open the possibility of many ways of being feminine. These models take the abstract behavioral patterns feminist psychologists such as Bem (1976), Bernard (1976), and Gilligan (1982) are studying, and present them in concrete form. The exploration of the pluralism and the multifaceted aspects of the feminine in an individual woman provides women with access to aspects of themselves which were denied in the early twentieth century. This denial limited women to elaborations of the peculiar roles I examined in Chapter One: angel, whore, mother, temptress, invalid, eternal child, or lunatic. The replacement of these with a composite, multifaceted, and well-rounded view is particularly well developed in the work of Harding, de Castillejo, Ulanov, Meador, Kast, and Wheelwright.

The recovery of lost aspects of the feminine and the reclamation of the dark side of the feminine provide a source of healing and power; they also release the energy and vitality which has until recently been unavailable — bound up as it was in internal and societal repression, disparagement, and condemnation. Jungians' reevaluation of what was until recently considered negative offers substantiation and validation for women struggling out from under the myths that have enveloped them. It also gives women access to a depth of self-understanding missing from much contemporary feminist psychology. Harding, de Castillejo, Ulanov, Whitmont, Woodman, Perera, Berry, Bradway, Meador, Kast, Wheelwright, and Young-Eisendrath and Wiedemann are important sources of this significant and exciting reevaluation and reinterpretation.

The increasing use by Jungians of pre-patriarchal feminine images and of images from diverse cultures expands knowledge of the range of the feminine and of woman's psychological possibilities. Jungian use of archetypal patterns to explore and elucidate specific psychological problems provides a clarity and depth that add greatly to the understanding of these problems and of the archetypes themselves. Woodman's work on eating disorders, Leonard's on the negative, sometimes devastating consequences that result from fathers' (and our culture's) anima projections onto young girls, Shuttle and Redgrove's work on menstrual problems, Perera's on depression and scapegoating, Ulanov's on envy — all are felicitous and important examples of the value of this approach.

It seems particularly significant (and appropriate) that women analysts are doing by far the most work on the feminine in contemporary Jungian circles. Along with creating new theory, they are increasingly exploring their own psychology and experience, as well as that of their patients, and then applying both of these to their practice and to their written work. They are examining themselves in the mirror and describing what they see. As Jung wrote, "every psychology . . . has the character of a subjective confession" (1929/1970, p. 336). It is this confession on the part of women which is starting to produce a long-awaited reconsideration of Jungian approaches to the feminine. What men write about the feminine derives in part from and is colored by their experience of the anima. This seemed to be the basis of much early writing on the feminine, with women often defining or disguising themselves according to its tenets. Women writing about women and about their own experience come from a different perspective; it is a perspective which may in fact be a renewal — breaking us free of tradition and forming a new, less restricted one that better mirrors our needs and our solutions.

Studying the feminine from the point of view of a woman's psyche is different from studying the feminine from a man's viewpoint; it demands a revision of Jung's theory. The influence of individual personality, gender, and socio-cultural conditions all contribute to both the choice and treatment of a subject. These exploratory studies — predominantly by women — on the archetypes of the feminine extend, enrich, deepen, clarify, and vivify what we know about the psychology of women; they provide their own hall of mirrors for the feminine.

CHAPTER NINE: TOWARD A PSYCHOLOGY OF WOMEN

Feminist psychology of women will generate no universal laws, promise no uncomplicated models of change, and offer no easy routes to undermining gender-based differentials. Feminist psychology can advance qualified psychological findings that recognize commonalities and differences across groups of women, incorporate an understanding of structural and economic influences on women's psychologies, produce complex, non-victim blaming analyses of women's conditions, and distinguish between ideologies and realities for distinct groups of women across different settings and in varied relationships.

> Michelle Fine: "Reflections on a Feminist Psychology of Women: Paradoxes and Prospects."

The analysis of a woman stands a better chance now of facilitating individuation than it used to.

> Judith Hubback, "Reflections on the Psychology of Women"

In previous chapters I discussed Jungian literature on the feminine in women and in the anima. In this chapter I will be concerned with the psychology of women and writers who have focused on this subject. Jung gave no detailed nor orderly description of women's psychology or process of development. Since his time, few analysts have attempted this task. When they do, they often fail to present a picture of women that is different from the anima, or they confuse the two. Until very recently, few have examined the nature and experience of women themselves and how these may differ from men's; fewer still consider how social and cultural factors color their view.

In the theories about women that have been suggested, three elements recur: the archetypal treatment of development as progressing from a relatively unconscious and undifferentiated state toward one of greater individuality and consciousness; the theme of integration and the discovery of the (feminine) Self in the individuation process; finally, individuation and development through initiation. In each case, the underlying processes are considered the same for men and women, but the paths often are gender-specific and quite different. Besides considering what has been written about specific paths for women, I will also briefly point to some recent changes in the traditional modes of Jungian therapy that incorporate a new understanding of the psychology of women and of women's particular needs.

In *The Way of all Women* (1933/1975), Harding depicts women's development occurring in relation to the anima and animus; this development aims toward wholeness and comes about through the discovery and integration of both feminine and masculine qualities. Harding takes Jung's definition of what is normal feminine behavior in women as typical only of the initial stages in women's development. In these first two stages a woman carries and lives out a man's anima projections, first naively then on a more conscious and sophisticated level. Harding portrays the naive anima-woman as psychologically undifferentiated and living a primarily unconscious life. At this stage she is "a nature product" (1933/1975, p. 10), instinctive, unconscious, primitive, and unaware of herself and even of men's projections onto her. In the second, sophisticated stage, the anima-woman's ego has awakened, though she may still consciously choose to hold and embody a man's projections in order to receive his attention or gain power. A woman at this stage lives through a man and fulfills his idea of who she is; she often gains prestige and stability thereby, and can create a good environment for him in the process, but she fails to discover and live her own life. Further development involves a woman in a new and precarious situation: "to sacrifice this power requires real devotion to a purpose or value which is superior to her own ego" (p. 11). Harding finds that this sacrifice constitutes a major step in a woman's individuation; it involves her in a profound exploration of her own nature, of the feminine principle, and of feminine spirituality.

Harding warns that the new interest in the suprapersonal often involves a transitional stage in which a woman functions not through a man but through identification with her own inner masculine, the animus. This is the stage during which many women repress their feeling function and often become overrational, over-frank, and outspoken. Harding finds this in the newly professional, often animus-identified or animus-possessed women of her time. She pays particular attention to the positive worth of this stage as well as to its negative aspects, and notes in passing the many cultural restraints and prejudices that make a professional woman's career and personal life so arduous. The stage beyond this is not well elaborated, though Harding's emphasis is on the integration of the masculine rather than identification with it. Here a woman, she feels, must develop a personal and individual moral attitude accompanied by personal responsibility. This enables a woman to look within herself for access to her own strength and to the development of her own sense of values.

In *Woman's Mysteries* (1935/1976), Harding again views women's psychological development as different from men's. The sequence she suggests for women is one of withdrawal from the world (and its conventional view of women), initiation, suffering, and endurance, rather than development through action in and with the world. She buttresses her argument with examples of this pattern for women in a vast range of mythological examples and symbols and through the dream imagery of her patients. Part of the lack of clarity in Harding's treatment of the final stage of women's development is that, in this more theoretical work, she follows Jung quite literally. She insists that feminine development occurs almost entirely through subjectivity, feelings, and relatedness with others, rather than through what she and Jung both designate as the more masculine path of separation and individuation—a path that, nonetheless, seems implicit in Harding's feminine schema of withdrawal, initiation, suffering, and endurance. The consequence is that Harding, following Jung, defines women as representing Eros and the unconscious. The conclusions she reaches seem to limit women's development accordingly and prohibit the higher stage of individuation she outlines from her own experience. Thus her theory does not mirror the reality of women like herself. By denying them and herself, at least theoretically, Harding obscures herself as the role model she could have been—an example of an individuated woman at a higher level of consciousness than the one acceptable to traditional Jungian theory. Harding thus confuses a woman's nature with her culture's definition of the feminine and the stringent limitations this placed on women; she ends with a comprehension of her own and women's independent possibilities, but then sacrifices them to relationship.

For the woman to achieve anything of value and permanence in the masculine world, she must be developed on both sides of her nature, but even when this has been done and she feels herself ready to put forth in a creative work the wisdom she has gained she will probably meet another barrier within herself. For, in order to speak openly about a woman's secret knowledge, she must overcome her fundamental instincts of modesty, passivity and reserve. To most women this seems well-nigh impossible. For it is in a woman's nature to hold herself in the background, to maintain a passive attitude, and, psychologically speaking, to veil herself and her reactions and to seek her goal only by a devious and largely unconscious route. For a woman to show herself clearly as an individual, to come into the open and say what she has to say, demands that she go contrary to this natural tendency. To do such a thing with real integrity involves a complete sacrifice to her ego and she can bring herself to make this sacrifice only for some very potent reason. (1933/1975, pp. 81-82)

Woman . . . is unconscious of her true aim. She thought she wanted independence and a career. This was a subsidiary though a very necessary phase in the movement toward her real goal, namely the creation of the possibility of psychic, or psychological, relation to man. (p. 87)

In *The Value and Meaning of Depression* (1970/1980), Harding focuses on the prevalence of depression in women (a depression which may have been a direct consequence of sacrifing independence for a "healthier" subservience). Harding looks at depression as a crisis which may give a woman the opportunity to turn toward her own inner needs and possibly discover a new path. It is perhaps a necessary counterpoint to and retreat from an over-masculinized society. As such, she sees depression aiding in the development and preservation of the feminine Self, which may then function compensatorily to masculine society.

Harding, like Jung, stresses the process of individuation as a life-long task. She is one of the first Jungians to view women's middle and old age constructively. The final chapter of Harding's (1933/1975) book is on women and old age. She portrays women, for the first half of their adult lives, as being necessarily occupied with children, family, and with both inner and outer adaptations to multiple tasks, and/or to making a way in the world; after this, she says, comes "the time of the beginning of wisdom" (p. 241). She finds this is only true for women who have passed through the three prior stages of psychological development, and are thus ready for a period of internal achievement and what she calls "downgoing." She criticizes our culture for its adolescent valuation of youth above old age, citing other cultures and Jung himself for their more enlightened views. Harding foresees that the many women in our culture who have not met their own psychological needs may have to pass through a period of midlife crisis full of anguish.

> To many a woman, coming to consciousness of her dual nature only at the age of fifty or more, it seems utterly impossible to create anything of value from the years that remain. The sense of having come to the end of the road, the sense of irreparable failure, may be so terrifying and obsessing, so intense and immanent that she can give her attention to nothing else. Depression and insomnia fall upon her. Nothing holds value or significance. It is as though she drops into a bottomless pit. . . . She has come to the period of downgoing and she does not know how to meet it. (p. 249)

Harding finds that many women remain stuck in one of the earlier psychological stages, while few are impelled to develop all sides and phases of themselves. The mother, for instance, may start to develop her Logos side, the professional woman her Eros side. Harding focuses on the necessity for inward-turning and introspection in some form of spiritual encounter, the analytic process being her paradigm for this process. She sees this as a way of making sense out of life and as a preparation for the journey toward death. An examined and fulfilled life is the goal — though one that women, with their many relationships and responsibilities, seldom achieve. A woman's work on her own integration, Harding concludes, relieves her offspring, family, and friends from bearing the negative consequences that follow from a woman's unreflective and eluded life.

In "A Few Thoughts on the Process of Individuation in Women" (1941), Toni Wolff examines the problems of contemporary women and the preponderance of women in analysis. She concludes that contemporary "women have been more estranged and have deviated further from their real nature than men, and that they are consequently more disoriented" (p. 81). She attributes this to the Judeo-Christian devaluation of the body and its rejection of sexuality, as well as to the absence in the culture of a feminine godhead or superior principle. In analysis, Wolff finds that women generally start with more diffuse and amorphous ego-development than men, and have greater trouble (culturally reinforced) in acknowledging their shadow and evil sides. "The uncertainty and disorientation of women with respect to themselves" (p. 85) is of paramount concern in their therapy.

In my previous chapter I described Wolff's (1934/1956) work on the

structural types in feminine psychology. As with Jung's description of
the four function types, the development and integration of all four of
these would seem to be necessary for psychological wholeness. However, Wolff does not develop the idea of transformation, development, and
growth in her representation of these types in women. Perhaps this is
because, as with Harding, neither writer had a theoretical model in which
to mirror an adult, complex, and differentiated female person. The socio-
cultural attitudes that produced this situation still prevail to a certain
extent. For instance, research done in the nineteen-seventies on
parameters of mental health echo Wolff and Harding. Researchers (e.g.,
Broverman, Broverman, Clarkson, Rosenkrantz, and Vogel, 1970) have
found psychological health and adulthood to be equated with male-
ness, while femaleness is seen as incongruent with both. Such attitudes
have until recently prevented the theoretical construct or description of
a healthy adult woman. Wolff, as I have mentioned, did note cultural
changes which allowed some progression for women. She remarks that
women of her generation usually were of a pronounced single type while
those of the generation that followed often combined two types. Thus
she saw that later generations of women could possibly manifest a more
"complex feminine psychology" (1941, p. 98) than women of her own
generation. This observation also allowed later writers to develop and
expand Wolff's original ideas into a more complex theory of the psychology of women.

Neumann has formulated perhaps the most comprehensive archetypal
scheme of developmental psychology of both men and women in analytical psychology. His theory involves stages of consciousness expressed
through archetypal images. The stages of consciousness as elaborated
in *The Origins and History of Consciousness* (1950/1954), are the *uroboric*, the *matriarchal*, and the *patriarchal*. Neumann alludes to, but
does not develop, the possibility that the present age could be a merging of both the matriarchal and the patriarchal. Like Jung, he places
women in an ahistorical, matriarchal stage of development and concludes
from this that "consciousness, as such, is masculine even in woman"
(p. 42).

In "The Moon and Matriarchal Consciousness" (1954), Neumann follows Harding's (1935) development of moon mythology as a paradigm
for feminine development. His particular emphasis, however, is again,
as in his earlier work, on the evolution of consciousness from matriarchy to patriarchy. In "The Psychological Stages of Feminine Develop-

ment" (1959), Neumann presents the masculine and the feminine as prototypes of the opposites. A female infant is described as confronted with a primary relationship with a similar (same gender) object as caregiver rather than a dissimilar one. Because of this the "bio-psychic difference between the two sexes" (p. 65) is emphasized, which in turn leads, in Neumann's view, to a woman's greater unconsciousness and less extensive ego development than a man's. (This is also the general idea in chapter four of Neumann's incomplete and posthumously published *The Child* [1973], where he again looks at a girl child's development.) A man, on the other hand, develops his ego as a consequence of confronting the dissimilar; he does so at the cost of isolation and "estrangement from himself" (p. 66), with subsequent severe relationship anxiety. The result of early childhood experience is that "ego and consciousness always appear archetypally as symbolized by the masculine" (p. 66) a masculine which needs to confront and overcome the mother. Because a woman does not have to confront the mother as "other," she can remain for her entire life "childish and immature . . . but not estranged from herself" (p. 67). A woman can be undifferentiated and unconscious but, in Neumann's view, still be psychologically healthy, harmonious, and complete within the all-enfolding, pre-matriarchal uroboros.

In Neumann's developmental scheme a woman can, but does not have to, progress from this first uroboric stage to a very different one—a woman-identified, male-excluding, Demeter-Kore phase. Neumann calls this the matriarchal stage and describes positive aspects of this "unthought life" (p. 69), but also notes the negative: a lack of relation to the masculine, an unrelated, Amazonian sexuality and/or frigidity and/or masochism, all of which lead to disturbances within marriage and contribute to the neurosis of the children.

Neumann's third stage is the first male-identified one. It involves a numinous, transpersonal, animus "invasion of the paternal uroboros" (p. 70), which appears as an impersonal "overpowering intoxication" by a "ravishing penetrator" (p. 71). As a result of this encounter, a woman is separated from the matriarchal, but also comes to equate marriage with death and the killing of her former mother-identified self. In examining this stage, Neumann appears to fall into an increasingly Romantic mixture of phallocentric fantasy and exaggeration concerning the feminine and women, which sounds suspiciously like anima projection. It is reminiscent of Jung on the feminine and may be diagnostic of that era's approach to the feminine; though it may also reflect some women's actual experience, in particular that of fathers' daughters. It has reverberated in much — even recent — work on the feminine (see Woodman, 1984), but is unfamiliar to my own experience and to many of my less patriarchally fathered women clients' experience of themselves. For example, Neumann writes:

> The woman meets this overpowering and super-dimensional maleness with a transpersonal feeling of insufficiency, with a sense of inferiority which has an impersonal and archetypal basis here. She feels herself too small in the face of the masculine. (1959, p. 72)

Neumann concludes that through self-surrender and acceptance of what actually is, or a woman may perceive as, violent rape, she is "led subjectively to the development, enrichment, and extension of consciousness" (p. 70). Women who lack this darkly convulsive experience, according to Neumann's theory, remain in the early part of the patriarchal stage, either identified with the masculine and the animus or as fathers' daughters. He describes this sort of woman as without a shadow, possessed by the animus, and estranged both from herself and from the archetype of the feminine, the Great Mother, whom she has lost. Neumann's final developmental stage for a woman in the patriarchy is her redemption by either an outer or an inner hero. In this stage, she is redeemed to consciousness by the masculine, who "becomes for the woman the representation of consciousness and of its development" (p.78). He finds that this representation underlies the superior position of males in our society and is what leads to the imbalance inherent in patriarchal marriage. This stage is accompanied by a necessary "depreciation of the feminine" (p. 78).

Neumann underscores the damage done to women and the feminine in a patriarchy. This is an essential and exciting part of his theory and one which is congruent with psychological findings today (e.g., Young-Eisendrath and Wiedemann, 1987; Gilbert and Gubar, 1988). He believes that there is no room for women's development here; instead a woman has to develop in secret (Neumann, 1959, p. 78). The consequences of normal patriarchal development are a necessary "catastrophe for the girl child who, under these patriarchal values, has to grow up in self-deprecation" (p. 81). He also notes that the feminine in its entirety is jeopardized. Neumann calls the negative repercussions of the patriarchy a vicious circle that threatens women's psychological health.

In it, "women experience a shrinking, and even stunting of femininity" (p. 81), become scapegoated as carriers of evil for men (p. 83), and are liable to invasion by the archetype of the raging and terrible mother (p. 87). This attitude toward the feminine is also detrimental for men, entailing as it does loss of soul, spiritual childishness, dependence on women for feeling values, and enmeshing both men and women in "the deadly battle of the sexes" (p. 86).

In a 1959 lecture, "Fear of the Feminine" (1959/1986), Neumann continues to examine the negative pressure exerted by the patriarchy on men's and women's development. A woman's fear of the feminine involves her in a heroic break from her mother and into overdetermined, patriarchal activity, while the mother often delivers her daughter over to the patriarchal world without any protection or the strength that could have been imparted if her own femininity had been respected and unfeared. Individuation involves a woman in self-discovery and liberation from patriarchal values: "the woman will and must conflict with the patriarchy if she wants to come into her own" (p. 25).

Thus Neumann, in statements that are often overlooked today, does not regard the patriarchal stage in the development of consciousness as static, normal, or healthy. He sees the psychology of his day and the personality development (especially of women) within it as pathological. A woman's position in Neumann's world and the pain and difficulty of her development are poignantly delineated. However, Neumann believes that this unbalanced situation is in flux, and that a large number of people are progressing beyond the patriarchal to a union of the masculine and feminine. He finds that his peers who are ready to advance in this direction are hampered by lack of knowledge of their feminine half and of the psychology of women. He describes women who seek individuation during this time as perhaps needing to withdraw completely from relationship so that they can have the psychic space in which to discover themselves. "The psychology of confrontation and individuation" is Neumann's next step in the development of consciousness; a step that, for both men and women, will result "in psychic conflict and can only be accomplished with the investment of the entire personality" (p. 90).

In *Amor and Psyche* (1962), Neumann takes up this psychology of confrontation and individuation within women and the anima, Psyche representing an active and transformative feminine archetype. Psyche separates from the Great Mother through sacrifice and a marriage with death in a "marriage situation [that is] an archetype and central figure of feminine psychic reality" (p. 65). In her pull toward individuation, Neumann describes Psyche as progressing through a confrontion with her shadow (her sisters), active redemption of both herself and her conventional, patriarchal marriage, and the saving and transfiguration of her mother-bound husband. Psyche accomplishes this through what Neumann describes as a feminine combination of the body and the spirit acting through love. "Psyche's subsequent development is nothing other than an attempt to transcend, through suffering and struggle, the separation accomplished by her act" (p. 83) in order to achieve a new and conscious union of the opposites.

Neumann takes the six tasks Psyche is given by the Great Mother to be representative of the psychological tasks through which a woman gains personal individuation. The first task is one in which Psyche (along with the individual woman who follows this path) orders, discriminates and selects, and in which animus and "masculine" Logos capacities are developed. The second involves a woman learning to combine patience with instinct in order to appreciate the value and timing involved in waiting, in actively seizing the appropriate moment and then engaging in vigorous action. The woman's next task is to give form to the formless and contain the flow of life, a process in which the feminine molds and contains a masculine that lacks form, and that can also, lacking the feminine, become uncontained excess. The fourth task involves a woman's descent to the underworld, where she develops a firm and strong-willed ego. This is a difficult and paradoxical task, for in it a woman learns to abjure the pity, empathy, and relatedness she has been taught. The final task is the patriarchally-demanded rejection of the archetypally feminine and the matriarchal; Psyche fails, by masculine standards, at this task. Neumann describes this defeat as ultimately a success through which the sixth task can be accomplished. By not denying the feminine, Psyche and her followers reunite with the Great Mother and integrate the feminine with the masculine, the matriarchy with the patriarchy, to bring about a further advance in consciousness.

Neumann (like Harding) describes the depressive components in women's psychological growth that accompany feminine development. They involve the feminine psyche in Psyche's depression and in her troublesome "recurring tendency to suicide" (p. 115). He analyzes these grave stresses on women and finds them to be consequences of the strains involved in women having to confront and differentiate from both the matriarchy and the patriarchy; the extraordinary difficulties and solitariness of a feminine hero's quest, with its loneliness, suffering, unsupported tenacity, and need for assimilation of much that her culture considers negative; and the quest itself, which tears a woman away from her home ground — the feminine and matriarchal — and propels her not only toward, but past the masculine, while her sisters remain safely anchored in a known home and culture.

Neumann's developmental schema has been criticized for confusing the development of the individual with the development of cultural and historical eras, neither of which proceeds in the clear pattern Neumann outlines. Giegerich (1975) questions the historical and empirical validity of Neumann's sequential outlook, pointing out that patriarchies have preceded matriarchies and that different cultures are at different developmental levels at the same historical time. He also suggests that the development of consciousness which Neumann elaborates is mythological rather than scientific. These myths in turn, as described by Neumann, limit individual and cultural development to only a few set archetypal scenarios.

Neumann's concepts can also be criticized for their common Jungian flaw of conflating the feminine and the anima with a woman herself, and for the lack of case studies or other empirical verification. However, when Neumann's ideas are seen as imaginal and archetypal portrayals of possible developmental stages in the individual or culture, I think his concepts retain their potency. Seen in this light, their subjective reality can be clinically verified. Again, when seen as only one of many possible forms of development, they are of value in delineating stages of development within therapy. Through his feeling response to the final stage and his acknowledgement of the perilous loneliness and difficulty inherent in a woman's search for an essentially new sense of herself, Neumann provides one of the few mirrors which reflect the anguish many women feel as they are impelled forward on their ambitious quest.

Neumann's concepts continue to generate elaborations by modern Jungians such as Ulanov (1971/1978, 1981) and Whitmont (1982a), and are the underpinnings of Woodman's (1980, 1982 and 1984) and Shorter's (1987) theoretical and clinical studies. It is regrettable that Neumann's (1962) exciting work on the development and individuation of the active feminine is seldom mentioned in the literature today, while views he limited to the patriarchal feminine have become part of traditional Jungian theory on the "normal" feminine.

Hannah (1957, 1962), Moreno (1965) and Ulanov (1971/1978) use Neumann's early (1959) work on the stages of feminine development in formulating their own theories about the feminine. They seek to incorporate the theory that Neumann was proposing in 1959 with the "normal" narcissistic and masochistic feminine types of Helene Deutsch's (1944) work. Women, Hannah states, need to develop the receptive, passive, and related feminine identity that Deutsch, Neumann, and Jung described. This is the era's idea of what a woman should be and is taken as signifying psychological health for her.

In contrast to Neumann's later vision of transformative feminine development, Moreno, in his article "Archetypal Foundations in the Analysis of Women" (1965), recapitulates Wolff's and Neumann's early schema of women's psychological development. He places Wolff's four types of the feminine within Neumann's (1959) stages of feminine development and also tries to incorporate Emma Jung's (1957/1974) stages of animus (here called Logos) development. He states that each of the stages he describes is mandatory for a woman's development and that each follows the other linearly, and may occur only after the integration of the preceding phase.

Moreno describes a woman in the first stage as being in an undifferentiated, matriarchal, uroboric stage governed by the archetype of the Great Mother. In this the woman's psychological attitude is described as one of self-conservation. Moreno equates this stage with Wolff's structural type of the Mother, and portrays the animus of a woman in this stage as fitting the archetype of the Son. Moreno's next stage for a woman's development is the patriarchal uroboric one. He defines this as governed by the archetype of the Great Father, and specifies the psychological attitude of a woman in this stage to be one of dedication. The structural type is the Amazon, who is seen in her form as a *puella* and a father's daughter; the animus appears as a father figure. In the following stage, which Moreno calls the patriarchate, the archetype and the animus are both the Hero, whom Moreno describes as often also acting as mediator. He portrays the psychological attitude here as concerned with union and marriage; for this stage he picks the Hetaira type. Moreno describes a final stage of encounter and individuation as governed by the archetype of the Self; the type is the Medium, but Moreno also has the Medium acting as a "man's woman." He says that the animus for this stage is the Magician or Wise Man.

Moreno views each stage primarily in reference to the male; for example, the Hetaira awakens a man's individual psychic life, the Medium his spirit. Moreno also says that his, and men's, interest has turned to the psychology of women in order to compensate for the patriarchal character of the culture and to help men "overcome the experience of solitude and so reach the totality of the self" (p. 174). He concedes that self-development is also an issue for women; for this he advocates incorporating Deutsch's stages of feminine development. He concurs with Deutsch (and Freud) that the goal for women is to

> change her primary object of infantile love (the mother) and substitute the father for it; displace the anatomical physiological basis and executive organs of sexuality, which from external (clitoris) must become internal (vagina); and hence pass from an initial para-masculine position to a properly feminine (passive masochistic) position. (p. 184)

Much in Moreno is unclear, open to debate and question, and culturally influenced by the attitudes (here particularly, attitudes toward women) endemic at the time of his writing. His theory uses arguments based on a biological and sexual theory of women that has since been found biologically unsound by, among others, Masters and Johnson (1966). Moreno presents his scheme as a foundation for the analysis of women, but gives no substantiating evidence and makes no reference to clinical validity. Though he notes sociocultural determinants, he also consistently confuses the terms women, feminine, and Eros, often using them interchangeably. Faulty logic arises from this confusion, as when Moreno concludes:

> Eros conduces therefore to identification, to the renunciation of one's own subjectivity. Hence the feminine existential pattern consists in turning oneself into object and in giving oneself to the world as mother, as daughter, as woman. (pp. 176-177)

Moreno asserts that his theory of feminine development is confirmed in his psychotherapeutic treatment of women. He says the stages are passages his women patients must undergo in order to resolve their neuroses and engage in the process "of feminine becoming" (p. 178). I wonder if it may also have been likely that his women patients conformed to these views and requirements in order to be accepted by Moreno and receive his care.

Irene de Castillejo's *Knowing Woman* (1973) was mainly written during the nineteen-fifties and, as I mentioned in the last chapter, was in the process of revision and updating when she died. In it de Castillejo uses some of the same sources as Moreno; she elaborates and expands on Wolff's four types of the feminine in the light of traditional Jungian concepts of the feminine as embodying feeling, Eros, and the unconscious. Yet at the same time and in contrast to Moreno, de Castillejo notes the change in women brought about through cultural ferment. She also observes that "woman's psyche is not just that of man the other way round" (p. 165); it is something no one has sufficiently explored, and which requires the focused attention of women—especially of women scientists and analysts. In her own exploration she presents no theory of the psychology of women, but instead writes about the integration of the shadow, the development of the animus, and the importance of women's role as mediator to the masculine in men and in themselves. De Castillejo explores the traditional differences between men and women and finds their different roles in life, when not hidebound, to be helpful in the expression of each's psychology and nature. Integration of the self is seen as a task for women as well as men. The particular task of older women is paid some attention, but again de Castillejo views the expression of Eros, love, as older women's paramount need. The book must have been helpful to women in the nineteen-fifties and early sixties because of de Castillejo's application of Jungian theory to the actual problems and expectations of womens' lives. De Castillejo herself remarks, however, on the changing times and the tentativeness of some of her conclusions.

Ulanov (1971/1978) updates Wolff's and de Castillejo's four feminine types; she, like de Castillejo, finds each type potentially present in every woman. Ulanov applies Neumann's stages of consciousness to personality development in a way that also uses Moreno's (1965) article. For women specifically, she proposes a detailed scheme which involves the integration of four modalities of feminine being. This model is based on a synthesis of prior work by Emma Jung, Wolff, Deutsch, Neumann, and Moreno. She envisions the stages in relation to a structural type, a dominant archetype, a woman's identity, her relation to man and to her animus.

Ulanov starts with the structural type of the Mother. The archetype is the nourishing or devouring Great Mother; the woman finds her identity through nourishing others or engaging in masochistic protest and denial. She relates to men as homemaker and/or mother to their personae. The animus archetype is the *puer aeternus,* as a revolutionary or as a projection onto the son. The next stage represents the Hetaira type. The archetype is that of the Great Father; the woman relates to him, either as an individual or is subsumed by him in identification with *his* anima and as a father's daughter. The woman finds her identity in her individual psychic life, or else she refuses a realistic adaptation to her feminine role and plays the temptress instead. Her relation to men is as daughter or as anima-catcher. Her animus is the saving or the ravaging Hero. Ulanov describes the next type as the Amazon, under the archetype of the Virgin, who is either self-contained or frigid and unrelated. The woman's identity is achieved either through the development of her own ego, or she remains identified with the mother's animus and/or shadow. In relationship she is the comrade of a man's ego; her animus is the Father as a spiritual guide or as a tyrant. The final type is what Ulanov calls the Medial Woman rather than the Medium. She manifests elements of the archetype of the Wise Woman, who positively furthers culture or else negatively furthers evil as a witch. Her identity is achieved through the development of a firm and discriminating ego, or is lost in the collective unconscious. She is the mediatrix to a man's anima, and can give it an objective form by carrying its image for him. Her animus is the Wise Man, for whom she mediates the unconscious, or the Magician, who tempts her into magic and inflation, especially an inflated sense of her own guilt.

The power of Ulanov's design is its comprehensive inclusion of both sides of each stage and the clarity of her organizing principle. Ulanov does not relate this scheme to her later developmental ideas. Instead she describes its usefulness to women in its Jungian symbolic approach and as a representation of the feminine in its psychic as well as its sexual and cultural determinants.

> The four types of women encompass almost every aspect of the feminine. What makes this a particularly useful typology is its close attention to the cultural contexts in which the Mother, the Hetaira, the Amazon, and the Medium appear and the mythological symbolism, always fundamental to Jungian theory, which best expresses both the types and their various environments. (p. 210)

Ulanov also details stages of anima and animus development which echo the work of Emma Jung, Harding, and Binswanger, and which I described in Chapter Six. In her 1981 work, Ulanov is one of the first U.S. analysts writing on the feminine to include child development in her theory. First, Ulanov states, there is a stage of infant uroboric non-differentiation of ego from its surroundings. Matriarchal consciousness prevails in early childhood, followed by the patriarchal consciousness of puberty and young adulthood. It is during puberty that the individual ego emerges and slowly becomes differentiated. A new integrative consciousness occurs, Ulanov says, only after the ego is strong and the adult clearly present and acting in the world. The development of integrative consciousness becomes a task for the second half of life, though in her descriptions of this integrative stage of consciousness, Ulanov (along with Neumann and Whitmont) does not deal with the issue of people being at different stages of consciousness at the same time in history. Limiting the growth of consciousness to specific biological ages also leads to some logical incongruities. For instance, having classes of people, such as the young adults, male and female alike, all destined to be going through the same stage of patriarchal behavior in psychological development, puts the most vital and dynamic group of an integral era in a patriarchal, pre-integrative stage.

Whitmont (1979, 1980, 1982a) elaborates on the varied types and possibilities inherent in the feminine, but he does not work out a detailed theory of women's development. He follows Neumann in seeing consciousness in both men and women as progressing through uroboric, matriarchal, and patriarchal stages. Again like Neumann, he posits the end of patriarchy and the emergence of what he calls a new integrative era which evolves beyond, though includes and synthesizes, the matriarchy and patriarchy. Like Ulanov, Whitmont parallels these three cultural eras with developmental stages in the child, using object-relations terminology, and insisting on the necessity of both men and women going through each stage. He concurs with Ulanov on the socio-historical causes for the evolution and the devaluation of the feminine, and presents an even wider array of archetypal examples of the feminine. He focuses especially on types which had been overlooked, suppressed, or rejected during the patriarchy, and clearly differentiates the feminine from matriarchal consciousness.

Following Wolff, de Castillejo, and Ulanov, Whitmont uses the four types of the feminine. However, he sees these types in a broader context, independent rather than relating to the masculine. Like Ulanov, he presents them as aspects manifested by and possible to all women and to men's anima-natures. The four differently conceived types that Whitmont proposes are equated with the phases of the moon; he names them Luna, Lila, Pallas, and Medusa. All these types have an active and a passive side. Whitmont (1982a) considers women's development as occuring through the integration of these aspects of the feminine, especially the powerful and creative dark phase of the Medusan and Dionysian, and that this integration is both an individual psychotherapeutic task and one for the culture at large.

Despite Whitmont's excellent discussion of feminine and masculine principles, he does not satisfactorily outline how they develop in the psychology of actual men and women, nor does he consider the implications of single-gender (female) nurturing as a possible source of developmental and behavioral differences between sexes in our culture. Dinnerstein (1977), N. Chodorow (1978), Hall (1980), and Rubin (1983) have all examined this question. Because of the nuclear family, the absence of the father or other masculine presence in day-to-day nurturing and care-giving, and the dominance of the mother in infant experience, they argue that the male who has to learn his difference from the mother is apt to experience a more traumatic development and also exhibit more fear of the feminine than females. This is a difference in experience which may inevitably reinforce patriarchal gender-typed behavior and make the integration of all aspects of the feminine more problematical for men in our culture than for women, and more difficult than Whitmont concludes.

Whitmont does extend Jung's approach to analysis through the incorporation of what Whitmont terms the feminine into the practice as well as the theory of analytical psychology. He adheres to the traditional Jungian view of seeing the earth, nature, body, and matter as feminine. Like Hillman (1972), he criticizes traditional Jungian analysis for its increasing tendency to be too cerebral, linear, judgmental, interpretive, Apollonic, and masculine. In contrast, and in order to develop the feminine in both men and women, he recommends what he describes as archetypally feminine modes: playful experiment, gestalt work, psychodrama, nonverbal enactment, body awareness, responsible touch and body contact, guided imagination, and analysis in a group as well as a private setting. He describes these "feminine" modalities as involved in experiment and as necessary for the creation of new myths and new rituals for a new integrative age (1982a and b). Through his breadth of perspective, Whitmont adds richness, complexity, respect for nuance (and blur), and openness to the unexpected possibilities inherent in the many forms in which the feminine mirrors and reveals itself.

Neumann, Ulanov, and Whitmont have all used object-relations terminology to describe developmental processes which fit well within the matrix of analytical psychology. Among members of the London School, Fordham (e.g., 1973) is perhaps the foremost Jungian proponent of object-relations theory. His theories extend Jung's by blending them with Kleinian psychology to form, in Plaut's (1975) and Henderson's (1975) term, a "Jung-Klein hybrid." Fordham's view of woman's development is essentially that held by Melanie Klein (and thus beyond the sphere of this book, though the "Jung-Klein hybrid" deserves attention and further study for its new and evolving ideas about early developmental psychology).

Analysts concerned with feminine development, such as the following three writers, show the value of Neumann's archetypal scheme when applied to specific developmental impairments. For example, Gerhard Adler (1959) conceives of the problems of a female agoraphobic in relation to her failed progresssion through Neumann's earliest stages. The patient had a disturbed primal relation to her mother, which left her open to attack from the masculine through an incestuous relationship to her father and through a transference to her male analyst whom she considered violently intrusive. Adler describes her development in analysis as progressing from Neumann's matriarchal uroboric state to a patriarchal uroboric one through the patriarchate and toward individuation.

Fritz Beyme (1967) uses Neumann's terminology to follow the dreams of a female patient (stuck in Neumann's early third stage) in connection with her "frigidity." The dreamer, at first enwrapped within the safety of the matriarchy, starts by feeling herself threatened. Then come dreams of dangerous men, male animals, and penetrating object. Beyme states that the form of her dream patterns are indicative of frigidity and blocked development. The dreams never progress beyond the feeling of threat and the negative, intrusive, and often anonymous masculine which the dreamer feels to be overpowing (the intrusion of the negative patriarchal stage). There is an absence of abysses, there are no masculine images that attract, and no lysis from anxiety to pleasure occurs. Beyme notes a possible traumatic or incestuous experience that may underlie the patient's feelings of threat, and her subsequent repressions of them.

Andrew Samuels (1980) writes of a more abstract "incest archetype" in analysis as a oneness that moves toward twoness. He equates the oneness with Neumann's uroboric stage, in which infantile uroboric omnipotence (whether in the infant or in the regressed or stuck patient) equals uroboric incest.

A fourth analyst is more classically a London School Kleinian. James Astor (1987) does not use Neumann's terms but describes a patient being stuck in a stage where resists violent patriarchal intrusion (in fantasy and also, Astor, postulates, in possible unremembered fact) through her infantile autistic (uroboric) and concertistically repetitive defences. He uses the word *claustrum* to describe a world view made up of fantasies of intrusive identification ("the inside of the object penetrated by intrusive identification" [p. 346]). The patient's encapsulation in this stage resulted in a characteristically schizoid character formation, two-dimensionality, and autoerotic sexuality. Analysis moved toward a maternal transference (the matriarchy) which in turn started to become negative as the woman developed enough to try to break out of the enveloping maternal and her defensive *claustrum* and toward warmth and three-dimensional contact with the positive masculine (again through her male analyst.)

Another London School analyst, Judith Hubback (1978/1988), uses clinical material from two patients to round out her brief but well-titled "Reflections on the Psychology of Women." After simply naming some of the topics covered in the general Jungian literature on women (mother and father archetypes, the anima and the animus, intersexual envies, masochism, sadism, bisexuality, homosexuality, gender identity, creativity, destructive forces, spirituality—with a note on new work on the animus and goddesses added to the updated 1988 form of the article) and naming representative writers (Emma Jung, Harding, Neumann, and Singer), Hubback declares that three problems or themes need to be addressed when considering the psychology of women. These, as I mentioned in Chapter Five, are whether anatomy is destiny; whether any material can be discussed apart from its social and cultural setting; and what the real nature of women is. Hubback's article raises important questions and reviews some findings; she sees the present as a time during which the psychological similarities and differences of men and women perhaps can be discovered. She finds that the challenging of cultural and social stereotypes leads to change both in and out of analysis, and argues for the necessity of the analysts' knowledge of the collective storehouse of the humanities, of a woman's specific social and cultural milieu, and of the women's movement.

At present, Hubback encounters women in analysis who are "afraid of the attacking and counterattacking forces in themselves" (1978/1988, p. 138) brought about by cultural change. She emphasizes the importance in a woman's psychology of consideration of woman's nature—made up in part by her femaleness, her sexuality, and her feminine gender identity. Hubback remarks on the need for clinical material that elucidates these themes. An analyst and writer who combines Jungian and object-relations theory most generatively, she writes that although there is "no question of disregarding" the effect of culture and society on women's psychology, "the liberalizing climate has not done away with the fundamental intrapsychic conflicts" (p. 139). Hubback finds examples of these conflicts in early mother-child responses, in a child's first perception of itself as an individual, in the child's same-sex/opposite-sex interactions, rivalries, and incestuous, oedipal conflicts. Analysis of women, she concludes, can fairly easily uncover these early experiences in themselves, in sibling rivalries, and in later sexual encounters and partnerships, especially through transference-countertransference dynamics. Hubback attributes this to women's generally clearer perception and articulation of their own experience, with the result that analysis of women "stands a better chance now of facilitating individuation than it used to" (p. 139). Hubback concludes, however, that at this stage in analytical psychology, findings such as she makes remain subjective and anecdotal. She considers that the study of animus and anima manifestation are, today, the most productive way toward understanding men's and women's psychological natures.

I have written about Greenfield's (1983), Young-Eisendrath's (1984), and Young-Eisendrath and Wiedemann's (1987) conceptualization of animus development in Chapter Seven. The latter two writers envision a comprehensive Jungian psychology of women in which the female Self reaches consciousness and power through integration of the animus complex and reclamation of the authority women project on it. In their schema, the animus image rises through five levels, each of which is accompanied by an increasing sense of Self—the matriarchy with the animus as intrusive, alien other; the patriarchy with a critical, judgmental animus as father, God or king; a heroic, patriarchal stage with a partner animus as a youth, hero, or lover; and the final two stages where women's authority is reclaimed and the animus becomes, first, the partner within and then, finally, integrated within the larger female Self, as androgyne. Androgyny is defined as "not simply taking on male roles and attitudes. Rather it is the ability to be essentially human, and to choose for oneself the most authentic masculine or feminine gender modes, depending on the current environment" (1987, p. 11). The archetypal myths Young-Eisendrath and Wiedemann use for these five stages are the rape of Persephone, the myths of Pandora and Zeus, Amor and Psyche, Ariadne's confrontation with the Minotaur, and Theseus and Dionysus. The final stage has no myth:

> For modern women, there is no wholly adequate story for the integration of the animus. The old matriarchal myths have been largely buried and lost to us. The Greek and Roman stories take us only part way—perhaps because the edge of our consciousness is still unfolding. (p. 156)

Along with Hubback, Young-Eisendrath and Wiedemann envision women's development today as deeply problematic and conflicted, with women's multifarious attitudes, roles, and ideas about self-worth all combating each other. Hubback, Wiedemann and Young-Eisendrath all focus on a central problem underlying the psychology and treatment of women, a problem which echoes Neumann's analysis of women in a patriarchy: the gender-identity into which girls and women are socialized today produces a negative self-concept, "significant feelings of inadequacy" (Young-Eisendrath and Wiedemann, 1987, p. 2), and an essential double-bind concerning the development of a female Self and female authority.

Female Authority is the title of Young-Eisendrath's and Wiedemann's book and the focus of their strong reinterpretation of Jungian theory. It is a courageous and important work. It buttresses Hubback's more anecdotal work and is verified by many current findings about women's psychology in other fields (e.g., Jackson, 1987; Hare-Mustin and Maracek, 1988). The two authors review contemporary theorists on personality development and gender research, though they markedly limit reference to Jungian material. They criticize the major current theories of personality development for putting too much emphasis on the personal mother rather than on the Jungian archetypal mother complex. This complex combines with the effects of "gender, race, social caste, the family members, support systems, physical environment, material resources and biological father (to name but a few)" (p. 216) as important influences on development. Rather than attempting a broad developmental theory, the authors criticize unhelpful ones and show how feminist Jungian therapy works pragmatically to assist women through the various stages of animus development, always toward increasing competence, self-esteem, authority, and awareness of the female Self.

> Our work on female authority has led us along two intertwining strands
> of interpretation in psychotherapy with women. The first is a deconstruc-
> tion of the animus complex, in terms of both its hidden and its expressed
> convictions of male superiority. The second is a revaluation of female so-
> cialization in terms of the myriad desires of women for their own ideal
> cultural forms. (p. 215)

The authors stress the importance of empathy, egalitarianism, and
active enhancement of competence as prerequisites for a psychotherapy
that promotes women's development. It is not clear how this type of
analysis would deal with early infantile wounds and the need for an analysand's regression, but I feel that the attitude they promote need not
be antithetical to these concerns. However, would it allow for the temporary loss of competence involved in regression—the step back in order to advance? I also wonder if the very clarity of the line of development
(like Geigerich's 1975 criticism of Neumann) perhaps is not too linear.
In my experience, women often circle around their animus problems
but meet the same figures at an increasingly more evolved level, though
the fact that animus figures change as women develop is incontroverti-
ble. Since animus forms develop along with women's development, I
would envision that different forms and models could be added to or
woven within Young-Eisendrath and Wiedemann's exciting prototype.

Another question is why Young-Eisendrath and Wiedemann's scholarly treatment of the non-Jungian fields of gender studies and developmental psychology is not matched by an equal consideration of Jungian
work on the feminine. They cite only Jung in any depth, omitting the
wider Jungian field except for cursory references to Neumann, de Castillejo, A. Stevens, and Woodman. These are minor criticisms of a valuable
book which brings the Jungian approach to women's psychology into
a developmental scheme congruent with women's present reality and
needs.

So far, I have discussed theories or case histories of women's psychological development that are presented as a more or less linear progression through stages toward greater individuality, consciousness, and sense
of Self. There is another major theme in Jungian literature on the
feminine—this is development and individuation through initiation (or
using the archetype of initiation as a paradigm for development in and
through the analytic process). As early as 1957 the importance of initia-

tion as a model for women's developmental psychology formed the core of Linda Fierz-David's seminar at the C. G. Jung Institute in Zürich, "Psychological Reflections on the Fresco Series of the Villa of the Mysteries in Pompeii" (1957), recently published as *Women's Dionysian Initiation* (1988). In the seminar, Fierz-David contemplates the pictures of an Orphic initiation ritual for women and explores the ritual's relevance to the psychological needs of contemporary women.

The developmental stages in this inner initiatory process parallel the frescoes. The first pictures depict a loss of the former extraverted relationship with the outer world and its consequent group-identification. Turning aside from this world, the next step is symbolized by dismemberment. Fierz-David makes the analogy between the tasks of this stage and those of the first stage of analysis; they involve a search for the personal unconscious, the shadow, and the animus. She (in a view that parallels Harding's) compares this stage to one during which a woman often lives through her animus in order to become conscious of and surmount it. The third stage involves a descent into the collective unconscious. It is a "mystery way" similar to Harding's "downgoing," where words are no longer of use. This stage requires a surrender of the rational that was so hard won in the animus stage and involves a loss of former consciousness. The symbols of music in the picture here denote the way to connect with a central and new symbol that is full of feeling.

Fierz-David then describes the next step, in which this passive, "feminine" surrender is no longer enough. This next stage is one full of fear and terror, subject to the God Dionysus, and accompanied by feelings of death as well as of ecstasy. At this stage a woman often feels panic, and wants to break off the initiation or analysis and run away. Fierz-David writes at length about the urge for women to rush away from initiation before they can progress further. She also describes this as the place in an initiation process where the realms of men's and women's experience diverge. (I am reminded of the uncanny similarity of this description with the Navajo girls' three-day puberty initiation ceremony, the Kinaaldá, during which the girl symbolically becomes the Navajo goddess, Changing Woman, and engages, during the first days of the initiation, in foot races with other girls in flight away from, and then finally back to, the ceremonial hut.) Fierz-David sees this as a time for testing, in which women have to sacrifice a life of relatedness in the world for loneliness, separation, self, and spirit (this again echoes Harding and Neumann). Fierz-David concludes that nothing in the culture supports women in this perilous step toward individuation.

The sixth scene is of Dionysus and Ariadne. Fierz-David calls this the core of the mystery, "the deepest place" (p. 108) which governs the rest. She explores the archetypal image of Ariadne and Dionysus together as representative of the archetype of the Self for women, as well as the way toward its realization. This point in the initiation is dealt with more briefly than any others, though it is deemed the most important, pervading all the rest. Fierz-David equates it with the journey to the lowest part of the underworld and the stage from which ascent and development become possible. To me it also represents the deepest stage of analysis and the *coniunctio* that can occur in analysis.

In the seventh scene the woman is represented as returning from the underworld wretched and exhausted. Fierz-David calls it a scene for women and only for women. In the mystery, the initiate is kneeling as if caught in a superhuman vision and is about to uncover the hidden and sacred phallus in the ceremonial winnowing basket. An angel with a whip stands in her way. Fierz-David amplifies this scene at length, concluding that the woman had returned from the depths of the mystery and, unthinking and inflated, was about to commit sacrilege; the higher power of the angel stops her. Fierz-David then discusses how, for women, the spirit can appear in Dionysian form in her own sexuality:

> It is truly a divine recognition that sex, too, can be holy. And for a woman it is truly one of the most important experiences that the creative spirit becomes alive for her when it reaches her bodily depths. . . . We can quote the often cited sentence of the alchemical *Tabula Smaragdina:* "What is below is as that which is above; and what is above is as that which is below; in order that the miracle of the *one* thing may be accomplished." (1988, p. 100)

Fierz-David adds that this is why the phallus has to be kept hidden and therefore symbolic, and why this initiation form is for and by women. It is only under these specific conditions that the secret avoids profanation. Fierz-David considers the extinguished torch that the woman carries in this scene as psychologically representative of a newly developed animus who now can act as guide and mediator between consciousness and the collective unconscious. The extinguished torch is also equated with the hidden and sacred phallus. Fierz-David describes the angel in this scene as representative both of the feminine aspect of Dionysus and of the higher and deeper morality that develops through individuation.

I concur with Fierz-David's general interpretation of this scene, but would add that the urge to uncover the basket could also be equated with scenes four and five in Jung's "The Psychology of the Transference" (1946/1975). Jung, in reference to these scenes, discusses the urge within analysis to concretize what has to remain inner and symbolic. Uncovering the basket and seizing the phallus is a graphic image of the pull toward concretization. The scene is also congruent with a more Freudian interpretation, as the wish for a penis in the sense that it represents power and authority in this culture (see Karen Horney, 1967). Here the image would reflect the desire to seize this masculine symbol from without rather than discovering, developing, and relating to the masculine within the woman herself.

The eighth scene is described as a return to consciousness. In it the initiate fully surrenders to the process and is without disguise. She leans against the lap of a priestess who contains her but does not interfere or attempt to soften the experience.

> The initiate has reached a point where she has experienced everything that she is *not*, where nothing remains to her but the feeling of terrible destitution and overpowering remorse for the profanation. But this profanation was, after all, by no means the first. Where people are unconscious, they always transgress. As long as a woman is identified with the world, she lays violent hands on it; as long as she is identified with the principle of relatedness, she lays violent hands on people and things; and as long as she is identified with the animus, she lays violent hands on the spirit. (1988, p. 121)

Fierz-David emphasizes the comfort other women as teachers, companions, and models can give in this situation, and other women's importance in assisting the discovery of a woman's feminine base. I am struck by the relevance of this scene to the analytic process and to the support given by the good and firm mothering that can occur silently at this stage of analysis.

Fierz-David concludes her discussion of these frescoes by using the penultimate scene as the basis for a long amplification of the Ariadne and Maiden archetypes as emblematic of a woman's discovery and recovery of her own feminine being. The final scene of the Roman matron Livia, who faces the Ariadne-Dionysus fresco, is described as a portrayal of the initiate who returns to the world but remembers and recalls how she has been changed.

Katherine Bradway, in a far shorter and more condensed work (1982b), is also drawn to the mysteries at Pompeii as an archetypal pattern for women's development through initiation. Bradway values these frescoes as pictures without words or history; they are therefore culturally unaffected by interpretation, yet also call for a personal response. She reaches many of the same conclusions as Fierz-David but presents them in a more scholarly way. She disagrees with Fierz-David in particulars, presents alternative interpretations, and cites many other sources. Her main disagreement is with Fierz-David's contention that the frescoes only apply to women's individuation. She concludes that they are symbolic of feminine individuation in both sexes. She also suggests that the angel with the whip is driving the initiate away from the masculine and toward the feminine. She joins Fierz-David in being moved by the frescoes and in making parallels between the experiences portrayed there and contemporary women's own search for their feminine ground. Bradway interprets the scenes as representative of the analytic process and responds to scene eight in much the same way I do. (I feel that this scene holds an especially powerful archetypal significance for a woman therapist who has undergone analysis herself.) Bradway writes:

> The already-initiated woman knows that nothing can, or should, protect the initiate from the stroke of the whip. It is part of what she has to endure in order to find an inner strength. She has to find her own god and her own goddess within herself. She has to realize her inner wholeness. This is the transformation which initiation fosters. (p. 26)

> The initiate . . . reconnects with her own feminine being through bodily contact with another woman who supports her through the ordeal, a woman who has been through the initiation and can offer empathy and comfort — but not, significantly, protection. We could describe this woman as containing the initiate. Just as the analytical relationship may form a container for the analysand, so this holding woman makes the initiate feel safe enough to endure the painful transforming experience. (p. 29)

In *Thresholds of Initiation*, Henderson (1967) is primarily concerned with the archetype of initiation as such. He too sees the experience of analysis as often paralleling the form of initiation. The pattern of development he discerns in both is from a pre-initiatory phase to submission, then a two-part stage of transformation—containment and liberation—with immanence or individuation the goal. He also describes these stages as separation from the mother's world, alliance with the father's world and the group, and then perhaps retreat, isolation, some inner quest, and a return to the group as an individual. Each of these passages involves some form of initiatory experience. Henderson compares the progression he sees in initiation with the developmental theories of Erikson. He also includes a brief discussion of fellow Jungians' developmental theories, including Neumann's stages of consciousness, Fordham's ideas on infant development, and Edinger's on adolescence.

Henderson seems most clear about, and mostly concerned with, the initiation experience of men and of patriarchal initiatory rites, though he states that "male and female find the same initiatory answer to their different questions" (p. 122). What he does say about woman seems to belong to Neumann's matriarchal stage and to the mother-daughter archetype.

> In modern women's dreams the theme of belonging to a group is much less marked than in the case of men, but it is no less important in its bearing upon the individual woman's life pattern. The idea of identifying with a women's group does not seem to appeal to most women except as a transitory phase. They may belong to women's clubs or other organizations, but these do not enjoy the solidarity of the men's equivalent groups. What a woman seems most frequently to need is a sense of her own individuality *as woman* in such a way as to feel developmentally contained in the mother-daughter archetype with its cyclical rhythm of union and separation so beautifully exemplified in the myth of Demeter and Kore. (p. 119)

Henderson subscribes to the Logos/discrimination/masculine and Eros/relatedness/feminine equations (p. 124). He is not very consistent in distinguishing feminine from women and masculine from men in actual usage, though he does make the distinction at a theoretical level. He also seems to limit specific qualities to specific gender. For example, while amplifying a dream he refers to the son of the woman who had the dream as having a presumably idiosyncratically masculine quality: creativity. Henderson contrasts him, as male, to his mother, as female, by alluding to his "specific masculine faculty, his inventive or creative mind" (p. 123). Henderson sees girls' initiations as limited primarily to an "unfolding sense of awakening" (p. 121) while boys' are trials of strength. He adds that though women may go through equivalent sorts of trials in primitive cultures, psychologically the initiation serves a different purpose for them. This purpose, he explains, has more to do with the Jungian concepts of feminine containment and relatedness than with a need for separation: "while women also undergo ordeals and trials of strength in tribal societies and women's mysteries, the specifically feminine experience seems to arrive at some form of inner containment" (p. 121). He concludes that though there are and always have been exceptional heroines, the heroic is not primarily a woman's way. Instead Henderson sees women as naturally at home in the liminal and the essence of woman herself as liminal. Because of this, women are capable of mediating the experience of initiatory borders, thresholds, and entryways to the realms of the unconscious.

Henderson's view is the classic one of Jung's time, and has great value for this verisimilitude except when it confuses socio-cultural prejudices with timeless psychological reality. Perhaps the women he is seeing today have evolved out of the developmental pattern delineated here and toward a more heroic yet innerly contained one similar to Neumann's (1962) ideas about Psyche — herself an example of the individuated feminine who, through her personal development, helps to take the culture a step beyond the levels of patriarchal development. The women in my far more limited experience today do have dreams of groups (often of dancing groups), and it is not unusual for them to have an interest in and allegiance to a small group of women that is profound, neither transitory nor idiosyncratic — though each, also, has encountered highly individual periods of downgoing, isolation, and return.

In my interview with Henderson, he noted that a major difference between Jung's time and today is in the number of women describing the feminine from out of their own experiences and with their own voices. As these experiences and voices are heard, men's and women's understanding and theory will be modified accordingly. (*Thresholds of Initiation* contains an appendix about the archetype of the bear, the great Artemisian symbol for young girl's initiation. It completes the book and balances it through the inclusion in symbol of this most powerful symbol of the initiatory feminine.)

Henderson writes of the importance of the descent to the kiva, the underground chamber, and the descent to the underworld both in initiation and as a stage in psychological development. Sylvia Perera (1981), Betty Meador (1984), and Jane Wheelwright (1984) have all written or spoken about this downward initiatory path as especially significant in women's psychological development. Perera, Meador, and Wheelwright connect this descent with the need, both in therapy and in our culture, for recovering the potency of all the dark, repressed, and rejected sides of the feminine. Because of our culture's alienation from these aspects of the feminine, a psychological need for withdrawal, descent, and even depression seems at this time to be an integral part of a woman's psychological development.

Bani Shorter, in *An Image Darkly Forming: Women and Initiation* (1987), combines and verifies much prior work on the feminine in Jungian psychology. Through five clinical vignettes, she writes of women's development through initiation and self-discovered, Self-enhancing rituals of initiation. Shorter often refers to Neumann's ideas about women's development and Henderson's ideas about initiation. Like Henderson and Fierz-David, she sees that patriarchal society (which she calls Western society) has ignored the liminal; women have had to find it within themselves through secret rituals and initiation. Following the tradition of Harding, Perera, Meador, and Wheelwright, she describes a time in a woman's development for downgoing — a necessary time in which a woman can break out of an outmoded concept of the feminine and toward a new sense of herself; "it can take the form of withdrawal, solitude, disorientation and disassociation and is mirrored clinically as depression" (1987, p. 66). Like Emma Jung, Harding, and the many Jungians through to Young-Eisendrath and Wiedemann, Shorter emphasizes an evolution of the animus that marks and parallels women's development. Along with the latter two authors, she notes that the change in inner male and female images also results in a woman's changed relationship to men. Shorter, perhaps more traditionally, emphasizes this relationship as a key marker in woman's development. As with Hubback, a central question for Shorter is how one becomes a woman and what this means psychologically. Along with Neumann, Hubback, and Young-Eisendrath and Wiedemann, she is attentive to the cultural moment — the conflicts within a woman at a particular historical time and the many competing influences on a woman who lives in a man's world.

> This raises the question as to whether, for a woman, such influences can ever be eliminated or if the initiatory period is not itself a time of confrontation with that which is patriarchal, resulting, for better or for worse, in altered images and changed likenesses of both male and female within the same person. (p. 56)

As in the writings of Berry, Perera, Woodman, and many contemporary analysts directly involved with patient care (Whitmont, Mindell, Jane Chodorow, and Anita Greene come immediately to mind), the importance of the body in women's analysis is stressed. Shorter believes that ritual has to include bodily awareness as well as mind and spirit, and that bodily awareness for women can be a gateway to, or an embodiment of, the spiritual. The rites of initiation result in a changed relationship between the patients' bodies and their spirits. Along with Young-Eisendrath and Wiedemann, Shorter stresses the special need for empathy and loving relationship in women's therapy; like them too, she sees a paramount need to help women empower themselves and increase their self-esteem. I am stressing all these similarities, for I believe this book and Young-Eisendrath's and Wiedemann's are a culmination of a long historical progression in Jungians' view about women — a progression that remains implicit rather than articulated. We do have a history and development in our approach to the psychology of women and the understanding of the feminine.

Like the majority of analysts' work on the feminine and on the psychology of women, Shorter's book is illustrated by and grounded in clinical experience. It exemplifies a difference in tone from many of her London School colleagues. Rather than choosing *one* among Samuels' (1985) descriptions of classical, developmental, and archetypal modes of analysis, Shorter includes all three in a way that I would suggest exemplifies a feminine rather than a masculine approach. Trained in Zürich and England, Shorter follows Jung in perceiving technique as necessary but not definitive. For her, technique is subject to the needs of the individual patient and to an analyst's particular style rather than being a dogma to be applied. In other words, the technique is at the service of the patient and can be modified according to her individual needs; the patient is not to be fitted into and used to verify a pre-defined *modus operandi*.

In each of Shorter's five cases, a long period of preparatory analysis takes place before the development through initiation occurs; then, at a critical juncture, the woman comes up with or is involved in a self-created initiatory experience which results in an abrupt and profound growth in her psyche. The rituals are neither regressive nor primitive. They do not "cure" pathology, but bring the woman into a new relationship with her own inner Self. Shorter describes the rituals as decisive, authentic, and full of their own creative authority. They involve simple yet profound actions: a woman with gender-identity problems pierces her ears and places gold hoops in them; a *puella* type anima-woman spends three days in ritual house-cleaning of an Ibsen-like fantasy doll's house before she leaves it; another woman and her partner conduct funeral rites for the death of an outer and inner child; the last woman recovers from and works through a failed initiation through the experience of being loved yet contained within a new initiatory analysis.

Shorter concludes that through rites of initiation, her patients face, make sense of, and transcend their psychological wounds.

> I have been particulary interested in the spontaneous ceremonies devised by women because of what they have shown me about the distinctive pattern of feminine transformation as well as for what they have revealed about what appears to be essential for the formation and transformation of psychic imagery. (pp. 12-13)

> The ceremonies employed by all five had certain features that I believe 'caused', in the sense of 'generated', their effectiveness. Moreover, they were 'specific', in the sense of 'designed' to achieve psychological transformation of image along with person. That is to say, a changed image and likeness of woman resulted in each instance and these changes apparently occurred coincidentally with the performance of the ceremonies rather than as a result of subsequent interpretation and experience. (p. 41)

Like Fierz-David, Shorter stresses the particular dramatic moment of change, rather than the slow, slogging initial stages of therapy. She also sees these "leaps" in women's psyches in a similar way that Kuhn (1970) envisions paradigm shift and Gould (e.g., 1981) makes sense of evolution — theories which combine acknowledgement of periods of slow development with sudden and abrupt periods of consolidation and change — ideas that are especially fruitful for further investigation in psychology.

Along with the reevaluation and broadening of our knowledge about the psychology of women such as I have described here, there are concurrent changes in the way some (predominantly female) Jungian analysts are practicing that reflect a further inclusion of what is considered the feminine (Whitmont, 1982b). These changes include a new interest in ritual, body work, touch, movement, sandplay, and group work as well as the former emphasis on art, guided imagination, and dreamwork. It is essential in reviewing work on the psychology of women to include them, for they show a concrete change of style and focus that reflects this psychology and the effect women are starting to have on its practice. These perhaps more feminine modalities exist side by side with a concurrent push toward a more scientific, Freudian, and object-relations approach, which Whitmont and Hillman see as reflective of a predominantly masculine, if not patriarchal, psychology.

Sandplay (Dundas, 1978/1989; Kalff, 1980; Bradway, 1981; Weinrib, 1983) unites Jung's emphasis on artistic representation and active imagination with the construction of sand worlds. Its purpose is to allow the unconscious to manifest itself and bring about development and healing more or less unrestricted by the more usual, rational, linear, and verbal mode of expression. A collection of articles on sandplay by Jungian analysts in the San Francisco Bay area (Bradway *et al.*, 1981/1989) presents a historical, theoretical, clinical, and methodological analysis of its current use in this area.

Weinrib's *Images of the Self* (1983) is a complete overview of the theory and practice of sandplay. She describes sandplay as a method which provides a strong impetus toward psychological development for both men and women. This development can be seen in the series of sand-tray pictures which emerge over time. Weinrib describes a regressive and restorative stage, the emergence of ego, transformative phases, and eventual signs of individuation. She sees the essence of sandplay as being its powerful, healing, and transformative qualities which evolve from reconnection with and development of the feminine. She writes that "the primary thrust of sandplay is the reestablishment of access to the feminine elements of the psyche in both men and women, elements that have been repressed in Western Judeo-Christian culture" (p. 37). Weinrib restricts the feminine to the concrete, the emotional, the unconscious, the intuitive, and the spontaneous. She allows for the presence of masculine and feminine in both genders, but often writes as if women and her definition of the feminine were interchangeable.

Group therapy (Whitmont 1961, 1974, 1982a, 1982b; Thayer Greene, 1982) is described as being more feminine, democratic, and less patriarchal and hierarchical than one-to-one analysis. Whitmont finds it to be reintegrative of the matriarchal, more in touch with the real world, and opening the analytic encounter to the body in a more permissive and less restricted way than conventional analysis. Both writers see the dilution of the transference phenomenon as a positive aspect of group therapy; both describe group therapy as an adjunct to, not a replacement for, private analysis.

Touch therapy is advocated by Woodman (1980, 1982), Perera (1981), and Anita Greene (1980) as perhaps particularly useful in the therapy of women and as an essentially feminine extension and amplification of Jung's method. Mindell (1982) and Whitmont (1972, 1982b) advocate the use of touch and body experience as a healing and integrating force. Mindell describes neurosis as visible and manifest in the physical body and subject to therapeutic intervention there. Whitmont is more concerned with the body's neediness and the harm done through our culture's body-mind split. All of these analysts note that in their practices they have found that the use of responsible touch mitigates rather than constellates erotic transference. Literature from the patients' viewpoint is lacking, as is consideration of possible gender differences, especially when the analyst is male and the analysand female (e.g., Henley, 1972, *The Politics of Touch*).

Fay (1977) introduces the parallels between dance therapy and Jungian theory. Much of her work rests on that of Mary Whitehouse, who combined depth psychology, active imagination, and polarity theory in pioneering dance movement therapy. Whitehouse's own (1979) article on Jung and dance therapy delineates how her theory derives from the union of her perception of her own needs and ideas with those of Jung's. Penny Bernstein (1980a, 1980b, 1981) studies the archetypes of the moon goddess, medium, and earth mother in relation to the woman therapist who uses dance and movement; she also describes the union of gestalt technique and active imagination in Jungian movement therapy. Joan Chodorow's (1982) ground-breaking article on dance movement therapy is the first time this mode has been given more or less official sanction in mainstream Jungian literature through its inclusion in a comprehensive book (M. Stein, [Ed.], 1982) on Jungian analysis. In it she places dance and body awareness on a firm historical and theoretical foundation within depth psychology, but notes its rareness and lack of development. She concludes, "it seems that as the Jungian collective turns its attention to the neglected feminine and to the shadow, it cannot avoid attending to the third aspect of this rejected trinity: the body" (p. 200). This was followed by the 1986 issue of *Chiron,* entitled *The Body in Analysis,* which contains articles by Chodorow, Perera, Hubback, and Mario Jacoby, among others, that speak directly to these themes.

Whitmont (1982a, 1982b) discusses psychodrama as an extension and improvement on the traditional Jungian active imagination. He sees it as more potent than active imagination and praises it for expanding the experiential and feminine dimension in analysis. He finds psychodrama to be suitable for either group or individual analysis, as well as useful as a new integrative ritual for self- or peer-exploration.

In this chapter I have presented and discussed those writers who have
dealt with the psychology of women in analytical psychology. I have con-
centrated on developmental theory and initiatory stages. I have also included changes in therapeutic approach brought about by the inclusion
of the feminine. Elements that continually recur are: the archetypal treatment of the process of development; development seen in stages leading from the relatively unconscious and undifferentiated toward increasing
consciousness and individuality; development through integration of the
contrasexual and other split-off parts of the psyche, leading toward the
recovery of the Self; and, finally, development through initiation. These
elements occur in both men and women, but there has been little research on the ways this development differs according to gender.

I have noted a variety of attitudes toward women and their development. Harding (though she does posit a possible further stage), Wolff,
Hannah, Moreno, Ulanov in her early (1971/1978) work, and Henderson all seem to restrict women to what Broverman, *et al.* (1970) have
typified as non-adult stages of merger, containment, and relatedness.
Neumann (1959) criticizes this sort of development and describes it as
a pathological requirement of the patriarchy. Ulanov (1981) and Whitmont propose that men and women evolve through the same developmental stages and levels of consciousness. Neumann, Fierz-David,
Bradway, Perera, and Wheelwright all delineate a separate path for the
psychological development of women or the feminine. All these writers
speak of transformation, individuation, and the gaining of self-awareness.
How women differ from men, why they do, and why their developmental path may be different, all remain largely unexplored until the work
of Hubback and Young-Eisendrath and Wiedemann.

A comprehensive, objective, and accurate Jungian psychology of women
in tune with current research remains to be written. Much of the material I have presented is of historical importance, but no longer fits with
women's idea of themselves as expressed in their novels, poems, paint-
ings, academic concerns, and in what they reveal in therapy. Much belongs to the time in which it was written and has little relevance to
modern women. This is especially true of theories which deny women
the right to relate directly to life rather than acting through men and
for men's benefit, or which restrict them to a less evolved developmental level than men's. There is a further confusion brought about by the
impreciseness of terminology. "Women" and "the feminine" are often
used interchangeably as concepts or are not adequately distinguished

from each other. Both are quite often mixed with the function of feeling, with relatedness, and with the archetype of Eros; the psychology of women is defined accordingly.

The extensive use of archetypal symbols as developmental and psychological exemplars is of value when it extends the possibilities open to women and gives them fuller access to their multiple potentialities. This symbolic approach can also help clarify and organize experience. However, when theories are used as facts and women are expected to conform and develop in accordance to theory, it becomes limiting and potentially harmful. There is still much too much confusion in analytic literature between cultural conditioning, gender expectations, and woman's own reality.

Areas that are especially interesting to me and of value in starting to evolve a psychology of women center around Nancy Chodorow's (1978) work on the difference between men's and women's affective development and object-relations, and Gilligan's (1982) work on the difference between men's and women's cognitive development; while biologists (such as Anne Fausto-Sterling, 1985) and neurologists (such as Bleier, 1984) are starting to emphasize the similarities of men and women before culture intervenes and to point out the inadequacies of former studies of gender differences. Anyone writing about the psychology of women today needs a knowledge of contemporary findings, such as the recent overviews by Cynthia Fuchs Epstein (*Deceptive Distinctions: Sex, Gender, and the Social Order,* 1988), by Hare-Mustin and Marecek ("The Meaning of Difference: Gender Theory, Postmodernism and Psychology," 1988) or by Michelle Fine ("Reflections on a Feminist Psychology of Women," 1985).

Neumann's (1962) proposal of an active and heroic feminine development remains persuasive. He describes a particularly feminine style in which Psyche develops through confrontation with her shadow, separation from the matriarchy, active redemption of herself along with the masculine, and reunion with the feminine, but in an individual way which propels her beyond both matriarchy and patriarchy as they are archetypally described within Jungian theory. Neumann also outlines specifically feminine tasks of discrimination (but describes this discrimination as animus development), of patience, of action at the right time, of containment and the capacity to give form to the formless, of descent, and, finally, after a denial of relatedness, of reunion at a higher level of consciousness.

Harding, Fierz-David, Neumann, Henderson, Perera, Bradway, Meador, Wheelwright, and Shorter all focus on the need and the positive value of withdrawal, descent, even depression, as necessary elements in women's development. The positive aspect of depression, which is so often seen in women, is that it can also be a way in the patriarchy for women to have time for the exploration of inner needs. Neumann views depression as the consequence of the loneliness and difficulty of the feminine struggle to face and surmount both matriarchal and patriarchal assumptions in the current world. Perera, Meador, and Shorter develop and extend both these ideas. Whether depression is an integral component of women's psychological development or whether this is a consequence of her present socio-cultural experience (with the introjection of external inequality causing low self-valuation and consequent depression) remains largely unexplored. Perera's important book on the scapegoat complex and the complexes' cultural derivatives in women's psychology remains a recent and strong exception.

Young-Eisendrath and Wiedemann's work on culture, authority, and women's self-esteem is the first full-scale effort to include social and cultural elements in a Jungian study of women's psychology. The authors frankly state their feminist perspective and make an effort to integrate Jungian theory with contemporary research in other fields. They bring Jungian psychology up to date in a way that may mark a fruitful postmodernist period in analytical psychology.

The study of women's mysteries and women's initiatory rites for clues to, or as analogies of, women's development is an exciting addition to psychological theory. Much more work needs to be done here, for example to explore other examples of women's rites which have largely been ignored in the literature of initiation. Girls' puberty ceremonies such as the three-day Navajo rite of Changing Woman or the African Bantu ceremonies deserve further study, as do the various African women's cults which Vera Bürhmann is starting to explore. All of these rites include both active and passive, outgoing and withdrawing elements as essential to women's ceremonies and to women's psychological needs. Personal experience and clinical examples also contain much that could be contributive both for their dream images and in woman's search for and experience of her own way.

One final question remains. Are the nonverbal and more experiential approaches to therapy that I have included here really more feminine modes and more suited to women, both as patients and as therapists?

The relationship between these modes, typology, personality and therapeutic outcome remains unexplored. Nonverbal and experiential therapies are being used in masculine, feminine, matriarchal, and patriarchal ways. As much depends on the personality and approach of the therapist as on the type of therapy employed. More work needs to be done in clarifying these areas and in establishing both facts and explanations.

Without current awareness of the history of the treatment of the feminine in analytical psychology, cultural stereotypes that are outmoded are still allowed to govern the treatment of women. Women's psychology becomes confused with temporary cultural definitions about the nature of women and the feminine. The analysis of both men and women depends both on knowledge of the images of the feminine in the collective psyche and on the reality of women living today. Valuable insights into this reality are emerging from analysts, often women, who have examined themselves, their patients, and archetypal sources in an extensive reevaluation of woman's power, her varied and multiple expressions of potentiality, and all sides of her being. Changes in therapy are occurring as women are discovering their own paths toward healing, and as analysts become more open to the incorporation of the feminine into their therapy.

CHAPTER TEN: THE WOMAN IN THE MIRROR

Conclusion

And out of what one sees and hears and out
Of what one feels, who could have thought to make
So many selves, so many sensuous worlds,
As if the air, the mid-day air, was swarming
With the metaphysical changes that occur,
Merely in living as and where we live.

Wallace Stevens

I found God in myself and I loved her, I loved her fiercely.

Ntozake Shange, 1975

The attitudes toward the feminine and about women that underlie Jungian practice determine the treatment of both men and women as patients. This book attempts to bring these attitudes into consciousness and to note what may be of lasting value and what may be outdated, androcentric, time- and culture-bound, and detrimental to the full development of personality. I believe that a complete and thorough examination of the literature on the feminine in analytical psychology is necessary before current theory can be generated and before responsible adoption, reconsideration, discussion, or amendment of the theory can take place. When contemporary scholars and analysts remain unaware of the alternatives that are available to them, but instead adhere to and teach an unexamined and outmoded view of the feminine contaminated by the prejudices of the time or by the writer's own biases, it can harm patients, students, and themselves. When they examine specific small areas of feminine psychology without a general knowledge of the entire area and without the necessary framework of historical or the-

oretical continuity, they risk confusing the particular with the general
and the stereotypical with the archetypal.

Jung's ideas about the feminine were conditioned by his era and its
beliefs and expectations, and by his own experience and psychology. I
have tried to separate and examine some of these elements. Jung, as
a man and a product of his time, tended to describe his own psychology
first and, adopting a dualistic and polarized mode of thinking, often
allocated the opposite of it to women and the feminine. Women
themselves—his patients, his family, the subjects of his studies and of
his romantic interest—were keenly observed, yet were not differentiated strongly enough from his own anima and his own projections and
needs.

Among Jung's own theoretical contributions of lasting value are his
exploration and description of the character and quality of the feminine as found in symbols, myth, and alchemy. Presentations of various
feminine archetypes, though often only alluded to by Jung, contain the
seeds of subsequent Jungian work on this subject. Jung made a crucial
differentiation between the feminine as a psychological concept and actual female gender; his affirmation of the presence and importance of
both masculine and feminine elements in each gender strongly affects
future theory and allows for the expression of the contrasexual in each
person. He analyzed the harm done to the psyche and to the world by
the repression and devaluation of the feminine, and emphasized the
psychological necessity for the reintegration and reevaluation of all sides
of the feminine, especially the neglected and misapprehended dark side.
Jung was one of the first psychologists to take women's sexuality seriously in and of itself. He also, within his practice, encouraged the full
expression and development of his analysands' individuality regardless
of their gender.

Jung's concept of psychological types, when the types are not restricted by gender expectations, broadens the possibilities inherent in human behavior through its elaboration of eight equally valid ways of
functioning in the world. His reevaluation of Eros and Logos modes,
when not gender-bound, adds to the variety of ways humans have of
knowing and perceiving. These offer men and women access to a wide
range of behavioral modes and broadens the concepts within which they
may seek to define themselves. Though affected by his own personal
biases and the historical and socio-cultural biases of his time, these contributions of Jung's remain powerful and useful elements in a contem-

porary psychology. They stand behind all later studies of the feminine in analytical psychology.

Some elements that have often seemed integral to Jungian theory on the feminine may no longer be useful or acceptable in present-day theory. These are the equation of the feminine with and the limiting of women to Eros rather than Logos, feeling rather than thinking, the contained instead of the container. Also unacceptable is treating women and the feminine as representative of either the unconscious or of diffuse consciousness, and limiting them to the related and passive mode. The contention that woman's psychology is opposite to and complementary to man's fails to mirror woman herself. Given the realities of industrial and post-industrial societies, the conceit that men and women belong in separate (though possibly equal) spheres is an ill-conceived anachronism. None of these ideas is viable today.

There is no clear pattern, either historically or today, to Jungians' thinking about women or the feminine. I believe this is because there has been no comprehensive, chronological, historical, and integrated treatment of this subject from which to build. Many analysts, scholars, and readers remain unaware of the developments and possibilities inherent within analytic psychology. A pattern is also difficult to determine and perceive during our present age because individuals are, perhaps more than at any other time, at such different stages of evolution of identity and consciousness; the age itself may be changing into a new level of awareness. There is the further problem of how to gain a perspective from which to evaluate one's own age.

What I hope I have elucidated in this book is the gradual shift away from a concept of women as adjuncts of men and toward a concept of them as independent and complex individuals. There has also been some movement (though with marked exceptions) away from the tendency to limit women to stereotypical gender-role definitions. There has been a continuation and expansion of Jung's emphasis on the presence of the contrasexual within each person, and an emphasis on its exploration and incorporation. This has been accompanied by a growing interest in the study of women themselves, usually by women, which often emphasizes the importance of personal experience as intrinsic to theory. From this study of and by women has come further exploration and reevaluation of what may be essentially feminine: a feminine voice which had been suppressed and is just now surfacing. This has in turn produced a marked interest in and encouragement of power and strength in women. Criticism of prior work on the feminine is emerging which emphasizes the interrelationship of attitudes with culture, circumstance, and time. Part of the problem is that even though women have been struggling for self-definition, this struggle necessarily takes place within an androcentric social order and is pervaded by all the explicit and unconscious beliefs that define that system. It is immensely difficult to mirror women's reality as women experience it in itself, free of all the ways the patriarchy images us — i.e., men's experience of women. The beliefs and practices of a system inevitably influence even those who are trying to change it. It is still much easier for women to collude or acquiesce and mold their reality and words into the faulty definitions we all are taught, rather than honor women's individual and supposedly aberrant reality.

A person's type and psychology also influence how he or she sees and describes the world. Many writers examine their own way of being and generalize from this. They tend to see people of their own gender as like themselves and give opposite attributes to the other sex. Thus a feeling type woman (statistically the majority of women in our society) describes *all* women as feeling types and delineates the function's characteristics rather than the gender's. A thinking type man (again in the majority) does the same thing from his perspective. These definitions and outlooks then tend to restrict all members of a gender to a narrow range of behavior and result in a confusion of gender with function type in a limiting way.

The difference between the concept of the feminine and the definition of woman remains unresolved. About all that can be said is that there is a difference both between actual concrete men and women, and among the abstract symbols associated with the masculine and the feminine — and usually, but not always, women express more of the feminine. What these differences are and how they arise remains unclear. Possible differences in biology and in the experience of same- and other-sex mothering may prove crucial. In addition, differences may rest on socio-cultural biases and arise from social conditioning; many may be transitory, deriving from a particular time and culture. Comparison of Jungian findings with research from other disciplines and paradigms is a necessity. My conclusion from such a reading is that the terms "masculine" and "feminine" are categories that bestow predominantly social and political meanings to gender difference and are rooted in a system whereby the former accrues power and autonomy to itself and denies it to the latter. The terms are often so tentative, relative, unclear, and

prone to stereotypical formulations that, without a socio-cultural cav-
eat and definition, they are no longer particularly useful concepts for
a modern psychology. However, no better terms (including the terms
Yin and Yang, which suffer from many of the same deficits and add
cross-cultural complications of their own) present themselves; it may be
time to go beyond these dualities toward common humanness.

An attempt has been made recently to free the archetypes from specific gender linkage; unconscious feminine and unconscious masculine
elements are accepted as present in both men and women. The linkage
between anima and animus, typology, and Eros and Logos has been harder to break. The animus, for instance, is all too often still equated with
a woman's thinking, while the anima is given both the man's emotions
and his feeling. Hillman has offered a subtle and brilliant reinterpretation of the anima; a thorough critique of the ideas raised by this interpretation is lacking. How the implications of Hillman's revisioning
of the anima logically affect the very foundations of Jungian psychology
remains unexamined. No such attention has been paid to the animus,
though the critique and analysis of the animus by Young-Eisendrath
and Wiedemann, Mattoon and Jones, and Douglas has laid the ground-
work for it.

Possible components of further reassessment would distinguish the
animus from both thinking and Logos, and would clarify the difference.
The animus' various manifestations would have to be linked with function type and explored accordingly. The way, for instance, the animus
of a predominantly thinking type would mediate between the ego and
the unconscious must be different from the way a feeling type's animus
would go about the same task; the same holds true for sensation and
intuition. Animus contamination by the shadow could raise very different problems, dependent again on typology. Many different forms of
the masculine need to be emphasized in this reassessment, notably those
that the patriarchy itself ignores. As the masculine changes in its outward manifestation in our culture, its inward forms change as well. Possibly by cultivating these new images of the inner masculine, their
appearance in the outer world may increase. There seems to be a growing interest among men, too, in different ways of being male. The mixture of anima and animus in each person irrespective of gender brings
further complication and balance to the conscious and unconscious personality. The possibilities inherent in this new view await the sort of
wholehearted attention Hillman gave to his reworking of the anima

concept.

Jungian psychology is particularly rich and original in the use of archetypal symbolism for the study of human nature. The increasingly wide variety of archetypal imagery of the feminine emerging today helps counteract the restricted view of women held by our culture. In the study of feminine archetypes, I think the recovery of lost aspects of the feminine and the reevaluation of the dark side of the feminine is profoundly important, restoring dynamic and powerful models for women today. Also of major interest is the increasing use of pre-patriarchal images as perhaps less contaminated by socio-cultural limitations of the feminine than those of the patriarchy.

Neumann and Whitmont have posited a theory of consciousness that depicts a matriarchy followed by patriarchy, possibly followed by an integral era. It is interesting to note that the pattern of archetypal images explored during the past fifty years follows a similar progression. The depiction of the unconscious, primodial feminine was first emphasized, then differentiated facets of the patriarchal feminine caught people's interest, while today more diffuse, complex, and many-sided feminine images come into view. It is as if the image of the feminine archetype has spiraled backward into the past and forward into the future to reintegrate both at a higher level of consciousness in the present. This seems to portend both progress and the reattainment of a feminine whole. It seems both natural and significant that, as more women are engaged in scholarly inquiry, it is women analysts who are doing by far the most work on the feminine in Jungian circles. They are showing the effects of the changing culture and the impact of feminism in that they are increasingly exploring their own psychology and experience as well as that of their patients, and then applying this to their practice and to their theory. The potency of the archetype and the releasing of women's energy (as well as their ability to effect a clearer imaging of the archetype) fructify each other.

I have presented and examined various developmental theories in the context of their time and have attempted to draw implications for a psychology of women that is in tune with current research. This psychology is tentative at best, though Hubback and Young-Eisendrath and Wiedemann, especially, have marked a strong beginning. Much of the material I have discussed belongs to the time in which it was written and contains outdated theories which see women's existence as subservient to men's needs, limit women to a non-adult developmental stage, or deny women the right to relate directly to life instead of expecting them to act through men and for men's benefit. These need to be replaced.

Many of the newer theories involve a wider use of new modalities of therapy, such as sandplay work, group analysis, and forms of body involvement. These have been considered to be more feminine modalities. They may be indicative of the changes in therapeutic practice that the inclusion of the feminine may require. It is interesting to note that their use is also consistent with a less patriarchal way of envisioning the therapeutic encounter. The use of these new modes concurrently with the more traditional ones may also synthesize the two and lead to a more unified and advanced approach which better meets the psychological needs of modern men and women. Both modes, however, can be used in restrictive matriarchal or patriarchal ways as well as in a more freeing integral way that increases self-empowerment; as much depends on the quality and attitude of the analyst as on the form the therapy takes.

I need to emphasize again that one of the biggest problems throughout my study has been the confusion brought about by the impreciseness of the terms used by the authors whose texts form the basis for my analysis and evaluation. "Women" and "the feminine" are often used as if they were synonymous in spite of the theoretical differentiation between the two. Theory is hopelessly muddied when the terms are used interchangeably or when one is used when the other is meant. Both "women" and "the feminine" are all too often used to denote the function of feeling and relatedness (which are also confused). The archetype of Eros is mixed with these concepts, while men's experience of their own animae further blurs what they are seeing. The psychology of women suffers from many Jungians' tendency toward sloppy and muddled thinking.

The extensive use of archetypal symbols to illustrate developmental and psychological processes is where Jungian psychology is most original. Illustrative usage of archetypal symbols has great value, providing new models of ways in which women can grow, opening possibilities of experience to them, and giving them fuller access to their potentialities. This symbolic approach can also help clarify personal experience by giving it a larger perspective. However, when specific archetypal images give rise to theories and the theories are then taken for facts, the map for the terrain, Jungian theory becomes not only muddled but potentially harmful. In some of this sort of theorizing, women are painfully unmirrored. They are expected to conform and develop themselves in relation to an image that accords with a biased and limiting theory of development, but is alien to their own experience and perception of themselves. There remains much confusion between cultural conditioning, gender expectations, archetypal illustrations, and woman's own reality.

Without current awareness of the history of the treatment of the feminine in analytical psychology, outmoded cultural stereotypes still influence the way women are treated. A woman's intrinsic nature — who she is and can be — becomes confused with cultural stereotypes and social roles. The analysis of both men and women depends on knowledge of the images of the feminine in the collective psyche and on women's reality in the late twentieth century. Valuable insights into this reality are emerging from analysts, often women, who have examined themselves, their patients, and archetypal sources in an extensive reevaluation of woman's power, her varied and multiple potentiality, and all sides of her being. Changes in therapy are occurring as women are discovering their own paths toward healing, and as analysts are more open to the incorporation of the feminine into their therapy and within themselves.

The inclusion in this study of important work by many women analysts and authors who have often been overlooked provides access to a cumulative female voice. Their inclusion may change both theory and the generation of theory. The biggest change discernible right now is the amount of new literature about the feminine by women, and the freedom with which women are talking about the reality of their own lives and struggling to express them as women, rather than molding them into male definitions of what women's experience should be. Women are now writing about the feminine from their own perspective. The consequences brought about by the inclusion of an increasing number of women writers and scientists — whose allegiance is to the exploration of their own sense of themselves as women as well as to their identity as scientists — must influence the field. The influence is already felt in the current interest in feminine empowerment, women's initiation, and female rites of passage.

The symbols of women's initiations, their difference from male rites, and the recent use of initiation as an archetype for a woman's individuation journey, are of great interest and require further study. This exploration of women's initiation may hold the key to some possible interesting differences in men and women in terms of psychological theorizing, practice of therapy, and training of therapists. Women's initiation rites as a paradigm for therapy is in marked contrast to the more bounded and primarily masculine model of the Jung-Klein paradigm that is also rising as an alternative within analytical psychology. (This latter is only one example of the new and varied representations of the masculine principle that also require study, exploration, and integration today.)

I started this book by presenting some of the social, cultural, and personal determinants behind Jung's thought and psychology. Jung's "Number One" character—the positivist, pragmatic Swiss bourgeois doctor, who was patriarchally dubious about his own feminine "inferior" — and Jung's "Number Two" character—Romantic, allied to the mountains, valleys, and rushing waters of his countryside, intrigued and entranced by the powerfully mysterious idealized feminine—both left their mark on his theories about the feminine and women. In the chapters that follow, I traced Jungians' theory on the feminine and women from Jung to the present. My aim, other than historical—to give readers some access to Jungian history on the feminine—has been to track the growth and evolution of this theory; another aim has been to try to separate the congruent from the contaminated. As I wrote in Part Two, my purpose has been to point out what helps psychological growth today and what may restrict. Jung's androcentric outlook is part of our inheritance; his and his era's positivist and Romantic view of human psychology, masculine and feminine, runs in our collective blood. Both views obscure Jung's affirmation of the individual and of his or her particular and idiosyncratic path. Both views are detrimental to women's psychological health and growth and to the perception of women as full adult human beings. In the few pages remaining, I want to make an urgent plea for reformulating analytical psychology toward better meeting women's needs.

Jung's breadth of view remains, as does his dedication to his patients, his belief in their individuality, his description of a healing path, along with his tentative mapping of the psyche and his understanding of the collective unconscious that links us all. In contrast to the cultural conservatism of many Jungians who take Jung's map of these territories as the reality of the terrain, the thing in itself, and who seek to conform people to the concrete specifics of Jung's map, turning the descriptive and speculative into the normative, I propose the following correctives.

Analysts need to vigorously reexamine the language of our theory and practice to eliminate words, ideas, and treatment which restrict men and women to preconceived notions of limitation—to one half of life, one side of a duality, one "right" way of being or doing—simply because they happen to be of a particular gender. We need to be aware of our own knowledge, conditioning, socio-cultural inheritance, and prejudices and how they can, verbally or attitudinally, affect our theory and the people we serve. Women and men are not simple and opposite classes of beings with a gender-specific homogeneity of experience. There are many more intra-gender differences than inter-gender; gender must be seen as intertwined with such things as a person's age, class, race, sexual orientation, culture—all the multifold aspects of identity. Reinterpretation of theory must also be relevant to homosexual as well as heterosexual perspectives. Maybe above everything else, Jungians need to not only examine their own field and experience, but reach outside to gain awareness of current social, biological, and psychological studies—in this case, studies by and about women today which mirror them more clearly. These need to be judiciously incorporated into an evolving sense of Jungian theory so that neither the feminine nor the masculine is devalued. Sticking to outmoded definitions can be soul-killing and harm rather than further individuation. We live in the real world as well as in theory, and need to see the particular problems with which women and other groups have to contend, and that add to or affect their functioning (e.g., Ulanov's study of envy, Perera's analysis of the scapegoat complex, Odajnyk's study of the effect of colonialism).

Much contemporary work on the feminine has explored our inherited hatred, fear, and devaluation of the feminine, and the ways women have internalized these through their own damaged self-esteem or active self-loathing; other work has studied the anima and men's projection of its split angel/whore, divine/demonic attributes onto women. The overwhelming impact of single sex mothering that underlies our gender conditioning has started to be noted by both Freudians and Jungians. Only recently have Jungians described, or had models for, a whole adult female human being in touch with her own feminine power and feminine self.

Contemporary work on the psychology of women tends to fall into two potential errors that Jungians need to be aware of as they listen to themselves and as they read. Hare-Mustin and Maracek (1988) have called these Alpha and Beta biases. The alpha bias is one of separatism, finding too much difference between men and women, and exaggerating their contrasting worlds and psychology (a tendency in some followers of Chodorow's and Gilligan's work, in the early Jungians, and in overestimation of either the feminine or the masculine); the beta bias minimizes difference and stresses similarity (as in some feminist extrapolations from the neurological and biological work of Bleier and Fausto-Sterling, and in some Jungian work on androgyny).

Analytical psychology needs to respect and explore men's and women's similarities and differences. The idea that men and women in this culture develop ego in the same way needs reevaluation as to its beta bias. At this particular time in history, rather than sacrificing the ego, I find a need for most women patients to relinquish a pseudo-masculine idea of ego and develop and strengthen their own more tensile feminine ego. This ego, at this cultural moment (Chodorow, Gilligan, D. Wehr, *et al.*), tends to be more fluid, more permeable, more connected, and less rigidly bound than a man's. Developing this ego means honoring it and building it up, not the cutting down and sacrifice that is sometimes prescribed. The feminine ego needs to learn how to connect without being engulfed, and how to differentiate without severing or splitting off. Women's development today seems to mainly derive from discerning, developing, and honoring what is feminine in them—what is so hard to discern and uncover under its many patriarchal veils. Taking these layers away, women's psyches seem to reveal what Chodorow has called their own particularly complex layering, having a "richer inner object-world and . . . greater continuity in their external object-relations" (1978, p. 169).

Many women, as Jane Wheelwright has also suggested, contain great internal richness; they have multiple aspects, sides, personalities; they are a unity that is made up of non-unity, a one that is several (see Irigaray, 1977), like the symbol of the moon in all its phases, or the triune goddess, maiden, mother, crone. Female sense of body, even a different ego-body, needs acknowledgement and development. This may be because women's bodies for so long have not belonged to them but been sexualized, valued, and defined by men's experience of them; thus objectified, women's connection with physical cycles, menstruation, pregnancy, birthing, and lactation has vanished under the mirror of man's projections and his limiting idealization or derogation. It is essential for women to see and value their own bodies and bodily reality anew.

To see herself clearly in the mirror, no longer obscured by denial or repression, the woman in the center of her own life has to free herself from both outer and inner definitions of what a woman is supposed to be so that she can embrace her own particular truth and her own self-image. This involves reseeing and reshaping both herself and the world. Carolyn Heilbrun, in her book on women writers (1988), calls daughters of the patriarchy "female impersonators," but also speaks of the great courage and suffering involved in discovering and expressing a different way of being. She finds that it may be easier for a woman to remove the culture's false female mask and examine who she really is as she ages. Heilbrun quotes an Isak Dinesen character who says, "Women when they are old enough to have done with the business of being women, and can let loose their strength, must be the most powerful creatures in the world" (1988, p. 25).

Women need a different form of analysis that builds from this kind of strength and toward this kind of strength; it involves the reclamation of women's self-esteem and self-respect. Though

the other side of this act of reclamation is to recognize the many ways in which our social institutions repress, brutalize and trivialize women. There is little hope for women to develop their creative potential without support from their environment. (Mattoon and Jones, 1987, p. 20)

Analysis as well as therapy must aid and encourage all aspects of psyche, including the expression of power and rage. Analysts, especially male analysts, need to free themselves of their dread of, or entrapment in, the engulfing personal mother and terrible archetypal mother. A whole person is not a masculine person; women may have to explore and experience different stages and different ways of development toward wholeness. Above all, I doubt whether the patriarchal *via negativa* of deprivation, excoriating interpretation, and obloquy works for most women, either in their training or in their analysis. Women and the feminine need to be seen and mirrored clearly rather than further brought low; this mirror needs to be cleansed of its Romantic idealization or corrosive derogation. Most women seem to need a more active and containing therapy than the classical psychoanalytic one—an embodied therapy. So many women I see, myself included, had no mother with a sense of her own worth, power, or self; these mothers brought up daughters with a profound sense of feminine inferiority and self-distrust. The daughters were taught to conform, while any urge toward something larger or freer was attacked with envy, rage, or ostracism. Little girls are all too often taught to be nice and obliging deficient objects instead of being taught how to stand up for themselves, or to see themselves clearly in the accurate mirroring of their mothers' eyes. Girls and women have seldom been taught how to grow themselves; so, in therapy, active support, containment, and remothering are necessary in order to build strength, power, authority, and sense of self (in the dosages, as Perera has noted, that a patient can handle, and differentiating this from the narcissistic mother's smothering). Women in analysis also need a sense of the female analyst's own self-worth as a woman, her own sense of power and authority. The woman analyst who has gone through such a process herself can then, like the image in the Pompeiian Villa of Mysteries, offer her lap to comfort and sustain the initiand. There is joy as well as pain in this reconnection to the dynamic feminine.

Since this is a Jungian study, it seems appropriate to close it with a dream I had as I was nearing the end of its first draft. The dream was about shamans and a woman's initiation rite. The dream was down to earth but also beyond words and involved with shape-shifting. It was a profound dream but also very matter of fact—neither grand nor noble. I dreamed there was a central fire in a circular place in the middle of a wide valley. It was in high country: red, ochre, sandstone, and violet hills encircled the horizon; there were four larger hills, one in each direction. What makes the dream so hard to describe is the way its elements interpenetrated, dissolved into each other and into the earth, and the earth into them. I'm sitting in the center by the fire with an Indian wise-woman I know from other dreams. We are preparing dinner; after a while there seem to be no boundaries or edges to anything. What's me, her, the rocks, the hills, what's standing on what, and who was who at the start of it all, is no longer clear. The lines of my book are somehow intermingled with the cooking, rising in the smoke of the fire and the steam from the pot.

The silent woman is telling me, or I am thinking, that the horses came to a man once but he turned away from them. It hurt the horses and angered them and hurt the hills, this beautiful earth, the fire, the woman, me—it is an open wound we still bear. Now the horses come back again, racing and dancing through the sky, one from each of the four directions. They are the horses from out of the four hills. I feel small, filled with fearful awe, but also with profound love. My task, if that's the word, is to be there and not to turn away from anything that happens. I need to sit in front of the fire, prepare the corn, and remain undivided. Yet right then and with all the power of my being I also need to turn toward the horses—to connect with, become, be each horse and all at the same time and completely and one the other—while maintaining my wholeness centered by the fire and occupied with my cooking pot. The dream also has something to do with a picture of da Vinci's Saint Anne I had used in a lecture I'd just given. The Indian woman (like the woman in Pompeii whose lap, Fierz-David and Bradway point out, was there for the initiand, and like Woodman's description of St. Anne supporting Mary) provided containment so the daughter could rest on, emerge from, grow out of her lap, and then reach out to the child, the Self. But in my dream, the Indian woman and I also were the horses, and they were us and this sharing, communion one with the other, was the vital part (and also contained the message of what we were about). Yet the message was also in the fire, that had to be tended, and in the cooking, and in the pot whose water mirrored all that was going on—mirrored me to myself. I have never felt so strongly centered and focused, yet somehow part of everything else.

The sense I make of all of this, and why I am including it here, is that I think the dream is saying a lot about the feminine that I couldn't get to any other way. Perhaps it also says why we are in such grave need of it. I'll say the weightiest thing first. I think we, as children of the patriarchy, *have* all turned from the horses, and this has wounded them and made them mad. It has also hurt the earth, the world, and all humanity, perhaps beyond repair. I can't help but think of two far grander visions that I connect most strongly with the patriarchy: the four horses of the apocalypse and Black Elk's (Neihardt, 1961) majestic horses. Both were signifying war and devastation. This signified a return.

It embarrasses me to bring these great classical dreams into a discussion of mine, but I need to point out the differences. My dream felt deep and profound, yet human, not inflated; some sort of archetypal hubris throbs around both of the others. Everything was so quiet and matter of fact in mine, almost domestic, yet also powerful; great noise and outward activity belonged to Black Elk's dream and to St. John's vision. The movement of mine came from the periphery and converged toward the center; the other two whirl further and further outwards. My horses came to a simple woman quietly preparing corn flour by a campfire; the others carried the dreamers away. Finally, mine allowed me to turn toward the horses with love and connect with them, but I had to do this and strongly remain my own self. This may speak about the feminine and why it's needed so badly now. It also may be saying something about the potency of the feminine — horses being one image of the power of the Great Mother — that must be reckoned with. My dream says a lot to me about a return, a reclamation of something that once was left behind. I believe we have lost a vital connection with our world and therefore have also lost our separation. In the dream there seems a way to work this out, a way to intermingle and interpenetrate, yet, in the process, hang on to our egos and all the consciousness the patriarchy has given us, but hang on strongly enough to yield to a connection with something greater than ego or consciousness. And maybe that's what the dream was working on, and what the feminine has to offer in order to prevent us turning away from the horses toward our destruction. And maybe it's the feminine in women and in men that bears this message at this point in time.

Using the dream, I would like to attempt to define my own sense of what is feminine. It does, after all, retain connection with earth and with bodily, daily tasks and duties like fire-tending, pollen preparation, child-bearing. I'm not prepared to say whether this is cultural or biological. I'm also sure there is a masculine way of being earthy, embodied and generative, too. The round of tasks given to woman in all cultures, the fact that she has historically accomplished them and still maintained her concentration, kept all the various things in mind at once, are examples of two aspects of the feminine acting in her. One is the bodily connection; the other the spiritual and mental capacity to keep all sorts of things sorted and simmering at one time. I see neither this nor the ability to fluidly connect and interpenetrate as examples of unconsciousness or diffuse consciousness, though men have described them that way. In my dream it required every bit of consciousness I had and something more. It required a combination of attention, acute awareness, and the ability to hold several things clearly in consciousness at once while being open to the unexpected and to interpenetration. Whether or not this is the right-brain, left-brain cross-access women are supposed to have more of than men (e.g., Kenevan, 1981), it is an aspect of the feminine I think women have right now more than most men do. Nurtured and released, it leads to access to great creativity. I think it may lead to just the kind of thinking that can bring up questions and answers the patriarchy couldn't envision.

The center, the hearth, the pot, the mirroring water, and the valley, these I'll take for feminine and even speak of Yin, though this concept, too, stems from a peasant patriarchy and is full of socio-cultural bias. The whole energy of the dream comes down and toward the center, is enfolded, connected with, vivified, and returned. This is feminine energy. It is full of what Harding wrote so longingly about: feminine action and feminine vigor. The enormous potency of the horses is feminine power. This power had them dancing through the air as well as on the ground. This feels like the way I feel sometimes—my only name for it is spiritual, but a feminine spirituality that belongs to and loves this planet, and connects from here and from within, out to the sublime. The horses needed food and water and care, but also were goddess' horses and carried a spiritual connection both from deep within the hills and from the sky. Above all else in the dream, they demanded acceptance from me and required my intense concentration and willingness to meet them and connect with them in the spirit while engaged in earthly tasks.

When the Indian woman appears in my dreams, she most often comes as a companion and a witness. She contains, nurtures, supports, and teaches, manifesting many of the qualities of the wise Sophia. She may be a solid earthy form of that archetype of feminine wisdom, perhaps, but also something more, for it is with her that shape-shifting comes and shamanic experiences—and bawdiness. All of which are part of the feminine, as is her sometimes more ambiguous, mercurial quality. In this dream, I feel that she was everywhere and in every part of it.

The sense of taking in and flowing toward what happened between me and each element of the dream also seems a feminine way of action, full of movement and shifts in perspective. Feminine sexuality and its particular result—gestation or birthing of an infant or one's self—is my first association. My second is that this fluid yet strong feminine ego can creatively blur boundaries, but is neither weak, neurotically borderline, nor psychotic. The difference is vast, though in the dream there definitely was a sense of risk. I could not have sat there concentratedly and allowed the horses to come into me and me go out to them without a very strong and resilient ego, nor without the Indian woman as midwife. There is a difference between the feminine here and the chaotic archaic feminine. The feminine Self, though, has to return from masculine developmental patterns to pick up something the masculine had foresworn (as in Neumann's description of Psyche's transformatively feminine task). The risk is there, as in any initiation; my risk was in fragmenting into each of the separate horses and then we'd all have been gone, blown sky-high. It didn't happen and wasn't

This brings me back to psychology. I think this is wh
of when they approach the feminine. If they try to assimilate thes
of it, they fear regression and dissolution—that the old chaotic unconscious vortex will have them at last. This isn't so if they've done their
patriarchal work. The feminine then brings not a regression, but the
promise of renewal at a higher level, and can be a guide to the future.
I believe men need this potent feminine within themselves as much as
women do—to bear and gestate and nurture themselves and their environment, the home planet—but it seems just now that women lead
the way. For women, too, the task involves honoring of the feminine.
It requires a search for it within themselves, by whatever name they want
to call it. And we also need models of other women, like my Indian
shaman woman, who have found their own feminine selves. Honoring
makes a difference. Respect for one's own feminine ground gives a woman
a better sense of herself as a complete human being. The right to be
this individual and the right to ask for what we want and need, and
to expect an answer, can follow. Occupying the ground we stand on and
deriving strength and authority from within ourselves helps us discover
who it is we are, and helps us see this and the world with our own, not
our culture's, eyes.

My book was in the smoke and in the pot, so this dream had also
to do with this study. What I have not mentioned is the passion and
love in the dream that went out from me to each aspect of it and from
each to me, and that includes this book. As a thinking type, one way
I can express my love is by putting it into words—doing what I have
done right here. I have done this by examining the history of women
and of the feminine in analytical psychology, my lineage, studying it
as carefully and caringly as I can, and seeing the feminine, women, and
myself in a clearer mirror that returns a sense of personal strength and
authority in the process—and then sharing what I have discovered. Looking in the mirror of the feminine, "I found God in myself and I loved
her, I loved her fiercely."

REFERENCES

Adler, G. (1959). Ego integration and patterns of coniunctio. *JAP*, 4, *1-2*, 153-159.

———. (Ed.). (1973). *C.G. Jung letters*, Vol. One, 1906-1950. Princeton: Princeton University Press.

———. (Ed.). (1973). *C.G. Jung letters*, Vol. Two, 1951-1961. Princeton: Princeton University Press.

———. (1974). *Success and failure in analysis*. New York: G.P. Putnam's Sons.

Alex, W. (1968). Depression in women. Unpublished lecture read before the Societies of Jungian Analysts of Northern and Southern California, March 14-17.

———. (1977) Archetype: The anima. In B.B. Wolman (Ed.), *International encyclopedia of psychiatry, psychology, psychoanalysis and neurology* (92-94). New York: Aesculapius Publishers.

Allenby, A. (1955). The father archetype in feminine psychology. *JAP*, 1, *1*, 79-92. Reprinted in Samuels (Ed.) 1985 *The father* (135-152). London: Free Association Books.

American Council of Learned Societies. (Eds.). (1954). Hinkle, Beatrice M., In *Dictionary of American biography*. 5th Supplement (301-303). New York: Scribners.

APA Task Force. (1975). Report of the task force on sex bias and sex-role stereotyping in psychotherapeutic practice, *American Psychologist*, 30, 1169-75.

Arieti, S. (1976). *Creativity: The magic synthesis*. New York: Basic Books.

Astor, J. (1987). Some aspects of female sexuality, psychopathology, and their relation to infantile states of mind. *JAP*, 32, 4, 345-358.

Auerbach, N. (1982). *Woman and the demon: The life of a Victorian myth*. Cambridge: Harvard University Press.

Aylward, J.C. (1968). *The person and presence of women*. Unpublished manu-script, property of the Kristine Mann Library, New York.

Bancroft, M. (1975). Jung and his circle. *Psychological Perspectives*,6, *2*, 114-127.

Banford, S. (1982). Linda Leonard's *The wounded woman* [review]. *SFJLJ*, 4, *1*, 1-15.

Bardwick, J. (1971). *Psychology of women: A study of biocultural conflicts*. New York: Harper & Row.

Bauer, J. (1982). *Alcoholism and women*. Toronto: Inner City Books.

Beebe, J. (1984). The father's anima as a clinical and symbolic problem. *JAP*, 29, *3*, 227-287.

————. (1987). *Psychological types*. San Fransisco Jung Institute Seminar (cassette recording property of Virginia Detloff library).

————. (Ed.). (1983). *Money, food, drink, and fashion in analytic train-ing*. Fellbach: Bonz.

Begg, E. (1985). *The cult of the black virgin*. New York: Routledge & Kegan Paul.

Bem, S.L. (1976). Probing the promise of androgyny. In A. Kaplan & J. Bean (Eds.), *Beyond sex-role stereotypes* (47-62). Boston: Little Brown.

Bennet, E.A. (1962). *C.G. Jung*. New York: Dutton.

————. (1985). *Meeting with Jung*. Zürich: Daimon.

Bernard, J. (1976). Sex differences: An overview. In A. Kaplan & J. Bean (Eds.), *Beyond sex-role stereotypes* (9-26). Boston: Little Brown.

Bernstein, P.L. (1980a). A mythological quest: Jungian movement therapy with the psychosomatic client. *American Journal of Dance Therapy* 2, *3*, 44-55.

————. (1980b). The union of the Gestalt concept of experiment and Jun-gian active imagination. *Gestalt Journal*, 2, 36-45.

————. (1981). *Moon goddess, medium and earth mother: A phenomeno-logical study of the guiding feminine archetypes of the dance movement therapist*. Paper presented at the 16th annual American Dance Therapy Association, Madison, Wisconsin. Unpublished manuscript, property of the Kristine Mann Library, New York.

Berry, P. (1975). The rape of Demeter/Persephone and neurosis. *Spring*, 186-198.

————. (1978). What's the matter with mother? London Guild of Pastor-al Psychology. Lecture no., 190.

————. (1982). *Echo's subtle body*. Dallas: Spring Publications.

————. (Berry-Hillman). (1982). Virginities of image. In Stroud and Tho-mas (Eds.). *Images of the untouched* (27-38). Dallas: Spring Publications.

Bertine, E. (1948). Men and women. *Spring*, 70-92.

————. (1949). *The conflict of modern woman*. Paper presented before the YWCA. Unpublished manuscript, property of the Kristine Mann Li-brary, New York.

————. (1952). Speaking of good and evil. *Spring*, 79-91.

————. (1960). The perennial problem of good and evil. *Spring*, 21-33.

Beyme, F. (1967). Archetypal dreams and frigidity. *JAP*, 12, *1*, 3-22.

Binswanger, H. (1963). Positive aspects of the animus. *Spring*, 82-101.

————. (1965). Ego, animus and persona in the feminine psyche. *Har-vest*, 1-14.

————. (1975). *Development in modern women's self-understanding*. C.G. Jung Memorial Lecture, Zürich. Unpublished manuscript, property of the Kristine Mann Library, New York.

Birkhauser-Oeri, S. (1988). *The mother: Archetypal image in fairy tales*. Toronto: Inner City Books.

Black, R.A. (1978). Implications of Jung's prefiguration of priestesses. *JAP,* 23, 2, 149-160.

Bleier, R. (1984). *Science and gender: A critique of biology and its theories on women*. New York: Pergamon Press.

Bloom, H. (1989). *Ruin the sacred truths*. Cambridge: Harvard University Press.

Blum, B.L. (Ed.). (1980). *Psychological aspects of pregnancy, birthing and bonding*. New York: Human Sciences Press.

Bolen, J.S. (1982). The alchemy of Aphrodite. Paper presented at symposium, *In celebration of the feminine spirit* [cassette recording]. C.G. Jung Institute of San Francisco.

————. (1984). *Goddesses in everywoman*. San Francisco: Harper & Row.

Boring, E.G. (1950). *A history of experimental psychology* (2nd Edition). Englewood Cliffs, New Jersey: Prentice-Hall.

Bradway, K. (1970). *And modern women*. Paper presented at The C.G. Jung Institute of San Francisco, (public seminar).

————. (1978). Hestia and Athena in the analysis of women. *Inward Light*, 91, 41, 28-42.

————. (1989). A woman's individuation through sandplay. In *Sandplay Studies: Origins, theory, practice*. Boston: Sigo Press. (Original work published 1981)

————. (1982a). Gender identity and gender roles: Their place in analytic practice. In M. Stein (Ed.), *Jungian analysis* (275-293). La Salle, Illinois: Open Court.

————. (1982b). *Villa of mysteries: Pompeii initiation rites of women*. San Francisco: The C.G. Jung Institute of San Francisco.

————. (1984). Feeling trapped; feeling angry; feeling strong; feeling freed. Paper presented at The Analytical Psychology Club of San Francisco.

Brand, R. (1952). *Erich Neumann's contribution to the development of feminine psychology*. Unpublished manuscript, property of the Kristine Mann Library, New York.

————. (1980). *The experiment*. San Francisco: The C.G. Jung Institute of San Francisco.

Briner, M. (1960?). *Problem of modern woman as reflected in dreams*. Unpublished manuscript, property of the Kristine Mann Library, New York.

Broverman, I.K., Broverman, D.M., Clarkson, F.E., Rosenkrantz, P.S., and Vogel, S.R. (1970). Sex-role stereotyping in clinical judgments of mental health. *Journal of Consulting and Clinical Psychology,* 34:1-7.

Brown, L.B. (1988). Feminist therapy perspectives on psychodiagnosis: Keynote address. International Congress on Mental Health Care for Women, Amsterdam.

Bruner, C. (1986). *Anima as fate*. Dallas: Spring Publications. (Original work published 1963)

Bührmann, M.V. (1981). Intlombe and Xhentsa: A Xhosa healing ritual. *JAP*, 26, 3: 187-203.

————. (1983). Training of analytical psychologists and Xhosa medicine men. In Beebe (Ed.), *Money, food, drink, and fashion in analytic training* (237-248). Fellbach: Bonz.

————. (1983). Archetypal transference as observed in the healing procedures of Xhosa indigenous healers. In Beebe (Ed.), *Money, food, drink, and fashion in analytic training* (249-259). Fellbach: Bonz.

————. (1985). Nature, psyche and a healing ceremony of the Xhosa. In *A testament to the wilderness* (78-86). Essays in honor of C. Meier. Santa Monica: Lapis Press.

————. (1987). The feminine in witchcraft, Part One. *JAP*, 32, 2: 139-156.

————. (1987). The feminine in witchcraft, Part Two. *JAP*, 32, 3: 257-277.

Byington, C. (1983). Symbolic psychotherapy, a post-patriarchal pattern in psychotherapy. In Beebe (Ed.), *Money, food, drink, and fashion in analytic training* (441-472). Fellbach: Bonz.

Carotenuto, A. (1982). *A secret symmetry*. New York: Random House.

————. (1986). *The spiral way: A woman's healing journey*. Toronto: Inner City Books.

de Castillejo, I.C. (1955). The animus: Friend or foe? *Harvest*, 1-16.

————. (1973). *Knowing woman: A feminine psychology*. New York: Putnam's.

————. (1986). Woman as mediator. In Tuby, M. (Ed.), *In the wake of Jung* (53-66). London: Coventure, Ltd. (Originally published in 1963)

Champernowne, H.I. (1959). Woman and the community. *Harvest*, 5, 50-70.

Chodorow, J. (1982). Dance/movement and body experience in analysis. In M. Stein (Ed.), *Jungian Analysis* (192-203). La Salle, Illinois: Open Court.

————. (1984). To move and be moved. *Quadrant*, 17, 2: 39-48.

Chodorow, N. (1978). *The reproduction of mothering: Psychoanalysis and the sociology of gender*. Berkeley: University of California Press.

Cixous, H., and Clement, C. (1987). *The newly born woman*. Minneapolis: University of Minnesota Press.

Cohen, E.D. (1976). *C.G. Jung and the scientific attitude*. Totowa, New Jersey: Littlefield, Adams and Co.

Colegrave, S. (1979). *The spirit of the valley: The masculine and feminine in human consciousness*. Los Angeles: J.P. Tarcher.

Colonna, M.T. (1980). Lilith: Or the black moon. *JAP*, 25, 4: 325-350.

Corsini, R. (Ed.). (1977). *Current personality theories*. Itaska, Illinois: Peacock.

Covitz, J. (1986). *Emotional child abuse*. Boston: Sigo Press.

Cowan, L. (1982). *Masochism, a Jungian view*. Dallas: Spring Publications.

————. (1982). Forever wilt thou love, and she be fair: Faulkner's image of virginity. In Stroud and Thomas (Eds.), *Images of the untouched* (65-84). Dallas: Spring Publications.

Curatorium of the C.G. Jung Institute, Zürich (Eds.). (1967). *Evil: Studies in Jungian thought.* Evanston, Illinois: Northwestern University Press.

Dallett, J. (1988). *When the spirit comes back.* Toronto: Inner City Books.

Derrida, J. (1976). *Of grammatology.* Baltimore: Johns Hopkins University Press.

Deutsch, H. (1944). *The psychology of women, a psychoanalytic interpretation.* New York: Grune Stratton.

Diamond, S.A. (1987). Rediscovering Rank. *SFJLJ,* 7, 3: 1-10.

Dieckmann, H. (1986). *Twice-told tales.* Wilmette, Illinois: Chiron Publications.

Dieckmann, U., Bradway, K., and Hill, G. (1974). *Male and female, feminine and masculine.* San Francisco: The C.G. Jung Institute.

Dijkstra, B. (1986). *Idols of perversity: Fantasies of feminine evil in fin-de-sicle culture.* New York: Oxford University Press.

Dilling, C., and Claster, B. (1985). *Female psychology: A partially annotated bibliography.* New York: Coalition for Women's Health.

Dinnerstein, D. (1977). *The mermaid and the minotaur: Sexual arrangements and human malaise.* New York: Harper & Row.

Douglas, C. (1983). Whitmont, Edward C.: Return of the goddess [Review]. *SFJLJ,* 4, 3: 1-18.

——— . (1985). Biology and archetypal theory. *SFJLJ,* 5, 4: 1-21.

——— . (1986). The animus: old women, menopause, and feminist theory. *SFJLJ,* 6, 3: 1-20.

——— . (1989). Christiana Morgan's visions reconsidered: A look behind. *The Visions Seminars. SFJLJ,* 8, 4: 5-27.

——— . (in press). Because I would not give my love to the druid named Dark. In Stein, M. (Ed.), *Interpretations of Fairy Tales.* Wilmette, Illinois: Chiron Publications.

Dundas, E. (1989). *Symbols come alive in the sand.* Boston: Sigo Press. (Original work published in 1978)

Dykes, A. (1986). The medusa archetype. In Tuby, M. (Ed.), *In the wake of Jung* (67-86). London: Coventure, Ltd. (Original work given as an APC lecture, December 1976)

Eckman, B. (1986). Jung, Hegel, and the subjective universe. *Spring,* 88-100.

Ehrenreich, B., and English, D. (1972). *Witches, midwives, and nurses: A history of women healers.* Old Westbury, New York: The Feminist Press.

——— . (1973). *Complaints and disorders: The sexual politics of sickness.* Old Westbury, New York: The Feminist Press.

——— . (1979). *For her own good: 150 years of the experts' advice to women.* New York: Doubleday.

Ellenberger, H.F. (1970). *The discovery of the unconscious: The history and evolution of dynamic psychiatry.* New York: Basic Books, Inc.

Encyclopedia Britannica. (1910-1911). 11th Edition. *I.* 519-522.

Epstein, C.F. (1988). *Deceptive distinctions: Sex, gender and the social order.* New Haven: Yale University Press.

Evans, R. (1964). *Conversations with Carl Jung.* Princeton: Van Nostrand.

Fausto-Sterling, A. (1985). *Myths of gender: Biological theories about men and women.* New York: Basic Books, Inc.

Fay, C.G. (1977). *Movement and fantasy: A dance therapy model based on the psychology of C.G. Jung.* Unpublished master's thesis, Plainfield, Vermont: Goddard College. Property of the Kristine Mann Library, New York.

Fierz-David, L. (1987). *The dream of Poliphilo.* Dallas: Spring Publications. (Original work published 1950)

————. (1957). *Psychological reflections on the fresco series of the Villa of Mysteries in Pompeii.* Zürich: Psychological Club of Zürich.

————. (1988). *Women's Dionysian initiation: The Villa of Mysteries in Pompeii.* Dallas: Spring Publications.

Fine, M. (1985). Reflections on a feminist psychology of women: Paradoxes and prospects. *Psychology of Women Quarterly* 9, 2: 167-183.

Fine, R. (1979). *A history of psychoanalysis.* New York: Columbia University Press.

Fordham, M. (1975). Memories and thoughts about C.G. Jung. *JAP,* 20, 2, 102-113.

————. (Ed.). (1963). *Contact with Jung: Essays on the influence of his work and personality.* London: Tavistock.

————. et al. (1973). *Analytical psychology: A modern science.* London: Heinemann.

————. et al. (1973). *Technique in Jungian analysis.* London: Heinemann.

Fowles, B.K. (1978). Thoughts about the tomgirl: A study in femininity. *JAP,* 23, 2: 161-174.

Franz, M.-L. von. (1964). The process of individuation. In C.G. Jung (Ed.), *Man and his symbols* (157-254). New York: Dell.

————. (1966). *Aurora consurgens.* New York: Pantheon Books.

————. (1967). The problem of evil in fairy tales. In Curatorium (Eds.), *Evil: Studies in Jungian thought* (83-119). Evanston, Illinois: Northwestern University Press.

————. (1970). *Apuleius' golden ass.* New York: Spring Publications.

————. (1975) *C.G. Jung: His myth in our time.* New York: Putnam's.

————. (1976). *Problems of the feminine in fairy tales.* Zürich: Spring Publications. (Original unpublished lecture series, 1958-1959, C.G. Jung Institute, Zürich)

————. (1980a). *Shadow and evil in fairy tales.* New York: Spring Publications. (Two original unpublished lecture series, 1957 and 1964, C.G. Jung Institute, Zürich)

————. (1980b). *Alchemy.* Toronto: Inner City Books.

————. (1981). *Puer Aeternus.* Boston: Sigo Press. (Original work published 1971)

————. (1986). Jung and society. In M. Tuby (Ed.), *In the wake of Jung* (27-40). London: Coventure, Ltd.

Franz, M.-L. von, and Hillman, J. (1971). *Lectures on Jung's typology.* New York: Spring Publications.

Frey-Rohn, L. (1967). Evil from the psychological point of view. In Curatorium (Eds.), *Evil: Studies in Jungian thought* (151-200). Evanston, Illinois: Northwestern University Press.

————. (1974). *From Freud to Jung*. New York: Dell.

Gardiner, J.K (1983). Power, desire and difference: Comment on essays from the *Signs* special issues on feminist theory. *Signs, 8*: 733-787.

Gay, P. (1984) Education of the senses. *The bourgeois experience: Victoria to Freud* (Vol. One). New York: Oxford University Press.

————. (1986). The tender passion. *The bourgeois experience: Victoria to Freud* (Vol. Two). New York: Oxford University Press.

————. (1988). *Freud: A life for our time*. New York: W.W. Norton.

Geer, G. (1981). *The humble animus*. Unpublished dissertation, New York: C.G. Jung Institute of New York. Property of the Kristine Mann Library, New York.

Giegerich, W. (1975). Ontogeny = phylogeny? A fundamental critique of Erich Neumann's analytical psychology. *Spring*, 110-129.

————. (1986). The rescue of the world: Jung, Hegel and the subjective universe. *Spring*, 107-115.

Gilbert, S.M., and Gubar, S. (1980). *The madwoman in the attic: The woman writer and the nineteenth-century literary imagination*. New Haven: Yale University Press.

————. (1988). *The war of the words. No man's land: The place of the woman writer in the twentieth century* (Vol. One). New Haven: Yale University Press.

————. (1989). *Sex changes. No man's land: The place of the woman writer in the twentieth century* (Vol. Two). New Haven: Yale University Press.

Gilligan, C. (1982). *In a different voice: Psychological theory and women's development*. Cambridge: Harvard University Press.

Goldberg, S. (1973). *The inevitability of patriarchy*. London: Maurice Temple Smith.

Goldenberg, N.R. (1976). A feminist critique of Jung. *Signs, 2*: 443-449.

————. (1979). *Changing of the gods: Feminism and the end of traditional religions*. Boston: Beacon Press.

Goodheart, W. (1984). C.G. Jung's "patient": On the seminal emergence of Jung's thought. *JAP, 29, 1*: 1-34.

Gould, S. (1981). *The mismeasure of man*. New York: W.W. Norton.

Greene, A. (1980). *The use of touch in analytical psychology: A case study*. Unpublished manuscript, New York: The C.G. Jung Institute. Property of the Kristine Mann Library, New York.

————. (1984). Giving the body its due. *Quadrant*, 17, 2: 9-24.

Greene, T.A. (1982). Group therapy and analysis. In M. Stein (Ed.), *Jungian analysis* (219-231). La Salle, Illinois: Open Court.

Greenfield, B. (1983). The archetypal masculine: Its manifestation in myth and its significance for women. *JAP, 28, 1*: 33-50.

Grinnell, R. (1973). *Alchemy in a modern woman: A case study in a contrasexual archetype*. Zürich: Spring Publications.

Guggenbuhl-Craig, A. (1970). Must analysis fail through its destructive aspect? Translated by J. Hillman, *Spring*, 113-140.

————. (1977) *Marriage—Dead or alive*. Zürich: Spring Publications.

————. (1982). *Power in the helping professions*. Dallas: Spring Publications.

Gustafson, F. (1979). The black madonna of Einsiedeln [cassette recording]. Evanston, Illinois: The C.G. Jung Center.

————. (1989). *The black madonna*. Boston: Sigo Press.

Haddon, G.P. (1986). Delivering yang-femininity. Spring, 133-142.

Hall, N. (1980). *The moon and the virgin*. New York: Harper & Row.

Hannah, B. (1957). *Feminine psychology in literature*. Course given at the C.G. Jung Institute, Zürich. Unpublished manuscript, property of the Kristine Mann Library, New York.

————. (1958). The problem of women's plots in "The evil vineyard." Guild lecture #51. London: The Guild for Pastoral Psychology. (Original lecture APC, Zürich, 1946)

————. (1962). *The problem of contact with the animus*. New York: Guild. (Original work published 1951)

————. (1976). *Jung, his life and work: A biographical memoir*. New York: Putnam's Sons.

————. (1989). *Striving toward wholeness*. Boston: Sigo Press. (Original work published 1971)

Harding, M.E. (1922, October). *The eros and logos values of modern woman*. Paper presented before the London Psychology Club. Unpublished, unsigned manuscript attributed to Harding (?), property of the Kristine Mann Library, New York.

————. (1946). *"She": A portrait of the anima*. Paper presented before the Analytical Psychology Club of New York. Unpublished manuscript property of the Kristine Mann Library, New York.

————. (1952). Anima and animus. *Spring*, 25-43.

————. (1961). The spiritual problem of woman. In E. Bertine (Ed.), *Three papers* (18-33). Unpublished typescript, property of the Kristine Mann Library, New York.

————. (1962). Jung's influence on contemporary thought. *Journal of Religion and Health* 1, 3: 247-257.

————. (1965). *The 'I' and the 'not-I.'* Princeton: Princeton University Press.

————. (1975). *The way of all women: A psychological interpretation*. New York: Harper and Row. (Original work published 1933)

————. (1976) *Woman's mysteries, ancient and modern*. New York: Harper and Row Colophon. (Original work published 1935)

————. (1980). The value and meaning of depression. *Psychological Perspectives* 12, 2: 113-136. (Original work published 1970)

Hare-Mustin, R., and Maracek, J. (1988). The meaning of difference: Gender theory, postmodernism, and psychology. *American Psychologist*, 43, 6, 455-464.

Harrell, M. (1983). *The hidden self: A study in the development of the feminine psyche*. Unpublished diploma thesis, C.G. Jung Institute of New York. Property of the Kristine Mann Library, New York.

Hart, D. (1978). The evolution of the feminine in fairy tales. *Psychological Perspectives,* 1, 9: 46-56.

Heilbrun, C.G. (1988). *Writing a woman's life.* New York: W.W. Norton.

Henderson, J. (1963). C.G. Jung: A reminiscent picture of his method. In M. Fordham (Ed.), *Contact with Jung.* London: Tavistock.

————. (1967). *Thresholds of initiation.* Middletown, Connecticut: Wesleyan University Press.

————. (1975). Analytical psychology in England. *Psychological Perspectives,* 2, 6: 197-203.

————.. (1984). *Cultural attitudes in psychological perspective.* Toronto: Inner City Books.

————. (1985). Memories of a time in Zürich: Origins of a theory of cultural attitudes. *Psychological Perspectives,* 16, 2: 210-220.

————. (1988). The cultural unconscious. *Psychological Perspectives,* 21, 2: 7-16.

Henley, N. (1972). The politics of touch. *Women, a Journal of Liberation,* 3, 1: 7-8.

Heydt, Von der, V. (1964). *On the animus.* Lecture 126. London: Guild of Pastoral Psychology.

Hill, G. (1975). Men, anima and the feminine [cassette recording]. Los Angeles: C.G. Jung Institute of Los Angeles.

————. (1978). *Patterns of immaturity and the archetypal patterns of masculine and feminine, a preliminary exploration.* Unpublished doctoral dissertation. Institute for Clinical Social Work, Berkeley.

Hillel, R. (1987). The story of Ruth: Myth and model for modern women in transition. Unpublished lecture read before the Analytical Psychology Club of New York, November 13, (reviewed in the APC *Bulletin* 49, 8).

Hillman, J. (1971). The feeling function. In M.-L. von Franz and J. Hillman, *Jung's typology* (75-150). New York: Spring Publications.

————. (1972). *The myth of analysis: Three essays in archetypal psychology.* New York: Harper Colophon.

————. (1973). Anima. *Spring,* 97-132.

————. (1974). Anima II. *Spring,* 113-145.

————. (1976). Some early background to Jung's ideas: Notes on C.G. Jung's medium, by Stefanie Zumstead-Preiswerk. *Spring,* 128-136.

————. (1982). Salt: A chapter in alchemical psychology. In Stroud and Thomas (Eds.), *Images of the Untouched* (111-138). Dallas: Spring Publications.

————. (1983). The bad mother: An archetypal approach. *Spring,* 165-182.

————. (1985). *Anima: An anatomy of a personified notion.* Dallas: Spring Publications.

————. (1987). A psychology of transgression drawn from an incest dream. *Spring,* 66-76.

————. (Ed.) (1980). *Facing the gods.* Dallas: Spring Publications.

Hinkle, B. (1920). Arbitrary use of the terms "masculine" and "feminine." In *Proceedings of the International Conference of Women Physicians* 4, 100-118. New York: The Woman's Press.

————. (1940). Evolution of woman and her responsibility to the world today. lecture, APC, New York.

————. (1949). *Recreating of the individual: A study of psychological types and their relation to psychoanalysis*. New York: Dodd, Mead. (Original work published 1923)

————. (1987). Why feminism? In Showalter (Ed.), *These modern women: Autobiographical essays from the twenties* (137-141). New York: The Feminist Press. (Original work published 1926)

Hinshaw, R. (Ed.). (1985). *Testament to the wilderness*: Essays in honor of C.A. Meier. Santa Monica: Lapis Press.

Homans, P. (1976). *Jung in context: Modernity and the making of psychotherapy*. Chicago: The University of Chicago Press.

Horner, M. (1970). Follow-up studies on the motive to avoid success in women. Symposium presentation, American Psychological Association, Miami.

————. (1981). President Horner's ninth annual report to the alumnae. *Radcliffe Quarterly*, September.

————. (1989). Quoted in McLeod, From the double bind to the double burden: women and the fear of success. *Radcliffe Quarterly*, June, 7-8.

Horney, K. (1967). *Feminine psychology*. New York: W.W. Norton.

Hosmer, M. (1968). *Kali: The black one*. Paper presented before the Analytical Psychology Club of New York. Unpublished manuscript, property of the Kristine Mann Library, New York.

Howes, E. (undated; c. 1945-1955). *The nature and function of the animus: A condensation of Mrs. Jung's paper and seminar on the animus*. Unpublished typescript, property of the Detloff Library, San Francisco.

Hubback, J. (1978). Reflections on the psychology of women. *JAP*, 23, 2: 175-185.

————. (1988). *People who do things to each other*. Wilmette, Illinois: Chiron Publications.

Hutt, C. (1972). *Males and females*. Harmondsworth: Penguin.

Irigaray, L. (1977). *The sex which is not one*. Ithaca: Cornell University Press.

Jackson, K. (1987). G. Lloyd's Man of reason: "Male" and "female" in western philosophy [review]. *Signs*, 13, 1: 165-168.

Jacobi, J. (1942). *The Psychology of Jung*. London: Routledge & Kegan Paul.

————. (1944). *Woman and the psyche* [unauthorized translation]. Unpublished manuscript, property of the Kristine Mann Library, New York.

————. (1958). The process of individuation. *JAP*, 3, 2: 95-114.

————. (1959). *Complex, archetype, symbol in the psychology of C.G. Jung*. Princeton: Princeton University Press.

————. (1976). *Masks of the soul*. Grand Rapids: Eerdmans. (Original work published 1967)

Jaffe, A. (1964). Symbolism in the visual arts. In C.G. Jung (Ed.), *Man and his symbols* (230-271). Princeton: Princeton University Press.

————. (1971). *From the life and work of C.G. Jung*. New York: Harper Colophon.

————. (1972). The creative phases in Jung's life. *Spring*, 162-190.

————. (1984). Details about C.G. Jung's family. *Spring*, 35-44.

James, W. (1943). *Essays on faith and morals*. New York: Dover. (Original work published 1890)

————. (1950). *The principles of psychology. Volume one*. New York: Dover. (Original work published 1890)

————. (1950). *The principles of psychology. Volume two*. New York: Dover. (Original work published 1890)

Jarrett, J. (1981). Schopenhauer and Jung. *JAP*, 26, *1*, 193-205.

Jensen, F. (Ed.). (1982). *C.G. Jung, Emma Jung, Toni Wolff: A collection of remembrances*. San Francisco: The Analytical Psychology Club of San Francisco.

Jones, E. (1955). *The life and works of Sigmund Freud*. New York: Basic Books, Inc.

Jung, C.G. (1934-1939). *Zarathustra* (Vols. 1-10). Unpublished seminars privately distributed. Zürich: C.G. Jung Institute of Zürich.

————. (1954). Marriage as a psychological relationship. In W. McGuire (Ed.), *CW* (Vol. 17, 187-201). Princeton: Princeton University Press. (Original work published 1925)

————. (1965). *Memories, dreams, reflections*. New York: Vintage Books.

————. (1966). Anima and animus. In W. McGuire (Ed.), *CW* (Vol. 7, 188-211). Princeton: Princeton University Press. (Original work published 1928, rev. ed. 1953)

————. (1966). The relations between the ego and the unconscious. In W. McGuire (Ed.), *CW* (Vol. 7. 123-304). Princeton: Princeton University Press. (Original work published 1928, rev. ed. 1935)

————. (1966). On the psychology of the unconscious. In W. McGuire (Ed.), *CW* (Vol. 7, 3-119). Princeton: Princeton University Press. (Original work published 1943)

————. (1967). *Symbols of transformation*. In W. McGuire (Ed.), *CW* (Vol. 5). Princeton University Press. (Original work published 1911-12, rev. ed. 1952)

————. (1967). Commentary on "The secret of the golden flower." In W. McGuire (Ed.), *CW* (Vol. 13, 1-56). Princeton: Princeton University Press. (Original work published 1929)

————. (1967). The philosophical tree. In W. McGuire (Ed.), *CW* (Vol. 13, 251-349). Princeton: Princeton University Press. (Original work published 1945, rev. ed. 1954)

————. (1968). Archetypes of the collective unconscious. Princeton: Princeton University Press. In W. McGuire (Ed.), *CW* (Vol. 9i, 3-41). (Original work published 1934)

————. (1968). Concerning the archetypes, with special reference to the anima concept. In W. McGuire (Ed.), *CW* (Vol. 9i, 54-72). Princeton: Princeton University Press. (Original work published 1936, rev. ed. 1954)

————— . (1968). Individual dream symbolism in relation to alchemy. In W. McGuire (Ed.), *CW* (Vol. 12, 39-223). Princeton: Princeton University Press. (Original work published 1936)

————— . (1968). Concerning rebirth. In W. McGuire (Ed.), *CW* (Vol. 9i, 113-147). Princeton: Princeton University Press. (Original work published 1940, rev. ed. 1950)

————— . (1968). Introduction to the religious and psychological problems of alchemy. In W. McGuire (Ed.), *CW* (Vol. 12, 1-37). Princeton: Princeton University Press. (Original work published 1944)

————— . (1968). The phenomenology of the spirit in fairy tales. In W. McGuire (Ed.), *CW* (Vol. 9i, 207-254). Princeton: Princeton University Press. (Original work published 1948)

————— . (1968). *Aion: Researches into the phenomenology of the self.* In W. McGuire (Ed.), *CW* (Vol. 9ii). Princeton: Princeton University Press. (Original work published 1951)

————— . (1969). Psychological aspects of the mother archetype. In W. McGuire (Ed.), *CW* (Vol. 9i, 75-110). Princeton: Princeton University Press. (Original work published 1938, rev. ed. 1954)

————— . (1969). Conscious; unconscious, and individuation. In W. McGuire (Ed.), *CW* (Vol. 9i, 275-289). Princeton: Princeton University Press. (Original work published 1939)

————— . (1969). Psychology and religion (The Terry lectures). In W. McGuire (Ed.), *CW* (Vol. 11, 3-105). Princeton: Princeton University Press. (Original work published 1940)

————— . (1969). The psychological aspects of the Kore. In W. McGuire (Ed.), *CW* (Vol. 9i, 182-203). Princeton: Princeton University Press. (Original work published 1941, rev. ed. 1954)

————— . (1969). A psychological approach to the dogma of the Trinity. In W. McGuire (ed.), *CW* (Vol. 11, 109-200). Princeton: Princeton University Press. (Original work published 1942, rev. ed. 1948)

————— . (1969). Foreward to the I-Ching. In W. McGuire (Ed.), *CW* (Vol. 11, 589-608). Princeton: Princeton University Press. (Original work published 1950)

————— . (1969). Answer to Job. In W. McGuire (Ed.), *CW* (Vol. 11, 355-470). Princeton: Princeton University Press. (Original work published 1952)

————— . (1970). The love problem of a student. In W. McGuire (Ed.), *CW* (Vol. 10, 97-112). Princeton: Princeton University Press. (Original work published 1922, rev. ed. 1964)

————— . (1970). Mind and Earth. In W. McGuire (Ed.), *CW* (Vol. 10, 29-49). Princeton: Princeton University Press. (Original work published 1927, rev. ed. 1931)

————— . (1970). Woman in Europe. In W. McGuire (Ed.), *CW* (Vol. 10, 113-133). Princeton: Princeton University Press. (Original work published 1927)

————— . (1970). Freud and Jung: Contrasts. In W. McGuire (ed.), *CW* (Vol. 4, 333). Princeton: Princeton University Press. (Original work published 1929)

————— . (1970). The meaning of psychology for modern man. In W. McGuire (Ed.), *CW* (Vol. 10, 134-156). Princeton: Princeton University Press. (Original work published 1933)

————— . (1970). Mysterium coniunctionis: An inquiry into the separation and synthesis of psychic opposites in alchemy. In W. McGuire (Ed.), *CW* (Vol. 14). Princeton: Princeton University Press. (Original work published 1955-1956)

————— . (1970). The undiscovered self (present and future). In W. McGuire (Ed.), *CW* (Vol. 10, 245-305). Princeton: Princeton University Press. (Original work published 1957)

————— . (1970). Good and evil in analytical psychology. In W. McGuire (Ed.), *CW* (Vol. 10, 456-468). Princeton: Princeton University Press. (Original work published 1959)

————— . (1971). *Psychological types.* In W. McGuire (Ed.), *CW* (Vol. 6). Princeton: Princeton University Press. (Original work published 1921)

————— . (1971) The worship of woman and the worship of the soul. In W. McGuire (Ed.), *CW* (Vol. 6, 221-240). Princeton: Princeton University Press. (Original work published 1921)

————— . (1972). Postscript to *The Visions Seminars*, 2nd edition. *Spring*, 213.

————— . (1975). The psychology of the transference. In W. McGuire (Ed.), *CW* (Vol. 16, 163-323). Princeton: Princeton University Press. (Original work published 1946)

————— . (1975). Psychological comments on kundalini yoga. *Spring*, 1-32.

————— . (1976). Psychological comments on kundalini yoga (part two). *Spring*, 1-31.

————— . (1976). *The visions seminars. Book one.* Zurich: Spring Publications. (Original work multigraphed 1933)

————— . (1976). *The visions seminars. Book two.* Zurich: Spring Publications. (Original work multigraphed 1933)

————— . (1978). On the psychology and pathology of so-called occult phenomena. In W. McGuire (Ed.), *CW* (Vol. 1, 3-88). Princeton: Princeton University Press. (Original work published 1902)

————— . (1980). Foreword to Harding's, *The way of all women*. In W. McGuire (Ed.), *CW* (Vol. 18, 807-810). Princeton: Princeton University Press. (Original work published 1948)

————— . (1980). Jung and religious belief. In McGuire (Ed.), *CW* (Vol. 18, 702-744). Princeton: Princeton University Press. (Extracts from H.L. Philip, *Jung and the problem of evil*, 1957)

————— . (1980). Foreword to Jung's, "Wirklichkeit der seele." In W. McGuire (Ed.), *CW* (Vol. 18, 768-769). Princeton: Princeton University Press. (Original work published 1933)

————. (1980). The Tavistock lectures. In W. McGuire (Ed.), *CW* (Vol. 18, 5-182). (Original work published 1935)

————. (1982). Aspects of the feminine (Bollingen series 20) Princeton: Princeton University Press. (From *CW* Vols. 6, 7, 9i, 9ii, 17).

————. (1983). *The Zofingia lectures*. In W. McGuire (Ed.), *CW* (Volume A). Princeton: Princeton University Press. (Original lectures given 1902)

————. (1984). *Dream analysis: Notes of the seminar given in 1928-1930*. In W. McGuire (Ed.). Princeton: Princeton University Press.

————. (1988). *Nietzsche's Zarathustra: Notes of the seminar given 1934-1939* (In two volumes). James L. Jarrett (Ed.). Princeton: Princeton University Press.

C.G. Jung Institute of Los Angeles. (1982). *Matter of heart* [film]. Los Angeles: The Film Project of the C.G. Jung Institute of Los Angeles.

C.G. Jung Institute of San Francisco. (1981/1989). *Sandplay studies: origins, theory, practice*. Boston: Sigo Press.

Jung, E. (1941). On the nature of the animus. *Spring*.

————. (1981). *Animus and anima*. Zürich: Spring Publications.(The Animus originally published 1957)

Jung, E., and von Franz, M.-L. (1986). *The grail legend*. Boston: Sigo Press. (Original work published 1958)

Kalff, D.M. (1980). *Sandplay: A psychotherapeutic approach to the psyche*. Boston: Sigo Press.

Kast, V. (1986). *The nature of loving: Patterns of human relationship*. Wilmette, Illinois: Chiron Publications.

Keller, T. (1982). Beginnings of active imagination: Analysis with C.G. Jung and Toni Wolff. *Spring*, 279-284.

Kenevan, P.B. (1981). Eros, logos and androgyny. *Psychological Perspectives*, 12, 3: 8-21.

Kiersey, D., and Bates, M. (1978). *Please understand me: An essay on temperament styles*. Del Mar, California: Prometheus Nemesis Books.

Kirsch, T.B. (1982). Carotenuto, Aldo: A Secret symmetry. Sabina Spielrein between Jung and Freud [review]. *SFJLJ*, 3, 3: 33-36.

Kluger, R.S. (1974). *Psyche and Bible: Three Old Testament themes*. Zürich: Spring Publications.

————. (1978). Old Testament roots of women's spiritual problem. *JAP*, 23, 2: 135-148.

Knipe, R. (1982). Pele: Volcano goddess of Hawaii. *Psychological Perspectives*, 13, 2: 114-126.

Kotschnig, E.P. (1968-1969). Womanhood in myth and life, Part I. *Inward Light*, 74, 31: 16-30.

————. (1969). Womanhood in myth and life, Part II. *Inward Light*, 78, 32: 5-22.

Koltuv, B.B. (1975). *Hestia/Vestia*. C.G. Jung Institute of New York. Unpublished manuscript, property of the Kristine Mann Library, New York.

————. (1980). *Lilith and the daughters of Eve*. Unpublished dissertation, C.G. Institute of New York, property of the Kristine Mann Library, New York.

————. (1983). Lilith. *Quadrant*, 16, *1*: 63-87.

————. (1986). *The book of Lilith*. York Beach, Maine: Nicholas Hayes.

Kuhn, T. (1970). *The structure of scientific revolutions*(2nd Edition). Chicago: The University of Chicago Press.

Lambert, K. (1977). Four "contacts with Jung." In McGuire and Hull (Eds.), *C.G. Jung speaking* (159-161). Princeton: Princeton University Press.

Lackoff, R. (1975). *Language and woman's place*. New York: Harper Colophon.

Lauter, E., and Rupprecht, C. (1985). *Feminist archetypal theory*. Knoxville: University of Tennessee Press.

Layard, J. (1982). The incest taboo and the virgin archetype. In Stroud and Thomas (Eds.), *Images of the untouched* (145-184). Dallas: Spring Publications. (Original work published 1945)

Lederer, W. (1970). *The fear of women*. New York: Harcourt Brace Jovanovich.

Leonard, L. (1978). Puella patterns. *Psychological Perspectives*, 9, *2*: 127-143.

————. (1979a). The puella and the perverted old man. *Psychological Perspectives*, 10, *1*: 7-17.

————. (1979b). Amazon armors. *Psychological Perspectives*, 10, *2*: 113-130.

————. (1982). *The wounded woman: Healing the father-daughter relationship*. Athens, Ohio: Swallow Press.

————. (1986). *On the way to the wedding*. Boston: Shambhala.

Lerman, H. (1986). *A mote in Freud's eye: From psychoanalysis to the psychology of women*. New York: Springer.

Lewontin, R.C., Rose, S., and Kamin, L.J. (1984). *Not in our genes: Biology, ideology, and human nature*. New York: Pantheon.

Lowinsky, N. (1984). Why can't a man be more like a woman? *SFJLJ*, 5, *1*, 20-30.

Maccoby, E.E., and Jacklin, C.N. (1974). *The psychology of sex differences*. Stanford: Stanford University Press.

MacFarlane, A. (1977). *The psychology of childbirth*. Cambridge: Harvard University Press.

Maduro, R., and Wheelwright, J.B. (1977). Analytical psychology. In Corsini (Ed.), *Current personality theories* (83-124). Itaska: Peacock.

Mahdi, L.C., Foster, S., and Little, M. (Eds.). (1987). *Betwixt and between: Patterns of masculine and feminine initiation*. La Salle, Illinois: Open Court.

Malamud, R. (1971). The amazon problem. *Spring*, 1-21.

Mankowitz, A. (1984). *Change of life*. Toronto: Inner City Books.

Marriot, K. (1983). Stevens, A.: *A natural history of the self* [review]. *JAP*, 28, *1*: 80-81.

Martinez, I. (1979). Women artists: Key to the female psyche. *Quadrant*, 12, *1*: 64-79.

Masters, W.H., and Johnson, V.E. (1966). *Human sexual response*. Boston: Little, Brown.

Mattoon, M.A. (1981). *Jungian psychology in perspective*. New York: Free Press.

————. (1983a). *Is the animus obsolete?* [cassette recording. Public seminar]. San Francisco: The C.G. Jung Institute of San Fransisco.

————. (1983b). *Femininity in a feminist era* [cassette recording. Public seminar]. San Francisco: The C.G. Jung Institute of San Fransisco.

————. (1984). *Archetypes: A natural history of the self*, by Dr. A. Stevens [review]. *Quadrant*, 17, *1*: 61-64.

————. and Jones, J. (1987). Is the animus obsolete? *Quadrant*, 20, *1*: 5-22.

McGuire, W. (1974). Jung's seminars. *Quadrant*, 16, *1*: 29-38.

————. and Hull, R.F.C. (1977). *C.G. Jung speaking: Interviews and encounters*. Princeton: Princeton University Press.

————. (Ed.). (1974). *The Freud/Jung letters*. Princeton: Princeton University Press.

McNeely, D. (1987). *Touching: Body therapy and depth psychology*. Toronto: Inner City Books.

McPhee, J. (1984). *La place de la concorde Suisse*. New York: Farrar, Straus & Giroux.

Meador, B. (1984a). The divine feminine and modern woman [cassette recording. Public seminar]. San Francisco: The C.G. Jung Institute of San Fransisco.

————. (1984b). Transference/countertransference between the woman analyst and the wounded girl child. *Chiron*, 163-174.

————. (1986). The Thesmophoria: A woman's ritual. *Psychological Perspectives*, 17, *1*: 25-45.

Meier, C.A. (1989). *Ancient incubation and modern psychotherapy*. Einsiedeln: Daimon Verlag. (Original work published 1967)

————. (1984). *The unconscious in its empirical manifestations*. Vol. One in *The psychology of C.G. Jung*. Translated by E. Rolfe. Boston: Sigo Press.

Merritt, D. (1988). Jungian psychology and science: A strained relationship. In New England Society of Jungian Analysts (Eds.), *The analytic life* (11-31). Boston: Sigo Press.

Mill, J.S. (1979). *The subjection of women*. Cambridge: The MIT Press. (Original work published 1869)

Miller, N.K. (1988). *Subject to change: Women's writing—feminist reading*. New York: Columbia University Press.

Mindell, A. (1967). Somatic consciousness. *Quadrant*, (14), 66-77.

————. (1982). *Dreambody: The body's role in revealing the self*. Boston: Sigo Press.

Money, J., and Ehrhardt, A. (1972). *Man and woman, boy and girl*. Baltimore: Johns Hopkins University Press.

Moore, N. (1983). Anima-animus in a changing world. In Zoja and Hinshaw (Eds.) *Differing uses of symbolic and practical approaches in practice and theory* (193-214). Zürich: Daimon Verlag.

Moreno, M. (1965). Archetypal foundations in the analysis of women. *JAP*, 10, 173-186.

Myers, I.B. (1962). *The Myers-Briggs type indicator*. Palo Alto: Consulting Psychologists Press.

Nagy, M. (1981a). Menstruation and shamanism. *Psychological Perspectives*, 12, 1: 52-68.

———. (1981b). *The moon and the virgin* [review]. *Quadrant*, 14, 2: 109.

Napier, P.S. (1985). *Demeter of Villarosa, Sicilia*. Unpublished diploma thesis, the C.G. Jung Institute of Zürich. Property of the Kristine Mann Library, New York.

Neie, W. (1986). *The princess and the sorcerer*. Unpublished dissertation, property of the Kristine Mann Library, New York.

Neihardt, J.G. (Flaming Rainbow). (1961). *Black Elk speaks: Being the life story of a holy man of the Oglala Sioux*. Lincoln, Nebraska: The University of Nebraska Press.

Neumann, E. (1954). *The origins and history of consciousness*. Princeton: Princeton University Press. (Original work published 1950)

———. (1954). The moon and matriarchal consciousness. *Spring*, 83-100.

———. (1955). *The great mother: An analysis of the archetype*. New York: Pantheon.

———. (1959). The psychological stages of feminine development. *Spring*, 63-97.

———. (1962). *Amor and Psyche. The psychic development of the feminine: A commentary on the tale by Apuleius*. New York: Harper.

———. (1986). Fear of the feminine. *Quadrant*, 19, 1: 7-30. (Original work published 1959)

———. (1973). *The child*. London: H. Karnac Books.

New England Society of Jungian Analysts (Eds.). (1988). *The analytic life: Personal and professional aspects of being a Jungian analyst*. Boston: Sigo Press.

Newman, R.D. (1986). The transformative quality of the feminine in the Penelope episode of *Ulysses*. *JAP*, 31, 1: 63-74.

Odajnyk, V.N. (1976). *Jung and politics: The political and social ideas of C.G. Jung*. New York: Harper & Row.

Osterman, E. (1963). C.G. Jung: A personal memoir. In Fordham (Ed.), *Contact with Jung* (218-220). London: Tavistock.

Perera, S.B. (1981). *Descent to the goddess: A way of initiation for women*. Toronto: Inner City Books.

———. (1986). *The scapegoat complex: Toward a mythology of shadow and guilt*. Toronto: Inner City Books.

Plaut, A.S. (1975). Recent developments in analytical psychology. Paper presented before the C.G. Jung Institute of Los Angeles.

Post, L. van der. (1975). *Jung and the story of our time*. New York: Random House.

Pye, F. (1974). Images of success in the analysis of young women patients. In Adler (Ed.), *Success and failure in analysis* (198-205). New York: Putnam's Sons.

Qualls-Corbett, N. (1988). *The sacred prostitute: Eternal aspects of the feminine*. Toronto: Inner City Books.

Roazen, P. (1984). *Freud and his followers*. New York: New York University Press.

Roberts, H. (Ed.). (1981). *Doing feminist research*. London: Routledge & Kegan Paul.

Rockwell, R. (1982). Carotenuto, Aldo: *A secret symmetry. Sabina Spielrein between Jung and Freud* [review]. *SFJLJ*, 3, 4: 1-14.

Roscher, W., and Hillman, J. (1972). *Pan and the nightmare*. Zürich: Spring Publications.

Rosencrantz, P.S., de Lorey, C., and Broverman, I. (1985). One half a generation later: Sex role stereotypes revisited. Paper presented at the annual meeting of the American Psychological Association, Los Angeles.

Rubin, L. (1983). *Intimate strangers: Men and women together*. New York: Harper & Row.

Rupprecht, C.S. (1974). The martial maid and the challenge of androgyny. *Spring*, 269-293.

Samuels, A. (1980). Incest and omnipotence in the internal family. *JAP*, 25, 1: 37-58.

————. (1985a). *Jung and the post-Jungians*. London: Routledge & Kegan Paul.

————. (1985b). Gender and psyche: Developments in analytical psychology. *Anima*, 11, 2:125-138.

————. (Ed.). (1983). *The father*. London: Free Association Books.

Sandner, D. (1983). Symbols of feminine development in Jung's *Visions Seminars*. Unpublished lecture. San Francisco: APC.

————. (1986). The subjective body in clinical practice. In Stein (Ed.), *The body in analysis* (1-18). Wilmette, Illinois: Chiron Publications.

Sanford, J.A. (1980). *The invisible partners: How the male and female in each of us affects our relationships*. New York: Paulist Press.

Satinover, J.A. (1985). Jung's relation to his mother. *Quadrant*, 18, 1: 9-22.

————. (1987). Samuels (Ed.): *The father* [review]. *Quadrant*, 20, 2: 79-82.

Schmidt. L. (1980). The brother-sister relationship in marriage. *JAP*, 25, 1: 17-36.

————. (1983). How the father's daughter found her mother. *Psychological Perspectives*, 14, 1: 8-19.

————. and Wheelwright, J.H. (1984). The power of the maiden: Psychological reflections by a daughter and her mother [cassette recording. Public seminar]. San Francisco: The C.G. Jung Institute of San Fransisco.

Schwartz, S. (1985). *Beyond puella?* Unpublished diploma thesis, the C.G. Jung Institute of Zürich. Property of the Kristine Mann Library, New York.

Scott-Maxwell, F. (1957). *Women and sometimes men*. New York: Knopf.

Seligman, M.E. (1975). *Helplessness: On depression, development and death*. New York: Wiley.

Serbin, D. (1984). In conversation with Joseph B. Wheelwright. *Psychological Perspectives*, 15, 2: 149-167.

Shapira, L. (1988). *The Cassandra complex*. Toronto: Inner City Books.

Shorter, B. (1983). The concealed body language of anorexia nervosa. In Beebe (Ed.). *Money, food, drink, and fashion in analytic training* (97-128). Fellbach: Bonz.

————. (1987). *An image darkly forming: Women and initiation*. New York: Routledge & Kegan Paul.

Showalter, E. (Ed.) (1989). *These modern women: Autobiographical essays from the twenties*. New York: The Feminist Press.

Shuttle, P., and Redgrove, P. (1978). *The wise wound: Menstruation and every-woman*. New York: Richard Marek.

Signell, K.A. (1989a). The use of sandplay with men. In C.G. Jung Institute of San Francisco (Eds.), *Sandplay studies: Origins, theory, practice* (101-132). Boston: Sigo Press.

————. (1989b). The sandplay process in a man's development. In C.G. Jung Institute of San Francisco (Eds.), *Sandplay studies: Origins, theory, practice* (133-156). Boston: Sigo Press.

Singer, J. (1972). *Boundaries of the soul*. New York: Knopf.

————. (1975). *Dreams of an emerging woman*. Unpublished manuscript, property of the Kristine Mann Library, New York.

————. (1989). *Energies of love: Sexuality revisioned*. Boston: Sigo Press. (Original work published 1983)

————. (1989). *Androgyny: Toward a new theory of sexuality*. Boston: Sigo Press. (Original work published 1976)

Smith, B. (1975). Ariadne, her thread [cassette recording]. Los Angeles: The C.G. Jung Institute of Los Angeles.

————. (1977). The mirror of Aphrodite [cassette recording]. Los Angeles: The C.G. Jung Institute of Los Angeles.

Spender, D. (1980). *Man made language*. London: Routledge & Kegan Paul.

Spiegelman, J.M. (1985). *The nymphomaniac*. Phoenix: Falcon.

Stein, L. (1955). Loathsome women. *JAP*, 1, *1*: 59-77.

————. (1959). *Loathsome women*. London: Weidenfeld and Nicolson.

Stein, M. (1977). Hera: Bound and unbound. *Spring*, 105-119.

————. (1985). The significance of Jung's father in his destiny as a therapist of Christianity. *Quadrant*, 18, *1*: 23-34.

————. (Ed.). (1982). *Jungian analysis*. La Salle, Illinois: Open Court.

Stein, R.M. (1970). The animus and impersonal sexuality. *Spring*, 126-132.

————. (1973). *Incest and human love*. Baltimore: Penguin.

Stern, D. (1985). *The interpresonal world of the infant: A view from psychoanalysis and developmental psychology*. New York: Basic Books.

Stevens, A. (1983). *Archetypes: A natural history of the self*. New York: Quill.

Stevens, W. (1972). *The palm at the end of the mind*. New York: Random House.

Stewart, C.T. (1989). The developmental psychology of sandplay. In C.G. Jung Institute of San Francisco (Eds.), *Sandplay studies: Origins, theory, practice* (39-92). San Fransisco: C.G. Jung Institute of San Fransisco.

Stewart, L.H. (1982). Sandplay and Jungian analysis. In Stein (Ed.), *Jungian analysis* (204-218). La Salle, Illinois: Open Court.

Stroud, J., and Thomas, G. (Eds.). (1982). *Images of the untouched*. Dallas: Spring Publications.

Te Paske, B.A. (1982). *Rape and ritual: A psychological study*. Toronto: Inner City Books.

Tiger, L., and Fox, R. (1972). *The imperial animal*. London: Secker and Warburg.

Tuby, M. (1986). Opposites and the healing power of symbols. In Tuby (Ed.), *In the wake of Jung* (87-111). London: Coventure, Ltd.

————. (Ed.). (1986). *In the wake of Jung*. London: Coventure, Ltd.

Ujhely, G.B. (1973). *An attempt at explaining some aspects of modern women's experience by means of Jungian psychology*. Unpublished manuscript, property of the Kristine Mann Library, New York.

Ulanov, A.B. (1977). The witch archetype. *Quadrant*, 10, 1: 5-22.

————. (1978). *The feminine in Jungian psychology and in Christian theology*. Evanston, Illinois: Northwestern University Press. (Original work published 1971)

————. (1979). Fatness and the female. *Psychological Perspectives*, 10, 1: 18-36.

————. (1981). *Receiving woman: Studies in the psychology and theology of the feminine*. Philadelphia: Westminster.

————. (1983). *Cinderella and her sisters: The envied and the envying*. Philadelphia: Westminster.

————. (1988). *The wisdom of the psyche*. Cambridge: Cowley.

————. and Ulanov, B. (1979). *The witch and the clown*. Wilmette, Illinois: Chiron Publications.

Vaughter, R. (1976). Psychology: Review essay. *Signs*, 2: 120-146.

Vitale, S., Hillman, J., Neumann, E., Von der Heydt, V. (1973). *Fathers and mothers*. Zürich: Spring Publications.

Vogelsang, E. (1985). The confrontation between Lilith and Adam: The fifth round. *JAP*, 30, 2: 149-164.

Von Der Heydt, V. (1964). On the animus. Lecture 126. London: The Guild of Pastoral Psychology.

Voogd, S. de. (1977). C.G. Jung: Psychologist of the future, "philosopher" of the past. *Spring*, 175-182.

Voss, J. (1986). *The wild pig goddess and her blood of life*. Unpublished diploma thesis, the C.G. Jung Institute of Zürich. Property of the Kristine Mann Library, New York.

Walker, B. (1981). Psychology and feminism. In D. Spender (Ed.), *Men's studies modified: The impact of feminism on the academic disciplines*. Oxford: Pergamon Press.

Walker, L.E.A. (1989). Psychological violence against women. In *American Psychologist*, 44, 4: 695-702.

Weaver, R. (1973). *The old wise woman*. New York: Putnam's Sons.

————. (1975). The feminine principle. *Quest* (44-76). Perth, Western Australia: Analytical Psychology Club.

Wehr, D. (1987). *Jung and feminism*. Boston: Beacon Press.

Wehr, G. (1971). *Portrait of Jung: An illustrated biography*. New York: Herder and Herder.

————. (1987). *Jung: A biography*. Boston: Shambhala.

Weinrib, E. (1983). *Images of the self*. Boston: Sigo Press.

Weinstein, N. (1971). Psychology constructs the female: Or the fantasy life of the male psychologist. In Gornick and Moran (Eds.), *Woman in sexist society*. New York: Basic Books, Inc.

Wesley, D. (1977). The animus. In Wolman (Ed.), *International encyclopedia of psychiatry, psychology, psychoanalysis, and neurology* (Vol. One) (95-98). New York: Aesculapius Publishers.

Wheelwright, J.B. (1963). An attempt at appreciation. In Fordham (Ed.), *Contact with Jung* (224-225). London: Tavistock.

————— . (1971). A tribute and some comments on the etiology of the animus and anima. In Kirsch (Ed.), *The well-tended tree* (197-203). New York: Putnam's Sons.

————— . (1975). A personal experience of Jung. *Psychological Perspectives, 6, 1*: 64-73.

————— . (1982). *St. George and the dandelion*. San Francisco: The C.G. Jung Institute of San Francisco.

Wheelwright, J.H. (1963). A personal experience. In Fordham (Ed.), *Contact with Jung* (226-228). London: Tavistock.

————— . (1978). *Women and men*. San Francisco: The C.G. Jung Institute of San Fransisco.

————— . (1982). Jung. In Jensen (Ed.), *C.G. Jung, Emma Jung, Toni Wolff: A collection of remembrances* (96-105). San Francisco: The APC of San Fransisco.

————— . (1984). *For women growing older: The animus*. Houston: C.G. Jung Educational Center.

————— . (1985). The ranch papers. In Hinshaw (Ed.), *A testament to the wilderness* (93-110). Santa Monica: Lapis Press.

————— . (1988). *The ranch papers*. San Francisco: The C.G. Jung Institute of San Francsico.

————— . and L. Schmidt. (1984). The power of the maiden: Psychological reflections by a daughter and her mother [cassette recording. Public seminar]. San Francisco: The C.G. Jung Institute of San Fransisco.

Whitehead, A.N. (1929). *The function of reason*. Princeton: Princeton University Press.

Whitehouse, M. (1979). C.G. Jung and dance therapy. In Bernstein (Ed.), *Eight theoretical approaches to dance-movement therapy* (51-70). Dubuque: Kendall/Hunt.

Whitmont, E.C. (1957). Magic and the psychology of compulsive states. *JAP, 2, 1*: 3-32.

————— . (1958). Religious aspects of life problems in analysis. *Spring*, 49-64.

————— . (1961). Individual and group. *Spring*, 59-79.

————— . (1964). Guilt and responsibility. *Spring*, 4-32.

————— . (1966). Role of the ego in the life drama. *Spring*, 39-59.

————— . (1967). *Changing ethical and religious values in this epoch*. (Lectures before the Analytical Psychology Club of New York, March 2, 9, 16, 23, April 6, 13, 20. Unpublished manuscript).

————— . (1969). The destiny concept in psychotherapy. *Spring*, 73-92.

————. (1970). On aggression. *Spring*, 40-67.

————. (1971). Nature, symbol, and imaginal reality. *Spring*, 64-83.

————. (1974). Analysis in a group setting. *Quadrant*, 16, *2*: 5-25.

————. (1977). Momentum of man. *Anima*, 3, *2*: 41-48.

————. (1978). *The symbolic quest: Basic concepts of analytical psychology*. Princeton: Princeton University Press. (Original work published in 1969)

————. (1979). Feminism and the evolution of consciousness [cassette recording. Public seminar]. San Francisco: The C.G. Jung Institute of San Fransisco.

————. (1980). Reassessing femininity and masculinity: A critique of some traditional assumptions. *Quadrant*, 13, *2*: 109-122.

————. (1982a). *Return of the goddess*. New York: Crossroad.

————. (1982b). Recent influences on the practice of Jungian analysis. In Stein (Ed.), *Jungian analysis* (335-364). La Salle, Illinois: Open Court.

Widengren, G. (1967). The principle of evil in Eastern religions. In Curatorium (Eds.), *Evil: Studies in Jungian thought* (19-55). Evanston, Illinois: Northwestern University Press.

Wiedemann, F. (1984). Mother, father, teacher, sister: Transference-countertransference issues in the first phase of animus development. *Chiron*, 175-190.

Willeford, W. (1975). Jung's polaristic thought in its historical setting. *Analytische Psychologie*, 6, 218-239.

————. (1976). The primacy of feeling: Part I. *JAP*, 21, *2*: 115-133.

————. (1977). The primacy of feeling: Part II. *JAP*, 22, *1*: 1-16.

————. (1988). *Feeling, imagination, and the self: Transformations in the mother-infant relationship*. Evanston, Illinois: Northwestern University Press.

Wilmer, H. (1985). Jung: Father and son. *Quadrant*, 18, *1*: 35-40.

Wilson, E.O. (1975). *Sociobiology: The new synthesis*. Cambridge: Harvard University Press.

Wittig, M. (1985). *Les guerrileres*. Boston: Beacon Press.

Wolff, T. (1956). *Structural forms of the feminine psyche*. Zürich: Spring Publications. (Original work mimeographed 1934)

————. (1941). A few thoughts on the process of individuation in women. *Spring*, 81-103.

Wolff-Windegg, P. (1976). C.G. Jung: Bachofen, Burkhardt and Basel. *Spring*, 137-147.

Wolman, B.B. (Ed.). (1977). *International encyclopedia of psychiatry, psychology, psychoanalysis, and neurology* (Vol. One). New York: Aesculapius Publishers.

Woodman, M. (1980). *The owl was a baker's daughter: Obesity, anorexia nervosa and the repressed feminine*. Toronto: Inner City Books.

————. (1982). *Addiction to perfection: The still unravished bride*. Toronto: Inner City Books.

————. (1983). Feminine consciousness as healer of perfectionism [cassette recording. Public seminar]. San Francisco: The C.G. Jung Institute of San Fransisco.

————. (1984). Psyche/soma awareness. *Quadrant,* 17, 2: 25-37.

————. (1985). *The pregnant virgin.* Toronto: Inner City Books.

————. (1987). Emergence of the feminine. In Mahdi et al. (Eds.), *Betwixt and between.* La Salle, Illinois: Open Court.

Woolf, V. (1957). *A room of one's own.* New York: Harcourt Brace Jovanovich. (Original work published 1929)

Woolger, R., and Woolger, J. (1987). Athena today. *Quadrant,* 20, 1: 23-48.

Yandell, J. (1977). *The imitation of Jung: An exploration of the meaning of "Jungian."* St. Louis: Centerpoint Foundation.

Young-Eisendrath, P. (1984a). *Hags and heroes: A feminist approach to Jungian psychotherapy with couples.* Toronto: Inner City Books.

————. (1984b). Demeter's folly: Experiencing loss in mid-life. *Psychological Perspectives,* 15, 1: 39-64.

————. and Eisendrath, M. (1980). Where's mother now? *Psychological Perspectives,* 11, 1: 70-82.

————. and Wiedemann, F. (1987). *Female authority: Empowering women through psychotherapy.* New York: The Guilford Press.

Zabriskie, B. (1982). Incest and myrrh: Father-daughter sex in therapy. *Quadrant,* 15, 2: 4-24.

Zabriskie, P. (1974). Goddesses in our midst. *Quadrant,* 17: 34-45.

————. (1979). The loathly damsel. *Quadrant,* 12, 1: 47-63.

Zumstein-Preiswerk, S. (1975). *C.G. Jung's medium: Die geschichte der Helly Preiswerk.* Munich: Kindler.

INDEX

SIGO PRESS

SIGO PRESS publishes books in psychology which continue the work of C.G. Jung, the great Swiss psychoanalyst and founder of analytical psychology. Each season SIGO brings out a small but distinctive list of titles intended to make a lasting contribution to psychology and human thought. These books are invaluable reading for Jungians, psychologists, students and scholars and provide enrichment and insight to general readers as well. In the Jungian Classics Series, well-known Jungian works are brought back into print in popular editions.

Other Titles from Sigo Press

The Unholy Bible *by June Singer*

Emotional Child Abuse *by Joel Covitz*

Dreams of a Woman *by Shelia Moon*

Androgyny *by June Singer*

The Dream-The Vision of the Night *by Max Zeller*

Sandplay Studies *by Bradway et al.*

Symbols Come Alive in the Sand *by Evelyn Dundas*

Inner World of Childhood *by Frances G. Wickes*

Inner World of Man *by Frances G. Wickes*

Inner World of Choice *by Frances G. Wickes*

Available from SIGO PRESS, 25 New Chardon Street, #8748A, Boston, Massachusetts, 02114. tel. (617) 526-7064

In England: Element Books, Ltd., Longmead, Shaftesbury, Dorset, SP7 8PL. tel. (0747) 51339, Shaftesbury.

DATE DUE

MAR 20 '97		
APR 0 9 1997		
6 1 97		
JAN 25 '98		
APR 29 1999		
NO 1 05		
DE 21 06		